T0332811

Optical Transmission and Networks for Next Generation Internet Traffic Highways

Fouad Mohammed Abbou
Al Akhawayn University, Morocco

Hiew Chee Choong
Kasatria, Malaysia

Information Science
REFERENCE
An Imprint of IGI Global

Managing Director:	Lindsay Johnston
Acquisitions Editor:	Kayla Wolfe
Production Editor:	Christina Henning
Development Editor:	Allison McGinniss
Typesetter:	Kaitlyn Kulp
Cover Design:	Jason Mull

Published in the United States of America by
Information Science Reference (an imprint of IGI Global)
701 E. Chocolate Avenue
Hershey PA 17033
Tel: 717-533-8845
Fax: 717-533-8661
E-mail: cust@igi-global.com
Web site: http://www.igi-global.com

Library of Congress Cataloging-in-Publication Data

Abbou, Fouad Mohammed, 1963-
  Optical transmission and networks for next generation internet traffic highways / by Fouad Mohammed Abbou and Hiew Chee Choong.
       pages cm
  Includes bibliographical references and index.
    ISBN 978-1-4666-6575-0 (hardcover) -- ISBN 978-1-4666-6576-7 (ebook) -- ISBN 978-1-4666-6578-1 (print & perpetual access) 1. Optical fiber communication. 2. Internet. I. Choong, Hiew Chee, 1981- II. Title.
  TK5103.592.F52A23 2015
  621.382'75--dc23
                              2014029329

British Cataloguing in Publication Data
A Cataloguing in Publication record for this book is available from the British Library.

All work contributed to this book is new, previously-unpublished material. The views expressed in this book are those of the authors, but not necessarily of the publisher.

Table of Contents

Section 1

Chapter 1

Chapter 2

Section 2

Chapter 14

Chapter 15

Preface

Telecommunications systems and networks of the future are expected to provide a wide range of integrated voice and data services to customers. Data services, especially those involving multimedia applications can often be bandwidth intensive and accessed concurrently by a large number of users. Therefore, a great deal of effort is underway in many countries to replace conventional network infrastructure, based on copper lines and coaxial cables, with fiber optic networks to meet these requirements. One of the key advantages is the capability to simultaneously multiplex a huge number of WDM channels into a shared fiber optic medium. In this context, various hybrid multiplexing techniques such as OCDM-WDM, SCM-WDM, and OTDM-WDM can be employed to achieve terabit per second transmission rates.

Due to the large bandwidth and the associated high bit rates of optical fiber communication, the multiplexing process is beyond the capabilities of purely electronic methods and has to be implemented optically, too. One important technique is Optical Time Domain Multiplexing (OTDM), which has demonstrated impressive bit rates (Nakazawa, 2000). Nevertheless, the most commonly used multiplexing technique lately has been Wavelength Division Multiplexing (WDM), which can fully utilize the available fiber bandwidth using 10 Gb/s channels with high spectral efficiency (Zhu, 2002; Gnauck, 2003). Recently, the push has been to increase the bit rate per WDM channel. Recent experiments have used Electrical Time Domain Multiplexing (ETDM) to achieve 40 Gb/s bit rates per WDM channel (Cai, 2002). In the long run, however, the potential bit rate per channel of ETDM is subject to the physical limitations in the speed of electronic devices. The reduction of WDM channels is favorable because it reduces costs by reducing the number of lasers or transmitters required. Another current trend is the pursuit of higher spectral efficiencies in Dense WDM (DWDM) and Ultra-Dense WDM (UDWDM) systems (Bosco, Carena, Curri, Gaudino, & Poggiolini, 2004; Srivastava, 2000). This is because increasing spectral efficiency is a convenient way to increase transmission capacity.

Extensive research carried out on OTDM-WDM system has shown tremendous potential capacity (Zhu, 2002; Gnauck, 2003; Weinert, 1999). OTDM-WDM is attractive from two opposing perspectives. Firstly, the integration of WDM in OTDM systems is required to maximize the bandwidth utilization as a pure OTDM system cannot achieve bit rates high enough to fully cover the potentially available bandwidth. Secondly, the integration of OTDM in WDM systems is required to increase the bit rate per WDM channel to reduce the number of WDM channels for reasons mentioned earlier. Thus, the solution looks to combine both OTDM and WDM such that WDM provides the higher hierarchy (high capacity) multiplexing while OTDM takes care of the lower hierarchy tributaries.

Propagation through the optical fiber is subject to a large number of naturally occuring physical phenomena within the optical fiber. Setting up a communication system using the optical fiber would subject the system to all these effects that will put a limitation to the potential capacity of a reliable communication system at the physical level. An OTDM-WDM system would, of course, be impaired by both the effects that more significantly impair OTDM as well as WDM transmission. Therefore, any attempt to optimize the system would need to take into account numerous effects. To reduce the complexity of the problem, it is essential to cut down the number of effects included in a model of the system to only the most significant ones. In this study, we focus on the use of Single Mode Fibers (SMF) as opposed to Multi Mode Fibers (MMF) as the SMF is the fiber of choice for high capacity links. This is because SMF does not suffer from the large penalties incurred through modal dispersion (Agrawal, 1997).

For optical fiber transmission in general, fiber attenuation (Agrawal, 1997; Keiser, 2000) is the first limitation. This is overcome in modern systems using optical amplifiers (Desurvire, 1994). However, amplifiers induce Amplified Spontaneous Emission (ASE) noise, which has become the dominant noise source in long distance fiber communication (Desurvire, 1994; Yamamoto, 2003). Next, fiber dispersion leads to significant errors that has been reduced through the use of new fiber types (Agrawal, 1997) and Dispersion Management (DM) (Pachnicke, Man, Spalter, & Voges, 2005; Duce, Killey, & Bayvel, 2004). However, the problem of dispersion has not been fully compensated for due to the limitations of present-day fibers in handling higher-order dispersion (Cai, 2002).

With the compensation of attenuation and dispersion, the new limitation to the performance of optical fiber communication are nonlinear effects (Tkach, Chraplyvy, Forghieri, Gnauck, & Derosier, 1995; Wu & Way, 2004). Specifically, these nonlinear effects are those caused by the nonlinear refractive index of the fiber also known as the Kerr nonlinearity. Many different effects originate from this same phenomenon, classified by the source and consequence of the effect. For a pure OTDM system, Self-Phase Modulation (SPM) is present (Kumar, Mauro, Raghavan, & Chowdhury, 2002). When dispersion is strong or when the bit rate is high, two subsets of SPM called the Intrachannel Cross Phase Modulation (IXPM) and Intrachannel Four Wave Mixing (IFWM) become significant (Kumar, Mauro, Raghavan, & Chowdhury,

2002). For a WDM system, the additional effects of interchannel XPM (Chiang, Kagi, Marhic, & Kazovsky, 1996; Cartaxo, 1999; Marcuse, Chraplyvy, & Tkach, 1994) and FWM (Tkach, Chraplyvy, Forghieri, Gnauck, & Derosier, 1995), that induces crosstalk between WDM channels become significant. This nonlinear crosstalk acts in addition to linear crosstalk caused by closely spaced WDM channels (Bosco, Carena, Curri, Gaudino, & Poggiolini, 2004).

Some other nonlinear scattering effects such as the Stimulated Raman Scattering (SRS) and the Stimulated Brillouin Scattering (SBS) have been ignored in this book, and a fiber phenomenon that has fast gained prominence but has been also ignored here are the effects of signal polarization and fiber birefringence (Wang, 1999; Liu, Xie, & van Wijngaarden, 2004). The consideration of arbitrary polarization within the optical fiber can lead to a variety of effects such as polarization dispersion (Born & Wolf, 1980; Liu & Enyuk, 1999; Menyuk, 1987). These effects become significant for high bit rate and long distance systems. However, the employment of polarization multiplexing or polarization interleaving may allow further increase of the potential capacity of fiber communication (Evangelides, Mollenauer, Gordon, & Bergano, 1992).

In order to evaluate the performance of a communication system, it is crucial to obtain reliable and simple methods to quantify the performance. To accomplish this, we look into different models used to evaluate performance in an OTDM-WDM system. Currently, there are no complete methods available that are applicable for all general scenarios, and this task is further complicated by the numerous effects that have to be taken into account. As such, the use of performance estimators have to be carefully chosen or tested for reliability. The obtained results are then used to optimize and analyze the performance of the system by varying important parameters such as signal pulse width, filter bandwidths, input signal power, modulation technique, bit rate, and spectral efficiency. These analyses will then help in the future design of OCDM-WDM, SCM-WDM, and OTDM-WDM communication systems.

As with any other communication system, there are many factors that limit the performance of the optical communication system. In this book, we specifically focus on physical effects within the optical fiber that impose limitations to transmission performance. Important effects that largely determine the limiting factors of present-day, long-distance optical communication systems will be examined in detail. Before looking at performance limitations, the criteria used to quantify the performance of a system are the system information rate (bit rate), bandwidth utilization (spectral efficiency, channel separation), transmission length, system reliability (bit error rate, required Optical Signal to Noise Ratio, OSNR), Dispersion Management (DM), Forward Error Correction (FEC), power consumption, and system cost.

It is important to make note of the quantifying criteria since they serve as yardsticks to help us evaluate system performance. This is turn helps us clearly observe the limitations that are imposed. The criteria stated above are standard criteria for any communication system, and an optical fiber-based system is no exception. When constructing a communication system, there generally has to be some trade-off among the five performance criteria listed above. For practical purposes, we would like to maximize the system information rate, bandwidth utilization, and transmission length. However, in pursuing these goals, system reliability will be steadily compromised while power consumption and system cost will increase. For this report, we ignore the implications of system cost since the mode of investigation is analysis and simulation. Given that freedom, the main factor that places a limit to the maximization of transmission rates and length is the need to maintain a certain threshold of system reliability. This trade-off will be a key feature of this book.

Therefore, whenever there is the presence of two or more competing requirements that trade off with each other, an optimum point exists. With respect to our analysis of the optical communication system, it means that we are looking for optimum performance points for these systems. In any analysis of optimal performance, the two main factors that need to be worked out are the equations that govern the behavior of the system and initial conditions (parameters) of the system.

In general, the equations are complex and have to be solved using numerical analysis. The use of numerical simulations leads naturally to questions of approximations and degree of accuracy. As such, these inaccuracies need to be quantified and minimized using rigorous methods of computation. For the second factor of initial system conditions, in our analysis, it means the setup or configuration of the optical communication system that we intend to analyze. Since the number of possible configurations is rather limitless, we have to place our own set of limits to the configurations that we intend to study.

The systems we have chosen to focus on are high performance, long distance systems. This is because these are the areas where system reliability will be most strained due to the requirements for high bit rates, high density, and large transmission lengths. These are also the areas where studies are still actively conducted to further maximize the transmission capabilities of the optical fiber. Since our research work is of an analytical nature, we can bypass the limitations of infrastructure cost. As such, it is ideal for research such as this one to focus on high-end, speculative systems to check the boundaries of performance limitations. This is to keep the performance analysis and optimization performed in this report relevant and useful for future deployments of actual systems.

So for example, in a typical OTDM-WDM system, there are generally a number of key parameters that has to be decided upon before a particular system setup can be implemented. Among them are transmission distance, amplification scheme, and dispersion management scheme. Then, signal modulation format, OTDM channel bit rate, WDM channel bit rate, and spectral efficiency can be varied or specified over a particular series of simulations.

After the system has been established, there are still a number of variables that have to be optimized in order to achieve optimal performance for a particular system configuration. Among these parameters are the signal pulse width, optical filter bandwidth, electrical post-detection filter bandwidth, and the input power into the transmission link that can be optimized for a particular system setup to obtain the optimal performance that the system is capable of.

Throughout this book, there are numerous references to either a back-to-back or a point-to-point system configuration, where back-to-back refers to a configuration whereby the signal from the transmitter is fed straight into the receiver without passing through a transmission fiber link. Optical noise can be added onto the signal just before the receiver to set the Optical Signal to Noise Ratio (OSNR) of the received signal to a required value. This approach is used to test the behavior of the signal in the presence of linear effects such as WDM linear crosstalk and Intersymbol Interference (ISI). By avoiding simulation of the fiber link, we can quickly optimize and analyze the system under a linear operating environment without fiber-related effects. Point-to-point refers to a configuration whereby the signal from the transmitter is fed through a transmission fiber link before reaching the receiver. Optical noise in this scenario is typically the result of accumulated ASE and this sets the received OSNR. This approach is a full simulation of a transmission system and takes into account all linear and nonlinear effects within the system. This is slower but a more complete test of the system behavior.

At present, complete description of the signal propagation is only available through numerical solutions to the basic modeling equations. Purely analytical solutions to complex systems that take into account both linear and nonlinear distortions are not available. At the same time, many of the linear and nonlinear effects in the optical fiber have become significant performance inhibitors as the limits to modern optical communication systems are pushed even higher.

As such, there is a need to obtain and verify reliable simulation techniques and methodologies. With a reliable set of tools, various high-speed, dense hybrid multiplexing systems such as OCDM-WDM, SCM-WDM, and OTDM-WDM can be studied and analyzed to optimize various system parameters to achieve performance gains.

Additionally, such analysis can be used for comparisons between competing communication schemes such as signal modulation or network topology. Numerical simulations using innovative models act as a reliable meter to gauge the comparative performance of different system configurations. Such results can be used to tailor future experimental work, which is expensive to undertake. Using data from numerical simulations, future experiments can rely on previous simulation results to target specific optimized results.

The present work attempts to enable technical managers, graduate students enrolled in the MS and PhD degree programs, engineers and technicians involved in the fiber-optics industry, and scientists working in the fields of optical communications to attain a broader perspective of the parameters involved in the transmission of optical signals using optical soliton system, OCDM-WDM, SCM-WDM, and OTDM-WDM.

The book is organized in five sections with 15 chapters. Chapter 1 focuses on the linear effects that occur at the physical medium. Specifically, much attention is paid to physical linear effects within the optical fiber that imposes limitations to optical transmission performance.

Chapter 2 presents an overview of important physical layer nonlinear effects impairments such as Self-Phase Modulation (SPM), Cross-Phase Modulation (XPM), Four-Wave Mixing (FWM), Stimulated Brillouin Scattering (SBS), and Stimulated Raman Scattering (SRS). It thus provides a framework for describing nonlinear phenomena in fiber optic transmission systems.

Chapters 3 through 6 of section 2, deal with high-speed and advanced optical transmission systems such as the optical soliton, SCM-WDM, OCDM-WDM, and OTDM-WDM. In this context, Chapter 3 gives an overview on the effect of Cross-Phase Modulation (XPM) on Dispersion Managed (DM) 40Gb/s direct detection optical soliton transmission system in the presence of Group Velocity Dispersion (GVD), Self-Phase Modulation (SPM), and Amplified Spontaneous Emission (ASE).

Chapter 4 is devoted to analyze semi-analytically the performance limitation of Subcarrier Multiplexing-WDM Passive Optical Network (SCM-WDM PON) in the presence of XPM and GVD.

Chapter 5 starts by discussing the operation principles of a phase-encoded OCDMA system and presents an analytical approach to study dispersion effects on optical pulse in fiber medium in order to obtain the properties of the phase encoded OCDMA signal as it propagates in a dispersive fiber transmission link.

Chapter 6 presents a detailed study on the XPM effect on the performance of dispersion managed 20Gb/s optical WDM transmission system using either OOK and DPSK modulation, in the presence of Group Velocity Dispersion (GVD), Self-Phase Modulation (SPM), and Amplified Spontaneous Emission (ASE).

In section 3, Chapter 7 presents a detailed description of the operation principle of OTDM-WDM transmission system.

Chapter 8 looks into the effects that impair OTDM-WDM propagation, particularly the nonlinear effects. Particular attention was given to model the major physical performance limitations to the system, especially within the optical fiber.

Chapter 9 provides a framework for OTDM-WDM system components modeling including all relevant devices. In this regard, successfully, high capacity, long distance, SMF, OTDM-WDM optical fiber communication systems, employing optical amplification and DM, have been deeply modeled and studied.

Section 4 deals with the performance analysis models and discusses the optimization of system design parameters. In this context, Chapter 10 starts by discussing the indirect performance evaluation methods such as the estimation of the eye penalty, calculation of Signal to Noise Ratio (SNR), as well as estimation of amplitude and timing jitter. Further, in order to complete the modeling of the network environment begun in pervious sections, a BER estimation model for optical networks is discussed using tools that have been developed earlier.

Chapter 11 is devoted to optimization of dense OOK OTDM-WDM systems for both RZ and NRZ modulation with signal bit rate, signal pulse width, optical filter bandwidth, and signal-to-noise ratio as parameters. Using polynomial fitting, an approximated expression for the optimal signal pulse duty cycle as a function of spectral density and OSNR is provided. Further, Chapter 12 discusses the MGF-BER estimation technique in details.

The book concludes with Section 5, which verifies the effectiveness of using the DP-Q as a performance estimation tool. In this regard, Chapter 13 provides a comparison of RZ-OOK and RZ-DPSK optimal performance in dense OTDM-WDM systems with varying spectral densities, WDM channel bit rates, and signal-to-noise ratios while optimizing the signal pulse widths and optical filter bandwidths.

Chapter 14 discusses the impact of a post-OTDM-Demux optical filter. In this context, a rigorous simulation is carried out to optimize the double-tier filter configuration and find out the conditions in which it provides performance improvement over the single-tier filter configuration.

Chapter 15 concludes the book by examining the impact of nonlinear effects on the BER performance of dense WDM, cross-connected networks using the Hot-Potato MS Network with deflection routing as a case study. A semi-analytical model, combining the hop distribution and node model with Nonlinear Schrodinger Equation (NLSE)-based simulation of the fiber interconnections is used to evaluate the network performance in the present of fiber nonlinear effects.

Fouad Mohammed Abbou
Al Akhawayn University, Morocco

Hiew Chee Choong
Kasatria, Malaysia

REFERENCES

Agrawal, G. P. (Ed.). (1997). *Fiber-optic communication systems*. New York: Wiley-Interscience.

Bergano, N. S. (2002). *640 gb/s transmission of sixty-four 10 gb/s wdm channels over 7200 km with 0.33 (bits/s)/hz spectral efficiency*. Academic Press.

Born, M., & Wolf, E. (Eds.). (1980). *Principles of optics*. Oxford, UK: Pergamon Press.

Bosco, G., Carena, A., Curri, V., Gaudino, R., & Poggiolini, P. (2004). Modulation formats suitable for ultrahigh spectral efficient wdm systems. *IEEE Journal of Selected Topics in Quantum Electronics, 10*(2), 321–328. doi:10.1109/JSTQE.2004.827830

Cai, J. X. (2002). Long-haul 40 gb/s dwdm transmission with aggregate capacities exceeding 1 tb/s. *Journal of Lightwave Technology, 20*(12), 2247–2257. doi:10.1109/JLT.2002.806770

Castanon, G. A., Tonguz, O. K., & Bononi, A. (1997). Ber performance of multi-wavelength optical cross-connected networks with deflection routing. *IEE Proc-Communications, 144*, 114-120.

Chiang, T. K., Kagi, N., Marhic, M. E., & Kazovsky, L. G. (1996). Cross-phase modulation in fiber links with multiple optical amplifiers and dispersion compensators. *Lightwave Technology, 14*(3), 249–260. doi:10.1109/50.485582

Desurvire, E. (1994). *Erbium-doped fiber amplifiers: Principles and applications*. New York: Wiley-Interscience.

Duce, A. D., Killey, R. I., & Bayvel, P. (2004). Comparison of nonlinear pulse interactions in 160-gb/s quasi-linear and dispersion managed soliton systems. *Lightwave Technology, 22*, 1483–1498.

Evangelides, S. G., Mollenauer, L. F., Gordon, J. P., & Bergano, N. S. (1992). Polarization multiplexing with solitons. *Lightwave Technology, 10*(1), 28–35. doi:10.1109/50.108732

Gnauck, A. H., Raybon, G., Bernasconi, P. G., Leuthold, J., Doerr, C. R., & Stulz, L. W. (2003). 1-tb/s (6 x 170.6 gb/s) transmission over 2000-km nzdf using otdm and rz-dpsk format. *IEEE Photonics Technology, 15*(11), 1618–1620. doi:10.1109/LPT.2003.818634

Keiser, G. (Ed.). (2000). *Optical fiber communications*. New York: McGraw-Hill.

Kumar, S., Mauro, J. C., Raghavan, S., & Chowdhury, D. Q. (2002). Intrachannel non-linear penalties in dispersion-managed transmission systems. *IEEE Journal of Selected Topics in Quantum Electronics*, 8(3), 626–631. doi:10.1109/JSTQE.2002.1016366

Liu, X., Xie, C., & van Wijngaarden, A. J. (2004). Multichannel pmd mitigation and outage reduction through fec with sub-burst-error-correction period pmd scrambling. *IEEE Photonics Technology Letters*, 16(9), 2183–2185. doi:10.1109/LPT.2004.833088

Marcuse, D., Chraplyvy, A. R., & Tkach, E. W. (1994). Dependence of cross-phase modulation on channel number in fiber wdm systems. *Journal of Lightwave Technology*, 12(5), 885–889. doi:10.1109/50.293982

Nakazawa, M. (2000). Solitons for breaking barriers to terabit/second wdm and otdm transmission in the next millenium. *IEEE Journal of Selected Topics in Quantum Electronics*, 6(6), 1332–1343. doi:10.1109/2944.902187

Pachnicke, S., Man, E. D., Spalter, S., & Voges, E. (2005). Impact of the in-line dispersion-compensation map on four-wave mixing (fwm) – impaired optical networks. *IEEE Photonics Technology Letters*, 17(1), 235–237. doi:10.1109/LPT.2004.838629

Srivastava, A. K., Radic, S., Wolf, C., Centanni, J. C., Sulhoff, J. W., Kantor, K., & Sun, Y. (2000). Ultradense wdm transmission in l-band. *IEEE Photonics Technology*, 12(11), 1570–1572. doi:10.1109/68.887758

Tkach, R. W., Chraplyvy, A. R., Forghieri, F., Gnauck, A. H., & Derosier, R. M. (1995). Four-photon mixing and high-speed wdm systems. *Journal of Lightwave Technology*, 13(5), 841–849. doi:10.1109/50.387800

Weinert, C. M., Ludwig, R., Pieper, W., Weber, H. G., Breuer, D., Petermann, K., & Kuppers, F. (1999). 40 gb/s and 4 x 40 gb/s tdm/wdm standard fiber transmission. *Journal of Lightwave Technology*, 17(11), 2276–2284. doi:10.1109/50.803020

Wu, M., & Way, W. I. (2004). Fiber nonlinearity limitations in ultra-dense wdm systems. *Journal of Lightwave Technology*, 22(6), 1483–1498. doi:10.1109/JLT.2004.829222

Zhu, B. (2002). *Transmission of 3.2 tb/s (80 x 42.7 gb/s) over 5200 km of ultrawave fiber with 100-km dispersion-managed spans using RZ-DPSK format*. Academic Press.

Acknowledgment

To my father, who instilled in me the passion for knowledge-seeking, may God bless his soul, forgive him, and grant him the highest levels of paradise. To my mother, wife, and children for their understanding, patience, and endless support throughout the production of this humble work.

Special thanks go to my MSc and PhD students who have, directly or indirectly, contributed to the completion of this work. I am indebted to all of them, and in particular, to my graduate students, Hiew Chee Choong and Chua Choon Hoe, and my colleague, Dr. Hairul Azhar Abdul-Rashid.

Fouad Mohammed Abbou
Al Akhawayn University, Morocco

Section 1

Chapter 1
Optical Transport Network:
A Physical Layer Perspective Part 1

ABSTRACT

Different linear effects that occur in the physical medium are studied and analyzed in this chapter. Specifically, much attention is paid to fiber attenuation, Amplified Spontaneous Emission (ASE) noise due to optical amplifiers, and fiber dispersive effects that cause pulse broadening, which may represent a serious problem in high-speed optical transmission systems. In order to reduce fiber dispersive effects effectively, dispersion compensation fiber is employed. Other effects such as linear crosstalk, which causes distortion and interferes with the filtered channel, can be reduced by optimizing the optical filter bandwidth and shape to obtain a compromise between WDM linear crosstalk and filter induced intersymbol interference (ISI).

INTRODUCTION

This chapter focuses on the linear effects that occur in the transmission medium when the optical transmission system is considered to be operating in a linear regime. It provides a clear picture about fiber attenuation and fiber dispersive effects that cause pulse broadening, which may represent a serious problem in high-speed optical transmission systems when dispersion management is not employed. In order to

DOI: 10.4018/978-1-4666-6575-0.ch001

maintain acceptable optical signal strength along the lightwave path, optical amplifiers are inserted to compensate for signal losses. Unfortunately, the optical amplification is accompanied by ASE noise which is accumulated along the transmission link and imposes additional limitation on the system performance. Other effect such as the linear crosstalk is also discussed and a solution to reduce its effect is presented.

FIBER ATTENUATIONS

Light traveling down an optical fiber experiences attenuation or loss as it propagates as shown in Figure 1. This is a fundamental limit on optical communications as it limits the possible distance of transmission. The attenuation or the fiber loss is defined as the ratio of the optical output power, P_{out} from a fiber of length L to the input power P_{in} and is expressed as

Figure 1. Signal progression through optical fiber with attenuation of 0.2 dB/km (Hiew, Abbou, & Chuah 2006)

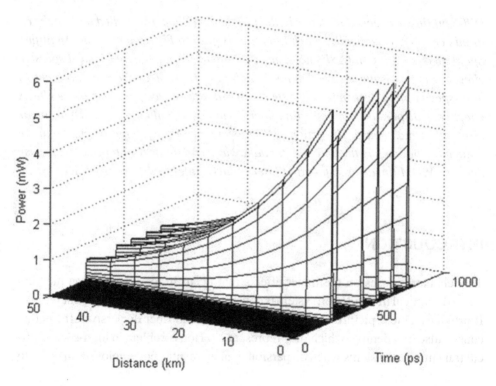

$$\alpha * L = 10 \log_{10} [P_{in} / P_{out}] \tag{1.1}$$

in units of decibels (dB). The loss of fiber is typically expressed using the attenuation factor α in units of dB/km

$$\alpha = 10 \log_{10} [(P_{in} / P_{out}) / L] \tag{1.2}$$

Thus, an optical signal propagating through the optical fiber will suffer a finite loss that can be described fully using the attenuation factor.

There are a few factors that lead to attenuation of the signal in an optical fiber. These factors are coupling losses between the source–fiber, fiber-fiber losses, fiber-detector losses, fiber bending losses, and losses due to absorption, scattering and radiation losses (Keiser, 2000).

Coupling losses between the source–fiber, fiber-fiber and fiber-detector and fiber bending losses are extrinsic in nature and not inherent properties of the optical fiber. However, these losses can add up to significant amounts in many real-life situations. For example, the coupling between the laser and the fiber leads to high losses due to aperture differences between the two mediums. However, these losses can be reduced with additional precaution being taken during system installation and are normally considered apart from the design of optical networks.

On the other hand, the losses due to scattering, absorption and radiation depend on fundamental characteristics of the fiber. Absorption of light in an optical fiber may be intrinsic or extrinsic. Intrinsic absorption is due to material absorption and electron absorption that are fundamental properties of the fiber medium. The extrinsic absorption is due to the presence of transition metal impurities known as impurity absorption. These impurities nowadays may be reduced to amounts that are negligibly small in effect for expensive, top-quality optical fiber that employs the latest fabrication and purification technology.

However, intrinsic absorption cannot be reduced, as it is property of the fiber material. Material absorption is a loss mechanism related to the material composition and the fabrication process of the fiber that results in the dissipation of some of the transmitted optical power into heat in the optical fiber. An absolutely pure silicate glass has little intrinsic absorption due to its basic material structure in the near infrared region and this is one of the advantages of optical fiber communication. It has two intrinsic absorption mechanisms at optical wavelengths that leave a low intrinsic absorption window over the 0.8 µm to 1.7 µm wavelength range that lies across the optical and infrared bands. Though the intrinsic loss is small, it is significant nowadays as it represents the last attenuation mechanism in optical fibers after the other mechanisms are dealt with, and thus becomes a limiting factor.

In silica fibers, the absorption peak occurs in the ultra-violet region at about 0.14 μm; however, the tail of this peak extends through to about 1 μm. In the infra-red and far-infrared region, the atomic bonds associated with the core material absorb long wavelength light. The absorption mechanism causes vibration of the molecules of the core materials and give absorption peaks at about 7 μm. The strong absorption bands occur due to oscillations of molecules such as Si-O (9.2 μm), P – O (8.1 μm), B – O (7.2 μm) and Ge – O (11.0 μm). The tails of the absorption mechanism are significant at or above 1.5 μm and are the cause of the most of the pure glass losses.

The effect of both these processes may be minimized by suitable composition of core and cladding materials. The optimization of all attenuation mechanism parameters leaves the silicon fiber with 'transmission windows' at certain ranges of wavelengths where fiber attenuation is low and optimum transmission can be achieved. Two of the commonly used windows are the ones centered at 1.33 μm and 1.55 μm. Today, a minimum attenuation factor of 0.20 dB/km is obtainable at wavelengths around 1.55 μm in silica fibers where the residual loss is caused by intrinsic loss and Rayleigh scattering loss, which will be discussed later. However, other fiber materials such as fluoride glasses have been discovered with lower losses at higher wavelengths. These fibers are still in an experimental stage and are not commercially implemented due to various reasons.

Linear scattering mechanisms cause the linear transfer of some or all of the optical power contained within one propagating mode into a different mode. This process tends to result in attenuation of the transmitted light as the transfer may be to a leaky or radiating mode which does not continue to propagate within the fiber core, but is radiated from the fiber. As the process is linear, there is no change in frequency due to scattering.

Linear scattering may be classified into Mie scattering and Rayleigh scattering. Mie scattering is due to inhomogeneities in the fiber that are comparable to the wavelength of light. It may be reduced significantly by reducing the impurity concentration in the fiber and using good fabrication techniques. On the other hand, Rayleigh scattering is the dominant intrinsic loss mechanism in the low absorption window between the ultraviolet and infrared absorption tails (Agrawal, 1997). It results from inhomogeneities of a random nature occurring on a small scale compared with the wavelength of light. These inhomogeneities manifest themselves as fluctuation in refractive index and arise from density and compositional variations that are frozen in the glass lattice on cooling. The compositional variation may be reduced by improved fabrication but the refractive index fluctuations caused by the freezing-in of density inhomogeneities are fundamental and cannot be avoided. Thus, Rayleigh scattering largely determines the minimum floor of the loss mechanism.

Though the attenuation spectrum of the optical fiber is not constant with frequency, we can normally assume a constant attenuation factor when specifying the parameters of the optical fiber. This is because optical transmission typically occurs only within a particular transmission window (for example, 1.55 μm) and within a window, the attenuation is approximately constant with respect to frequency.

OPTICAL AMPLIFIERS

Transmission along the optical fiber experiences attenuation and like any other transmission medium, this places a severe limiting factor to the maximum length of the communication system. The attenuation is low for high quality silicon fiber (as low as 0.20 dB/km) compared to free space medium but it becomes significant for transmission over long lengths. It is in the interest of optical communication systems design to fully maximize the potential transmission length of the fiber and to overcome the limits placed by fiber loss. For a long-haul lightwave system, the loss limitation has traditionally been overcome using optoelectronic repeaters in which the optical signal is first detected and converted into an electric current, which is used to guide the regeneration of the optical signal using a new set of transmitters (Agrawal, 1997). Such regenerators have to be placed at every set amount of distance and can become quite complex and expensive for multi-channel, long distance optical systems. An alternative approach makes use of optical amplifiers, which amplify the optical signal directly without requiring conversion to the electric domain (Desurvire, 1994).

The development of optical amplifiers has coincided with the need for changes in the telecommunication industry. Research in semiconductor optical amplifiers began earnestly fifteen years ago. At that time, optical amplifiers were considered to be a potential solution for amplification in optical communication systems. The performance of optical amplifiers relies critically on their gain characteristics, optical power output and energy consumption. An amplifier basically consists of an amplifying medium, the connecting transmission fiber through which the pump is delivered, and a pump source. The gain of an amplifier, G is normally set to counteract the attenuation suffered by the signal while transmitting through the optical fiber and the various other devices such that

$$G = 1/L \tag{1.3}$$

where L is the total loss to be compensated for. Optical amplifiers include semiconductor laser amplifiers (SLA) or semiconductor optical amplifiers (SOA), fiber Raman amplifiers, fiber Brillouin amplifiers, optical parametric amplifiers and erbium doped fiber amplifiers (EDFA).

Semiconductor diode laser amplifiers are usually used for high-speed optical amplification and all-optical switching in telecommunication systems. Applications including broadband semiconductor lasers will require knowledge of their ultra-fast gain and index dynamics. Ultra-fast gain nonlinearities affect the modulation bandwidth and the saturation behavior of semiconductor amplifiers whereas ultra-fast refractive index nonlinearities influence spectrum and chirp of the amplified pulses. Semiconductor optical amplifiers are considered complementary alternatives because they are inexpensive, miniature, extremely wavelength flexible and can be used as external modulators or as switches in networks. The main drawback of the SOAs is their relatively narrow gain bandwidths. This is a major issue in high capacity OTDM-WDM transmission as the total multiplexed signal bandwidth is large and consequently a large gain bandwidth is required to fully amplify the signal over its entire spectrum.

Doped fiber amplifiers make use of rare-earth elements as a gain medium by doping the fiber core during the manufacturing process. Many rare-earth ions such as erbium, holmium, neodymium, samarium and also thulium can be used to realize fiber amplifiers. One of the amplifiers that have attracted most attention is the erbium-doped fiber amplifier (EDFA) (Desurvire, 1994). EDFAs can operate and maintain a flat gain over a large bandwidth with low induced noise. This has revolutionized optical communication by enabling the implementation of multi-channel, high capacity, ultra long distance, and repeater-less systems. In spite of their usefulness, EDFAs can be deployed in only limited types of applications. They are very expensive, which means they are economical only for long-haul systems. Their large size means they are not monolithically integrable with other devices. However, much active research in recent years has been geared towards solving the problems of applying EDFAs. Despite its high cost, EDFAs have managed to increase the repeater-less length of optical transmission and remains the most viable alternative for long distance multi channel transmission. In this book, we will use the EDFA as the amplifier of choice since we are dealing with long-distance, multi-channel systems that require a large gain bandwidth. Figure 2 shows the signal loss with ideal periodic amplification using EDFAs as inline amplifiers.

Another type of amplifier coming to the fore is the Raman fiber amplifier (Agrawal, 2001; Bouteiller, Leng, & Headley, 2004; Zhou & Brik, 2004). This amplifier operated based on the SRS effect, which will be discussed briefly later. It utilizes the scattering of the pump wave through SRS into the probe signal to amplify the probe. A key advantage of Raman amplifiers is the inherently large bandwidth of the Raman gain spectrum, resulting in a large almost-flat gain bandwidth for the amplifier. Another advantage is that Raman amplification occurs within any regular optical fiber and this means that the optical fiber itself can be used as an amplifier so long as the right pump is provided. The Raman amplification

Figure 2. Signal loss with ideal periodic amplification (loss = 0.2 dB/km) (Hiew, Abbou, & Chuah 2006)

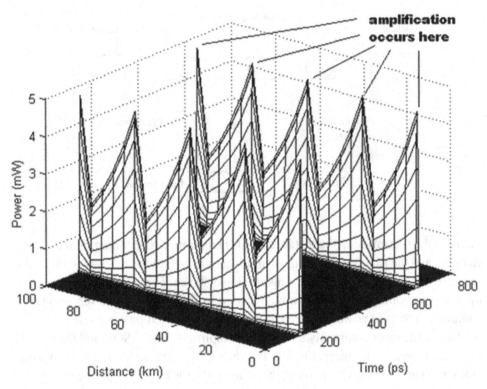

process is normally performed over a long distance, which is typically the length of the fiber span. As such, the gain of the amplifier is low as it does not rely on sharp, instantaneous gains. This helps keep the noise induced by the amplifier low. In recent years, a proposed solution uses Raman fiber amplifiers together with EDFAs to improve the amplification bandwidth and strength, while reducing the accumulated noise (Zhou & Brik, 2004). This could help reduce the cost of amplification and increase the flexibility of a system. However, the subject on the use of Raman amplifiers is beyond the scope of this study. Since the Raman amplifier is used as an additional device over existing optical systems, it serves as future work to see how the addition of the amplifier changes the behavior of the optical system.

There are various system designs that can be implemented using amplifiers. Among these are: inline amplifiers, power boosters and preamplifiers as shown in Figure 3. Inline amplifiers are used to replace optoelectronic repeaters. The amplifier is placed at strategic spots along the fiber transmission to boost power levels that have decreased due to attenuation. Power boosters are used to increase the transmitter power by placing the amplifier just after the transmitter. A power amplifier can

Figure 3. Various implementations of amplifiers in an optical system (Hiew, Abbou, & Chuah 2006)

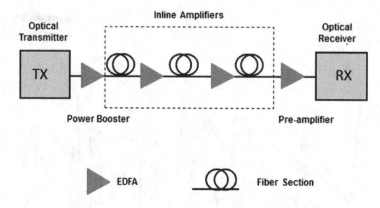

increase the transmission the distance by 100 km or more depending on the amplifier gain and the fiber loss. Putting an amplifier just before the receiver to boost the received power can also increase transmission distance. These amplifiers are called optical preamplifiers and are commonly used to improve the receiver sensitivity (minimum received power required to maintain a specified bit error rate).

Two of the most commonly used optical amplifiers are the SOA and the EDFA. For both devices, the internal configuration relies on the same mechanisms, one similar in nature to the operation of the semiconductor laser. Within the amplification medium, there is an excess of electron-hole pairs generated (population inversion) by pumping the amplifier with either electrical current (SOA) or a pump light on a frequency different from the input probe signal (EDFA). The propagation of the input probe light signal through the amplification medium causes the recombination of electron-hole pairs while releasing photons that are coherent to the input signal, known as stimulated emission. The addition of coherent photons provides the amplifying mechanism.

Amplified Spontaneous Emission Noise

The dominant noise generated in an optical amplifier is amplified spontaneous emission (ASE) (Yamamoto & Inoue, 2003; Agrawal, 1997). The origin of ASE is the spontaneous recombination of electrons and holes in the amplification medium, known as spontaneous emission. This spontaneous emission travels through the amplifying medium along with the probe signal resulting in its amplification. This gives rise to the name ASE and it is significant because the relatively small initial spontaneous emission is amplified by the time it reaches the amplifier output. Generally, the ASE generated is a random process characterized by a flat noise power spectrum also called the white noise spectrum.

When inline amplifiers are used, the signal propagates together with mixed noise resulting in various effects. The general shape of the noise spectrum generated using the above method is shown in Figure 4 where it is generally flat, with random spikes (Figure 4(a)). The autocorrelation obtained from an ideally flat noise spectrum (Figure 4(b)) is an impulse function and it is shown in Figure 4 (c) that the generated ASE noise autocorrelation has an almost ideal impulse response with a small margin of error. Detailed study of the ASE mechanism reveals that the spectrum is not exactly flat over the amplifier's entire gain bandwidth but depends among other things on the pump light used but actual derivation of the noise is complex involving rate equations (Desurvire, 1994; Yamamoto & Inoue, 2003), so it can be replaced in most cases by the flat spectrum approximation without much loss of accuracy.

ASE is a dominant limiting factor to the performance of optical communication systems whenever optical amplification is required. This is especially true for long distance systems where high amplifier gain is required to offset the signal loss along the long stretch of fiber. In most cases, the ASE generated by optical amplifiers tends to be much higher than the receiver noises such as the shot noise and thermal noise. Therefore, in the analysis of long distance (thousands of kilometers) optically amplified systems, the shot and thermal noises are often insignificant in comparison and ASE also known as optical noise becomes the chief concern (Bosco, Carena, Curri, Gaudino, & Poggiolini, 2002).

ASE cannot be avoided in the design of optical systems because the optical amplifier is necessary to sustain the optical signal for long distances. However, system design can be optimized to reduce its effects by controlling the placement of the amplifiers. The simplest way to place an optical amplifier for a certain length of fiber (e.g. 1000 km) would be to place one either at the front or at the end. The

Figure 4. ASE Noise (a) Intensity in time domain, (b) Power spectral density in frequency domain and (c) Autocorrelation (Hiew, Abbou, & Chuah 2006)

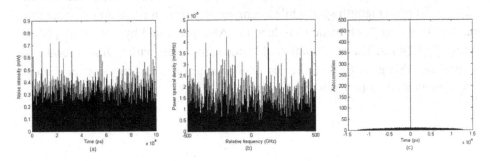

single amplifier would then need to have a gain equal to the total loss of the fiber length. In practice, it is hard to obtain an amplifier that can operate well with such high gains required. Even if we could, placing a single amplifier over such a long length of fiber is bad system design. This is because if placed only at the front (power booster), the fiber input signal power will be very high and becomes extremely susceptible to nonlinear effects, which we shall study in detail later. When placed only at the back (preamplifier), the signal at the input of the amplifier will be very weak and very easily distorted by the ASE generated. This is because the signal power is then comparable to the spontaneous emission power.

Thus, the practical solution in the design of long distance systems is to separate the length of fiber into multiple amplifier spans (also called multi-span amplification). Each span, normally of equal lengths (periodic amplification), would either begin or end with an optical amplifier as shown in Figure 5 and Figure 6. In this way, the task of amplifying the signal is distributed among many different amplifiers and the signal power is maintained along the fiber. However, ASE is still present and is generated by each amplifier in each span. The ASE generated will accumulate along the fiber length and increase in power. This will result in the reduction of the signal to noise ratio (SNR) as the signal propagates along the multiple amplifier spans. Ultimately, this represents a limit to the number of spans and the total length of fiber that the signal can propagate across to maintain a certain amount of signal reliability in terms of bit error rate (BER). Still, this solution is better than just using a single preamplifier (lumped amplification) for long range systems. In practice, the amplifiers are placed in an optimized arrangement before transmission, as inline amplifiers and before the receiver. Simulations of the signal with ASE comparing a fully lumped and fully periodic amplification system are shown in Figure 5 and Figure 6.

Research has shown that shorter amplifier spans result in better system performance. This is because the power of ASE noise is proportional to the gain of the amplifier and shorter spans lead to smaller gains required. However, the number of amplifier spans cannot be increased indiscriminately as each amplifier represents added cost and coupling to the amplifier introduces its own loss that implies a minimal limit to the amplifier gain required. Thus, it is normally required to maximize the amplifier length span while maintaining a certain BER. At the same time, many efforts have been made to reduce the ASE generated by optical amplifiers, especially EDFAs. The combination of Raman amplifiers with EDFAs promises to reduce the ASE generated further by distributing the gain process over a longer length and reducing the gain required in the EDFAs.

Figure 5. System block diagram and ASE effect on signal employing (a) lumped amplification with only a preamplifier (Hiew, Abbou, & Chuah 2006)

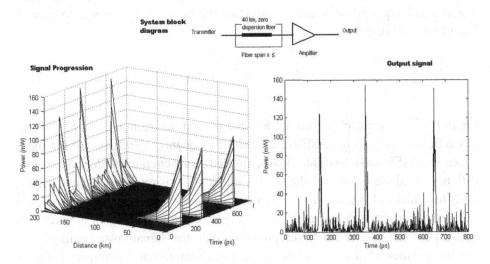

Figure 6. System block diagram and ASE effect on signal employing periodic amplification (Hiew, Abbou, & Chuah 2006)

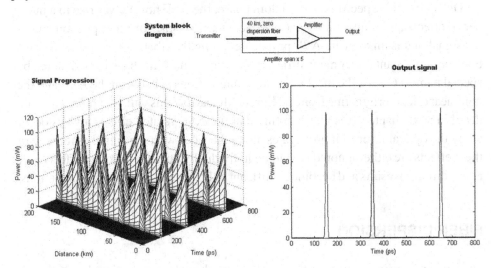

11

Due to the wide spectrum of ASE, it generates many beating (mixing) effects. At the receiver, a signal mixed with ASE noise is detected by the photodetector that acts as a square-law detector converting the optical signal power to current. The general result is

$$I_P = R\left(E_{signal} + E_{ASE}\right)^2 = R\left(E_{signal}^2 + E_{ASE}^2 + 2E_{signal}E_{ASE}\right) \tag{1.4}$$

where I_P is the output photocurrent, R is the photodiode responsivity, E_{signal} is the signal field and E_{ASE} is the ASE noise field. Consequently, the current of the signal mixed with ASE noise has additional terms that represent the beating of the signal with noise and the beating of the noise with itself. This method has been used to study the impact of ASE on the performance of optical systems. The current terms are used because the decision process made on the received signal is performed on the photocurrent. When signal power is high, the signal-noise beating is the dominant source of noise while the noise-noise beating only becomes significant when signal power is low. Furthermore, the noise-noise beating may be reduced significantly through the use of a bandpass optical filter before the photodetector to isolate the signal from the noise.

Due to its wide spectrum and random phase, the ASE noise gives rise to a number of effects and it also mixes and interacts with all sorts of other phenomena as the signal that is mixed with ASE propagates along the fiber. Some of these effects become significant under many different situations and some have been denoted by special names. One of the most interesting interactions is between the ASE and the nonlinear effects originating from the Kerr nonlinearity. This will be explored in more detail in next chapter. It is worth noting that the ASE-related effects always occur along the optical fiber as it propagates along the fiber with the signal, but many of these effects are either ignored or studied individually because different effects give rise to different results and become significant only in their own particular situations.

FIBER DISPERSION

Dispersion is a linear process that leads to the broadening of signal pulses as it propagates down the fiber. This broadening causes intersymbol interference between neighboring signal pulses. The interference caused here represents a limit imposed on the bit rate of transmission, as we would need to place pulses further apart, thus increasing the bit period (refer to Figure 7 and Figure 8). As such, OTDM signals

Figure 7. Dispersion effect on signal for lossless fiber with Dispersion D = 8 ps/nm/km (Hiew, Abbou, & Chuah 2006)

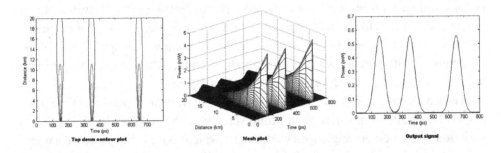

Figure 8. Dispersion effect on signal for lossless fiber with dispersion D = 2 ps/nm/km (Hiew, Abbou, & Chuah 2006)

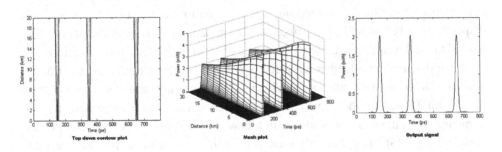

are particularly sensitive to dispersion due to its high bit rates and consequently small bit periods. Dispersion in optical fibers can be classified into two major types (Agrawal, 1997; Keiser, 2000): intermodal dispersion and intramodal dispersion.

Intermodal dispersion occurs only in multimode fibers. In multimode fibers, different modes travel at different group velocities due to the different path links used, and the output pulse width is dependent on the transmission times of the slowest and fastest modes. Multimode step-index fibers exhibit a large amount of intermodal dispersion, which gives the greatest pulse broadening of all dispersion types. However, inter-modal dispersion in multi-mode fibers may be reduced by adopting an optimum refractive index profile, which is provided by a near para-bolic profile of most graded index fibers. As mentioned earlier, our study avoids multimode fibers in favour of single mode fibers to avoid the problem of intermo-dal dispersion. The use of single-mode fibers is prevalent in most modern, long distance, high capacity optical systems.

Intramodal dispersion occurs in both multimode and single mode fibers. It in turn can be classified into material dispersion and waveguide dispersion. Material dispersion may occur in all types of optical fibers and may result from finite spectral width of the optical source and the fact that the refractive index of an optical fiber is not constant with respect to wavelength. The different emitted wavelengths of the optical source will travel at different group velocities due to different refractive index for different wavelengths. As a result, the different wavelengths arrive at the destination at different times leading to pulse broadening. The variation of refractive index with wavelength is dependent on the glass material.

The waveguiding of the fiber may also create intramodal dispersion. Waveguide dispersion results from variation of group velocity with wavelength. This is due to variation of the incident angle with wavelength, which consequently leads to a variation in the transmission times for the rays with different incident angles. Waveguide dispersion is a function of the structure of the optical waveguide and, as such, may be altered by suitable changes in the waveguide structure. This can be done by adding more core or cladding layers or by changing the refractive index profile of the core or cladding. This has turned out to be a boon for engineers as the waveguide dispersion can be controlled to counteract the fundamental material dispersion. This has led to the development of new fiber types with desired dispersion characteristics.

A regular single mode fiber has zero dispersion at a wavelength of approximately 1.33 μm. However, this does not coincide with the minimum attenuation wavelength of 1.55 μm. Thus, new fiber types have been designed where the waveguide dispersion is manipulated in such a way to obtain a new total dispersion curve. A dispersion shifted fiber (DSF) is commonly used, where the zero dispersion wavelength has been shifted to a higher wavelength (1.55 μm). A dispersion-flattened fiber has a dispersion that is evened out over a large range of wavelengths.

The use of fibers with zero dispersion at the operating transmission wavelength would seem to solve the problem of dispersion completely. However, since the dispersion is only zero at one particular wavelength and not over a large range of wavelengths, it still poses a problem because, though the optical signal is centred at one wavelength, its power is spread across its entire signal bandwidth (Marcus, 1991). For a WDM signal, this becomes a major issue as the multiplexed signal is spread across a wide bandwidth. As such, even though one WDM channel may experience zero dispersion, its neighbouring channels would still suffer from finite dispersion values (Konrad, 2002; Wang & Petermann, 1992).

Higher-Order Dispersion

It is often tempting to treat the dispersion of the optical fiber as if it were constant over all wavelengths. This is obviously not true. In reality, dispersion is a function of the signal wavelength and this becomes a major consideration in WDM systems.

The wavelength dependence originates from the wavelength dependence of the mode propagation constant, $\beta(\omega)$ of the optical signal, which can be expanded into a Taylor series about the center frequency ω_0 (Agrawal, 2001)

$$\beta(\omega) = n(\omega)\frac{\omega}{c} = \beta_0 + \beta_1(\omega - \omega_0) + \frac{1}{2}\beta_2(\omega - \omega_0)^2 + \frac{1}{3}\beta_3(\omega - \omega_0)^3 + \cdots \tag{1.5}$$

where $n(\omega)$ is the wavelength/frequency dependent refractive index, ω is the angular frequency, and

$$\beta_m = \left(\frac{d^m\beta}{d\omega^m}\right)_{\omega=\omega_0} \quad m = 0, 1, 2, 3, \ldots \tag{1.6}$$

where each β term is the mth order of the wavelength dependent propagation constant. β_0 is the constant portion of the propagation constant, β_1 is inversely proportional to the pulse group velocity, v_g which is the velocity of movement of the pulse envelope, β_2 is related to pulse broadening (dispersion), β_3 is related to the dispersion slope (rate of change of dispersion with wavelength) and the higher orders are related to correspondingly higher orders of dispersion though they become more insignificant due to their smaller values and the larger division factor in (Eq (1.5)). Relations for the more commonly used β terms are

$$\beta_1 = \frac{n_g}{c} = \frac{1}{v_g}$$
$$\beta_2 = -\frac{\lambda^2}{2\pi c}D \tag{1.7}$$
$$\beta_3 = \frac{\lambda^2}{(2\pi c)^2}\left(\lambda^2 Sl + 2\lambda D\right)$$

where n_g is the group refractive index, λ is the wavelength, D is the dispersion parameter and Sl is the dispersion slope ($Sl = \partial D / \partial\lambda$).

The series can theoretically be expanded into infinite terms but in practice it is only significant up to the fourth term at most. In most of this study, we would in fact only use up to the third term. These higher order terms are commonly known by their order such as third-order dispersion or fourth-order dispersion. The common name for third-order dispersion is dispersion slope and it has become increasingly significant as the second-order dispersion is overcome through new techniques. It is also the main reason why using DSF with zero second-order dispersion at the signal centre wavelength is not a sufficient solution. This is because a finite dispersion slope would result in non-zero dispersion at wavelengths other than the signal centre wavelength. Thus, higher frequency components of the signal would still be affected by dispersion. This factor is not so important in OTDM signals but very significant when WDM is included as well. This is because the WDM signal is spread over a wide spectrum and the second-order dispersion is only zero at one particular wavelength. If this is located at the centre of the channels, the channels at the edges would encounter significant amounts of second order dispersion as the dispersion slope would increase/decrease the dispersion beyond the zero-dispersion wavelength according to

$$D_{res}\left(\lambda\right) = \left(\lambda - \lambda_0\right)Sl \tag{1.8}$$

where $D_{res}(\lambda)$ is the residual dispersion at wavelength λ, λ_0 is the zero dispersion wavelength and Sl is the dispersion slope. The residual dispersion at the edge channels would accumulate as they propagate down the fiber. As such, some WDM channels would experience more dispersion compared to others. The residual dispersion can quickly become a source of errors for the WDM channels located on the edges.

In addition, the residual dispersion slope by itself can also become significant in distorting the signal. Figure 9 shows the trademarks of a third-order dispersion distorted signal. For most practical dispersion slope values, third-order dispersion only becomes significant over long distances. In Figure 9, the total fiber length is 1020 km and even then, a high dispersion slope, $Sl = 0.5$ was required for its effects to be clearly seen. Alternatively, the effects of residual dispersion slope are more significant when the signal pulses or bit periods are very short (short picosecond to femtosecond range) (Murakami, Matsudab, Maeda, & Imai, 2000). The uncompensated Sl causes the typical effects of the formation of a pedestal at the front of the pulse, a slight pulse broadening (causing a decrease in amplitude) and a shift of the pulse center towards the side of the pedestal. The pedestal can lead to interference with adjacent pulses if the bit period is small while the shift of the pulse center causes timing jitter on the signal which can lead to significant detection errors.

As second-order dispersion is compensated for through the use of DSFs, third-order dispersion becomes the new limiting factor especially for WDM signals. Thus, new fibers and methods have been invented whereby the third-order dispersion is also compensated for (Mu, Yu, Grigoryan, 2002).

Figure 9. Third order dispersion effects. Second-order dispersion, D in ps/nm/km is fully compensated while amplifiers are assumed to be noiseless (Hiew, Abbou, & Chuah 2006).

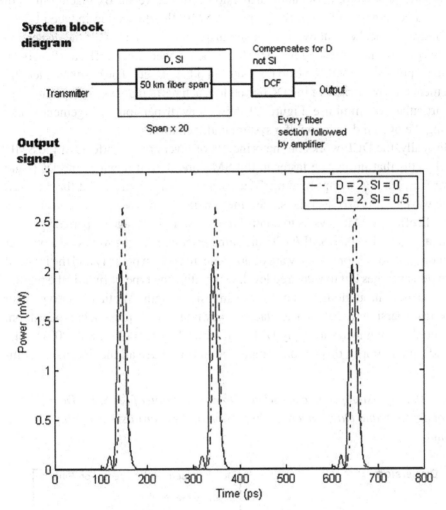

Dispersion Management (DM)

Another way to reduce dispersion effectively in optical communication systems is through dispersion management (DM) (Pachnicke, Man, Spalter, & Voges, 2005; Duce, Killey, & Bayvel, 2004). This method involves the use of dispersion compensation fiber (DCF) that has been fabricated to possess a dispersion that has opposite polarity to the dispersion of the regular fiber used in the majority of the fiber link. Therefore, if the regular fiber used has negative or normal dispersion, the DCF used should have positive or anomalous dispersion and vice versa. By placing links of DCF of a certain length after every span of SMF, the dispersion induced by the SMF may be cancelled out by the opposite dispersion in the DCF. If the dispersion is fully compensated, the original signal may be recovered perfectly, as dispersion is a linear process, provided we do not factor in other effects. The optimized length, placement and magnitude of the DCF used for each particular system are subject to the particular system in use. Figure 10 shows how dispersion management works to bring the overall dispersion of a system under control.

Basically, the DCF works on the principle of reversing the effects of the SMF. Wavelengths that propagate faster in the SMF are slowed down in the DCF and slower wavelengths are speeded up. Thus, when the signal arrives at the receiver, all the wavelengths arrive at the same time. Therefore, no overall dispersion is induced. In effect, DM allows us to control the amount of average dispersion present within a system. Besides SMF/DCF, the same principle of DM works on any other fiber combination as long as they are of opposite dispersion polarity and the induced dispersion averages out to a desired level. Generally, one type of fiber is the regular fiber type used throughout most of the transmission length. Another fiber type with opposite dispersion would then be placed at key points as dispersion compensation.

There are many ways to apply DM to an optical system (Agrawal, 2001). One method called lumped dispersion compensation is to place all the dispersion com-

Figure 10. Dispersion parameters where Dp = dispersion of the SMF, Dc = dispersion of the DCF and Dav = average dispersion of the overall system (Hiew, Abbou, & Chuah 2006)

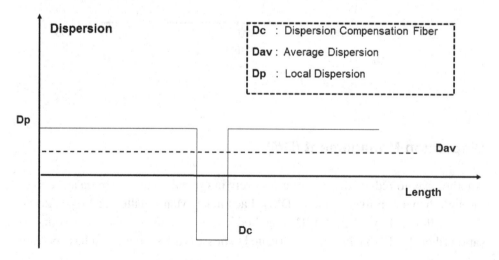

pensation at the front (called pre-dispersion compensation), at the back (called post-dispersion compensation) or in the middle. Another method is distributed dispersion compensation similar in concept to periodic amplification. In fact, it is often used in tandem, whereby each amplifier span is divided into two sections: the first is the regular fiber type and the second is the dispersion compensation. Some examples of DM configurations are shown in Figure 11, Figure 12 and Figure 13.

In DM systems, a few new terms are used to describe the nature of the dispersion under discussion:

1. **Local Dispersion:** Refers to the dispersion of the current fiber span where D_{pn} is dispersion of fiber span, n.
2. **Total Dispersion**: Refers to the total dispersion of all the fiber spans in the system such that Dtotal = D_{p1} + D_{p2} + ... + D_{pN} where N is the total fiber spans.
3. **Average Dispersion:** D_{av} = Dtotal / L where L is the total fiber length of the system.

Figure 11. Signal and block diagram (total length = 255 km, D = 2 ps/nm/km, loss fully compensated by amplifiers with ASE) for lumped DM (Hiew, Abbou, & Chuah 2006)

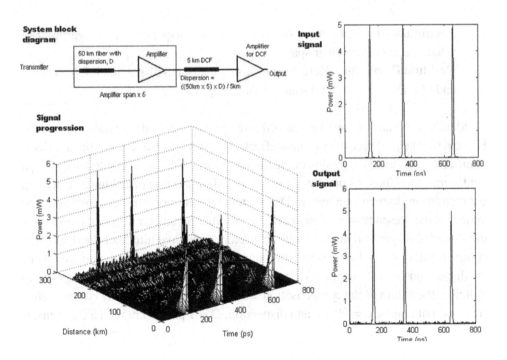

Figure 12. Signal and block diagram (total length = 255 km, D = 2 ps/nm/km, loss fully compensated by amplifiers with ASE) for distributed DM (Hiew, Abbou, & Chuah 2006)

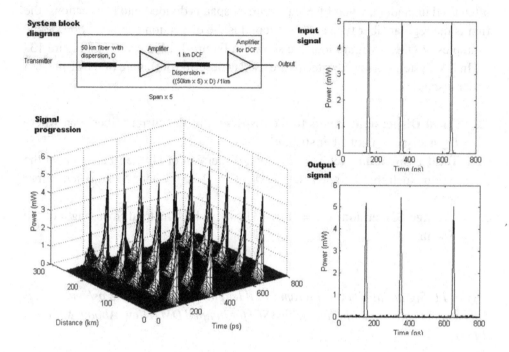

4. **Accumulated Dispersion:** Refers to the total dispersion up to the point of reference or current fiber span.
5. **Residual Dispersion:** Refers to any uncompensated dispersion left over at the end of a DM span or total transmission length.

Ideally, using any of the different DM arrangements should give the same results. However in the presence of nonlinear effects, this is not true as the nonlinear effects interact with the local dispersion of the fiber resulting in different results for different configurations. Thus, in practice, a mixture of lumped and distributed dispersion compensation (known as a hybrid DM system) is commonly used to optimize the system in the presence of nonlinear effects. Another parameter to consider in DM is the so-called dispersion map strength that refers to the magnitude of the dispersion compensation used. Alternatively, this can also be said to refer to the magnitude of the dispersion swing from the SMF to the DCF within each DM span. This property indicates the nature of the compensation. For instance, we could fully compensate a fiber span of length, $L = 90$ km and dispersion, $D = 1$ ps/nm/km with a compensat-

Figure 13. Signal and block diagram (total length = 255 km, D = 2 ps/nm/km, loss fully compensated by amplifiers with ASE) for mixed DM (Hiew, Abbou, & Chuah 2006)

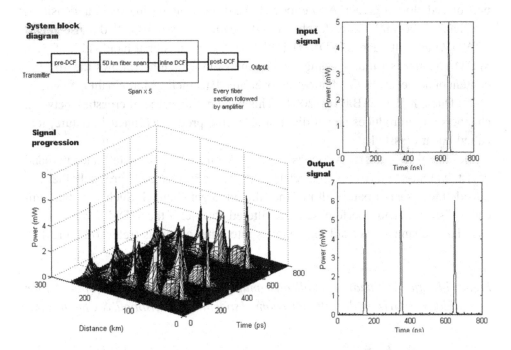

ing fiber span of $L = 10$ km and $D = -9$ ps/nm/km. We could achieve the same full compensation with a $L = 90$ km, $D = 10$ ps/nm/km span balanced with a $L = 10$ km, $D = -90$ ps/nm/km span. These two dispersion maps have different strengths but obtain the same full dispersion compensation result over the same transmission lengths. Thus, it would seem that any configuration would give the same results. This is true for a fully linear system, but once again different results are obtained when nonlinear effects are accounted for.

As stated in the previous section, new fibers have been devised to compensate for higher order dispersion as well. Such fibers are an extension of the regular DCFs where they can compensate for both dispersion and dispersion slope at the same time, and are called inverse/reverse dispersion fibers. An inverse/reverse fiber (D-) is slope matched with a positive dispersion fiber (D+) in a hybrid fiber span. Both the second and third order dispersions are matched so as to almost completely cancel each other. Such hybrid spans are part of a new generation of high performance DM systems.

WDM LINEAR CROSSTALK

Linear crosstalk occurs due to the overlap of the spectral content of WDM channels placed close together. As we move towards ever increasing spectral densities, the channels become more closely packed together in systems called dense WDM (DWDM) and ultradense WDM (UDWDM). Since the signal bandwidth of each WDM channel is finite, placing the channels close together allows the spectral content of adjacent WDM channels to overlap ((Pachnicke, Man, Spalter, & Voges, 2005; Duce, Killey, & Bayvel, 2004). This becomes a source of crosstalk between channels and introduces signal distortion. As the process is linear in nature, it is called linear crosstalk.

In general, there are two varieties of crosstalk, out-of-band crosstalk and intraband crosstalk. Out-of-band crosstalk refers to the adjacent channels' crosstalk that lies outside the essential bandwidth of the filtered target channel. Such crosstalk will cause distortion and interfere with the filtered channel if the WDM demultiplexer used has a channel filter tail that extends into other channels (refer to Figure 14).

Figure 14. Effect of linear crosstalk on demultiplexed WDM channels (optical filter bandwidth = 90 GHz) under different channel spacing (Hiew, Abbou, & Chuah 2006)

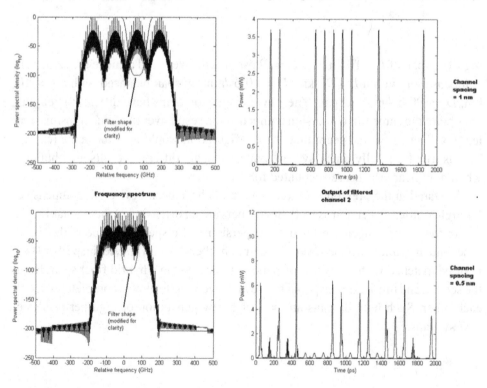

Thus, in order to reduce this effect, we can design filter shapes that have very sharp drop-off rates or use matched filters. However, for UDWDM systems where the channels are very closely packed together, intraband crosstalk is dominant. This is the case when the spectral content of adjacent channels directly overlaps the target filtered channel's essential bandwidth. Such crosstalk is mixed together with the spectral content of the target channel causing waveform distortions.

With such tightly spaced WDM channels, the optical filter bandwidth, used to demultiplex the individual WDM channels from the overall signal, needs to be optimized, where a balance needs to be achieved (Bosco, Carena, Curri, Gaudino, & Poggiolini, 2002; Winzer, Pfennigbauer, Strasser, & Leeb, 2001). This is because when the filter bandwidth is large intraband crosstalk occurs resulting in the wave-form distortions seen earlier. On the other hand, reducing the optical filter bandwidth to very small values to reduce linear crosstalk would result in the slicing off of channel spectral content, resulting in a phenomenon known as intersymbol interfer-ence (ISI). ISI occurs because the spectral content removed is the high frequency

Figure 15. Effect of ISI on demultiplexed WDM channels (channel spacing = 0.5 nm) under different optical filter bandwidths (Hiew, Abbou, & Chuah 2006)

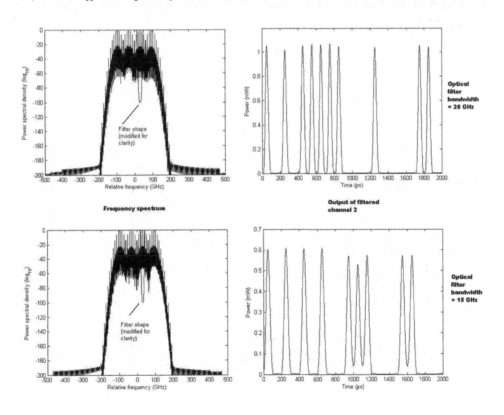

portions of the channel baseband signal. As a result, the received baseband signal would spread in the time domain causing adjacent pulses/symbols to overlap (refer to Figure 15).

This type of distortion is undesirable as well. Therefore, the optical filter bandwidth and shape need to be optimized to obtain a compromise between WDM linear crosstalk and filter induced ISI. An example to optical filter bandwidth optimization is shown in Figure 16.

SUMMARY

The linear effects that occur in optical fibers were discussed. Some of them, such as ASE noise and dispersion can degrade the system performance through the pulse shape distortion and signal spectrum broadening. In order to reduce dispersion effectively in an optical communication system, dispersion compensation fiber (DCF) is used either in a lumped-dispersion compensation arrangement, post-

Figure 16. Optimization of optical filter bandwidth, BWwdm for 40 Gb/s back-to-back signal (-10 dBm optical noise added just before receiver) (Hiew, Abbou, & Chuah 2006)

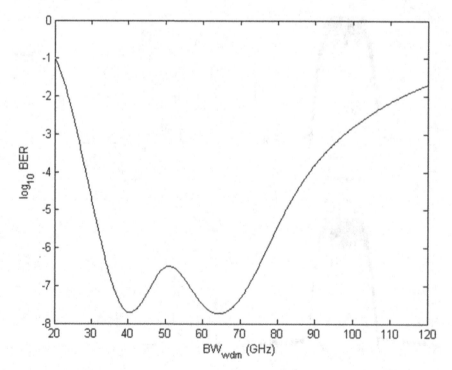

dispersion compensation, or middle-dispersion compensation. Another method is the distributed-dispersion compensation arrangement, whereby each amplifier span is divided into two sections; the first is the regular fiber type and the second is the dispersion compensation fiber. Other effect such the linear crosstalk, which causes distortion and interferes with the filtered channel can be reduced by optimizing the optical filter bandwidth and shape to obtain a compromise between WDM linear crosstalk and filter induced ISI.

REFERENCES

Agrawal, G. P. (Ed.). (1997). *Fiber-Optic Communication Systems*. Wiley-Interscience.

Agrawal, G. P. (Ed.). (2001). *Nonlinear Fiber Optics*. Academic Press.

Bosco, G., Carena, A., Curri, V., Gaudino, R., & Poggiolini, P. (2002). On the Use of nrz, rz and csrz Modulation at 40 gb/s with Narrow dwdm Channel Spacing. *Journal of Lightwave Technology, 20*(9), 1694–1704. doi:10.1109/JLT.2002.806309

Bouteiller, J. C., Leng, L., & Headley, C. (2004). Pump-pump Four-wave Mixing in Distributed Raman Amplified Systems. *Journal of Lightwave Technology, 22*(3), 723–732. doi:10.1109/JLT.2004.824459

Desurvire, E. (1994). *Erbium-doped Fiber Amplifiers: Principles and Applications*. Wiley-Interscience.

Duce, A. D., Killey, R. I., & Bayvel, P. (2004). Comparison of Nonlinear Pulse Interactions in 160-gb/s Quasi-linear and Dispersion Managed Soliton Systems. *Journal of Lightwave Technology, 22*, 1483–1498.

Hiew, C. C., Abbou, F. M., & Chuah, H. T. (2006). *Performance Analysis and Design of an Optical TDM-WDM Transmission System and Network* (Tech. Rep. No. 1). Malaysia: Multimedia University and Alcatel Network Systems.

Keiser, G. (2000). *Optical Fiber Communications*. McGraw-Hill.

Konrad, B., Petermann, K., Berger, J., Ludwig, R., Weinert, C. M., Weber, H. G., & Schmauss, B. (2002). Impact of Fiber Chromatic Dispersion in High-speed tdm Transmission Systems. *Journal of Lightwave Technology, 20*(12), 2129–2135. doi:10.1109/JLT.2002.807777

Marcus, D. (1991). Bit-error rate of Lightwave Systems at the Zero-dispersion Wavelength. *Journal of Lightwave Technology, 9*(10), 1330–1334. doi:10.1109/50.90931

Mu, R. M., Yu, T., Grigoryan, V. S., & Menyuk, C. R. (2002). Dynamics of the Chirped Return-to-zero Modulation Format. *Journal of Lightwave Technology, 20*, 608–617. doi:10.1109/50.996580

Murakami, M., Matsuda, T., Maeda, H., & Imai, T. (2000). Long-haul wdm Transmission Using Higher Order Fiber Dispersion Management. *Journal of Lightwave Technology, 18*(9), 1197–1204. doi:10.1109/50.871695

Pachnicke, S., Man, E. D., Spalter, S., & Voges, E. (2005). Impact of the In-line Dispersion Compensation Map on Four-wave Mixing (fwm) – Impaired Optical Networks. *IEEE Photonics Technology Letters, 17*(1), 235–237. doi:10.1109/LPT.2004.838629

Wang, J., & Petermann, K. (1992). Small Signal Analysis for Dispersive Optical Fiber Communication Systems. *Journal of Lightwave Technology, 10*(1), 96–100. doi:10.1109/50.108743

Winzer, P. J., Pfennigbauer, M., Strasser, M. M., & Leeb, W. R. (2001). Optimum Filter Bandwidths for Optically Preamplified rz and nrz Receivers. *Journal of Lightwave Technology, 19*(9), 1263–1273. doi:10.1109/50.948273

Yamamoto, Y., & Inoue, K. (2003). Noise in Amplifiers. *Journal of Lightwave Technology, 21*(11), 2895–2915. doi:10.1109/JLT.2003.816887

Zhou, X., & Brik, M. (2004). New Design Method for a wdm System Employing Broad-band Raman Amplification. *IEEE Photonics Technology Letters, 14*(3), 912–914. doi:10.1109/LPT.2004.823726

KEY TERMS AND DEFINITIONS

Absorption: Occurs in optical fibers due to the presence of impurities introduced during the manufacturing process.

Amplified Spontaneous Emission (ASE) Noise: when spontaneous emission is used to perform signal amplification in an optical fiber amplifier, ASE noise is produced by spontaneous emission.

Attenuation: Refers to the loss of the optical signal power caused by absorption, scattering, microbends, connectors, splices, and splitters, etc. It is expressed in dB or dB/km.

Chromatic Dispersion (CD): Is the combined effect of material dispersion and waveguide dispersion. Material dispersion arises because different frequency components of light travel at different velocities in the same medium.

Erbium Doped Fiber Amplifiers (EDFAs): EDFA is an optical amplifier doped with laser-active rare-earth erbium ions to amplify optical signals in the 1550 nm transmission window.

Extrinsic Absorption: Is caused by impurities such as iron, nickel, and chromium, cobalt, copper and from OH ions. These are introduced into the fiber material during fabrication.

Extrinsic Loss: In a fiber interconnection, the portion of loss due to imperfect joining of a connector or splice.

Fiber Attenuation: Attenuation is the loss of optical power as light travels along the fiber. It is caused by absorption, scattering, and bending losses.

Intrinsic Absorption: Refers to the scattering loss mechanism caused by the interaction of photons with the fiber glass itself.

Linear Scattering Loss: occurs as a result of microscopic variations in the material density of the glass fiber. It includes Rayleigh scattering loss and Mie scattering loss.

Mie Scattering Loss: A loss which results from the compositional fluctuations and structural inhomogeneities introduced during fiber fabrications.

Rayleigh Scattering: A fundamental loss mechanism that contributes to the attenuation of light in glass which is due random variations of the molecular positions in glass which create random refractive index inhomogeneities that act as scatter particles.

Chapter 2
Optical Transport Network:
A Physical Layer Perspective Part 2

ABSTRACT

The purpose of this chapter is to discuss two major categories of nonlinear effects related either to nonlinear refractive index or to nonlinear stimulated scattering effects. The effects related to nonlinear refractive index occur due to the dependence of the refractive index on the optical signal intensity. On the other hand, stimulated scattering effects are caused by interaction between light and material. As many wavelength signal channels travel through the optical fiber, they encounter many of those nonlinear effects impairments that affect the signal power level and hence degrade sharply the quality of the signal resulting in interference among signals carried by different wavelength channels. Therefore, before delving into the optical transmission performance issues, a physical picture of how optical signals behave in the presence of the most important nonlinear effect impairments is drawn.

INTRODUCTION

Nonlinear effects are normally intensity or power dependent and thus can lead to a variety of complicated interactions and behavior. An example of an optical nonlinearity that affects only the phase of the propagating signal is the nonlinear refractive index of the fiber material, also known as the Kerr nonlinearity. This property converts optical power fluctuations in a lightwave to phase fluctuations.

DOI: 10.4018/978-1-4666-6575-0.ch002

Phase modulation in silica fibers exists because of an intensity dependent refractive index. The refractive index of most transparent solids has the form (Uetsuka, 2004).

$$n = n_1 + n_2 I \qquad (2.1)$$

where n_1 is the ordinary refractive index associated with the material, n_2 is the intensity dependent (nonlinear) refractive index typically about 1.5×10^{-20} to 3×10^{-20} m²/W and I is the optical intensity.

The dependence of the refractive index to the intensity can have a serious effect on the propagating signal. This is because intensity fluctuations are commonplace due to intensity modulation, attenuation and amplification. The corresponding induced phase fluctuations can have detrimental effects and is a subject of detailed study in this report. It becomes more significant in modern systems where amplifiers are used to boost the signal power to very high levels in order to withstand the attenuation over a long fiber span.

In practice, the Kerr nonlinearity can affect the propagation of the communication system in many different ways depending on the properties of the system. These effects all originate from the nonlinear refractive index, but have been classified into different categories because they arise due to different sets of conditions or system parameters and have different consequences. These effects, which will be studied in detail, include self phase modulation as well as cross phase modulation and four wave mixing, where the latter two only occurs in systems with WDM. These effects impose a significant limiting mechanism to the potential of long distance, high capacity systems and thus have been extensively studied.

SELF PHASE MODULATION

Self phase modulation (SPM) is the nonlinear effect caused by the change of the nonlinear refractive index due to the intensity of the incident signal on itself. This means that the power of the signal acts to alter the refractive index of the fiber causing a phase modulation on the signal. This would not cause any problems if the intensity of the signal is constant as it would then only induce a constant phase shift over the entire signal. However, for an intensity modulated system, the signal intensity is not constant, but changes according to the modulation guided by bit sequence, thus generating phase shifts that change along the signal. These phase shifts occur almost instantaneously and are dependent on the current signal intensity because the nonlinear phase shift is an ultrafast process. Thus, any fluctuations in intensity create an almost instant fluctuation in phase.

The induced phase shift, $\phi_{SPM}(z,T)$ is distance and time dependent and can be approximated for a single fiber configuration by (Uetsuka, 2004)

$$\varphi_{SPM}\left(z,T\right) = \left|E\left(0,T\right)\right|^2 \left(\frac{1-\exp\left(-\alpha z\right)}{\alpha}\right)\left(\gamma P_0\right) \tag{2.2}$$

where $E(0,T)$ is the signal field envelope at distance $z = 0$, α is the fiber loss (attenuation) parameter, P_0 is the pulse peak power and γ is the nonlinearity coefficient given by

$$\gamma = \frac{n_2 \omega_0}{cA_{eff}} \tag{2.3}$$

where n_2 is the nonlinear refractive index, ω_0 is the signal center frequency and A_{eff} is the fiber effective area. From (Equation (2.2)), we can see that the SPM induced phase shift increases with power and distance, but the distance factor is limited by the exponential term associated with the fiber attenuation. In fact, for a distance L, the effective distance is defined as

$$L_{eff} = \left(\frac{1-\exp\left(-\alpha L\right)}{\alpha}\right) \tag{2.4}$$

The effective distance describes the distance over which intensity dependent nonlinear effects such as SPM are significant. The significance of SPM diminishes as the signal power decreases with attenuation. Beyond the effective distance, the SPM effect is pretty much insignificant. On the other hand, Equation (2.2), also shows that the SPM effect is dependent on the signal pulse shape given by $E(0,T)$. If we assume that the signal shape does not change throughout its propagation except for losses due to fiber attenuation, Equation (2.2) is sufficient to compute the induced SPM phase shift.

The fluctuations in phase would ideally not cause any distortion to the intensity of the signal and thus, would not induce any additional errors in intensity modulated systems where the phase of the signal is inconsequential. However, in practice, the induced phase fluctuations would interact with dispersion and be converted to intensity distortions (Uetsuka, 2004). This is because the phase fluctuations cause different frequency chirps over different sections of the signal. As dispersion is a function of frequency, this will alter the dispersion acting on different parts of the signal causing distortion of the signal.

Typical effects of SPM on a signal pulse are shown in Figure 1, Figure 2, and Figure 3. The type of effect shown depends on the power of the signal. Also, these effects only appear on a signal intensity plot when the fiber has a finite dispersion so that SPM-dispersion interplay leads to intensity fluctuations as shown in Figure 1 obtained using high powers over short distances. The spikes at the top of the SPM-affected pulses are indicative of the usual intensity distortion caused by the frequency chirp.

The interplay between SPM and dispersion takes on a further dimension when we consider that the SPM phase shift interacts directly with the dispersion term (Uetsuka, 2004)

$$
j \frac{\partial U}{\partial \xi} = \text{sgn}\left(\beta_2\right) \frac{1}{2} \frac{\partial^2 U}{\partial \tau^2} - N^2 \left|U\right|^2 U
$$
$$
N^2 = \frac{\gamma P_0 T_0^2}{\left|\beta_2\right|}
$$

(2.5)

Figure 1. SPM effects under a variety of circumstances (D = 4 ps/nm/km, Sl = 0, noiseless amplifiers) comparison of SPM with and without dispersion (Hiew, Abbou, & Chuah, 2006)

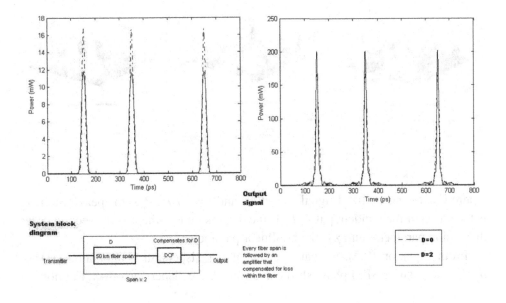

Figure 2. SPM effects under a variety of circumstances (D = 4 ps/nm/km, Sl = 0, noiseless amplifiers) pulse broadening in DM systems (Hiew, Abbou, & Chuah, 2006)

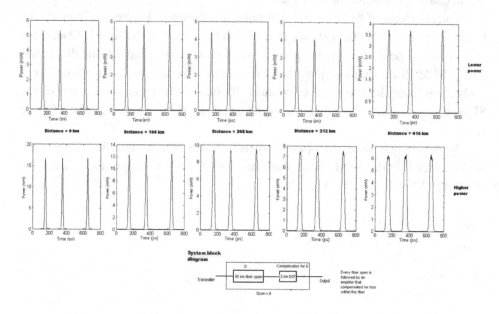

Figure 3. SPM effects under a variety of circumstances (D = 4 ps/nm/km, Sl = 0, noiseless amplifiers) countering dispersion with SPM in non-DM systems (Hiew, Abbou, & Chuah, 2006)

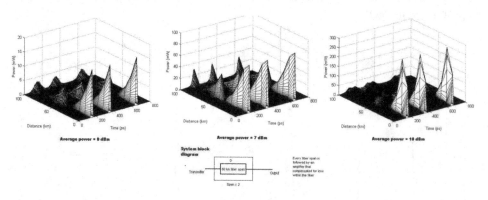

where U is the normalized signal, $\xi = z / L_D$ and $\tau = T / T_0$. P_0 is the peak power, T_0 is the width of the incident pulse, L_D is the dispersion length, β_2 is the second order dispersion parameter and γ is the nonlinear parameter.

From Equation (2.5), we can see that if the dispersion if anomalous ($D>0$, $\beta_2<0$), the positive SPM phase shift can diminish the dispersion effect. For normal dispersion ($D<0$, $\beta_2>0$), the SPM phase shift will increase the dispersion. Figure 2 examines lower powers over longer distances for an optimal DM system, and it is found that the SPM counters the dispersion in the fiber, thus upsetting the balance of the optimal DM, causing a residual dispersion that leads to pulse broadening as the signal progresses. This effect becomes more pronounced as the power increases causing an increase in the induced SPM phase shift. However, SPM may cause either an increase or decrease in pulse peak amplitude as seen in Figure 1 depending on its interplay with dispersion. Thus, occasionally, SPM caused by high powers can counter dispersion and actually improve signal performance by increasing pulse peak amplitude through a "sharpening" of the pulse shape (referred to occasionally as a soliton-like effect) as can be seen in Figure 3 without the use of DM. This works because the high SPM phase shift counters the anomalous dispersion of the fiber as given in Equation (2.5). However, it can be observed that increasing the power too much can lead back to distortion of the signal and the inducement of pulse pedestals.

Thus, when applying this principle to DM systems, the dispersion compensation can be decreased to take into account the SPM effects. However, in practice SPM depends on many other factors such as the signal pulse shape as illustrated in (2.2). The dependence on pulse shape indicates that different pulse shapes will behave differently under the influence of SPM and may not lead to exact compensation of dispersion with SPM. Generally, for most pulse shapes, SPM does not lead to exact compensation of dispersion. Thus, in most systems, the general design rule is to keep power low such that nonlinear effects are small so that it may be accommodated into the system design or DM configuration.

SPM occurs in any optical multiplexing system whether it is single channel, OTDM, WDM or OTDM-WDM. The fast time response of SPM means it behaves instantaneously even for ultra high bit rate OTDM transmission. Previously, we mentioned the use of power boosters to overcome the effect of ASE. Nonlinear effects such as SPM represent an upper limit to the amount of power that we can input into an optical system. Input power that is too high will suffer increased distortion due to SPM while input power that is too low will be distorted by ASE. Therefore, unlimited increases in input system power will not result in unlimited increased in system performance and thus, optimization of input power in a nonlinear optical fiber becomes a key design issue.

Various methods have been proposed to evaluate the effect of SPM on a system analytically to assist in system optimization (Uetsuka, 2004). This is possible because SPM is only dependent upon the signal power, pulse shape, distance, fiber loss and fiber dispersion. If we assume that the pulses are not overly altered by dispersion in such a way as to leak into their neighboring pulses, or overly distorted by ASE, the evolution of each signal pulse as it propagates along the fiber can be independently evaluated and described by the same equation. More importantly, this equation is deterministic as there are no random (stochastic) processes involved.

The deterministic nature disappears when we start to consider the effects of neighboring pulses on each other. The distortion induced on a pulse due to 'leakage' from its neighboring pulses is generally known as intersymbol interference (ISI). This could be caused by factors such as dispersion. When a pulse is affected by its neighboring pulses through dispersion, then the evolution of the pulse is no longer deterministic. This is because the ISI is determined by the bit sequence which is a random stream of symbols. For binary transmission, it is a random stream of ones and zeros. Thus, the effect of SPM would need to be averaged over the possible bit sequences and analytical solutions become more difficult. If the accumulated dispersion along the fiber never exceeds a small magnitude, the ISI may be safely ignored or dealt with through small perturbation approaches. However, when the accumulated dispersion attains high magnitudes such as in high dispersion strength DM, the overlapping pulses due to dispersion causes severe distortion to the pulse shape. This in turn changes the SPM effect whereby the overlapping pulses causes its own SPM phase shift on the overlapped pulse. The deterministic property also disappears when the accumulated ASE or optical noise becomes largely relative to the signal. This is because the ASE is a random process, and the SPM it induces is consequently random in nature.

OPTICAL SOLITON

In a way, SPM can be said to act hand-in-hand with dispersion in governing the evolution of the signal pulse. In fact, the two factors can be linked together as in Equation (2.5). Observe that if the two factors due to dispersion and SPM cancel out, the resulting signal is undistorted by either effect. This then is the concept of the optical soliton. The soliton phenomenon was first observed in traveling water waves and is always based on the interaction of a nonlinear effect with a linear process, to create a signal that could ideally travel undistorted over infinite distances. In the case of the optical soliton, SPM is the nonlinear process and dispersion is the linear process. Due to the potential of the soliton system (infinite distance), it has been extensively studied (Haus, 1993; Nakazawa, *2000*). The basic idea for a soliton system is to launch a signal with a certain shape and power to enable it to counteract the dispersion. The pulse shape required to do this has been solved and is found to be the hyperbolic-secant pulse. For this pulse shape, the power of the signal determines the magnitude of the SPM phase shift and this has to be balanced with the dispersion of the fiber. For a constant dispersion and for the fundamental soliton (first order soliton), the power of the signal should approximately be (Uetsuka, 2004)

$$P_1 = \frac{|\beta_2|}{\gamma T_0^2} \tag{2.6}$$

In practice, other propagation effects intrude upon this delicate balance of SPM and dispersion. The chief effect that causes the breakdown of this balance is fiber loss. Attenuation causes the gradual change of the signal power leading to smaller SPM phase shifts while dispersion is maintained. This would offset the balance and ultimately cause significant distortion. As attenuation is unavoidable, one solution calls for the gradual decrease of the fiber dispersion at the same rate as signal power using so-called dispersion decreasing fibers. This solution is potentially an ideal solution provided that the fiber can be manufactured with ideal characteristics. Another method requires the maintenance of an almost constant signal power over the length of transmission through finely distributed amplification using technologies such Raman fiber amplifiers. This solution depends on the ability of the Raman amplifiers to maintain the ideal constant signal power. All these methods are difficult to maintain in practice.

Even then, such signals can be badly distorted in WDM systems through the effects of cross phase modulation (XPM) and four wave mixing (FWM). For a purely OTDM system, soliton pulses can be a good solution due to the absence of XPM and FWM. However, in such a situation, care has to be taken to accommodate the effects of ASE, particularly a subset of ASE-related effects known as the Gordon-Haus jitter (Gordon & Haus, 1986; Marcuse, 1992). For the OTDM-WDM system, XPM and FWM are present since WDM is used and thus, ideal soliton propagation is not a good solution.

Nowadays, another method of transmission has been reached as a compromise on the soliton concept. This method is the dispersion managed soliton (DMS). In this system, the soliton pulse is not propagated through a constant dispersion fiber but through DM fiber spans. The soliton pulse would not stay constant in this system but would change accordingly within the fiber span. However, the output pulse at the end of each fiber span is more or less constant. Thus, the signal can be said to be soliton-like in nature. In such a system, the linear and nonlinear effects interact with one another, resulting in operation in the quasi-linear regime where the signal seems to behave linearly after the nonlinear effects are factored in (Mu, Yu, Grigoryan, & Menyuk, 2002). The pulses that operate in this regime have been found to be Gaussian pulses.

Recently, a study has suggested that the DMS system has effectively converged with the ordinary intensity modulated system (Mu, Yu, Grigoryan, & Menyuk, 2002). This is because intensity modulated systems have changed in recent years from non-return-to-zero (NRZ) pulses with lumped dispersion compensation to the use of return-to-zero (RZ) pulses with Gaussian-like pulse shape and periodic, distributed dispersion compensation. The characteristics of both systems are quite similar, and it has been shown that both systems operate in the quasi-linear regime and display similar behavior. In this book, the RZ Gaussian pulse and DM is often used in the simulated experiments. In doing so, we do not aim to create a soliton system; rather, we are trying to simulate the parameters of modern intensity modulated optical systems. It is similar to a DMS system only because the line between the soliton and non-soliton system has narrowed in recent years. Further, more discussion on the optical Soliton system is given in chapter 3.

Gordon-Mollenauer Noise

For phase modulated systems, SPM represents a major concern as it induces phase fluctuations. This is a direct source of distortion to the phase modulated system. At the same time, the phase modulated system is also disturbed by the ASE noise, which has a random phase. In addition to all this, SPM and ASE interact causing further phase distortion known as the Gordon-Mollenauer noise (Gordon & Mollenauer, 1990). In this process, the fluctuations of the signal intensity caused by ASE results in fluctuations in the SPM induced phase shift. This phase shift is in addition to the one caused directly by the random ASE phase or by the SPM-induced phase fluctuations due to the modulated pulse shape. The phase shift fluctuates randomly as it originates from the ASE noise and in effect, compounds the ASE noise effect in phase modulated systems. The Gordon-Mollenauer noise is one of the most significant problems in phase modulated systems and was one of the reasons why phase modulation was previously overlooked in practical systems. Recently though, DPSK modulation has shown promising performance in the presence of Gordon-Mollenauer noise (Gnauck & Winzer, 2005; Xu, Liu, & Wei, 2004).

CROSS PHASE MODULATION

A WDM signal consists of numerous WDM channels located at different center frequencies separated by a channel spacing specified in frequency Δf or wavelength $\Delta \lambda$. At the same time, the Kerr nonlinearity originates from the dependence of the fiber refractive index on the signal intensity. Thus, all the WDM channels would affect the total signal intensity in the fiber at the same time. Therefore, the fiber refractive index would change in response to all the different WDM channels. The altered refractive index will in turn change the behavior of all the different WDM channels. In this way, the behavior of one WDM channel can affect all the other WDM channels and vice versa, the behavior of each channel is dependent on all the other channels. Such behavior leads to crosstalk between the different WDM channels. Since it originates from the nonlinear property of the fiber, it is known as nonlinear crosstalk. Two main effects that originate from this property affecting WDM systems are the cross phase modulation (XPM) and four wave mixing (FWM) (Uetsuka, 2004).

In a WDM system, XPM is the nonlinear phase shift on one channel caused by the change of the nonlinear refractive index due to the intensity of another channel. This is because all WDM channels in a system propagate through the same optical fiber and the refractive index of the optical fiber, which is intensity dependent, is altered by the intensity of all the WDM channels. From the perspective of a single channel of interest, this means that a phase shift is induced upon it by all the other WDM channels that are propagating together with it. All the WDM channels will thus induce as well as undergo phase shifts due to all the other channels. Therefore, in a WDM system, XPM acts in addition to SPM.

It is worth pointing out here that the effective nonlinear refractive index, n_2 for XPM is two times the corresponding n_2 for SPM (Uetsuka, 2004). This means that the effect of XPM should be twice more significant. Coupled to this is the fact that the XPM induced phase shift is caused by the sum of the intensity of all the other channels. This means that in a high capacity WDM system with channels up to 100, empirically, the XPM effect should be much larger than the SPM effect. However, in practice, this is not always true because there is another factor that influences the magnitude of the XPM effect that has to be taken into account, which is the walk-off factor. The XPM induced phase shift of one channel (pump) on another (probe) can be approximately given by (Chiang, Kagi, & Marhic, 1996)

$$\Delta \varphi_{XPM} = 2\gamma P_m \sqrt{\eta_{XPM}} L_{eff} \qquad (2.7)$$

where P_m is the amplitude of the pump channel, L_{eff} is the effective fiber length equal to $(1-e^{-\alpha L})/L$ where L is the actual fiber length and η_{XPM} is the XPM efficiency given by (Chiang, Kagi, & Marhic, 1996)

$$\eta_{XPM} = \frac{\alpha^2}{\omega^2 d_{12}^2 + \alpha^2} \left[1 + \frac{4 \sin^2 \left(\omega d_{12} L / 2 \right) e^{-\alpha L}}{\left(1 - e^{-\alpha L} \right)^2} \right] \qquad (2.8)$$

Equations (2.7) and (2.8) describe the effect of XPM induced by a sinusoidally modulated pump on a continuous wave (CW) probe signal. Although this is different from the practical case of a random intensity modulated pump and probe, the governing factors are similar and results have validated the use of these equations.

As stated earlier, Equation (2.7) shows that the XPM induced phase shift is proportional to the pump power. Thus, like SPM, most of the XPM effect occurs at the beginning of the fiber before the signal power becomes insignificant due to attenuation. Further, notice that the XPM efficiency in (2.8) is a function of the walk-off factor between the probe channel (channel 1) and the pump channel (channel 2), d_{12}. The walk-off factor is in turn a function of the channel separation (channel spacing) and the dispersion characteristics of the fiber. These two factors determine the walk-off of a signal (channel j) with respect to another signal (channel k) given by (Uetsuka, 2004)

$$d_{jk} = \left(v_{gj} \right)^{-1} - \left(v_{gk} \right)^{-1} = \int_{\lambda_k}^{\lambda_j} D(\lambda) d\lambda \approx D \cdot \left(\lambda_j - \lambda_k \right) \tag{2.9}$$

where v_{gj} and v_{gk} are the group velocities of channels j and k respectively, $D(\lambda)$ is the wavelength dependent dispersion parameter while λ_j and λ_k refers to the center wavelengths of those channels. The final approximation holds when second order dispersion is dominant over all other orders of dispersion such that $D \gg Sl$ or $Sl \approx 0$ where Sl is the dispersion slope. A more accurate approximation, including the effects of dispersion slope would be

$$d_{jk} \approx D \left(\lambda_j - \lambda_k \right) + \frac{Sl}{2} \left(\lambda_j - \lambda_k \right)^2 \tag{2.10}$$

Figure 4 shows the walk-off process between three channels, each separated by $\Delta\lambda = 1$ nm. The dispersion is a constant, $D = 2$ ps/nm/km. From (2.9), the walk-off factor, $d_{12} = d_{23} = 2$ ps/km. If one of the channels is taken as the time reference (position constant with time), the relative timing difference between the two channels at distance z compared to the initial point, z_0 is given by

$$\Delta\tau = d_{jk} \left(z - z_0 \right) \tag{2.11}$$

Using the arrows on Figure 4 as the focal points and Channel 2 as the reference (stationary with time), the relative movements of the pulses can be clearly seen.

Figure 4. WDM signal walk-off in time domain (channel spacing, $\Delta\lambda = 1$ nm) (Hiew, Abbou, & Chuah, 2006)

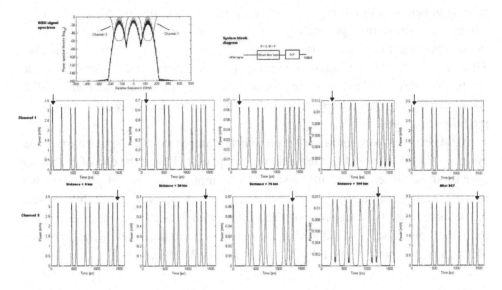

Channel 1 is leading (moving to the right) while channel 3 is lagging (moving to the left). The relative timing difference changes according to the walk-off factor. In this way, a channel can "move over" another channel as they propagate down the dispersive fiber. The XPM induced phase shift between two channels depends on this walk-off factor as shown in (Equation (2.8)). As the walk-off factor increases, the induced phase shift decreases quickly and rapidly becomes insignificant. This happens because a large walk-off factor indicates that the two channels have a large propagation velocity difference. This means that one channel will move past the other channel quickly. In such a scenario, the induced phase shift will not be coherent and will tend to cancel out as the negative and positive intensity of the sinusoid induces phase shifts that negate one another. For regular OOK signals, there is no negative intensity, so the induced phase shifts would not cancel out but rather average out to give a constant phase shift across the entire signal. The end result is the same as a constant phase shift induces no additional errors to the signal.

Thus, the expectedly large XPM induced phase shift is kept low by this factor. Looking at the dependence on channel spacing in (Equation (2.10)), this means that channels that are further apart in terms of frequency or wavelength have less effect on one another. Therefore, only the adjacent WDM channels have the most significant effect on a particular channel. On the other hand, the induced phase shift increases with reduced channel spacing. In order to increase spectral density, the channel spacing has to be decreased. Thus, in high capacity OTDM-WDM systems, the effect of XPM becomes more significant and is a subject of close study (Leibrich, C. Wree and W. Rosenkranz, 2002; Jiang and C. Fan, 2003). The presence of XPM puts an upper limit to the input power of an optical system (in addition to SPM) while, at the same time, presenting a limit to the spectral density. In effect, XPM induces nonlinear crosstalk between WDM channels that are close together. Like SPM, this crosstalk is in terms of phase fluctuations that are converted to magnitude fluctuations through the dispersion process (Cartaxo, 1999). Thus, similar to SPM, XPM affects phase modulated systems directly but only indirectly affects intensity modulated systems.

XPM becomes more significant in periodically amplified multi-span transmission systems. This is because the attenuation is compensated for at the end of each fiber span by an amplifier. The resultant signal at the input to the next fiber span is high in power, and according to (Equation (2.7)), the resultant XPM phase shift is high. At the same time, it also depends on the accumulated dispersion at the beginning of each fiber span. The XPM induced phase shift for a periodically amplified, multiple identical span system is given by (Chiang, Kagi, & Marhic, 1996)

$$\varphi(NL, t) = \sum_{l=1}^{N} \Delta\varphi \cos\left\{\omega\left(t - \frac{NL}{v_g}\right) + \theta + \omega(l-1)d_{12}L + \phi\right\}$$

$$= \Delta\varphi_N \cos\left\{\omega\left(t - \frac{NL}{v_g}\right) + \theta + \omega(l-1)d_{12}L + \phi\right\} \tag{2.12}$$

$$\Delta\varphi_N = \eta_{link}\Delta\varphi$$

$$\eta_{link} = \left|\frac{\sin\left(N\omega d_{12}L/2\right)}{\sin\left(\omega d_{12}L/2\right)}\right| \tag{2.13}$$

where $\Delta\Phi$ is the phase shift induced in a single span, $\Delta\Phi_N$ is the total phase shift and η_{link} is the link enhancement factor.

On the other hand, the walk-off factor depends on the polarity of the dispersion parameter. Thus if the dispersion changes polarity, the direction of relative movement will also change. Based on (Equation (2.11)), we can deduce that the relative time shift between channels is linked to the accumulated dispersion at a given point. For example, we consider two channels with $\Delta\lambda = 1$ nm. After traveling through an NZ-DSF link of $L = 100$ km and $D = 2$ ps/nm/km, $\Delta\tau = 200$ ps. If this is a periodic DM system with full compensation at each span, the signals might then pass through a DCF link of $L = 2$ km and $D = -100$ ps/nm/km, resulting in a $\Delta\tau$ of -200 ps. The total time shift at the end of the DM span is $200 - 200 = 0$ ps. Thus, in fully periodic DM systems, the relative channel positions are reset to their original positions after full compensation is achieved as in Figure 4. This reduces the effect of walk-off, resulting in increased XPM effect. This occurs as the XPM induced phase shifts induced within each DM span adds up coherently and accumulates to a large magnitude by the end of the total transmission link. With coherent addition, the total XPM induced phase shift is roughly equivalent to the multiple of the XPM induced in each DM span multiplied by the number of DM spans.

In Figure 5, we observe the XPM effect on a channel through a periodic DM system. When only a single channel is launched, there is only a slight decrease in pulse amplitude due to SPM. When 3 channels are launched, XPM occurs, and

Figure 5. Signal progression with and without the XPM effect for different channel spacing (different walk-off factor) and channel position for a periodic DM system with noiseless amplifiers (D = 1 ps/nm/km and total system length = 306 km) (Hiew, Abbou, & Chuah, 2006)

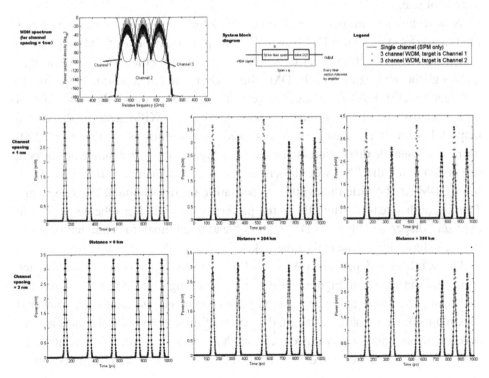

some of the pulses experience an additional drop in amplitude (target channel set as channel 1). Only some pulses are affected because only some pulses are occupying the same position as a logic '1' pulse of other WDM channels during propagation. As the positions are reset at each compensation span, the same pulses continuously experience XPM while others which share the same position as the logic '0' of other WDM channels are unaffected. Increasing the walk-off by increasing the channel spacing helps decrease the magnitude of the XPM-induced pulse amplitude reduction by reducing the length of fiber where the pulses may interact coherently before they walk-off from one another. By the time the pulses "walk-over" to the next bit position, the pulses already suffer from heavy dispersion, thus reducing its impact on other bit positions. As such, only pulses that initially share the same position as pulses from other WDM channels suffer greatly from the XPM effect.

The distortion of the pulses creates a problem similar to that experienced with SPM. In addition, the effects of XPM can be worse because it tends to affect some pulses more than others as shown previously. This creates large differences of amplitudes among equal symbols such as the '1' pulse. This is detrimental to system performance as it introduces an uncertainty to the received pulse amplitude known as the amplitude jitter that complicates bit decision at the receiver. When the target channel is set as the center channel (channel 2), the pulses experience greater amplitude changes due to an increased XPM effect as it has two adjacent channels instead of one.

New techniques are being used to counter XPM. One involves the use of new modulation formats such as DPSK, which shows promise of better XPM suppression (Gnauck, & Winzer, 2005; Xu, Liu, & Wei, 2004). Another more obvious technique is through the optimization of the DM scheme (Bergano & Davidson, 1996; Suzuki & Edagawa, 2003). As noted earlier, we could use a zero dispersion fiber or DM with weak dispersion map strength. However, to counter XPM, a strong dispersion map DM is preferred. This is because the XPM efficiency as in (Equation (2.8)) decreases when the dispersion increases. So, a high value of instantaneous or local dispersion along the fiber would increase walk-off and decrease the XPM effect. Strong DM can provide this while compensating for dispersion at the same time. This is another reason why DM is the preferred transmission scheme at present over zero dispersion fibers as $D = 0$ would lead to a tremendous amount of XPM induced phase shift at the end of the link.

On the other hand, periodic DM where full compensation is achieved within each compensation span as in Figure 5 results in the resetting of the pulse positions after each span. Therefore, at the beginning of each compensation span where power is maximum, due to the amplification, the pulses of different WDM channels are coherent with one another, leading to increased XPM, as noted earlier. To counter this, a combination of lumped and distributed dispersion compensation (hybrid scheme) is commonly used to maintain a degree of accumulated dispersion within the WDM signal throughout the fiber transmission link and full compensation is only achieved after the final post-DCF at the receiver. In this way, the accumulated dispersion is never zero throughout the fiber link except at the beginning and at the end. Thus, coherent addition does not occur from span to span within the transmission system.

FOUR WAVE MIXING

Another phenomenon that arises due to the same Kerr nonlinearity and becomes significant mainly in WDM systems is four wave mixing (FWM) (Tkach, Chraplyvy, Forghieri, Gnauck, & Derosier, 1995). FWM is caused by the beating (mixing) terms that arise between separate WDM channels. When a combination of two signals is squared together, besides the appearance of the intensities of each individual channel, the channels also interact with one another, such as in the situation below where two channels are mixed and the intensity is computed.

$$|U|^2 U = |U_1 + U_2|^2 (U_1 + U_2)$$

$$= |U_1|^2 U_1 + |U_2|^2 U_2 + 2|U_2|^2 U_1 + 2|U_1|^2 U_2 + U_2^* U_1^* + U_1^* U_2^2 \qquad (2.14)$$

The first two terms are linked to SPM, the second two terms are linked to XPM and the last two terms are the beating terms, and the same principle applies to the FWM process.

The mixing of channels belongs to a category of effects known as parametric processes (Uetsuka, 2004). FWM is a subset of these effects and is generally the only parametric process that becomes significant in optical communication systems. Parametric processes become significant when the channels mix coherently to generate new signals that are reinforced due to the coherence. Without coherence, any new signal generated cannot be sustained. FWM is the process whereby two or three WDM channels in an optical fiber mix and produce a third or fourth signal on a new frequency. When the new signal's frequency falls within the bandwidth of another WDM channel not involved in the current mix, it represents a nonlinear crosstalk to that channel. When it falls outside the bandwidth of any other WDM channel, it still causes some distortion as the mixing channels (called the pump signals) are depleted to form the new signal. This is known as pump depletion. In general, pump depletion is not a major concern as its effect is small and similar to general attenuation. It is the nonlinear crosstalk which is significant as it can distort the pulses on the affected channel. Note that FWM can occur even between two channels (called a two-tone product) to create a third signal, contrary to the name of the process. When this occurs, it is referred to as a degenerate case. When three channels mix (called a three-tone product), a fourth signal is generated (non-degenerate case).

The power of the generated FWM signal, P_g is given by

$$P_g = \frac{1024\pi^6}{n^4\lambda^2 c^2}\left(\frac{N\chi_{1111}L_{eff}}{A_{eff}}\right)^2 P_i P_j P_k e^{-\alpha L}\eta_{FWM} \tag{2.15}$$

where P_i, P_j and P_k are the mixing signals' powers, n is the refractive index, χ_{1111} is the nonlinear susceptibility ($\approx 4 \times 10^{-15}$ esu), N is a constant equal to 3 for two-tone products or 6 for three-tone products and η_{FWM} is the FWM efficiency given by

$$\eta_{FWM} = \frac{\alpha^2}{\Delta\beta^2 + \alpha^2}\left[1 + \frac{4\sin^2\left(\Delta\beta L/2\right)e^{-\alpha L}}{\left(1 - e^{-\alpha L}\right)^2}\right] \tag{2.16}$$

where $\Delta\beta$ is the difference of the propagation constants of the various waves, due to dispersion and for a two-tone product with channel spacing Δf is given by

$$\Delta\beta = \beta_g + \beta_k - \beta_j - \beta_i = \frac{2\pi\lambda^2}{c}\Delta f^2\left(D + \Delta f\frac{\lambda^2}{c}\frac{dD}{d\lambda}\right) \tag{2.17}$$

Once again these equations are derived for sinusoidally modulated signals but have been shown to be applicable to intensity modulated signals. As can be seen, the equation for FWM is similar to that for XPM (just replace ωd_{12} with $\Delta\beta$). In fact, the efficiency of both processes relies on the same factors as $\Delta\beta$ is dependent on channel spacing and dispersion, similar to d_{12}. Generally, a parametric process such as FWM is harder to occur than XPM due to the requirement of coherence. However, when strong coherence of signals is present, the effect is often more severe for intensity modulated systems, as FWM induces new signals that will directly interfere with the magnitude of the affected channels directly, whereas XPM only induces a phase fluctuation that needs to be converted by dispersion into magnitude fluctuations.

All channels in a WDM system may become pumps for the FWM process. Each channel can undergo the FWM process with any number of other channels at the same time, as long as they interact coherently. Whether or not, the channels may interact coherently depend on their frequencies. Given the set of pump signal frequencies, the generated FWM signal frequency is given by Tkach, Chraplyvy, Forghieri, Gnauck, & Derosier, 1995)

$$f_g = f_i + f_j - f_k \tag{2.18}$$

where f_i, f_j, f_k are the center frequencies of the pump channels and f_g is the center frequency of the generated FWM signal. The total number of new FWM signals generated, M_{FWM} is given by (Tkach, Chraplyvy, Forghieri, Gnauck, & Derosier, 1995)

$$M_{FWM} = \frac{1}{2}\left(N^3 - N^2\right) \tag{2.19}$$

where N here is the number of channels launched into the fiber.

As can be seen, the potential number of FWM signals generated is immense and increases tremendously with increasing WDM channels. Many of the new signals generated according to Equation (2.18) will occur at the same frequencies. In such cases, the generated FWM signals will simply add up. It is possible for the generated signals to interact again with the WDM channels and other generated signals to induce new FWM processes. However, such second stage FWM processes are generally insignificant as the generated signals are much smaller in magnitude than the WDM channels, and would not act as significant pumps.

Figure 6 shows the effect of FWM under various scenarios. In Figure 6(a), the generation of the FWM products can be clearly seen, though the generated signals do not fall on an existing channel and no crosstalk occurs. The FWM products are relatively small compared to the channels but increases over the propagation length. In Figure 6(b), the nonlinear refractive index, n_2 is set to zero, thus the Kerr nonlinear effects do not occur. In this scenario, no new signals are generated, proving that FWM is the source of the generated signals. With no FWM, the center channel's output signal is clean with no significant amplitude jitter. In Figure 6(c), the Kerr nonlinear effects are switched on and once again the FWM products can be seen. With three channels, more products are generated. More importantly, one of the FWM products fall within the center channel's bandwidth, thus resulting in crosstalk. From the output signal, it can be seen that the FWM crosstalk causes significant amplitude jitter as some pulses experience gain and some do not. In Figure 6(d), the channel spacing is increased to increase the walk-off. Consequently, the FWM products decrease in magnitude, and the amplitude jitter caused by the crosstalk decreases as well.

Figure 6. FWM effect (D = 2 ps/nm/km, periodic DM, noiseless amplifiers) (a) log power spectral density (psd) for 2 channel system (channel spacing = 2 nm), (b) log psd and center channel output signal for 3 channel system without nonlinear effects, (c) log psd, output spectrum and center channel output signal for 3 channel system with nonlinear effects (Δλ = 1 nm) and (d) log psd, output spectrum and center channel output signal for 3 channel system with nonlinear effects (Δλ = 3 nm) (Hiew, Abbou, & Chuah, 2006)

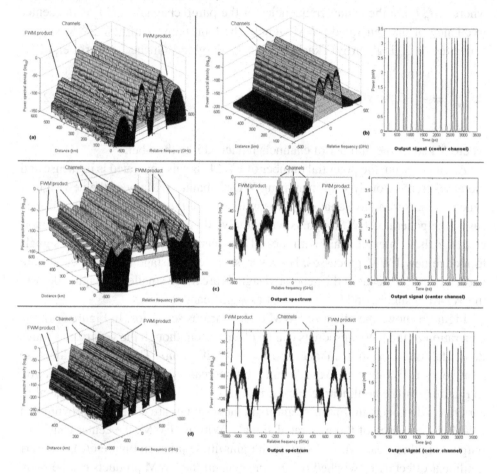

As seen in (Equation (2.15))-(Equation (2.17)), the same factors such as the walk-off factor, dispersion and channel spacing affect FWM the same way as XPM. Thus, FWM presents the same upper limits on input power and spectral density as XPM, while the same techniques that reduce the effect of XPM such as strong DM and a hybrid DM scheme to reduce signal coherence between DM spans works as well to reduce FWM (Pachnicke, Man, Spalter, & Voges, 2005; Bergano & Davidson,1996; Suzuki & Edagawa, 2003). In fact, these methods, which help reduce the coherency of channels are frequently more effective at reducing FWM compared to XPM as FWM explicitly requires signal coherency to occur in the first place. Another novel method to reduce the effects of FWM in a WDM system is the use of unequal channel spacing (Bogoni & Poti, 2000). Normally, in our discussions so far, we have implicitly assumed the use of equal channel spacing between the WDM channels, which is the normal practice for most systems. However, equal channel spacing facilitates the coherent mixing of channels for FWM. At the same time, the generated signals according to (Equation (2.18)) would then fall within the bandwidth of other WDM channels causing intraband nonlinear crosstalk. By adopting unequal channel spacing determined by algorithms such as in (Bogoni & Poti, 2004), the generated FWM signals would fall outside the bandwidth of existing WDM channels. Therefore, while FWM still occurs, it does not generate the nonlinear crosstalk that is the main source of distortion.

Parametric Gain (PG)

Previously, we have said that significant FWM interaction mainly occurs between WDM channels in a WDM system. This may be true but occasionally other FWM interactions can be of interest. Due to the wide spectrum of ASE noise, it can also interact with the WDM channels and/or with itself through the FWM process. ASE-ASE interaction through the FWM process does not lead to significant changes as the ASE is an almost white spectrum. As such, all frequency components can interact with all other frequency components through FWM and all components generally experience equal amounts of gain and pump depletion. As the ASE is basically random noise anyway, this process does not lead to significant changes.

However, interaction between ASE noise and the WDM channels can lead to an interesting effect known as the parametric gain (PG) (Bosco, *2000*). In this process, the FWM interaction between the WDM channels would generate new signals at certain frequencies. Even when no WDM channel is present at those frequencies, there is ASE noise. For long range systems where ASE noise is propagated along with the channels, this process would lead to the increase of noise at these particular frequencies. As ASE noise becomes more significant towards the latter parts of the transmission fiber length, the noise at these frequencies may interact back with the WDM channels through FWM. A simple scenario involving the propagation of two WDM channels is shown in Figure 7. Note that high channel powers are required for PG to become significant in the presence of ASE noise. This is because the generated FWM products need to be of higher magnitude than the accumulated ASE noise for the effect to significantly alter the ASE noise spectrum.

In practical systems, with many WDM channels, the combined effects would be more difficult to analyze. However, the end result is the same. The ASE noise that

Figure 7. Examination of PG effect through 2 channel WDM propagation with (a) input average power per channel, Pin = 5 dBm and (b) Pin = -2 dBm (Hiew, Abbou, & Chuah, 2006)

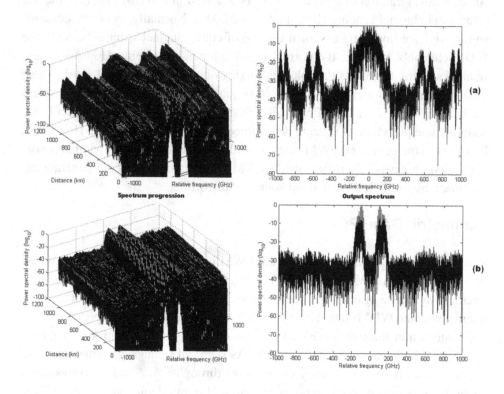

appears at the receiver no longer has a flat (white) spectrum but shows increased magnitude at frequencies that coincide with the frequencies of generated FWM signals. This process presents problems in the analytical analysis of receiver performance as a flat (white) noise spectrum is much easier to account for. However, since the resultant changes to the noise spectrum in most systems is not too significant, the white noise approximation is still used in many analyses.

Intrachannel XPM and FWM

From the previous sections, we have suggested that the use of strong dispersion maps in a DM system (large local dispersion) is preferred to increase WDM channel walk-off and consequently reduce the effects of the interchannel nonlinear distortions XPM and FWM. However, doing this leads to another problem. This is because the use of large local dispersion leads to increased SPM effect caused by the wide spreading of pulses within the transmission system (Pachnicke, Man, Spalter,

& Voges, 2005; Striegler & Schmauss, 2004). This class of SPM phenomena has attracted enough interest that it has been classified into two new effects known as the intrachannel cross phase modulation (IXPM) and the intrachannel four wave mixing (IFWM) (Matsumoto, 1998; Mecozzi, Clausen, & Shtaif, 2000). These two effects are different from the regular XPM and FWM discussed earlier, which were 'inter'-channel in nature. The word 'intrachannel' is used to differentiate the effects and it means that both IXPM and IFWM occur within a single wavelength (WDM) channel. It is worth keeping in mind that both IXPM and IFWM are effectively just subsets of SPM, and they have been studied separately in recent years mainly due to their significance in modern systems.

Fundamentally, the two processes originate from the SPM effect. Most of the time, when we discuss SPM, it refers to a situation as discussed earlier. Observe that mostly it is assumed that the SPM-induced phase shift on a pulse is caused by

Figure 8. Pulse spreading due to dispersion, D = 5 ps/nm/km with noiseless amplification and no dispersion compensation

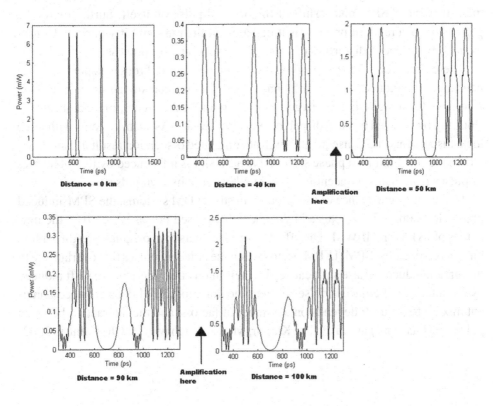

intensity of the pulse itself. However, when a signal undergoes strong dispersion, the pulses spread out and then eventually lose all shape as they completely meld into one another as in Figure 8. In such a situation, the information in the pulses is not completely lost, as it can still be recovered when the dispersion is compensated for in a DCF later. As dispersion is a linear process, the recovery can be performed no matter how much the original pulse has already been dispersed.

When the pulse (occupying one bit slot) is heavily dispersed, its intensity is spread over its many adjacent bit slots on both sides. This 'leakage' intensity can then induce a phase shift on the original pulse located within the adjacent bit slot through SPM. This occurs at all the bit slots 'leaked' into as the pulse is dispersed. This occurs for all the dispersed pulses and each pulse is spread across more bit slots as the accumulated dispersion increases. This is particularly significant in strong DM systems where the accumulated dispersion can reach values above 1000 ps/nm/km at certain points along the fiber link. It becomes more significant when the pulses are amplified while the signal is in its dispersed state because it increases the power that can facilitate the SPM process. The additional SPM phase shift caused by the 'leakage' pulses on a bit slot causes additional distortion on top of the self-induced SPM phase shift of the original pulse on itself. Furthermore, the phase shift is a random process as it depends on the random bit sequence. Consequently, the induced distortion on a pulse is also a random process.

Therefore, even when the original pulses are recovered through dispersion compensation, the induced phase shifts has already altered the signals at each bit slot. It follows from logic that the larger the dispersion of the signal, more adjacent bit slots will be affected by each dispersed pulse's intensity. As such, systems with large local dispersions and consequently high accumulated dispersion result in a situation where the SPM induced phase shift on each bit slot is influenced by the intensities of pulses from many adjacent bit slots in addition to its own pulse.

Due to the significance of this process in strong DM systems, the SPM-induced phase shifts on a bit slot caused by adjacent dispersed pulses were given the new names of IXPM and IFWM. The effect of a pulse on its own original, pre-dispersion bit slot is still called SPM. IXPM occurs when the adjacent pulses that overlap due to dispersion induce a phase shift caused by their intensities. It is a phase shift induced by the intensity of adjacent pulses in the time domain. IXPM does not need coherent mixing to occur. It depends on a number of factors, and the interaction between pulses in slots i and j are given by (Kumar, Mauro, Raghavan, & Chowdhury, 2002)

$$\frac{dp_i}{dz} = p_i C_i \beta_2$$

$$\frac{dC_i}{dz} = -4\beta_2 p_i^4 + C_i^2 \beta_2 - \sqrt{2}a^2\gamma p_i^3 \cdot \left[A_i^2 + 2A_j^2 + 2p_i^2\Delta T^2 \exp\left(-p_i^2\Delta T^2\right) \right]$$

$$\frac{d\Omega_i}{dz} = 4A_i^2 a^2 \gamma \Delta T p_i^3 \exp\left[-\left(p_i\Delta T\right)^2 \right]$$

$$\frac{dT_i}{dz} = \beta_2 \Omega_i$$

$$\Delta T = T_i - T_j$$

$$a^2(z) = \exp\left(-\int_0^z \alpha(s)\,ds\right)$$

$$(2.20)$$

where p_i, C_i, Ω_i and T_i are the inverse pulsewidth, chirp, angular frequency and pulse center of the pulse in slot i respectively, while $\alpha(z)$ is the fiber loss. Using the equations in (2.20), the pulsewidth and timing change of the pulse in slot i is calculated by summing over all pulse pair interactions involving the pulse in slot i.

Intrachannel XPM depends on the power of the pulses, dispersion of the fiber and the pulsewidth. A larger dispersion would lead to pulses from further off affecting each other. However, it is the pulses closest that cause the most significant effect. The pulsewidth determines how far the pulses are from one another analogous to the channel spacing for interchannel XPM.

Besides inducing a phase shift, the overlapping pulses can also generate new signals when they mix coherently at particular bit slots. This is the IFWM. When overlapping pulses at a bit slot beat coherently, either with each other or the original pulse, it can generate new signals, which will become a source of distortion to the original pulse at that bit slot when the signal is recovered. This would only occur in certain bit slots where coherence is achieved and it causes an increase in power at these slots while the pulses involved in the mixing suffer depletion. The energy of the pulse changes in IFWM whereas in IXPM and pure SPM, the energy does not change. The standard deviation of power change after a propagation distance L due to intrachannel FWM can be calculated as follows (Kumar, Mauro, Raghavan, & Chowdhury, 2002)

$$\left\langle \partial P\left(L\right)^2 \right\rangle \equiv P_0^4 \left| r\left(L\right) \right|^2 \sum_{p+q-r=0} \sum_{i+j-k=0} \left\langle m_i m_j m_k m_p m_q m_r \right\rangle X_{ijk} X_{pqr}$$

$$r\left(z\right) = \frac{T_0^2}{T_0^2 - is\left(z\right)} \qquad\qquad\qquad (2.21)$$

$$s\left(z\right) = \int_0^z \beta_2\left(s\right) ds$$

where $P(L)$ is the power after distance L, P_0 is the input peak power, T_0 is related to the FWHM pulsewidth and $\left\langle m_i m_j m_k m_p m_q m_r \right\rangle = 2^{-6}$ if $i \neq j \neq k \neq p \neq q \neq r$ or $\left\langle m_i m_j m_k m_p m_q m_r \right\rangle = \left(2^{6-r} + 1\right)^{-1}$ if any r indices are equal.

When the signal is highly dispersed, more pulses overlap with one another, fueling the effects of IXPM and IFWM (Matsumoto, 1998; Mecozzi, Clausen, & Shtaif, 2000). An issue of concern is that IXPM and IFWM are expected to become more significant as the OTDM signal bit rate increases, as the corresponding pulsewidths would become shorter. Note the manner in which IXPM and IFWM are analogous to the interchannel XPM and FWM with the difference being one occurs in the time domain while the other occurs in the frequency domain. This is the reason why the names IXPM and IFWM are generally used to describe these new subsets of SPM.

Figure 9 shows the effects of intrachannel XPM and FWM using a system that employs both lumped and distributed dispersion compensation (hybrid DM system) in a purely OTDM system. The inline DCFs compensate for 80% of the dispersion while the pre and post-DCFs combine for another 20% (10% each: split ratio is half). Without nonlinear effects, it is clearly seen that the pulses remain undistorted at the output and at the center of the propagation length (distance = 262.5 km) where the dispersion is totally compensated for. With nonlinear effects, after total dispersion compensation is performed at the output, the pulses display significant amplitude jitter due to accumulated IXPM and IFWM along the system. The progression of the signal also shows that the pulses actually increase in amplitude towards the center of the propagation as the pulses become thinner due to the soliton-like SPM effect. When the non-zero dispersion shifted fiber (NZDSF) dispersion is increased (increase in dispersion map strength), the output pulses display even larger amplitude jitter at the output after total dispersion compensation. In fact, significant amplitude jitter is already present at the halfway point.

Figure 9. Effects of Intrachannel XPM and FWM in a single channel, hybrid DM system with noiseless amplifiers. (a) System block diagram. (b) Signal without nonlinear effects. Signal with nonlinear effects having NZDSF dispersion, (c) D = 5ps/nm/km and (d) D = 10 ps/nm/km (Hiew, Abbou, & Chuah, 2006)

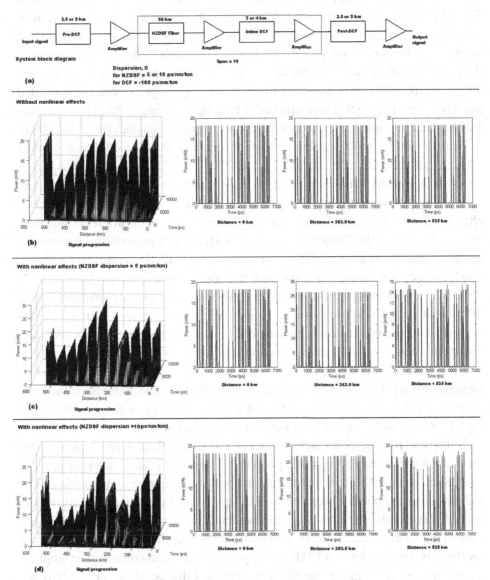

NONLINEAR SCATTERING

Optical waveguides do not always behave as completely linear channels whose increase in output optical power is directly proportional to the input optical power. Several nonlinear effects occur usually at high optical power levels. The nonlinear scattering causes transfer of optical power from one mode to the same or other mode in either the forward or backward direction at a different frequency. It depends on the power density within the fiber and becomes significant above threshold power levels. The most important types of nonlinear scattering in optical fiber are stimulated Brillouin scattering (SBS) and stimulated Raman scattering (SRS) both of which are observed in single-mode fibers at high optical power densities (Uetsuka, 2004).

Stimulated Brillouin scattering may be regarded as the modulation of light through thermal molecular vibrations within the fiber and scattered light appear as upper and lower sidebands, which are separated from the frequency of the incident light by the modulation frequency. The incident photon in this process produces a phonon of acoustic frequency as well as a scattered photon of different frequency. This produces an optical frequency shift (~ 11 GHz), which varies with the scattering angle because the frequency of the sound wave varies with the acoustic wavelength. The frequency is a maximum in the backward direction and reduces to zero in the forward direction making SBS a backward process. An important characteristic of SBS is that the spectral width of its gain spectrum is very narrow (~ 10 MHz). This property has been used as a mechanism for frequency selection. SBS can become a major detriment to optical communication systems as its threshold power is low (~ 1 mW). However, this threshold power increases with increasing signal bandwidth, meaning that it is less easily achieved in modern, high bit rate systems. At the same time, nonetheless, modern systems typically use high powers within the fiber making SBS a potential problem (Kovalev & Harrison, 2004).

Stimulated Raman scattering is similar to SBS except that a high frequency optical phonon rather than an acoustic phonon is generated in the scattering process. Also, SRS can occur both in the forward and backward directions in an optical fiber and may have an optical power threshold of up to three orders of magnitude higher than SBS in a particular fiber. On the other hand, the scattered photon in SRS has a much higher frequency shift (~ 13 THz) and the spectral width of the SRS gain spectrum is much wider (~ 40 THz). This property has been utilized as an amplifying mechanism in so-called Raman fiber amplifiers discussed earlier that have the advantage of large gain bandwidths. However, if two different optical waves are injected into an optical fibre, the lower frequency optical signal will experience optical gain generated by the high frequency optical signal. SRS causes power depletion in the shorter wavelength channel.

SUMMARY

The nonlinear effects that occur in optical fibers were discussed in detailed. It is found that Self phase modulation converts the optical power fluctuations into phase fluctuations, which would interact with dispersion and be converted to intensity distortions. However, when multiple wavelengths are propagating in a single fibre, fibre nonlinearities can lead to interactions and crosstalk between wavelengths due fibre nonlinearities such as four-wave mixing, cross-phase modulation, Stimulated Raman scattering, and Stimulated Brillouin scattering. Each of these nonlinearities will affect the optical transmission system in different ways. In general, due to cross-phase modulation, a nonlinear phase shift on one channel is caused by the change of the nonlinear refractive index due to the intensity of another channel and acts in addition to SPM. From the perspective of a single channel of interest, this means that a phase shift is induced upon it by all the other WDM channels that are propagating together with it. All WDM channels will thus induce as well as undergo phase shifts due to all the other channels. Four-wave mixing is another nonlinear effect that occurs when light of three different wavelengths is launched into a fibre, giving rise to a new signal. When the new signal's frequency falls within the bandwidth of another WDM channel not involved in the current mix, it represents a nonlinear crosstalk to that channel. When it falls outside the bandwidth of any other WDM channel, it still causes some distortion as the pump signals are depleted to form the new signal. Further, the use of strong dispersion maps in a DM system to increase WDM channel walk-off and consequently reduce the effects of the interchannel nonlinear distortions may lead to intrachannel nonlinear distortions.

REFERENCES

Bergano, N. S., & Davidson, C. R. (1996). Wavelength Division Multiplexing in Long-haul Transmission Systems. *Journal of Lightwave Technology, 14*(6), 1299–1308. doi:10.1109/50.511662

Bogoni, A., & Poti, L. (2004). Effective Channel Allocation to Reduce Inband fwm Crosstalk in dwdm Transmission Systems. *IEEE Journal on Selected Areas in Communications, 10*, 387–392.

Bosco, G., Carena, A., Curri, V., Gaudino, R., Poggiolini, P., & Benedetto, S. (2000). A Novel Analytical Method for the ber Evaluation in Optical Systems Affected by Parametric Gain. *IEEE Photonics Technology Letters, 12*(2), 152–154. doi:10.1109/68.823500

Bosco, G., Carena, A., Curri, V., Gaudino, R., Poggiolini, P., & Benedetto, S. (2001). A Novel Analytical Approach to the Evaluation of the Impact of Fiber Parametric Gain on the Bit Error Rate. *IEEE Transactions on Communications*, *49*(12), 2154–2163. doi:10.1109/26.974262

Gnauck, A. H., & Winzer, P. J. (2005). Optical Phase-shift Keyed Transmission. *Journal of Lightwave Technology*, *23*(1), 115–130. doi:10.1109/JLT.2004.840357

Gordon, J. P., & Haus, A. H. (1986). Random Walk of Coherently Amplified Solitons in Optical Fiber Transmission. *Optics Letters*, *11*(10), 665–667. doi:10.1364/OL.11.000665 PMID:19738722

Gordon, J. P., & Mollenauer, L. F. (1990). Phase Noise in Photonics Communications Systems Using Linear Amplifier. *Optics Letters*, *15*(23), 1351–1355. doi:10.1364/OL.15.001351 PMID:19771087

Haus, A. (1993). Optical Fiber Solitons, Their Properties and Uses. *Proceedings of the IEEE*, *81*(7), 970–983. doi:10.1109/5.231336

Hiew, C. C., Abbou, F. M., & Chuah, H. T. (2006). *Performance Analysis and Design of an Optical TDM-WDM Transmission System and Network* (Tech. Rep. No. 1). Malaysia: Multimedia University and Alcatel Network Systems.

Jiang, Z., & Fan, C. (2003). A Comprehensive Study on xpm- and srs-induced Noise in Cascaded im-dd Optical Fiber Transmission Systems. *Journal of Lightwave Technology*, *21*(4), 953–960. doi:10.1109/JLT.2003.810076

Kovalev, V. I., & Harrison, R. G. (2004). Spectral Broadening of Continuous-wave Monochromatic Pump Radiation Caused by Stimulated Brillouin Scattering in Optical Fiber. *Optics Letters*, *29*(4), 379–381. doi:10.1364/OL.29.000379 PMID:14971759

Kumar, S., Mauro, J. C., Raghavan, S., & Chowdhury, D. Q. (2002). Intrachannel Nonlinear Penalties in Dispersion-managed Transmission Systems. *IEEE Journal on Selected Areas in Communications*, *8*, 626–631.

Leibrich, J., Wree, C., & Rosenkranz, W. (2002). Cf-rz-dpsk for Suppresion of xpm on Dispersion-managed Long Haul Optical wdm Transmission on Standard Single-mode Fiber. *IEEE Photonics Technology Letters*, *14*(2), 155–157. doi:10.1109/68.980482

Marcuse, D. (1992). An Alternative Derivation of the Gordon-haus Effect. *Journal of Lightwave Technology*, *10*(2), 273–278. doi:10.1109/50.120583

Marcuse, D., Chraplyvy, A. R., & Tkach, E. W. (1994). Dependence of Cross-phase Modulation on Channel Number in Fiber wdm Systems. *Journal of Lightwave Technology*, *12*(5), 885–889. doi:10.1109/50.293982

Matsumoto, M. (1998). Analysis of Interaction Between Stretched Pulses Propagating in Dispersion-managed Fibers. *IEEE Photonics Technology Letters*, *10*(3), 373–375. doi:10.1109/68.661414

Mecozzi, A., Clausen, C. B., & Shtaif, M. (2000). System Impact of Intra-channel Nonlinear Effects in Highly Dispersed Optical Pulse Transmission. *IEEE Photonics Technology Letters*, *12*(12), 1633–1635. doi:10.1109/68.896331

Mu, R. M., Yu, T., Grigoryan, V. S., & Menyuk, C. R. (2002). Dynamics of the Chirped Return-to-zero Modulation Format. *Journal of Lightwave Technology*, *20*, 608–617. doi:10.1109/50.996580

Nakazawa, M. (2000). Ultrahigh-speed Long-distance tdm and wdm Soliton Transmission Technologies. *IEEE Journal on Selected Areas in Communications*, 6.

Pachnicke, S., Man, E. D., Spalter, S., & Voges, E. (2005). Impact of the In-line Dispersion-compensation Map on Four-wave Mixing (fwm) – Impaired Optical Networks. *IEEE Photonics Technology Letters*, *17*(1), 235–237. doi:10.1109/LPT.2004.838629

Striegler, A. G., & Schmauss, B. (2004). Compensation of Intrachannel Effects in Symmetric Dispesion-managed Transmission Systems. *Journal of Lightwave Technology*, *22*(8), 1877–1882. doi:10.1109/JLT.2004.832419

Suzuki, M., & Edagawa, N. (2003). Dispersion-managed High-capacity Ultra-long-haul Transmission. *Journal of Lightwave Technology*, *21*(4), 916–929. doi:10.1109/JLT.2003.810098

Tkach, R. W., Chraplyvy, A. R., Forghieri, F., Gnauck, A. H., & Derosier, R. M. (1995). Four-photon Mixing and High-speed wdm Systems. *Journal of Lightwave Technology*, *13*(5), 841–849. doi:10.1109/50.387800

Uetsuka, H. (2004). Awg Technologies for Dense wdm Applications. *IEEE Journal on Selected Areas in Communications*, *10*, 393–402.

Xu, C., Liu, X., & Wei, X. (2004). Differential Phase-shift Keying for High Spectral Efficiency Optical Transmissions. *IEEE Journal on Selected Areas in Communications*, *10*, 281–293.

Zhu, B. (2002). *Transmission of 3.2 tb/s (80 x 42.7 gb/s) over 5200 km of Ultrawave Fiber with 100-km Dispersion-managed Spans Using RZ-DPSK Format*. Academic Press.

KEY TERMS AND DEFINITIONS

Cross Phase Modulation (XPM): Refers to the change in the optical phase of a lightwave signal in a nonlinear medium induced by another optical field propagating at a different wavelength.

Four Wave Mixing (FWM): Is a nonlinear optical effect caused by the dependence of the refractive index on the intensity of the optical power. When three electromagnetic waves with different carrier frequencies co-propagate inside the fiber simultaneously, they generate a new electromagnetic wave whose frequency does not coincide with any of the three frequencies.

Gordon-Mollenauer Noise: Due to the nonlinear interplay between the signal and the amplified spontaneous emission (ASE) emitted by the inline amplifiers.

Interchannel Nonlinear Effects: Represent interchannel nonlinear effects such as four-wave mixing (FWM) and cross-phase modulation (XPM).

Intrachannel Nonlinear Effects: Represent nonlinear effects such as selfphase modulation (SPM), intrachannel FWM (IFWM) and intrachannel XPM (IXPM).

Intrachannel FWM (IFWM): In the presence of high dispersion, the energy is transferred to the middle of a neighboring bit slot, causing either a ghost pulse in an empty bit slot or an amplitude jitter in a nonempty bit slot.

Intrachannel XPM (IXPM): Caused by the modulation of a pulse phase by nonlinear interaction with neighboring optical pulses within the channel resulting in timing jitter.

Kerr Effect: Refers to the change in the refractive index of a material in response to an applied electric field.

Self Phase Modulation (SPM): Is the change of the phase of an optical pulse resulting from the nonlinearity of the refractive index of the material medium caused by its own optical intensity.

Stimulated Brillouin Scattering (SBS): SBS is a nonlinear process that arises from the interaction of light with acoustic phonons. At high input powers SBS converts transmitted light in the fiber to a strong scattered, Stokes-shifted (downshifted) wave propagating in the backward direction.

Stimulated Raman Scattering (SRS): SRS effect is an inelastic scattering of a photon with an optical phonon resulting from a finite response time of the third order nonlinear polarization of the optical fiber glass material. If two different optical waves are injected into an optical fiber, the longer wavelength channel will experience optical gain generated by the shorter wavelength channel.

Section 2

Chapter 3
Optical Soliton Transmission System

ABSTRACT

Performance analysis is carried out to evaluate the effect of XPM on a Dispersion Managed (DM) 40Gb/s optical soliton transmission using direct detection, in the presence of Group Velocity Dispersion (GVD), Self-Phase Modulation (SPM), and Amplified Spontaneous Emission (ASE) in this chapter. It is found that for a distance of 2000 km, a power penalty of 1.9 dB is required to achieve a BER of 10^{-9} when XPM is taken into consideration. This power penalty increases with increasing neighbouring channel power and decreases with increasing channel separation. The system performance is also shown to be dependant on the system dispersion whereby the optimum dispersion is linked to the channel input power.

INTRODUCTION

High-speed, medium-haul and long-haul transmission using optical fiber communication has been greatly improved through the development of solitons and Erbium Doped Fiber Amplifiers (EDFAs). The usefulness of such optical amplifiers with optical soliton systems has been experimentally investigated (Aubin, 1995; Ramaswami & Humblet, 1990). The RZ-based, 40Gbit/s, optical soliton systems using optical amplifiers are expected to be a viable new generation for medium distance, high capacity communication systems, in which fiber dispersion effects such as Group Velocity Dispersion (GVD) and nonlinear effects such as Self Phase Modulation

DOI: 10.4018/978-1-4666-6575-0.ch003

(SPM) are very important to system performance. Their unwanted effects can be minimized by using dispersion management (Shimoura & Seikai, 1999). Furthermore, this new generation, high capacity systems are also expected to employ wavelength division multiplexing (WDM) for which Cross-Phase Modulation (XPM) represents a potential limiting factor (Ting, Kagi, Marhic, & Kazovsky, 1996). At the same time, employment of the aforementioned optical amplifiers in the communication system introduces amplified spontaneous emission (ASE) which results in crosstalk due to beating of different channels during simultaneous amplification of dense WDM signals (Olsson,1989; Abbou, Chuah, & Majumder, 2000).

This chapter attempts to give an overview of 40 Gbps optical soliton transmission system in the presence of group velocity dispersion (GVD), self-phase modulation (SPM) and amplified spontaneous emission (ASE). Performance analysis is presented to evaluate the effect of Cross-Phase Modulation (XPM) on a dispersion managed (DM) 40Gb/s direct detection optical soliton transmission system. Numerical simulation analysis on XPM effect on the performance of a WDM, Dispersion Managed, direct detection, optical soliton transmission system in the presence of GVD, SPM and ASE effects are presented. The relative performance is determined in terms of the Bit Error Rate (BER) with special attention paid to the BER less than 10-9. The input signal power required to sustain error-free transmission would then determine the relative merits of the system as the XPM effect would introduce a power penalty through an increase in required input signal power. The effect of the power penalty caused by XPM is then explored by variation of parameters that affect XPM, such as channel wavelength separation, neighbouring channel power and channel dispersion (Ting, Kagi, Marhic, & Kazovsky, 1996; Cartaxo, 1999).

THEORETICAL ANALYSIS

Using the slowly-varying envelope approximation, the propagation of the two channels along the transmission medium is governed by the Nonlinear Schröndinger Equation (NLS). For this analysis, we consider the attenuation factor, the second and third order dispersion coefficients (linked to GVD), the Raman shift as well as the SPM and XPM effects given as follows:

Channel 1:

$$\frac{\partial A_1}{\partial z} + \frac{\alpha_1}{2} A_1 + \frac{i}{2} \beta_{21} \frac{\partial^2 A_1}{\partial T^2} - \frac{1}{6} \beta_{31} \frac{\partial^3 A_1}{\partial T^3} = i\gamma_1 \left[\left| A_1 \right|^2 + 2\left| A_2 \right|^2 - T_{R1} \frac{\partial \left| A_1 \right|^2}{\partial T} \right] A_1$$

(3.1)

61

Channel 2:

$$\frac{\partial A_2}{\partial z} + \frac{\alpha_2}{2} A_2 + d_{12} \frac{\partial A_2}{\partial T} + \frac{i}{2} \beta_{22} \frac{\partial^2 A_2}{\partial T^2} - \frac{1}{6} \beta_{32} \frac{\partial^3 A_2}{\partial T^3} = i\gamma_2 \left[|A_2|^2 + 2|A_1|^2 - T_{R2} \frac{\partial |A_2|^2}{\partial T} \right] A_2$$

(3.2)

where α_n represents the nth channel's attenuation parameter, β_{2n} represents the nth channel's second order dispersion parameter, β_{3n} represents the nth channel's third order dispersion parameter, γ_n represents the nth channel's nonlinearity coefficient, T_{Rn} represents the nth channel's Raman shift, and d_{12} represents the walk-off parameter between channels 1 and 2.

The first two terms on the right hand side of equations (3.1) and (3.2) are the nonlinearity factors that arise due to the nonlinear refractive index of the fiber. The XPM effect is modeled in the same manner as the SPM effect by introducing another term on the nonlinear portion of the NLS equation, and since there are only two co-propagating channels, the magnitude of one channel affects the other channel and vice versa. The effective nonlinear refractive index, n_2 of the XPM effect is twice that of the SPM effect. This leads to a factor of 2 applied to the magnitude of the neighboring channel in the NLS. Furthermore, the XPM effect is modeled by the addition of the walk-off parameter, d_{12} given by: $d_{12} = \left(v_{g1} \right)^{-1} - \left(v_{g2} \right)^{-1}$, where v_{gn} is the nth channel's group velocity. This is because the XPM-induced phase shift depends on the difference in velocity of the co-propagating channel. If the channel velocities are not equal, there will be a walk-off factor that tends to reduce the XPM-induced phase shift. The third parameter on the right hand side of the NLS (equations 3.1 and 3.2) is caused by the Raman shift, T_R that becomes significant for short pulses in the range of femtoseconds. Similarly, the third order dispersion term also becomes significant only for short pulses. The two-channel NLS equations (3.1) and (3.2) are solved over the entire fiber length using the split step Fourier method. In this method, the NLS equations are first split into its linear and nonlinear portions which are then applied separately. These equations for both channels are as follows:

$$\frac{\partial}{\partial z} A_n = \left[D_n + N_n \right] A_n : \text{General NLS}$$

(3.3)

$$D_1 = -\frac{\alpha}{2} A_1 - \frac{i}{2} \beta_2 \frac{\partial^2 A_1}{\partial T^2} + \frac{1}{6} \beta_3 \frac{\partial^3 A_1}{\partial T^3} : \text{Linear (Channel 1)} \qquad (3.4)$$

$$D_2 = -\frac{\alpha}{2} A_2 - \frac{i}{2} \beta_2 \frac{\partial^2 A_2}{\partial T^2} + \frac{1}{6} \beta_3 \frac{\partial^3 A_2}{\partial T^3} - d_{12} \frac{\partial A_2}{\partial T} : \text{Linear (Channel 2)} \qquad (3.5)$$

$$N_1 = i\gamma \left[|A_1|^2 + 2|A_2|^2 - T_R \frac{\partial |A_1|^2}{\partial T} \right] : \text{Nonlinear (Channel 1)} \qquad (3.6)$$

$$N_2 = i\gamma \left[|A_2|^2 + 2|A_1|^2 - T_R \frac{\partial |A_2|^2}{\partial T} \right] : \text{Nonlinear (Channel 2)} \qquad (3.7)$$

The input signal into the fiber consists of a stream of chirped Gaussian pulses given by

$$U(0,T) = \sqrt{\frac{P_{in}}{S}} \exp\left[-\frac{(1+iC)}{2} \frac{T^2}{T_0^2} \right] \qquad (3.8)$$

where P_{in} is the maximum pulse power, S is the surface area of the fiber, C is the chirp parameter, and T_0 is the half width of pulse at $1/e$ intensity point. The Gaussian pulse used as the input signal has an initial chirp because it has been reported that a chirped pulse enhances the power margin and dispersion tolerance (Morita, Suzuki, Edagawa, Tanaka, & Yamamoto, 1997). The bit stream will be intensity modulated into RZ-chirped Gaussian pulses before transmission.

System Model

The system model used for the analysis is depicted schematically in Figure 1. It consists of two channels, in which one is operating at a wavelength of 1552 nm and the other is separated by a small spacing $\Delta\lambda$. The two channels are multiplexed together using a WDM multiplexer (MUX). For analysis, the signal sources (Tx) assumingly consist of a laser source and a modulator for each channel. The laser source generates a stream of chirped Gaussian pulses that represent the intensity modulated bit stream. An optical amplifier (AMP) is placed after each section of the fiber and the amplifier is immediately followed by an optical filter (Filt). This pattern is repeated along the fiber link. After a number of amplifier spans, a dispersion compensation fiber (DCF) is placed just before the next amplifier. At the direct detection receiving

Figure 1. System block diagram (Hiew, Abbou, Chuah, & Majumder, 2005)

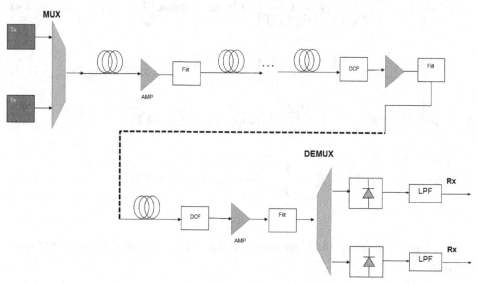

side, the two channels are demultiplexed with a WDM demultiplexer (DEMUX). The two channels are detected with separate photodetectors (Photo Det.). These photodetectors are immediately followed by low pass filters (LPF).

BIT ERROR RATE THROUGH THE Q-MAP METHOD

The system performance is quantified in terms of the bit error rate (BER). In this analysis, the BER is computed using the Q-factor method. Q-factor contour mapping has been shown to be a practical method to analyze optical transmission systems (Sahara, Kubota, & Nakazawa, 1996). Q-factor represents the signal-to-noise ratio at the receiver decision circuit. Equation (3.9) below shows the definition of Q-factor applied to NRZ systems. This definition is adopted to the RZ system used in our analysis by modifying the system bandwidth. We used 1.4 times the base band frequency for the simulations. This definition considers interaction and jitter effects. Relatively short bit patterns can then be used for simulations, as the interaction between adjacent pulses is dominant in soliton systems (Shimoura & Seikai, 1999; Sahara, Kubota, & Nakazawa, 1996).

$$Q = \frac{\mu_1 - \mu_0}{\sigma_1 + \sigma_0} \tag{3.9}$$

where μ_1 and μ_0 are the mean values of bit currents 1 and 0 respectively, and σ_1 and σ_0 are the standard deviations of bit currents 1 and 0 respectively. The bit error rate (BER) is calculated from the Q-factor as follows:

$$BER = \frac{1}{2} \, erfc\left(\frac{Q}{\sqrt{2}}\right) \tag{3.10}$$

NOISE MODEL

The noise modeled in the system includes the amplified spontaneous emission (ASE) noise, thermal noise and shot noise due to random arrival of photons at the receiver. The amplified spontaneous emission is considerd to be additive white Gaussian noise with zero mean and variance given by

$$\sigma_{sp}^2 = hf \, \eta_{sp}(G-1)B_o \tag{3.11}$$

where B_o represents the optical filter bandwidth, the parameter η_{sp} represents the spontaneous emission factor, h is the Planck's constant, f is the optical frequency and G is the optical amplifier gain. To include the effect of in-line amplifier noise, the real and imaginary components of the amplified spontaneous emission are modeled as zero mean white Gaussian noise and added to the signal field after each amplifier. The thermal noise is calculated for a perfectly matched resistive load. The shot noise is modeled using the bandwidth of the receiver after a low-pass baseband filter.

PARAMETERS USED IN SIMULATION

The simulated system is chosen to operate at a bit rate of 40 Gbit/s with the first channel operating at a wavelength of 1552 nm and the second channel is separated by a small wavelength separation $\Delta\lambda$. The input pulse has a chirp factor of 0.4 and each pulse in the bit sequence has a full width half maximum (FWHM) of 5 ps. The input signal is assumed to be a 10-bit pattern of "0101110110" and the single mode fiber used in the simulation has an effective core area of 50.0 μm^2, an attenuation factor of 0.20 dB/km and a Raman shift of 5 fs.

The nonlinear coefficient γ is 2.24×10^{-20} m²/W and the total length of the fiber used in the system is 2000 km. Furthermore, two terms are used regularly to describe the dispersion in the system, which are the local dispersion D_p and the average dispersion D_{av}. The average dispersion is defined as the local dispersion over a certain length plus the amount of dispersion compensation fiber (D_c, shown diagrammatically in Figure 2 and is defined as

$$D_{av} = \frac{\left(D_p \times L\right) + D_c}{L} \tag{3.12}$$

where L is equal to the distance between successive dispersion compensation fibres. The amplifier gain used is 20 dB. This corresponds to an amplifier span of 100 km as the only loss is the fiber attenuation. The amplifier has a noise figure of 4 dB. The filters used are Gaussian filters with a bandwidth of 3nm. The dispersion management scheme used in the system consists of dispersion compensation fibers of -30 ps/nm/km placed at distances of 5 amplifier spans apart and the fiber is operating in the anomalous dispersion region.

Figure 2. Dispersion map (Hiew, Abbou, Chuah, & Majumder, 2005)

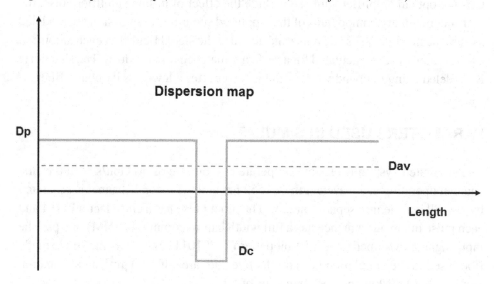

RESULTS AND DISCUSSIONS

Following the theoretical analysis presented earlier, performance analysis of cross-phase modulation effects on a direct detection dispersion managed optical soliton in the presence of GVD, SPM and ASE noise is studied by solving numerically the nonlinear Schröndinger equation (NLSE) using the beam propagation method. The results are evaluated at a bit rate of 40 Gb/s. The plots of BER versus input power with XPM and without XPM as a parameter are shown in Figure 3. As a result, the required input power required to achive a BER of 10^{-9} when XPM is not inculded is 3.5 dBm. However when XPM is taken into consideration, the required input power increases to about 5.4 dBm, which leads to a power penalty of about 1.9 dB.

Note that the graph in Figure 3 shows that the transmission is error-free within a certain range of input powers and an increase or decrease of the input power would eventually lead to a high BER. This is due to the delicate balance in the soliton system where the nonlinear effects caused by the signal intensity balances out the

Figure 3. BER versus input power with and without XPM Effect (Hiew, Abbou, Chuah, & Majumder, 2005)

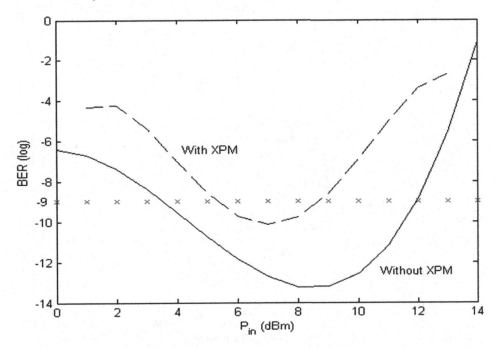

dispersion effects. However, here we notice that the XPM effect reduces the range of acceptable input signal power by increasing the minimum input signal power required for error-free transmission. In order to get a better insight into the balancing act of signal power and dispersion in a soliton system, we use the Q-map contour plot. A Q-factor of 6 and above corresponds to error-free transmission.

We show the Q-map contour plot with and without XPM effect in Figure 4 and Figure 5. The contour plots show that error-free transmission only lies within narrow ranges of input signal power (P_{in}) and average dispersion (D_{av}). The two parameters are related and, generally, the larger the average dispersion the higher the required input signal power. Taking XPM effect into account reduces the range of acceptable input signal powers by generally decreasing the Q-factor. This produces an increase of input signal power needed to sustain error-free transmission for the same value of average dispersion.

Figure 4. Q-map contour plot for transmission without XPM (Hiew, Abbou, Chuah, & Majumder, 2005)

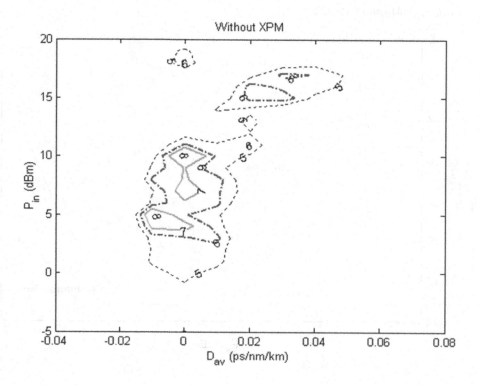

Figure 5. Q-map contour plot for transmission with XPM (Hiew, Abbou, Chuah, & Majumder, 2005)

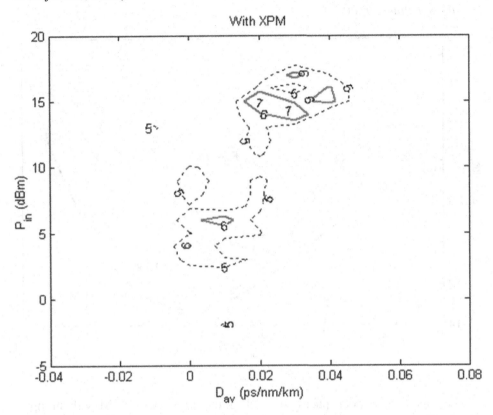

Figure 6 depicts the impact of input power variation of channel 2 on the BER performance as a function of channel 1 input power for three different input power levels; 1 mW, 2 mW and 4 mW. It is found that increasing the input signal power of Channel 2 increases the BER of channel 1 by shifting the BER vs. P_{in} curve higher. This increases the minimum input power required for error-free transmission and leads to a power penalty of 1.3 dB for $P_2 = 1$ mW and 1.9 dB for $P_2 = 2$ mW. In some cases when the input power of the copropagating channel is very high, XPM effect becomes more significant and consequently causes additional broadening due XPM-induced phase shift, leading to degradation of system performance and thus high values of the BER. This situation occurs for an input power of 4 mW of Channel 2 as shown in Figure 6. It can be seen that the transmission fails to meet the error-free criteria for all values of input power of Channel 1 (P_{in}).

Figure 6. BER versus input power for fiber length of 2000 km and for different input powers of channel 2; P2 = 1 mW, P2 = 2 mW, and P2 = 4 mW (Hiew, Abbou, Chuah, & Majumder, 2005)

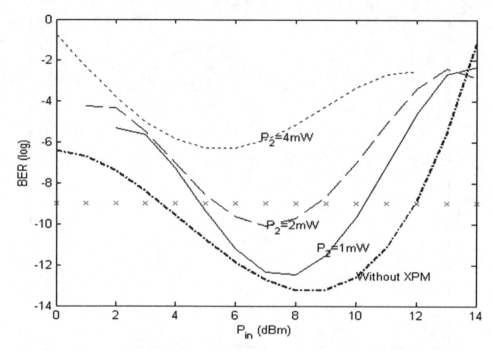

The impact of channel spacing on BER in the presence of XPM with an input power of 1 mW for channel 2 is shown in Figure 7. The BER is calculated by varying channel 1 input power for three different channel spacings; $\Delta\lambda = 2$ nm, $\Delta\lambda = 4$ nm and $\Delta\lambda = 6$ nm. The results show that decreasing the channel spacing increases the BER and leads to a power penalty for each case of approximately 0.7 dB for channel spacing of $\Delta\lambda = 6$nm, 1.3 dB for $\Delta\lambda = 4$nm, and 1.7 dB for $\Delta\lambda = 2$nm. This means that closely spaced channels lead to higher XPM-induced phase shifts due to less walk-off between channels.

Referring to the contour plots of Figure 4 and Figure 5, we can see that the transmission quality is strongly dependent on the fiber average dispersion. Therefore, based on BER results from Figure 6, we would not expect to obtain an error-free transmission for an input power of 6 mW for channel 2. However, by varying the average dispersion (D_{av}) and using a channel spacing of 4 nm and an input signal

Figure 7. BER versus input power for fiber length of 2000 km and for different. Channel spacings; $\Delta\lambda = 2$ mW, $\Delta\lambda = 4$mW, and $\Delta\lambda = 6$ mW (Hiew, Abbou, Chuah, & Majumder, 2005)

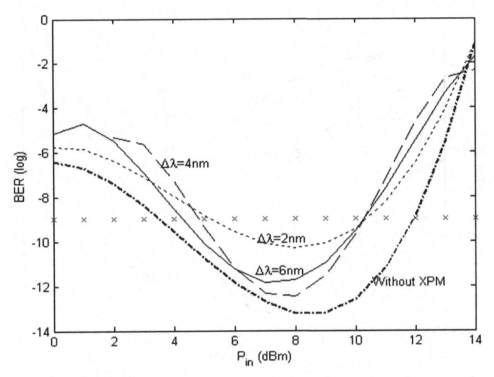

power of 6 mW for channel 2, as shown in Figure 8, when the average dispersion (D_{av}) is increased to 0.02, the BER decreases and error-free transmission is achieved over a very small window in the 11-13 dBm interval. However, further increasing the average dispersion does not improve the BER but it worsens it, which suggests the existence of an optimum value of the average dispersion that lies within a certain interval for which the error-free transmission is met.

SUMMARY

Performance analysis is carried out to evaluate the effect of cross-phase modulation on a dispersion managed 40Gb/s optical soliton transmission using direct detection, in the presence of group velocity dispersion (GVD), self-phase modulation (SPM) and

Figure 8. BER versus input power for fiber length of 2000 km and for different fiber average dispersion coefficients; Dav = 0, Dav = 0.02, and Dav = 0.03 (Hiew, Abbou, Chuah, & Majumder, 2005)

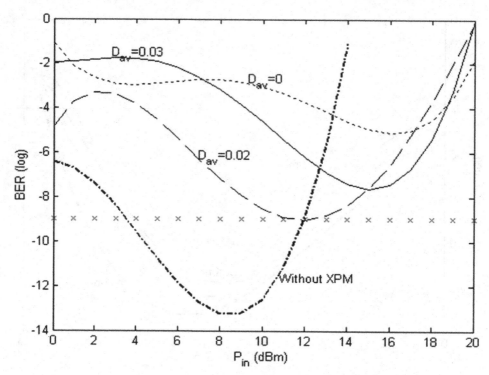

amplified spontaneous emission (ASE). It is found that XPM effect causes a power penalty that increases with increasing neighbouring channel power in the shared transmission link. At the same time, smaller channel separations also lead to larger power penalties. The system performance is also linked to the system dispersion with the appearance of an optimal dispersion window for a given input channel power.

REFERENCES

Abbou, F. M., Chuah, H. T., & Majumder, S. P. (2000). Limitations of Soliton Transmission in a Cascaded Optical Amplifier System. *Journal of Optical Communications*, *21*(5), 165–170.

Aubin, G. (1995). 20 gb/s Soliton Transmission over Transoceanic Distances with 105 km Amplifier Span. *Electronics Letters*, *21*(13), 1079–1080. doi:10.1049/el:19950755

Cartaxo, A. V. T. (1999). Cross-phase Modulation in Intensity Modulation-direct Detection wdm Systems with Multiple Optical Amplifiers and Dispersion Compensators. *Journal of Lightwave Technology*, *17*(2), 178–190. doi:10.1109/50.744218

Hiew, C. C., Abbou, F. M., Chuah, H. T., & Majumder, S. P. (2005). Analysis of Cross-phase Modulation Effects on a Direct Detection Optical Soliton Transmission System in the Presence of GVD, SPM, and ASE noise. *Journal of Optical Communications.*, *26*(2), 17–23.

Morita, I., Suzuki, M., Edagawa, N., Tanaka, K., Yamamoto, S., & Akiba, S. (1997). Performance Improvement by Initial Phase Modulation in 20 gbit/s Soliton-based rz Transmission with Periodic Dispersion Compensation. *Electronics Letters*, *33*(12), 1021–1022. doi:10.1049/el:19970714

Olsson, N. A. (1989). Lightwave Systems with Optical Amplifiers t. *Journal of Lightwave Technology*, *7*(7), 1071–1082. doi:10.1109/50.29634

Ramaswami, R., & Humblet, P. A. (1990). Amplifier Induced Crosstalk in Multi-channel Optical Networks. *Journal of Lightwave Technology*, *8*(12), 1882–1896. doi:10.1109/50.62886

Sahara, A., Kubota, A., & Nakazawa, M. (1996). Q-factor Contour Mapping for Evaluation of Optical Transmission Systems: Soliton against nrz against rz Pulse at Zero Group Velocity Dispersion. *Electronics Letters*, *32*(10), 915–916. doi:10.1049/el:19960590

Shimoura, K., & Seikai, S. (1999). Two Extremely Stable Conditions of Optical Soliton Transmission in Periodic Dispersion Compensation Lines. *IEEE Photonics Technology Letters*, *11*(2), 2. doi:10.1109/68.740703

Ting, K. C., Kagi, N., Marhic, E. M., & Kazovsky, L. G. (1996). Cross-phase Modulation in Fiber Links with Multiple Optical Amplifiers and Dispersion Compensators. *Journal of Lightwave Technology*, *96*, 3.

KEY TERMS AND DEFINITIONS

Chirp: Refers to time dependence of the instantaneous frequency of an optical pulse.

Full Width Half Maximum (FWHM): FWHM refers to full width half maximum values of a light Pulse's peak power and spectral width at the 3 dB points.

Group Velocity Dispersion (GVD): Due to group velocity dependence on wavelength, different parts of an optical signal will travel at different group velocities.

Non-Return-to-Zero (NRZ): Refers to a form of line coding technique in which 1s are represented by a positive voltage and 0s are represented a negative voltage, with no rest condition.

Optical Soliton: Refers to an optical pulse that can propagate undistorted over long distance communication without changing its shape because the fiber dispersive effects are balanced by fiber nonlinearities.

Return-to-Zero (RZ): A line coding technique used in telecommunications signals in which the signal returns to zero during the second half of each bit.

Walk-Off Parameter: Refers to the difference between the reciprocal group velocities of two optical pulses.

Chapter 4
A Detailed Analysis of Cross–Phase Modulation Effects on OOK and DPSK Optical WDM Transmission Systems

ABSTRACT

Performance analysis is carried out to evaluate the effect of XPM on a dispersion managed 20Gb/s optical WDM transmission system using either On-Off Keying (OOK) or Differential Phase Shift Keying (DPSK) modulation, in the presence of GVD, SPM, and ASE noise in this chapter. It is found that to achieve a BER of 10^{-9} at a distance of 160 km, a 1.0 dB XPM power penalty is incurred for input channel power of 3 dBm in OOK transmission and 7 dBm in DPSK. The power penalty increases with input channel powers, but it is inversely proportional and exhibits oscillations with respect to channel separation. The oscillation is evenly spaced for DPSK but not for OOK and suggests the presence of optimum separation values. XPM penalty decreases when high dispersion fiber is used, and it also increases linearly with increasing dispersion slope. Small residual dispersion can reduce the penalty of nonlinear effects.

DOI: 10.4018/978-1-4666-6575-0.ch004

INTRODUCTION

In this chapter, we carry out a detailed simulation of the XPM effect on the performance of dispersion managed 20Gb/s optical WDM transmission system using either OOK and DPSK modulation, in the presence of GVD, SPM and ASE noise. The use of dispersion management is to minimize the effects of dispersion in nonzero dispersion fibers. The system uses either a coherent detection scheme employing direct-detection DPSK or a simple OOK for comparison, both of which are Non-Return-to-Zero (NRZ). The relative performance is determined in terms of the bit error rate (BER) with special attention paid to BER<10^{-9} (criteria for error-free transmission). The minimum received power required to sustain error-free transmission would then determine the relative merits of the system, as the XPM effect would introduce a power penalty by increasing the minimum received power required, leading to a loss of receiver sensitivity. The magnitude of the power penalty caused by XPM is then explored by variation of channel power, channel wavelength separation and fiber dispersion characteristics for comparison between the two modulation schemes.

SYSTEM MODEL

The system model used for the analysis is depicted schematically in Figure 1. It consists of two or more channels, one of which is operating at a wavelength of 1548 nm and the others are each separated by a small channel spacing of $\Delta\lambda$. The channels are multiplexed together using an ideal WDM multiplexer (MUX). For analysis, the signal sources (Tx) are assumed to consist of an ideal laser source and a modulator for each channel. The channels are modulated from a pseudorandom bit stream to be either an OOK or a DPSK signal. The fiber used is a nonzero dispersion shifted fiber (NDSF) with small residual dispersion in the anomalous region. This is because zero dispersion fibers facilitate phase matching that introduces interchannel interference.

Figure 1. System block diagram (Abbou, Hiew, Chuah, Ong, & Abid, 2008)

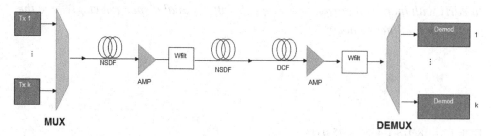

An optical amplifier (AMP) is placed after the first section of fiber, at the midway stage and at the end of the transmission path just before the receiver. A wideband optical filter follows each amplifier. Lumped dispersion compensation is employed whereby a span of dispersion compensation fiber (DCF) is placed just before the final amplifier. Lumped dispersion compensation has been shown to reduce XPM-induced penalties by maintaining the incoherence between channels over most of the fiber length (Marhic, Kagi, Chiang, & Kazovsky, 1996). At the receiving side, the channels are demultiplexed by wavelength separation with a WDM demultiplexer (DEMUX). The received power used in our analysis is measured just after the WDM demultiplexer before demodulation or photodetection. Each channel is then fed to their respective demodulators (Demod) that are different for OOK or DPSK modulation.

For OOK demodulation, the channels are detected by separate envelope detectors, each consisting of a photodetector (Photo Det.), that is immediately followed by a low pass filter (LPF) to produce the baseband signal (Rx), shown in Figure 2. For DPSK demodulation, we use direct detection delay demodulation receivers. This is shown in Figure 3 using a two-filter model (Sahara, Kubota, & Nakazawa, 1996). The received signal is time delayed by one bit period (T). The original signal and the delayed signal are then summed and subtracted in two separate adders. These signals are detected directly with envelope detectors. At the end of the low pass filters are the baseband signal and its inverse respectively. These two signals are compared to make the bit decision.

Figure 2. OOK demodulator block diagram (Abbou, Hiew, Chuah, Ong, & Abid, 2008)

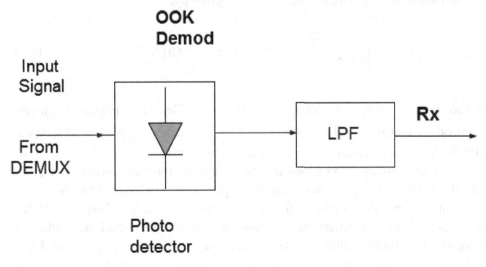

Figure 3. DPSK demodulator block diagram (Abbou, Hiew, Chuah, Ong, & Abid, 2008)

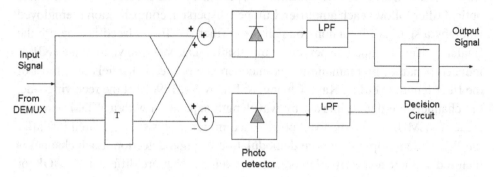

THEORETICAL ANALYSIS

The input signal launched into the fiber depends on the modulation scheme used. For the OOK modulated transmission system, the input signal is an NRZ signal given by:

$$E_{in}\left(t\right) = \sqrt{P_{in}} \sum_{v=-\infty}^{\infty} a_v rect\left(\frac{t-vT}{T}\right) \exp\left(j\omega_c t\right) \qquad (4.1)$$

where P_{in} is the maximum input pulse power with $a_v = \pm 1$ representing the vth information bit, *rect(t)* is the rectangular pulse shape used in OOK modulation, ω_c is the optical carrier angular frequency, T is the bit period. For the DPSK modulated transmission system, the input signal is given by:

$$E_{in}\left(t\right) = \sqrt{P_{in}} \exp\left[j \sum_{v=-\infty}^{\infty} \pi\left(1-s_v\right) rect\left(\frac{t-vT}{T}\right)\right] \exp\left(j\omega_c t\right) \qquad (4.2)$$

where $s_v = s_{v-1}$ if $a_v = 1$ and $s_v = s'_{v-1}$ if $a_v = 0$. Here, s'_v represents the inversion of s_v, that is $s'_v = 1 - s_v$ where $s_v \in \{0,1\}$ (Sahara, Kubota, & Nakazawa, 1996). All other parameters here are as explained before.

The beam propagation method is used to simulate the transmission. Using the slowly varying envelope approximation, the propagation of the channels along the transmission medium, is governed by the Nonlinear Schrodinger Equation (NLS). For this analysis, we consider only the attenuation factor, the second and third order dispersion coefficients (linked to GVD), the Raman shift as well as the SPM and XPM effects in the NLS, given as follows for an arbitrary channel:

Channel k:

$$\frac{\partial A_k}{\partial z} + \frac{\alpha_k}{2} A_k + \frac{1}{v_{gk}} \frac{\partial A_k}{\partial t} + \frac{i}{2} \beta_{2k} \frac{\partial^2 A_k}{\partial t^2} - \frac{1}{6} \beta_{3k} \frac{\partial^3 A_k}{\partial t^3} = i\gamma_k \left[|A_k|^2 + 2\sum_{\substack{j=1 \\ j \neq k}}^{N} |A_j|^2 - T_{Rk} \frac{\partial |A_k|^2}{\partial t} \right] A_k$$

(4.3)

where k is the current channel under consideration and N is the total number of channels.

α_k represents the kth channel's attenuation parameter, β_{2k} represents the kth channel's second order dispersion parameter (governs GVD), β_{3k} represents the kth channel's third order dispersion parameter, γ_k represents the kth channel's nonlinearity coefficient, T_{Rk} represents the kth channel's Raman shift, and v_{gk} represents the kth channel's group velocity. The first two terms on the right hand side of Equation (4.3) are the nonlinearity factors that arise due to the nonlinear refractive index of the fiber. The XPM effect is modeled in the same manner as the SPM effect by introducing another term on the nonlinear portion of the NLS equation. This term sums the effect of XPM caused by all other channels. The effective nonlinear refractive index, n_2 of the XPM effect is twice that of the SPM effect. This leads to a factor of 2 applied to the magnitude of the sum. The third parameter on the right hand side of Equation (4.3) is caused by the Raman shift, T_{Rk} which becomes significant for short pulses in the range of femtoseconds. Similarly, the third order dispersion term, β_{3k} also becomes significant only for short pulses. The NLS Equation (4.3) is solved over the entire fiber length using the split step Fourier method for all channels. In this method, the NLS equation is first split into its linear and nonlinear portions that are then applied separately. These equations for an arbitrary channel k are as follows:

$$\frac{\partial}{\partial z} A_k = \left[D_k + N_k \right] A_k : \text{General NLS}$$

(4.4)

$$D_k = -\frac{\alpha_k}{2} A_k - \frac{1}{v_{gk}} \frac{\partial A_k}{\partial t} - \frac{i}{2} \beta_{2k} \frac{\partial^2 A_k}{\partial t^2} + \frac{1}{6} \beta_{3k} \frac{\partial^3 A_k}{\partial t^3} : \text{Linear}$$

(4.5)

$$N_k = i\gamma_k \left[\left|A_k\right|^2 + 2\sum_{\substack{j=1 \\ j\neq k}}^{N} \left|A_j\right|^2 - T_{Rk} \frac{\partial \left|A_k\right|^2}{\partial t} \right] : \text{Nonlinear} \qquad (4.6)$$

A common problem that occurs in attempting to simulate the XPM effect using Equations (4.4), (4.5) and (4.6) is the consideration of the group velocity, v_{gk} within the time frame reference used. The respective channels' group velocities govern the walk-off factor between pulses of different channels that tend to reduce the XPM-induced phase shift by limiting the XPM interaction. If only two channels are present, a simplified model is often utilized whereby the effect of the difference of group velocity between two channels is given by the walk-off factor

$$d_{12} = \left(v_{g1}\right)^{-1} - \left(v_{g2}\right)^{-1}$$

that is included in the channel 2 equation and the time reference is set to

$$T = t - \frac{z}{v_{g1}},$$

which follows the propagation of channel 1 (Agrawal, 1995). This time reference needs to be common to both channels to properly model the relative velocity difference between the two channels. This method is extended here for a more generalized analysis. Furthermore, in simulation, it is often easier to use a time frame reference

$$T_k = t - \frac{z}{v_{gk}},$$

which follows the propagation of the kth channel when solving for that particular channel. First, we use a set of simplified Split-Step Fourier equations from (4.5) and (4.6) given by:

$$D_k = -\frac{\alpha_k}{2} A_k - \frac{i}{2}\beta_{2k} \frac{\partial^2 A_k}{\partial T_k^2} + \frac{1}{6}\beta_{3k} \frac{\partial^3 A_k}{\partial T_k^3} : \text{Linear} \qquad (4.7)$$

$$N_k = i\gamma_k \left[\left| A_k \right|^2 + 2 \sum_{\substack{j=1 \\ j \neq k}}^{N} \left| \hat{A}_j \right|^2 - T_{Rk} \frac{\partial \left| A_k \right|^2}{\partial T_k} \right] : \text{Nonlinear} \qquad (4.8)$$

Note the omission of the group velocity term and the use of a time reference T_k that follows the kth channel's propagation individually. We only take into consideration the XPM effect and ignore other third order nonlinear effects between channels such as Four Wave Mixing. The walk-off effect between channels is included by altering the second term on the right of Equation (4.6) that governs the XPM effect, such that A_j is changed to $\hat{A}_j$ in (4.8) where $\left| \hat{A}_j \right|^2$ is the magnitude-squared curve of the slowly varying envelop of the jth channel shifted in time to incorporate the relative time gap between channels k and j caused by their different group velocities at the current evaluation distance. Mathematically, $\hat{A}_j$ is given by:

$$\hat{A}_j = A_j \left(t + \Delta t_{jkm} \right) \qquad (4.9)$$

$$\Delta t_{jkm} = d_{jkm} \left(D_{curr} \right) + \sum_{n=1}^{m-1} \left(d_{jkn} - d_{jkm} \right) \left(L_n \right) \qquad (4.10)$$

where m is the current fiber section under consideration, Δt_{jkm} and d_{jkm} is the relative time gap and walk-off factor respectively between channels k and j at fiber section m, D_{curr} is the total distance already travelled by the signal at the current step distance and L_n is the length of the nth fiber section. To practically perform this alteration, we compute the walk-off factor, d_{jkm} given by (Chiang, Kagi, Marhic, & Kazovsky, 1996):

$$d_{jkm} = \left(v_{gjm} \right)^{-1} - \left(v_{gkm} \right)^{-1} = \int_{\lambda_k}^{\lambda_j} D_m \left(\lambda \right) d\lambda \qquad (4.11)$$

If the dispersion coefficient curve for the mth fiber section, $D_m \left(\lambda \right)$ is approximated by

$$D_m \left(\lambda \right) = \left(Sl_m \times \lambda \right) + c \qquad (4.12)$$

where Sl_m = dispersion slope, λ = wavelength and c is a constant of proportionality. The walk-off factor is then approximated by,

$$d_{jkm} \approx D_m \left(\lambda_k - \lambda_j \right) + \frac{Sl_m}{2} \left(\lambda_k - \lambda_j \right)^2 \tag{4.13}$$

where D_m = dispersion coefficient of channel with smaller wavelength at m^{th} fiber section. The walk-off factor is computed for each combination of j and k ($j \neq k$) and each fiber section m. Note that d_{jkm} can be positive or negative and thus the shifted curve $\left| \hat{A}_j \right|^2$ can be to the left or right. The technique used here assures that bit position and interaction effects are accounted for as the XPM effect on each individual pulse of a channel is due only to the corresponding pulses of other channels that occur simultaneously in time at the present distance.

The first advantage of this technique is the ability to include multiple channels while retaining the relative velocity difference between each and every channel to determine the XPM effect of one particular channel on another. The drawback is that the number of computations grows multiplicatively with the number of channels. Secondly, it easily enables us to keep track of the change in-group velocities of the channels when it travels between fibers with different dispersion values (such as from NDSF to DCF).

The error inherent in this technique is in the process of time shifting the channel pulses. By necessity, we have to model the pseudorandom bit pattern length of each channel as a finite value. Thus, when shifting the pulses, we have to maintain a window of interest. By assuming that the bit pattern repeats itself along the stream, any section of the pulse pattern that is shifted out of the window on one side is put back onto the other side (as in a circular shift). This causes an error as we have neglected the interpulse effects between the pulses at the edge of the window and those that theoretically lie just outside the window while modeling the propagation. However, the error can be reduced by using a long bit pattern length so that the portion at the edge of the window is only a small percentage of the total bit pattern length.

The system performance is quantified in terms of the bit error rate (BER). In this analysis, the BER is computed through the Q-factor method. Q-factor computations have been shown to be a practical method to analyze optical transmission systems (Sahara, Kubota, & Nakazawa, 1996). Q-factor represents the signal-to-noise ratio at the receiver decision circuit. Equation (4.14) below shows the definition of Q-factor as applied to NRZ systems:

$$Q = \frac{\mu_1 - \mu_0}{\sigma_1 + \sigma_0} \tag{4.14}$$

where μ_1, σ and μ_0 are the mean values of bit currents 1 and 0 respectively, and σ_1 and σ_0 are the standard deviations of bit currents 1 and 0 respectively. The Q-factor is calculated based on the received baseband signal. The bit error rate (BER) is calculated from the Q-factor as follows:

$$BER = \frac{1}{2} erfc\left(\frac{Q}{\sqrt{2}}\right) \tag{4.15}$$

The noise modeled in the system includes the amplified spontaneous emission (ASE) noise, thermal noise, photodetector dark current noise and shot noise due to random arrival of photons at the receiver. The amplified spontaneous emission is considered to be additive white Gaussian noise with zero mean and variance given by

$$\sigma_{sp}^2 = hf\,\eta_{sp}(G-1)B_o \tag{4.16}$$

where B_o represents the optical filter bandwidth, the parameter η_{sp} represents the spontaneous emission factor, h is the Planck's constant, f is the optical frequency and G is the optical amplifier gain. To include the effect of in-line amplifier noise, the amplified spontaneous emission is further modeled as having random phase and added to the signal field after each amplifier. The thermal noise is given as

$$\sigma_{th}^2 = \frac{4kTB_E}{R_L} \tag{4.17}$$

where k is the Boltzmann's constant, T is temperature in Kelvin, B_E is the electrical bandwidth and R_L is the load resistance. The shot noise is given as

$$\sigma_{sh}^2 = 2eR_d P_{rec} B_E \tag{4.18}$$

where e is the electron charge and P_{rec} is the received power. The phase noise and intensity noise of the laser source have been neglected by assuming an ideal laser source with negligible linewidth.

RESULTS AND DISCUSSIONS

Following the theoretical analysis presented earlier, performance analysis of cross-phase modulation effects on the dispersion managed optical transmission systems using OOK or DPSK, in the presence of GVD, SPM and ASE noise, is studied by solving numerically the nonlinear Schrodinger equation (NLSE) using the beam propagation method. The simulated system is chosen to operate at a bit rate of 20 Gbit/s with the first channel operating at a wavelength of 1548 nm and the second channel is separated by a small wavelength separation $\Delta\lambda$. Both input signals are modulated with pseudorandom bit sequences (PRBS) of length 512 bits. The length of the single mode fiber (NDSF) used in the system is 80 km before the first amplifier, 76 km after the amplifier and this is followed at the end with 4 km of dispersion compensation fiber (DCF) that provides lumped dispersion compensation bringing the total system length to 160km. For both types of fiber, the Kerr coefficient is 2.24×10^{-20} m²/W, the effective core area is 50.0 µm² and the attenuation factor is 0.20 dB/km. The amplifier gain used is 16 dB. This corresponds to an amplifier span of 80 km if assuming that the only loss is the fiber attenuation. The amplifier has a Noise Figure (NF) of 4 dB. The filters used are first-order Gaussian-shaped filters where the wideband filters after the amplifiers have a bandwidth of 500 GHz and the baseband filters have a bandwidth of 25 GHz. The results are evaluated for two channels, with channel spacing, $\Delta\lambda$ of 0.5 nm. For the NDSF, the dispersion coefficient, D is set to a low value of +1.5 ps/nm/km with a dispersion slope, Sl of zero. The dispersion is fully compensated with the DCF leading to an average dispersion of zero for all channels since the dispersion slope is zero. All these parameters are kept constant until stated otherwise.

For Figure 4, the observed probe channel (Channel 1) has an input power, P_1 of 3 dBm and the neighbouring copropagating channel (Channel 2) also has an input power, P_2 of 3 dBm for OOK modulation. For DPSK modulation, $P_1 = P_2 = 7$ dBm. All transmitted and received powers mentioned in this section refer to the average power of the signal. The plots of BER versus received power, P_R for both OOK and DPSK modulation, with or without XPM are shown in Figure 4.

The minimum received power (receiver sensitivity) required to achieve a BER of 10^{-9} for OOK modulation when XPM is not included: −30.3 dBm. However, when XPM is taken into consideration, the minimum received power required increases to about −29.3 dBm, which leads to a power penalty of about 1.0 dB. For DPSK modulation, the minimum received power required for error-free transmission is about −35.5 dBm without XPM. When XPM is taken into consideration, it increases to −34.5 dBm, which leads to a power penalty of about 1.0 dB. First of all, the graph shows that DPSK modulation provides much better receiver sensitivity

Figure 4. BER versus received power PR for both OOK and DPSK modulation with and without the XPM effect. (Two channels, total length = 160 km, input powers, P1 = P2 = 3 dBm for OOK, P1 = P2 = 7 dBm for DPSK, channel separation, $\Delta\lambda$ = 0.5 nm, D = +1.5 ps/nm/km) (Abbou, Hiew, Chuah, Ong, & Abid, 2008)

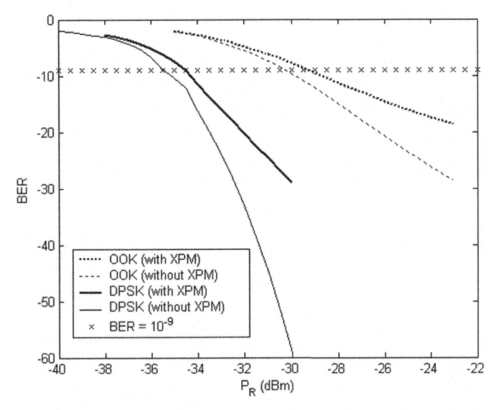

with an improvement of about 5.2 dB without XPM. Secondly, OOK modulation is more affected by XPM compared to DPSK since it requires less input power to incur the same penalty (1.0 dB).

Next, we take a look at the penalties caused without XPM (1 channel propagation) due to input power variation. We do this by comparing the receiver sensitivities of transmission for varying input powers compared to the case where P_I = 0 dBm. The result in Figure 5 gives us a good view of the factors affecting one channel transmission. Transmission at low powers incurs a power penalty due to the increasing significance of ASE noise. Transmission at high powers incurs a penalty due to the increasing significance of SPM-induced noise. It can be seen that OOK transmission is severely more affected by both ASE and SPM induced noise. This concurs with other results (Vassilieva & Hoshida, 2001) as the pattern independent intensity modulation of DPSK can suppress degradation caused by SPM and the

Figure 5. Power penalty caused by SPM and ASE versus input power of Channel 1, P1 with P1 = 0 dBm taken as the reference receiver sensitivity (power penalty = 0 dB). (One channel, total length = 160 km, D = +1.5 ps/nm/km) (Abbou, Hiew, Chuah, Ong, & Abid, 2008)

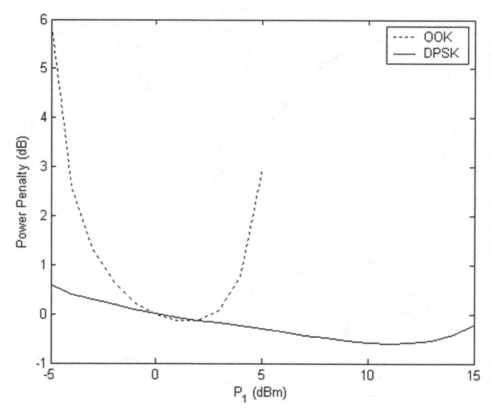

phase-encoded information is less susceptible to ASE fluctuations. The interplay between ASE and SPM produces an optimum input power of about 1 dBm for OOK and 11 dBm for DPSK.

From Figure 5, we have computed the additional power penalty caused by XPM over the other effects present by comparing the minimum receiver sensitivity for error-free transmission with or without XPM. The same method is used for all subsequent plots to compute the power penalty incurred by XPM under given conditions. Care is taken to make sure that all other parameters remain the same when comparing the minimum received power required for cases with or without XPM to obtain the power penalty. Firstly, Figure 6 depicts the power penalty caused by the XPM effect on Channel 1, for both OOK and DPSK modulation, due to the input power variation of channel 2. The input power of channel 1 is kept constant

Figure 6. Power penalty caused by XPM versus input power of Channel 2, P2 for both OOK and DPSK modulation. (Two channels, total length = 160 km, input power, P1 = 1 dBm, channel separation, $\Delta\lambda$ = 0.5 nm, D = +1.5 ps/nm/km) (Abbou, Hiew, Chuah, Ong, & Abid, 2008)

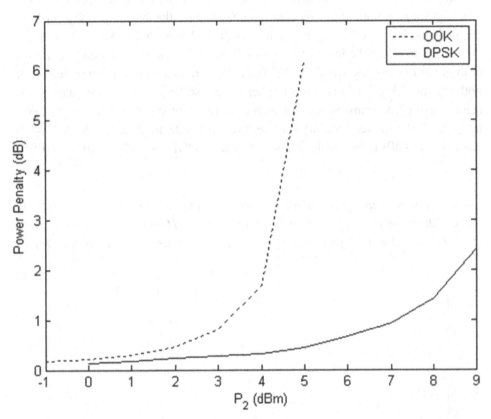

at 1 dBm. It is found that increasing the input signal power of channel 2 increases the XPM power penalty on channel 1 for both OOK and DPSK modulation but OOK modulation is more severely affected. The increasing penalty is because the increase in neighbouring channel power induces a larger XPM phase shift that directly distorts the phase encoded information in DPSK modulation. On the other hand, the intensity encoded information in OOK modulation is distorted when the XPM phase shift is converted to intensity variations (pulse broadening) through the GVD parameter. At low powers, both OOK and DPSK modulation suffer negligible XPM penalty but at P_2 = 4 dBm, the penalty is about 1.8 dB for OOK and only 0.3 dB for DPSK. The pattern independent intensity of DPSK modulation that helps suppress SPM degradation works for XPM as well.

Next, we move on to a more practical situation where both P_1 and P_2 are the same. Both the input powers are varied together to obtain Figure 7 for channel spacing of 0.5 nm and 1 nm. As expected, the XPM power penalty increases with increasing input powers and is larger for the case of smaller channel spacing. However, by varying both input powers simultaneously, the power penalty on both channels has increased compared to the results in Figure 6 for $\Delta\lambda = 0.5$ nm. Increasing both channels' input powers simultaneously lead to increased total power in the fiber that causes overall XPM effects to increase due to the mutual effect of both channels' high powers on each other. As a result, the system only manages to achieve error-free transmission for a smaller range of input power values. Once again, the XPM induced penalty is more severe for OOK modulation. At $\Delta\lambda = 0.5$ nm and $P_2 = 4$ dBm, the penalty is about 4.5 dB for OOK and only 0.5 dB for DPSK.

Figure 7. Power penalty caused by XPM versus input powers P1 = P2 for both OOK and DPSK modulation. (Two channels, total length = 160 km, channel separation, $\Delta\lambda = 0.5$ nm, D = +1.5 ps/nm/km) (Abbou, Hiew, Chuah, Ong, & Abid, 2008)

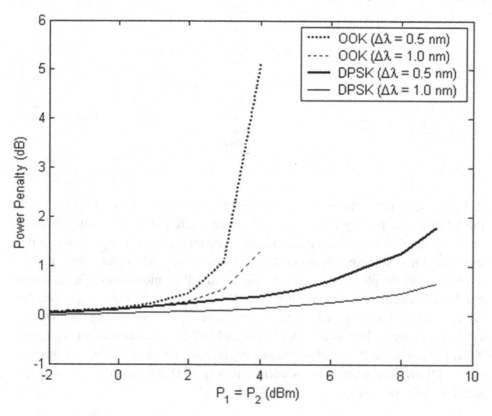

The impact of channel spacing, $\Delta\lambda$ on power penalty caused by XPM is shown in Figure 8. The input power, P1 used is 3 dBm for OOK modulation and 7 dBm for DPSK modulation. The respective powers used are selected based on the penalty-input power characteristics shown in Figure 7. On a rough scale, the XPM power penalty for both OOK and DPSK modulation decreases with increasing channel separation (almost inverse relation), becoming very small for $\Delta\lambda > 1.5$ nm. Generally, the DPSK penalty is smaller than the OOK penalty at large channel separations. On a finer scale, both the OOK and DPSK curves exhibit oscillations though the characteristics of their oscillations are different. The DPSK curve's oscillations are found to follow the XPM efficiency given as (Chiang, Kagi, Marhic, & Kazovsky, 1996).

Figure 8. Power penalty caused by XPM versus channel separation, $\Delta\lambda$ for both OOK and DPSK modulation. (Two channels, total length = 160 km, input powers, P1 = P2 = 3 dBm for OOK, P1 = P2 = 7 dBm for DPSK, D = +1.5 ps/nm/km) (Abbou, Hiew, Chuah, Ong, & Abid, 2008)

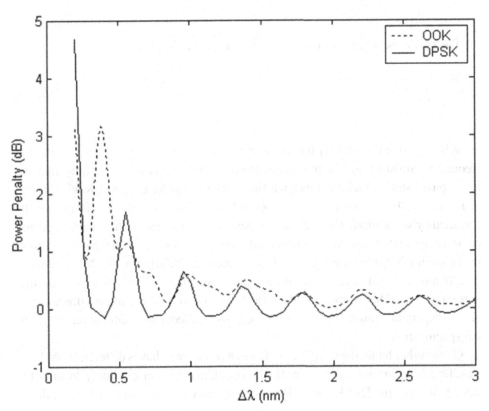

$$\eta_{XPM} = \frac{\alpha^2}{\omega^2 d_{jkm}^2 + \alpha^2} \left[1 + \frac{4\sin^2\left(\dfrac{\omega d_{jkm} L_m}{2}\right) e^{-\alpha L_m}}{\left(1 - e^{-\alpha L_m}\right)^2} \right] \qquad (4.19)$$

for fiber link m and modulation angular frequency, ω. From (Equation (4.19)), we can see that the XPM efficiency experiences a minimum when

$$\sin^2\left(\frac{\omega d_{jkm} L_m}{2}\right) = 0$$

and a maximum when

$$\sin^2\left(\frac{\omega d_{jkm} L_m}{2}\right) = 1.$$

The period between successive minimums or maximums is

$$\Delta\lambda_p = \frac{1}{f D_m L_m} \qquad (4.20)$$

Where (Equation (4.13)) has been used with $Sl = 0$ and f is the modulation frequency. Substituting for the values used in simulation and assuming that the XPM phase shift contributed by each fiber link is additive (Marhic, Kagi, Chiang, & Kazovsky, 1996), the period is about 0.42 nm. This corresponds to the results obtained by simulation. The presence of periodic minimums in the channel spacing curve suggests that system designers could use channel separations that correspond to minimum XPM efficiency based on (Equation (4.20)) for WDM systems to greatly reduce XPM induced penalties. At the same time, we should take note that variation of the fiber dispersion also affects the location of the minimums where a larger dispersion would lead to shorter periods and more oscillations on the channel spacing curve.

On the other hand, the oscillation of the OOK curve behaves differently. At large wavelength separation ($\Delta\lambda > 1$ nm), the oscillation period gradually follows the same pattern as the DPSK curve. However, at short wavelength separations, this is not true with the initial oscillation period close to two times of the DPSK curve producing instances when a maximum of the OOK corresponds to the minimum of the DPSK. All this suggests that the conversion of the XPM phase shift to intensity variation through the GVD parameter leads to new terms that become significant at small wavelength separations. The exact mathematical expression for the variance of the XPM induced intensity variation through GVD would need to be derived to obtain a better picture of the behavior of the OOK channel spacing curve.

We have also performed some simulations using high dispersion fiber ($D = +16.5$ ps/nm/km) and the result was lower XPM penalties. This is because the high dispersion leads to greater walk-off between the channels causing lower XPM efficiency as given by (Equation (4.19)). However, it is worth noting that at extremely small channel spacings ($\Delta\lambda < 0.2$ nm for DPSK and $\Delta\lambda < 0.3$ nm), the XPM penalty was very high causing error-free transmission to become impossible. Even at such small channel spacings, the walk-off factor is still reasonably large as the D value here is large (comparable to $\Delta\lambda < 2$ nm in the NDSF). Therefore, the large XPM penalty induced here is due to the pulse intensity distortion caused by large local GVD that is converted to phase distortion in neighboring channels through the Kerr nonlinearity. This effect is compounded by the fact that the system here uses lumped dispersion compensation where distorted signal pulses are amplified by the first amplifier without first undergoing dispersion compensation. The lumped dispersion compensation scheme is used to maintain the walk-off effect between neighboring channels throughout the fiber link so as to minimize XPM efficiency, but the simulations here show that it could be detrimental when high dispersion fiber is used together with extremely small channel spacings.

Next, we introduce a dispersion slope, Sl to the NDSF fiber to simulate actual fiber conditions. The dispersion slope would change four things. Firstly, it will cause the third order dispersion term, β_{3k} to be more significant. Secondly, it will alter the average dispersion of Channel 2 to something other than zero. Thirdly, it will change the dispersion of Channel 2 as compared to Channel 1. Fourthly, it will change the walk-off factor. The first effect is still negligible, because the pulse width is relatively large (not in the femtosecond range). The second effect is negated through individual compensation of each channel, whereby the increase in dispersion for Channel 2 due to a positive slope of the NDSF is compensated by a corresponding negative slope in the DCF to arrive at a constant average dispersion of zero for all channels. The effect of varying dispersion slope on the XPM power penalty is shown in Figure 8. Increase in dispersion slope leads to increase of power penalty for both OOK and DPSK modulation. The effect is approximately linear and the increase in power penalties due to the slope is small. For instance, at a practical slope of 0.07 ps/nm²/km, the increase of penalty is about 0.01 dB and

0.10 dB for OOK and DPSK modulation, respectively. The result shows that increase in local GVD induced pulse distortion, which is transferred between channels through XPM, can lead to an increase in XPM penalty even when it is accompanied by a small increase in the walk-off factor. However, for most practical slope values the additional penalty is negligible.

Lastly, we take a look at the potential of using residual dispersion in the system to reduce the power penalty induced by the nonlinear effects in Figure 9. As shown, OOK modulation has better receiver sensitivity for small values of positive average dispersion with an optimal value of about +0.2 ps/nm/km. On the other hand, DPSK modulation has better receiver sensitivity for both small values of positive and negative average dispersion, but the optimal value is positive at about +0.3 ps/nm/km. The improvements shown by adding residual dispersion are small at about 0.1

Figure 9. Power penalty caused by XPM versus dispersion slope, Sl for both OOK and DPSK modulation with individual channel compensation. (Two channels, total length = 160 km, input powers, P1 = P2 = 3 dBm for OOK, P1 = P2 = 7 dBm for DPSK, channel separation, $\Delta\lambda$ = 0.5 nm, D = +1.5 ps/nm/km) (Abbou, Hiew, Chuah, Ong, & Abid, 2008)

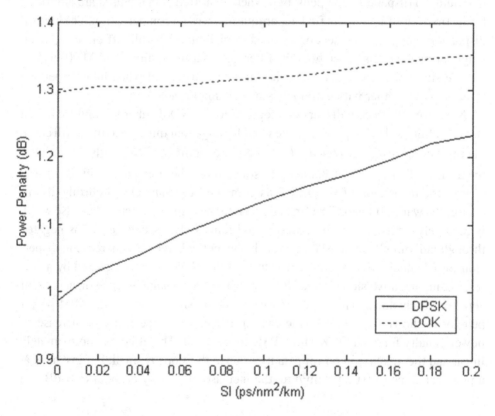

dB for OOK and 0.45 dB for DPSK. The effects accounted for in the penalty curve here refers to all the effects (GVD, SPM, XPM and ASE) acting together. Thus, a small positive average dispersion helps to partially counteract the effects of SPM and XPM in a soliton-like interaction. Further increase of average dispersion leads back to increased penalties because the GVD induced penalty then becomes dominant.

SUMMARY

Performance analysis is carried out to evaluate the effect of cross-phase modulation on a dispersion managed 20Gb/s optical WDM transmission system using either

Figure 10. Power penalty caused by all effects versus average dispersion for both OOK and DPSK modulation with average dispersion = 0 taken as the reference receiver sensitivity (power penalty = 0 dB). (Two channels, total length = 160 km, input powers, P1 = P2 = 3 dBm for OOK, P1 = P2 = 7 dBm for DPSK, channel separation, $\Delta\lambda = 0.5$ nm, D = +1.5 ps/nm/km) (Abbou, Hiew, Chuah, Ong, & Abid, 2008)

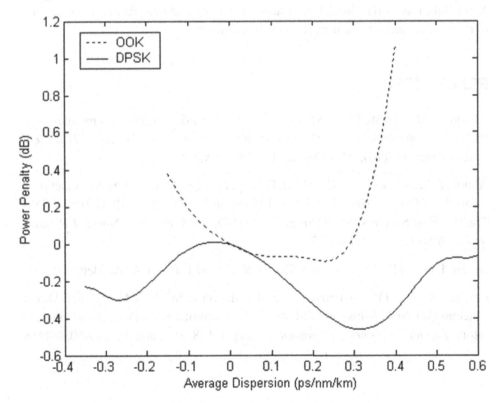

OOK or DPSK modulation, in the presence of group velocity dispersion (GVD), self-phase modulation (SPM) and amplified spontaneous emission (ASE). On the whole, the DPSK modulated signal displayed better receiver sensitivity along with better SPM and XPM tolerance compared to the OOK signal. It is found that the XPM effect causes a power penalty that increases with increasing channel power in the shared transmission link for both OOK and DPSK, with OOK modulation being more severely affected. For 1 dB penalty, input channel powers equal to 3 dBm for OOK and 7 dBm for DPSK. At the same time, the power penalty is inversely proportional to the channel separation for DPSK and OOK modulation on a large scale. On a fine scale, it exhibits oscillations. This oscillation follows the XPM efficiency curve for DPSK modulation with a constant period based on the walk-off factor. For OOK modulation, it follows the period of the DPSK curve at large channel spacing but is different for small channel spacing as a result of conversion of the XPM phase shift to intensity through the GVD parameter. The oscillations show the presence of optimum separation values where XPM induced penalty is at a minimum, and this is evenly spaced for DPSK. Also, the XPM penalty decreases when high dispersion fiber is used due to increased walk-off. On the other hand, the XPM-induced power penalty increases linearly with fiber dispersion slope suggesting that small GVD induced pulse distortion can be transferred through the XPM shift. Lastly, the simulation results show that residual dispersion can be used to reduce the penalties incurred by nonlinear effects.

REFERENCES

Abbou, F. M., Chuah, H. T., Majumder, S. P., & Abid, A. (2006). Semi-analytical BER Performance of a Direct Detection Soliton Transmission System. *IEICE Electronics Express*, *3*(10), 203–208. doi:10.1587/elex.3.203

Abbou, F. M., Hiew, C. C., Chuah, H.T., Ong, D. S., & Abid, A. (2008). A Detailed Analysis of Cross-Phase Modulation Effects on OOK and DPSK Optical WDM Transmission Systems in the Presence of GVD, SPM and ASE Noise. *J R Laser Research Springer, 29* (1), 57-70.

Agrawal, G. P. (1995). *Nonlinear fiber optics*. Sand Diego, CA: Academic.

Cartaxo, A. V. T. (1999). Cross-Phase Modulation in Intensity Modulation-Direct Detection WDM Systems with Multiple Optical Amplifiers and Dispersion Compensators. *Journal of Lightwave Technology*, *17*(2), 178–190. doi:10.1109/50.744218

Chiang, T. K., Kagi, N., Marhic, M. E., & Kazovsky, L. G. (1996). Cross-Phase Modulation in Fiber Links with Multiple Optical Amplifiers and Dispersion Compensators. *Journal of Lightwave Technology, 14*(3), 249–260. doi:10.1109/50.485582

Elrefaie, A. F., & Wagner, R. E. (1991). Chromatic Dispersion Limitations for FSK and DPSK Systems with Direct Detection Receivers. *IEEE Photonics Technology Letters, 3*(1), 71–73. doi:10.1109/68.68052

Elrefaie, A. F., Wagner, R. E., Atlas, D. A., & Daut, D. G. (1988). Chromatic Dispersion Limitations in Coherent Lightwave Transmission Systems. *Journal of Lightwave Technology, 6*(5), 704–709. doi:10.1109/50.4056

Hamaide, J. P., & Gabriagues, J. M. (1990). Limitations in Long Haul IM/DD Optical Fiber Systems Caused by Chromatic Dispersion and Nonlinear Kerr Effect. *Electronics Letters, 26*(18), 1451–1453. doi:10.1049/el:19900931

Iannone, E., Locati, F. S., Matera, F., Romagnoli, M., & Settembre, M. (1993). High-Speed DPSK Coherent Systems in the Presence of Chromatic Dispersion and Kerr Effect. *Journal of Lightwave Technology, 11*(9), 1478–1485. doi:10.1109/50.241938

Killey, R. I., Thiele, H. J., Mikhailov, V., & Bavyel, P. (2000). Prediction of Transmission Penalties due to Cross-Phase Modulation in WDM Systems Using a Simplified Technique. *IEEE Photonics Technology Letters, 12*(7), 804–806. doi:10.1109/68.853506

Marhic, M. E., Kagi, N., Chiang, T. K., & Kazovsky, L. G. (1996). Optimizing the Location of Dispersion Compensators in Periodically Amplified Fiber Links in the Presence of Third-Order Nonlinear Effects. *IEEE Photonics Technology Letters, 8*(1), 145–147. doi:10.1109/68.475807

Sahara, A., Kubota, H., & Nakazawa, M. (1996). Q-factor Contour Mapping for Evaluation of Optical Transmission Systems: Soliton against NRZ against RZ Pulse at Zero Group Velocity Dispersion. *Electronics Letters, 32*(10), 915–916. doi:10.1049/el:19960590

Vassilieva, O., Hoshida, T., Choudhary, S., Castanon, G., Kuwahara, H., Terahara, T., & Onaka, H. (2001). Numerical Comparison of NRZ, CS-RZ and IM-DPSK Formats in 43 Gbits/s WDM Transmission. *Lasers and Electro-Optics Society, 2*, 673–674.

KEY TERMS AND DEFINITIONS

Differential Phase Shift Keying (DPSK): Refers to a modulation technique in which the information is coded by using the phase difference between two neighboring bits.

Gaussian Noise: A statistical noise having a probability density function known as the Gaussian distribution.

Shot Noise: A random fluctuation in electrical current caused by the discrete nature of electron charge.

Thermal Noise: Refers to the thermal agitation of electrons inside an electrical conductor at equilibrium.

Wavelength Division Multiplexing (WDM): A method of combining multiple signals on laser beams at various wavelengths for transmission along one fiber optic cable.

Chapter 5
SCM–WDM PONs in Presence of XPM and GVD

ABSTRACT

In this chapter, a semi-analytical approach is used to evaluate and analyse the performance limitation of a SCM-WDM Passive Optical Network (PON) in the presence of Cross Phase Modulation (XPM) and Group Velocity Dispersion (GVD). In this context, a general expression for electrical average crosstalk noise power due to XPM and GVD was derived to measure the system performance for increasing number of WDM channels. Using the expression, it is found that XPM and GVD causes crosstalk in the system and imposes a power penalty as the WDM channels increases for a given channel spacing and modulating frequency. These results are extended to show that the system can be optimized to achieve a minimum BER of 10^{-9} by controlling the channel spacing and modulating frequency as the number of WDM channels increases.

INTRODUCTION

Fiber-to-the-Home (FTTH) has been the main concern in the telecommunication industry. Direct fiber connection has always been viewed as the long awaited solution due to the large bandwidth and low maintenance. However in order for FTTH to remain competitive, a passive optical network is required. SCM is a potential solution for transmission in PONs (Gross & Olshansky, 1990). The combination of SCM and WDM is a viable method to further increase the transmission capacity in PONs (Feldman, 1994).

DOI: 10.4018/978-1-4666-6575-0.ch005

SCM-WDM systems, however, suffer from non-linear effects in fiber. These non-linearities cause crosstalk between subscribers on different wavelengths. In a dispersive fiber like SSMF, one of the dominant fiber non-linearities that cause crosstalk is XPM. The phase crosstalk is converted to intensity crosstalk due to GVD. The effects of XPM and GVD in SCM-WDM video transmission systems while considering two WDM channels were reported in (Wang, 1995). The same system was analyzed by Yang (2000), both analytically and experimentally. Analytical investigation was extended in Subramaniam (2005) while considering three WDM channels.

The following section theoretically analyzes the performance limitation due to XPM and GVD by deriving the optical power fluctuation, average crosstalk noise power, normalized crosstalk, carrier-to-noise ratio (CNR) and bit-error-rate BER. Results from the theoretical analyses are plotted and discussed for various design parameters. Further, the performance limitation of the system is visualized in terms of normalized crosstalk, BER and power penalty. The results are extended to show that the system can be optimized to achieve a BER of 10^{-9} by controlling the channel spacing, modulating frequency, length and launched optical power as the number of WDM channels increase.

THEORETICAL MODEL

The theoretical analysis is extended from (Wang, 1995; Yang, 2000; Subramaniam, 2005). Consider N optical waves with the same polarization, co-propagating in a single-mode fiber. Assuming each optical wave is modulated with the same single subcarrier, the optical power at the input of the fiber can be expressed as:

$$P_k = P_b \left[1 + m \cos \left(\omega_s t + \varphi \right) \right] \tag{5.1}$$

where k denotes the center channel in an N channel WDM system, with wavelengths $\{\lambda_1, \lambda_2, \lambda_3 \ldots \lambda_N\}$ and $\lambda_1 > \lambda_2 > \lambda_3 > \lambda_N$. The center channel is evaluated since it represents the worst case. P_b is the average output power of each of the laser; m, ω_s, ϕ are, respectively the modulation index, angular frequency and initial phase of the subcarrier. For simplicity, we assume the subcarrier to be unmodulated and ignore the initial phase.

Let $A_k(z,t)$ denote the slowly varying complex field envelope of each wave, normalized so that $|A_k|^2 = P_k$. The coupled equations that describe XPM under the slowly varying envelope approximation are (Agrawal, 1995):

$$\frac{\partial A_k}{\partial z} + \frac{1}{V_{gk}} \frac{\partial A_k}{\partial t} = \left\{ -i2\gamma \left(\sum_{\substack{n=1 \\ n \neq k}}^{N} P_n \right) - \frac{\alpha}{2} \right\} A_k$$

.

. (5.2)

.

$$\frac{\partial A_N}{\partial z} + \frac{1}{V_{gN}} \frac{\partial A_N}{\partial t} = \left\{ -i2\gamma \left(\sum_{n=1}^{N-1} P_n \right) - \frac{\alpha}{2} \right\} A_N$$

where V_{gk} and V_{gN} is the group velocity for the optical wave transmitted at λ_k and λ_N respectively; γ is the nonlinearity coefficient, typically of the order of 10^{-3} W^{-1}m^{-1}. The general solution to Equation (5.2) can be expressed as:

$$A_k(z, \tau_k) = A_k(0, \tau_k) e^{-\alpha z/2} e^{j\phi(z,t)}$$ (5.3)

where

$$\phi(z, t) = \sum_{\substack{n=1 \\ n \neq k}}^{N} -2\gamma \int_0^z P_n \left(0, t - \frac{z}{V_{gn}} + d_{nk} z' \right) e^{-\alpha z'} dz'$$ (5.4)

is the phase crosstalk induced by XPM. However, through GVD, the phase modulation is converted to intensity modulation via the relation (Petermann, 1990)

$$\frac{dP_k(z, \tau_k)}{dz} = -\ddot{\beta}_k P_k(0, \tau_k) e^{-\alpha z} \frac{d^2 \phi(z, \tau_k)}{d\tau_k^2}$$ (5.5)

where $\ddot{\beta}_k$ is the second order fiber dispersion coefficient. This is an incremental change in the instantaneous power over a small segment dz. Over the entire length L of the fiber, each incremental modulation at point z along the fiber will be attenuated by $e^{-\alpha (L-z)}$ due to fiber loss.

Power Fluctuation

One can find the power fluctuation in WDM channel k at the output of the fiber by integrating over length L while assuming equal channel spacing $\Delta\lambda$ and equal dispersion coefficient D for all channels. The walk-off parameter can then be approximated by as $D\Delta\lambda$. Observing from (Wang, 1995; Yang, 2000), we can assume that $\alpha < \omega_s D\Delta\lambda$ and only consider the dominant terms in the numerator. The Fourier Transform of the power fluctuation $\Delta P_k(L,\omega)$ can then be approximated as (Hairul, 2006):

$$\Delta P_k\left(L,\omega\right) \approx \frac{-jm\gamma\ddot{\beta}_k\omega_s P_b^2 L2\sqrt{2\pi}e^{-\alpha L}\delta\left(\omega+\omega_s\right)}{D\Delta\lambda}\Psi_k \tag{5.6}$$

where (Hairul, 2006):

$$\Psi_k = \begin{cases} \left(\ln(N-k)+\dfrac{1}{2(N-k)}+\varepsilon\right) & \text{if } k=1 \\[2ex] \left(\ln(k-1)+\dfrac{1}{2(k-1)}+\varepsilon\right) & \text{if } k=N \\[2ex] \left(\ln(N-k)(k-1)+\dfrac{N-1}{2(N-k)(k-1)}+\varepsilon\right) & \text{otherwise} \end{cases}$$

with values of ε tabulated below for N number of WDM channels (Hairul, 2006):

Normalized Crosstalk

The power fluctuation can also be normalized by the modulation magnitude of the neighboring channels, each approximated by $mP_b e^{-\alpha L}$, to produce the total normalized XPM and GVD electrical crosstalk level, XT_c (Wang, 1995; Yang, 2000; Subramaniam, 2005).

Table 1. Ultra short optical pulse generation techniques

N	2	3	16	64	128	512	1000
ε	0.55685	0.56805	0.57689	0.57719	0.57721	0.57721	0.57722

$$XT_c = \left| 2 \sum_{n=1}^{(N-1)/2} \frac{-2\ddot{\beta}_c \omega_s^2 \gamma P_c}{\left(\alpha - j\omega_s D\Delta\lambda n\right)^2} \left\{ \begin{array}{l} \left[e^{-\alpha L} \cos(\omega_s D\Delta\lambda Ln) - 1 + \alpha L \right] \\ + j\left[e^{-\alpha L} \sin(\omega_s D\Delta\lambda Ln) - \omega_s D\Delta\lambda Ln \right] \end{array} \right\} \right|^2$$

(5.7)

Equation (5.7) gives the total intensity modulation fluctuation in the center channel c, which assumes equal channel spacing $\Delta\lambda$ and equal dispersion coefficient D for all channels. The magnitude of XPM and GVD crosstalk from neighboring channels is governed by the walk-off parameter, which has been approximated as $D\Delta\lambda$. Using the same approximations in Equation (5.6), the total crosstalk in any WDM channel k, XT_k can be written as (Hairul, 2006):

$$XT_k \approx \left| \frac{j2\gamma\ddot{\beta}_k \omega_s P_b L}{D\Delta\lambda} \Psi_k \right|^2$$

(5.8)

Average Crosstalk Noise

The electrical average noise power due to XPM and GVD can be determined by first expressing the electrical power spectral density due to the power fluctuation $\Delta P_k(L,\omega)$ as

$$S_k\left(L,\omega\right) = \Re^2 \Delta P_k^2\left(L,\omega\right)$$

(5.9)

where $\Re$ is the responsivity of the photodetector. The electrical average noise power due to XPM and GVD can be expressed by:

$$\begin{aligned} \sigma_{xpm,k}^{\ 2} &= \int_{\omega_1}^{\omega_2} S_k\left(L,\omega\right) d\omega \\ &= 8\left(\frac{m\gamma\ddot{\beta}_k \omega_s P_b^2 L\Re e^{-\alpha L}\sqrt{\pi}}{D\Delta\lambda} \Psi_k \right)^2 \end{aligned}$$

(5.10)

where $\omega_2 - \omega_1 = \Delta\omega$, the electrical bandwidth of the receiver and $\omega_2 > \omega_s > \omega_1$.

Carrier-to-Noise Ratio (CNR) and Bit-Error-Rate (BER)

In evaluating the BER, electrical average noise power due to XPM and GVD is added to the CNR equation as a source of noise. Assuming a subcarrier with BPSK modulation and the total noise power consists of detector noise (shot noise, σ_{sh}^2 and thermal noise σ_{th}^2), light source noise (relative intensity noise, σ_{RIN}^2) and noise due to XPM and GVD crosstalk, $\sigma_{xpm,k}^2$. The CNR is expressed as:

$$ CNR = \frac{\dfrac{\left(m\Re P_b\right)^2}{8}}{\sigma_{th}^2 + \sigma_{sh}^2 + \sigma_{RIN}^2 + \sigma_{xpm,k}^2} \tag{5.11} $$

The BER is given as:

$$ BER = \frac{1}{2} erfc\left(\sqrt{\frac{CNR}{2}}\right) \tag{5.12} $$

Approximations

The following figures demonstrate the approximations made in the expressions for normalized crosstalk and subsequently in the average crosstalk noise, CNR and BER. The performance of the SCM-WDM PON is analyzed for N number of WDM channels using the derived expressions in Equations (5.6) to (5.12). The SCM-WDM system is simulated for a system with launched optical power $P_b = 20$ mW, transmission length $L = 50$ km, channel spacing $\Delta\lambda = 4$ nm and standard single mode fiber (SSMF) with dispersion coefficient $D = 16$ ps/km.nm.

In Figure 1, the total normalized crosstalk XT_k is plotted for each WDM channel in a 50- channel SCM-WDM system. Normalized crosstalk is expressed in units of dBc, which denotes the relative crosstalk power in channel k to the signal power in the other WDM channels, assuming equal received optical power. It is clear that XT_k using the approximated expression is close to XT_k using the full expression since the condition $\alpha < \omega D\Delta\lambda$ is met.

In the following figures, the normalized crosstalk (dBc) in the center channel c, which represents the worst case, is evaluated for a SCM-WDM PON with increasing number of WDM channels. The figures are drawn from both the full and ap-

Figure 1. Normalized crosstalk (dBc) for each channel in a 50 channel SCM-WDM system using the full and approximated expression (Hairul, 2007)

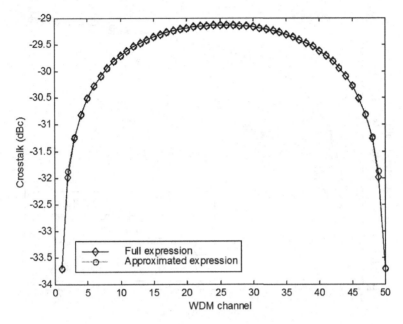

proximated expressions in Equation (5.7) and (5.8) respectively. The modulating frequency, length, launched optical power and channel spacing is varied respectively in Figures 2 to 5 (Hairul, 2006).

In Figure 2, the approximated XT_c is closer to the actual XT_c when the modulating frequency is 900 MHz. The same observation is made in Figure 5 and 6, when the channel spacing and dispersion coefficient is respectively higher. This is due to fulfillment of the condition $\alpha < \omega D \Delta \lambda$.

However, in Figures 3 and 4, the approximated XT_c is not influenced by the change in launched optical power and transmission length. This is due to the condition $\alpha < \omega D \Delta \lambda$.is independent of both the launched optical power and transmission length.

SEMI-ANALYTICAL RESULTS

The performance of the SCM-WDM PON is semi-analytically analyzed for *N* number of WDM channels using the derived expressions in Equation (5.6) to (5.12). The SCM-WDM system is simulated for a system with launched optical power P_b

Figure 2. Normalized crosstalk (dBc) for different modulating frequencies using the full and approximated expression

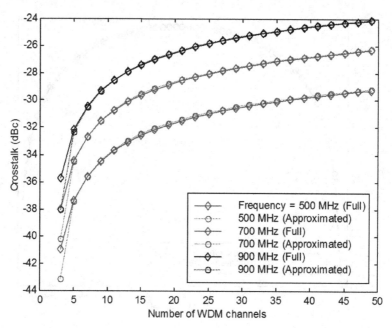

Figure 3. Normalized crosstalk (dBc) for different lengths using the full and approximated expression

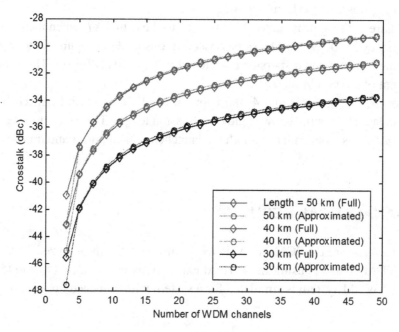

Figure 4. Normalized crosstalk (dBc) for different launched optical power using the full and approximated expression

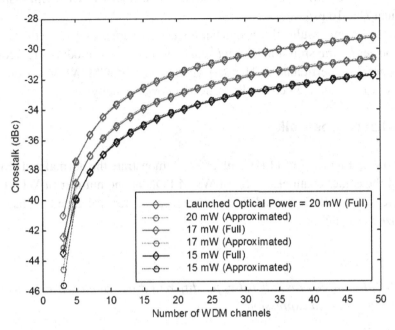

Figure 5. Normalized crosstalk (dBc) for different channel spacing using the full and approximated expression

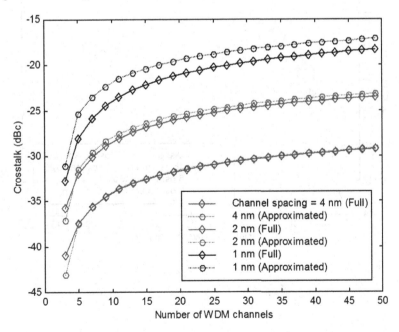

= 20 mW, transmission length L = 50 km, channel spacing $\Delta\lambda$ = 4 nm, modulating frequency f = 500 MHz and standard single mode fiber (SSMF) with dispersion coefficient D = 16 ps/km/nm.

In the following results, the design parameters that are changed are the launched optical power P_b, transmission length L, channel spacing $\Delta\lambda$, modulating frequency f and dispersion coefficient D. The performance of the SCM-WDM system is observed for the normalized crosstalk, BER and power penalty.

Normalized Crosstalk

The following Figures 7 to 11 (Hairul, 2006) demonstrate the normalized crosstalk (dBc) of the center channel in a SCM-WDM PON as the number of WDM channels increase. In each figure, a different design parameter is changed to observe the normalized crosstalk.

Figure 6. Normalized crosstalk (dBc) for different dispersion coefficient using the full and approximated expression

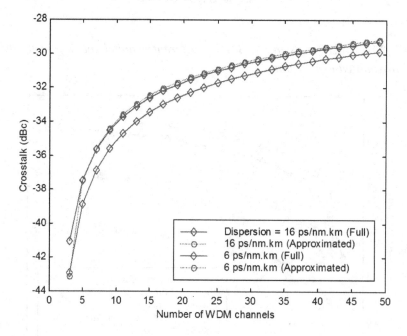

Figure 7. Normalized crosstalk (dBc) for different launched optical power

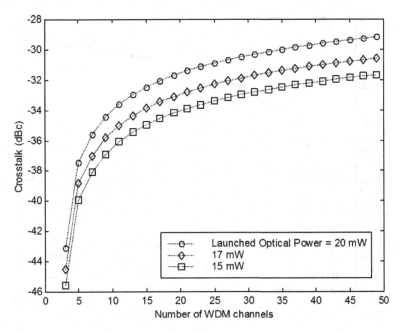

Figure 8. Normalized crosstalk (dBc) for different channel spacing

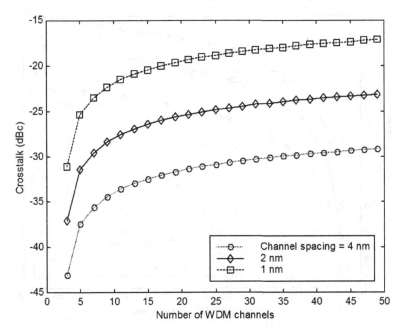

Figure 9. Normalized crosstalk (dBc) for two different dispersion coefficient

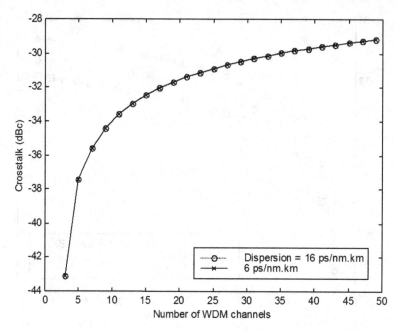

Figure 10. Normalized crosstalk (dBc) for different modulating frequencies

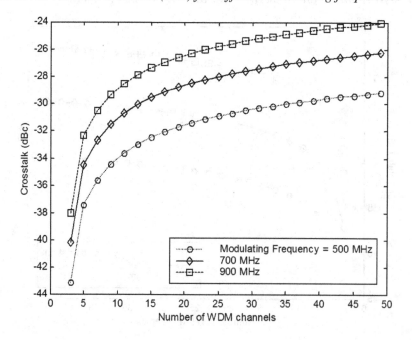

Figure 11. Normalized crosstalk (dBc) for different transmission lengths

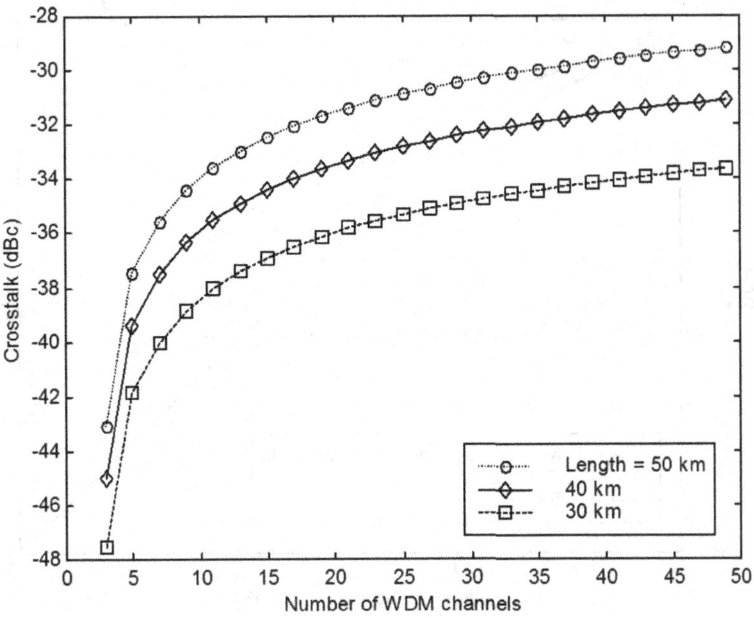

Bit-Error-Rate

The following Figures 12 to 16 (Hairul, 2007) demonstrate the BER against the received optical power for the center channel in an 11-channel SCM-WDM PON. In each figure, a different design parameter is changed to observe the BER performance.

Power Penalty

In the following Figures 17 to 21 (Hairul, 2007), the power penalty (dB) at a BER of 10^{-9} of a SCM-WDM PON is evaluated as the number of WDM channels increases and a different design parameter is changed to observe the shift in power penalty.

ANALYSIS AND DISCUSSION

The SCM-WDM PON is analyzed with increasing number of WDM channels using the derived expressions in Equations (5.6) to (5.12) and Figures 7 to 21 that describe the normalized crosstalk, average crosstalk noise, CNR, BER and power penalty respectively.

Figure 12. BER vs. received optical power (dBm) for different modulating frequencies

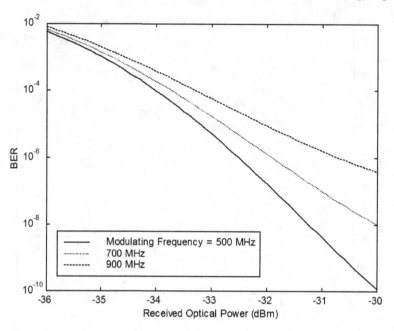

Figure 13. BER vs. received optical power (dBm) for different transmission lengths

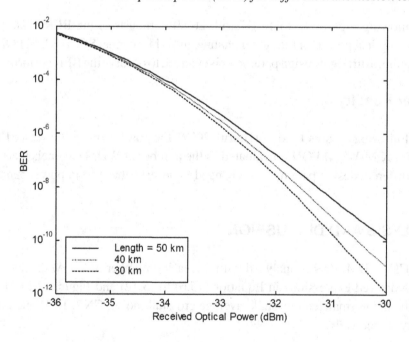

*Figure 14. BER vs. received optical power (dBm) for two different dispersion coef-
ficients*

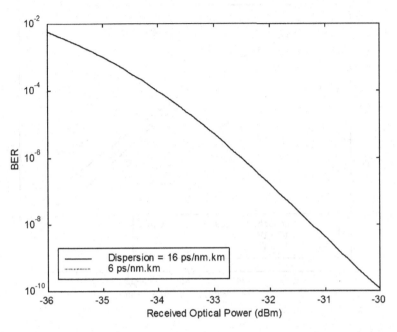

Figure 15. BER vs. received optical power (dBm) for different channel spacing

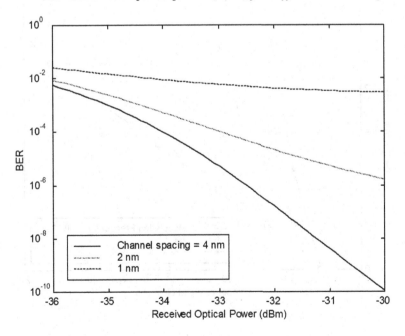

Figure 16. BER vs. received optical power (dBm) for different launched optical power

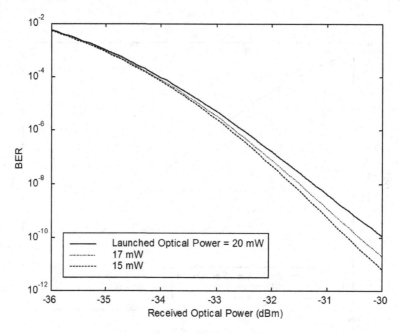

Figure 17. Power penalty (dB) for different modulating frequencies

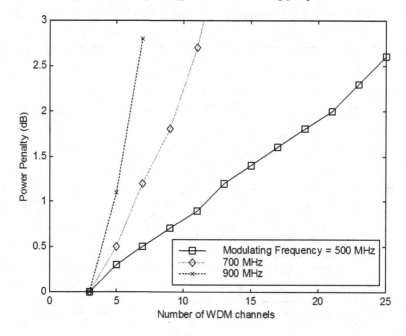

Figure 18. Power penalty (dB) for different transmission lengths

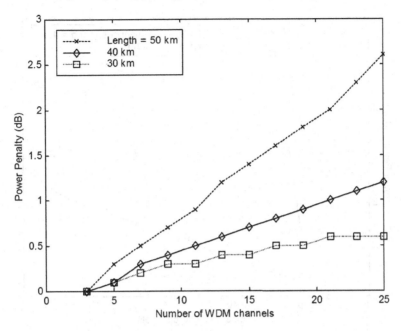

Figure 19. Power penalty (dB) for different dispersion coefficients

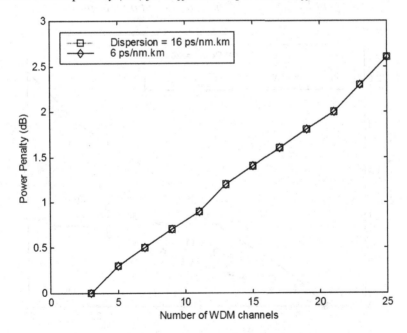

Figure 20. Power penalty (dB) for different channel spacing

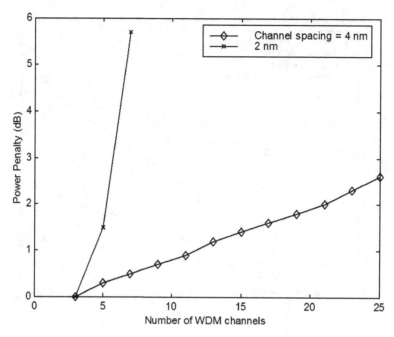

Figure 21. Power penalty (dB) for different launched optical power

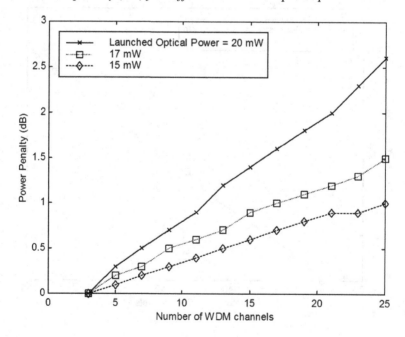

Normalized Crosstalk

In Figure 7, the normalized crosstalk XT_c in the center channel of the SCM-WDM system is analyzed against increasing number of WDM channels for three different values of launched optical power; 20 mW, 17 mW and 15 mW. The normalized crosstalk is expressed in units of dBc, which denotes the relative crosstalk power in the center channel to the signal power in the other WDM channels, assuming equal received optical power. It is clear that XT_c increases with increasing number of WDM channels and launched optical power. This is due to the accumulated crosstalk from each WDM channel on the center channel, as shown in Equation (5.7), which represents the worst case. XT_c also increases with the launched optical power since it is one of the dominant terms in increasing the XPM efficiency as described by Equation (5.4).

Figure 8 evidently shows that XT_c increases with increasing number of WDM channels and modulating frequency. This is due to the accumulated crosstalk from each WDM channel on the evaluated channel, as described by Equation (5.7). XT_c also increases with the modulating frequency f because it is one of the dominant terms in the phase to intensity conversion due to GVD expression in Equation (5.5).

XT_c increases with increasing number of WDM channels and transmission length, as shown in Figure 8. This is due to increasing transmission length, which is one of the dominant factors in both the XPM efficiency and in the phase to intensity conversion due to GVD, as expressed in Equation (5.4) and (5.5) respectively.

In Figure 9, it is also clear that XT_c increases with both increasing number of WDM channels and closer channel spacing. This is due to the accumulated crosstalk from each WDM channel on the center channel, as shown by Equation (5.7). XT_c also increases with closer channel spacing since it increases the XPM efficiency as the walk-off effect increases. This is depicted in Equation (5.4).

When two dispersion coefficients, 16 ps/nm.km and 6 ps/nm.km are used in Figure 10, no clear difference in normalized crosstalk is observed. This can be attributed to higher XPM efficiency but lower phase to intensity conversion due to GVD when the dispersion coefficient is lower at 6 ps/nm.km. When the dispersion coefficient is 16 ps/nm.km, the XPM efficiency is lower but the phase to intensity conversion rate due to GVD is higher. This results in minimal change in the normalized crosstalk as the dispersion coefficient is changed. Both these attributes are illustrated in Equation (5.4) and (5.5).

Bit-Error-Rate

The BER performance of the SCM-WDM PON that is shown in Figures 11 to 16 clearly demonstrates the effect of crosstalk due to XPM and GVD as different design parameters are changed. The average crosstalk noise $\sigma_{xpm,k}^2$ changes with launched optical power, channel spacing, modulating frequency and transmission length. Increase in the average crosstalk noise will deteriorate the BER performance and vice versa. When $\sigma_{xpm,k}^2$ increases with increasing launched optical power, modulation frequency and transmission length, the BER performance deteriorates as demonstrated by Figures 16, 12 and 13 respectively. The reduction of $\sigma_{xpm,k}^2$ due to wider channel spacing improves the BER performance as illustrated in Figure 15. The unaffected BER performance in Figure 14 when the dispersion coefficient is changed can be attributed to the unchanged average crosstalk noise $\sigma_{xpm,k}^2$. These trends in BER performance can be explained by expressions in Equations (5.10) to (5.12).

Power Penalty

The degree of change in the BER when different design parameters are changed is measured in terms of the power penalty as shown in Figures 17 to 21. It is clear that the power penalty increases faster when the average crosstalk noise $\sigma_{xpm,k}^2$ increases with higher modulating frequency, longer transmission length, closer channel spacing and higher launched optical power. These are evidently shown in Figures 17, 18, 20 and 21 respectively. Figure 19 illustrates how the change in dispersion coefficient does not alter the power penalty of the SCM-WDM PON, as discussed earlier.

DESIGN OF SCM-WDM PON

The BER approaches an error floor after a certain received optical power as shown clearly in Figure 15. By analyzing the sources of noise in the CNR expression in Equation (5.11), one can observe that the average crosstalk noise $\sigma_{xpm,k}^2$ increases with the fastest rate with respect to received optical power, compared to the other sources of noise. The combined increasing rate of the noise power is comparable to the increasing rate of subcarrier power as the received optical power increases. This causes the CNR to maintain the same ratio at higher received optical power, hence the error floor shown in Figure 15.

Based on the observation above, the system performance can be optimized by deducing diagrams to show the relationship between the maximum or minimum values of one design parameter against increasing number of WDM channels while maintaining an error floor lower than 10^{-9}. The relationship between the optimized channel spacing, modulating frequency, launched optical power and transmission length and increasing number of WDM channels are respectively demonstrated in Figures 22, 23, 24 and 25 (Hairul, 2007).

Figure 22. Maximum transmission length (km) against maximum number of WDM channels

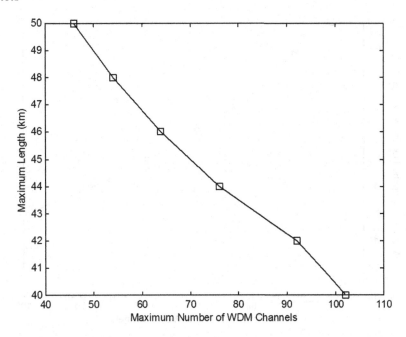

Figure 23. Maximum modulating frequency (MHz) against maximum number of WDM channels

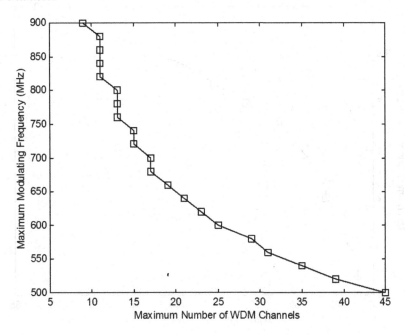

Figure 24. Maximum launched optical power (mW) against maximum number of WDM channels

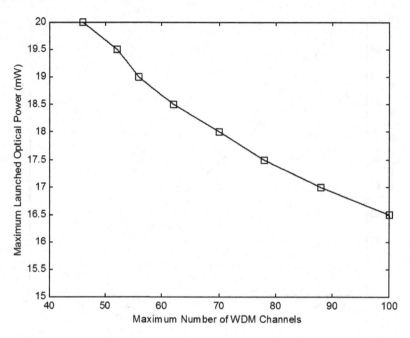

Figure 25. Minimum channel spacing against maximum number of WDM channels

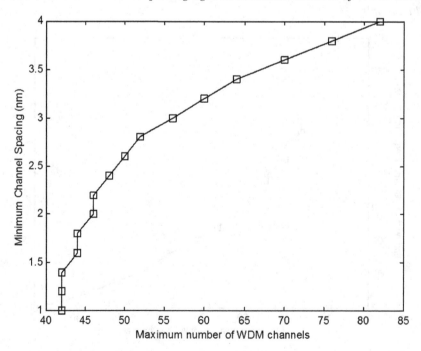

SUMMARY

The performance of a SCM-WDM PON is semi-analytically analyzed under the influence of XPM and GVD. A general expression for optical power fluctuation, electrical average noise power and electrical crosstalk level due to XPM and GVD for *N* number of WDM channels in an SCM-WDM PON is derived. By carefully approximating the derived expression, a closed form expression that can be used as a design tool for SCM-WDM PONs is produced. It is clear that the crosstalk level due to XPM and GVD increases with the number of WDM channels, modulating frequency and closer channel spacing. The performance limitation of the SCM-WDM PON is also shown in terms of the normalized crosstalk, BER and power penalty. Finally, it was shown that the SCM-WDM PON can be optimized by carefully selecting the channel spacing, modulating frequency, transmission length and launched optical power for a specific number of WDM channels in the system while sustaining a BER better than 10^{-9}.

REFERENCES

Agrawal, G. P. (1995). *Nonlinear fiber optics*. Sand Diego, CA: Academic.

Feldman, R. D. (1994). Cost Effective, Broadband Passive Optical Network System. *OFC Technical Digest*, 18-20.

Gross, M., & Olshansky, M. (1990). Multichannel Cherent fsk Experiments Using Subcarrier Multiplexing Techniques. *Journal of Lightwave Technology*, *8*(3), 406–415. doi:10.1109/50.50737

Hairul, A. A., Abbou, F. M., Chuah, H. T., Moncef, B. T., Malik, T. A., & Sivakumar, L. (2006). System performance optimization in SCM-WDM passive optical networks in the presence of XPM and GVD. *IEEE Communications Letters*, *10*(9), 670–672. doi:10.1109/LCOMM.2006.1714540

Hairul, A. B. A. R. (2007). *Design and Performance Analysis of Subcarrier Multiplexing Passive Optical Networks*. (Unpublished doctoral dissertation). Multimedia University, Malaysia.

Petermann, K. (1990). Fm-am Noise Conversion in Dispersive Single Mode Fibre Transmission Lines. *Electronics Letters*, *26*(25), 2097–2098. doi:10.1049/el:19901350

Subramaniam, S., Abbou, F. M., Chuah, H. T., & Dambul, K. D. (2005). Performance Evaluation of scm-wdm Microcellular Communication System in the Presence of xpm. *IEICE Electronics Express*, *2*(6), 192–197. doi:10.1587/elex.2.192

Wang, Z. (1995). Effects of Cross Phase Modulation in Wavelength Multiplexed scm Video Transmission Systems. *Electronics Letters*, *31*(18), 1591–1592. doi:10.1049/el:19951074

Yang, F. S., Marhic, M. E., & Kazovsky, L. G. (2000). Nonlinear Crosstalk and Two Countermeasures in scm-wdm Optical Communication Systems. *Journal of Lightwave Technology*, *18*(4), 512–520. doi:10.1109/50.838125

KEY TERMS AND DEFINITIONS

Crosstalk Noise: Crosstalk is any phenomenon by which a signal transmitted on one channel of a transmission system creates an undesired effect in another channel.

Carrier to Noise Ratio (CNR): The CNR is defined as the ratio of RMS carrier power to RMS noise power at the receiver.

Fiber to the Home (FTTH): A high-speed optical access network uses fiber optic links all the way to each house to provide broadband multimedia services to customers.

Passive Optical Network (PON): A type of fiber-optic access network that uses point-to-multipoint fiber to the premises to reduce the amount of fiber and central office equipment required compared with point-to-point architectures.

Polarization: The orientation of the electric and magnetic field vectors of a propagating electromagnetic wave. An electromagnetic wave theory describes in detail the propagation of optical signals (light).

Power Penalty: Determines the signal power increment (in dB) required to maintain the same bit error rate in the presence of impairments.

Subcarrier Multiplexing (SCM): Is a method for multiplexing many radio-frequency (RF) signals so that they can be transmitted along a single optical fiber.

Chapter 6
Phase Encoded Optical Code Division Multiplexing Access System

ABSTRACT

Phase encoded optical code division multiple-access system is evaluated in a dispersive fiber medium in this chapter. An approximate analytical expression for the root mean square (rms) width of the phase encoded signal (pseudorandom optical signal with low intensity) propagating in linear dispersive fibers is derived. Bit-Error Rate (BER) analysis of the system is performed in the case of both ordinary Single-Mode Fiber (SMF) and Dispersion-Shifted Fiber (DSF). The numerical results demonstrate that even though system performance improves due to the smaller width of initial Gaussian optical pulse, the effect from dispersion is higher. Larger code length reduces the effect of dispersion and the use of DSF greatly increases the transmission distance.

INTRODUCTION

Phase-encoded optical code-division multiple-access (OCDMA) communication system has been the subject of recent research (Salehi, Weiner, & Heritage, 1990). Such a system imposes less stringent requirements on light sources compared to other implementation schemes such as direct time spread and frequency hopping

DOI: 10.4018/978-1-4666-6575-0.ch006

OCDMA systems. Spectral phase encoding/decoding of the optical signal can be performed using fiber Bragg gratings (Tsuda, 1999) or high-resolution arrayed-waveguide grating (Grunnet-Jepsen, 1999). The performance of such a system has been analyzed (Ma, Zuo, Pu, & Lin, 2002) without considering the effect of the dispersive nature of the fiber channel. In that analysis, the phase-encoded optical signal was treated as a random process, with a variance, which was found to be inversely proportional to code length. The rms width of the phase-encoded optical signal was derived to be proportional to the width of initial optical pulse and code length. Thus, in order to achieve better system performance, one needs to have as large a code length and as short an initial optical pulse as possible. In this chapter, we incorporate second and third-order fiber dispersion effects of the channel into the performance analysis. we start by discussing the operation principles of a phase-encoded OCDMA system. In this contest, a system diagram and description of a typical phase encoded OCDMA communications system are presented. Further, a derivation of the time domain form of the phase encoded OCDMA signal and the physical and statistical properties of the signal are presented. Having established the fundamentals, two methods for analytical study of dispersion effects on optical pulse in fiber medium are reviewed and used to obtain the properties of the phase encoded OCDMA signal as it propagates in a fiber transmission link. Finally, an expression for calculation of bit error rate is derived for the phase encoded OCDMA performance considerations.

SYSTEM BLOCK DIAGRAM AND DESCRIPTION

A phase encoded OCDMA communication system can be modeled using the block diagram shown in Figure 1 (Chua, Abbou, Chuah, & Majumder, 2004). The transmitter consists of a pulse generator, a data generator and a spectral phase encoder. The pulse generator outputs an ultrashort pulse which is multiplied by the data generator. A data source takes on either "0" or "1" for on-off keying (OOK). When a data is "0", the ultrashort pulse is not transmitted. While, when a data is "1", the encoder multiplies the Fourier transform of the ultrashort pulse with the spectral phase code. An inverse Fourier transform then converts the resultant spectral waveform back to the temporal domain as a phase-encoded signal. The phase-encoded signal is transmitted over a fiber link, which we can assume is loss-compensated by a series of optical amplifiers. Fiber dispersion effects and interfering signal from other users (the MAI) are added onto the phase-encoded signal. The receiver consists of a conjugate spectral phase code generator, a photodetector, and data decision circuit. At the receiver, the phase code of the mth decoder is the conjugate code of the mth encoder.

Figure 1. Block diagram of phase encoded OCDMA communication system (Chua, Abbou, Chuah, & Majumder, 2004)

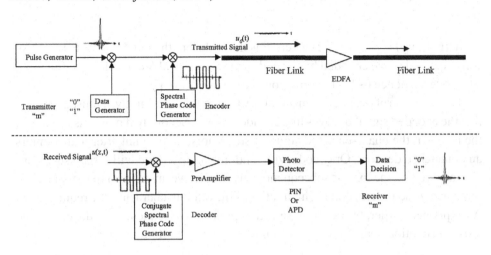

Assume the pulse generator generates an initial Gauss optical pulse

$$f(t) = e^{-\left(t^2 / 2T_0^2\right)} \tag{6.1}$$

The spectral shape of the pulse can be expressed as

$$F(\omega) = \sqrt{2\pi}T_0 e^{-\left(\omega^2 T_0^2 / 4\right)} \tag{6.2}$$

Assume that the appendix phase to the spectrum by the spectral phase encoder can be written as (Ma, Zuo, Pu, & Lin, 2002):

$$M(\omega) = \begin{cases} C_j & -\dfrac{\Omega}{2} + \dfrac{\Omega}{F}j \le \omega < -\dfrac{\Omega}{2} + \dfrac{\Omega}{F}(j+1) \\ & 0 \le j \le F-1, \quad C_j \in \{1,-1\} \\ 0 & otherwise \end{cases} \tag{6.3}$$

We can express the appendix phase, in the temporal domain, as Chua, Abbou, Chuah, & Majumder, 2004):

$$m(t) = \Im^{-1}\left[M(\omega)\right] = \sum_{j=0}^{F-1} C_j \frac{\delta\omega}{2\pi} Sa\left(\frac{\delta w}{2}t\right) e^{iv(j)\delta\omega t} \tag{6.4}$$

In (6.4), $v(j) = j - ((F-1)/2)$ where F is the code length, and $dw = W/F$, where W is the spectral range encoded by the code sequence C_j and $Sa(\cdot)$ is the sinc function. The code sequence $(+1, -1)$ corresponds to phase of $(0, p)$.

The selection of phase code must satisfy two conditions. Firstly, it must guarantee that the encoded signal behaves like a random noise. Secondly it must ensure that, at the receiver, the phase-encoded signal is still a noise-like signal after it encounters an unmatched decoder. Only code with random characteristic will satisfy such conditions. We assume for our subsequent analyses that we are using a maximal length sequence (m sequence) code, which satisfies the random characteristic requirement. As explained earlier, by carefully selecting preferred m sequences as the codes, the cross-correlation peaks of any two pair of sequences will be bounded.

THEORETICAL ANALYSIS OF PSEUDORANDOM OPTICAL SIGNAL

The output phase-encoded optical signal expressed in the temporal domain, $u_0(t)$, can be found from the inverse Fourier transform of $[M(w)F(w)]$(Chua, Abbou, Chuah, & Majumder, 2004):

$$u_0(t) = \int_{-\infty}^{+\infty} m(\tau)f(t-\tau)d\tau \approx \frac{\delta\omega}{\sqrt{2\pi}} T_o \sum_{j=1}^{F} C_j Sa\left(\frac{\delta\omega}{2}t\right) e^{iv(j)\delta\omega t} \tag{6.5}$$

We have made the assumption that $dw \dagger W$ in arriving at the approximation in (2.5). This can be considered reasonable as we make $f(t)$ an ultrashort pulse, resulting in a large spectral width.

Writing out the real and imaginary parts of the signal as:

$$\text{Re}[u_0(t)] = u_R(t) = \frac{\delta\omega}{\sqrt{2\pi}} T_o \sum_{j=1}^{F} C_j Sa\left(\frac{\delta\omega}{2}t\right) \cos\left(v(j)\delta\omega t\right) \tag{6.6}$$

$$\text{Im}[u_0(t)] = u_I(t) = \frac{\delta\omega}{\sqrt{2\pi}} T_o \sum_{j=1}^{F} C_j Sa\left(\frac{\delta\omega}{2}t\right) \sin\left(v(j)\delta\omega t\right) \tag{6.7}$$

We make an assumption that the spectral width encoded by code length F is equivalent to the spectral width at 1/e intensity. So we find that

$$\delta\omega = \frac{2\sqrt{2}}{T_0 F} \tag{6.8}$$

Substituting equation (6.8) into (6.6) and (6.7), we can derive the intensity of the phase-encoded signal as:

$$I(t) = \left|u_0(t)\right|^2 = u_R^2(t) + u_I^2(t) = k_1^2 Sa^2(\frac{\delta\omega}{2}t)\left[F + \sum_{i,j} C_i C_j \cos(i-j)\delta\omega t\right] \tag{6.9}$$

where

$$k_1 = \frac{2}{F\sqrt{\pi}}$$

The first interesting observation we can make here is that the intensity of the phase-encoded signal is the sum of two parts, one that is dependent on code length (but not on the choice of phase code) and the other which is dependent on choice of phase code. In our case, we have assumed random coding so the intensity will be random by observation of equation (6.9). We can also quickly deduce that the intensity of optical signal has been lowered in relation to the original input Gauss pulse, by a factor inversely proportional to code length. Therefore, we can now safely argue that the phase-encoded output is a pseudorandom optical signal of low-intensity.

Before we continue with our analysis, we take note that the phase-encoded signal is theoretically infinite in temporal domain. Because the amplitude of the signal is negligible outside the first zero points of the function $Sa((dw/2)t)$, we will limit our analysis to within the bounds of these points (Ma, Zuo, Pu, & Lin, 2002). To find the temporal width of this pseudorandom optical signal, we use the concept of rms width (Agrawal, 2002):

$$T_\sigma = \left[\left\langle T^2 \right\rangle - \left\langle T \right\rangle^2\right]^{1/2} \tag{6.10}$$

where

$$\left\langle T^n \right\rangle = \frac{\int_{-\infty}^{\infty} t^n \left| u_0(t) \right|^2 dt}{\int_{-\infty}^{\infty} \left| u_0(t) \right|^2 dt} \tag{6.11}$$

Using equations (6.9), (6.10) and (6.11) and performing the integration within the limits of the first zero points of $Sa((dw/2)t)$ which is [2p/dw, -2p/dw], we find (Chua, Abbou, Chuah, & Majumder, 2004):

$$T_\sigma = \frac{2}{\delta\omega} \sqrt{1 - \frac{1}{2F} \sum_{i-j=1} C_i C_j} \tag{6.12}$$

For the m sequence CDMA codes used here, we can say that $S_{i-j=1} C_i C_j$ is bounded. If we now also assume that F is typically large, we can approximate equation (6.12) as (Chua, Abbou, Chuah, & Majumder, 2004):

$$T_\sigma = \frac{T_o F}{\sqrt{2}} \tag{6.13}$$

We have also used equation (6.8) in arriving at this expression. We observe that T_s is proportional to code length F. So the ultrashort pulse has been transformed into an optical signal that is widened in the temporal domain, due to the process of spectral phase encoding. This feature together with its random, low intensity profile characterizes the main physical properties of the OCDMA signal in a fiber optic network.

We now turn our attention to the statistical properties of the OCDMA signal. In order to do this, we will not attempt to be mathematically rigorous. Instead we will make some generalized arguments to derive the probability distribution function (pdf) for the intensity of the phase-encoded signal. To do that, we first rewrite $u_0(t)$ as the product of two signals:

$$u_0(t) = G(t)V(t) \tag{6.14}$$

where

$$G(t) = Sa\left(\frac{\delta\omega}{2}t\right) \tag{6.15}$$

and

$$V(t) = k_1 \sum_{j=1}^{F} C_j e^{iv(j)\delta\omega t} \tag{6.16}$$

The signal $G(t)$ is a real envelope function which determines the temporal shape of the encoded signal, while $V(t)$ is the periodic pseudonoise signal whose temporal shape is determined by the code sequence C_j (Salehi *et al.*, 1990). So to derive the statistical properties of $u_0(t)$, it's sufficient to only consider $V(t)$. By introducing two random variables t' and x to represent the ambiguities in transmission time and the initial phase of the encoded light, we can rewrite (6.16) as

$$V(t - t') = \alpha_x(t - t') + i\alpha_y(t - t') \tag{6.17}$$

Here, a_x and a_y are the real and imaginary parts of the complex amplitude $V(t\text{-}t')$ and are defined accordingly as

$$\alpha_x(t - t') = k_1 \sum_{j=1}^{F} C_j \cos\left(v(j)\delta\omega(t - t') + \xi\right) \tag{6.18}$$

and

$$\alpha_y(t - t') = k_1 \sum_{j=1}^{F} C_j \sin\left(v(j)\delta\omega(t - t') + \xi\right) \tag{6.19}$$

The intensity $I(t\text{-}t')$ is now expressed as

$$I(t - t') = k_1 Sa^2\left(\frac{\delta\omega}{2}t\right)\left[\alpha_x^2(t - t') + \alpha_y^2(t - t')\right] \tag{6.20}$$

To derive the pdf for I, it is thus sufficient to find the joint distribution for a_x and a_y. We notice that both a_x and a_y resemble the steady state output of multimode laser light with no phase locking (Goodman, 2000). It has been shown that if the number of modes for such an output is sufficiently large, then the pdf of the signal will approach a Gauss shape. By using equivalence of F in our case here to the modes of the laser light, we can infer that a_x and a_y are both Gaussian random processes.

In addition, we can prove that the time averages for the real and imaginary parts of $u_0(t)$, within the rms width, is zero:

$$\left\langle u_R(t) \right\rangle = \int_{-T_\sigma/2}^{+T_\sigma/2} u_R(t)\,dt = 0 \tag{6.21}$$

and

$$\left\langle u_I(t) \right\rangle = \int_{-T_\sigma/2}^{+T_\sigma/2} u_I(t)\,dt = 0 \tag{6.22}$$

If we assume that $u_0(t)$ is a stationary, ergodic process, then the ensemble average of $u_0(t)$ within the rms width of the signal is also zero (Peebles, 2001). Assuming that the variances for both real and imaginary parts of $u_0(t)$ is $s^2/2$ and knowing the fact that both parts have Gaussian distributions, we can easily derive using statistical theory, the pdf for $I(t)$ as an exponential function given as

$$p(x) = \frac{1}{\sigma^2} e^{-(x/\sigma^2)} \tag{6.23}$$

To calculate the variance of the pdf, we first find the energy of input Gauss pulse:

$$E = \int_{-\infty}^{+\infty} \left| f(t) \right|^2 dt = \sqrt{\pi} T_o \tag{6.24}$$

If we note that the energy of the phase encoded signal within the first zero points of the function $Sa((dw/2)t)$ accounts for more than 90% of the whole signal energy (Ma, Zuo, Pu, & Lin, 2002), we can use the following relation [½ (Energy/interval)= average power] to find s (Chua, Abbou, Chuah, & Majumder, 2004):

$$\frac{1}{2}\left(\frac{0.9\sqrt{\pi}T_o}{T_\sigma}\right) = \frac{\sigma^2}{2} \tag{6.25}$$

$$\sigma = 1.263\sqrt{\frac{T_o}{T_\sigma}} \tag{6.26}$$

From (6.13) and (6.26), we note that the variance of the pdf is inversely proportional to code length F.

Dispersion Analysis of Pseudorandom Optical Signal

Several methods have been developed to find properties of optical pulses under the effect of dispersion as they propagate in fibre medium. Some of the methods involved numerical solutions of the wave equation describing the propagation of the optical pulse, while others are purely analytical solutions which require that one only needs to know the form of the original input pulse before it's coupled into the fiber link. One frequently used method was developed by Marcuse and involves evaluating the nth moment $<T^n>$ of t in the frequency domain (Agrawal, 2002). This is done by doing a Fourier transform of the original input signal to obtain an expression for the signal in the frequency domain. Next, the dispersion effect of the fiber is formulated in the form of a transfer function. In doing so, we can find the rms width of the distorted pulse by staying completely in the frequency domain. This method has been proven to be quite accurate when evaluating Gaussian pulse distortion in second and third-order dispersive fiber. It can be used for cases where the original input pulse is either chirped or unchirped.

In our case since the appendix phase $M(w)$ is not a continuous function, doing the analysis of dispersion on $u_0(t)$ in the frequency domain is not an attractive option. We would rather keep the analysis completely in the temporal domain.

Anderson and Lisak have shown that for an optical pulse propagating along a dispersive optical fiber, the rms width varies parabolically with distance, irrespective of initial pulse form and frequency chirp variation (Andersen & Lisak, 1987). This result is true to any dispersive order and is a very useful tool. Furthermore it is also shown that fiber loss does not affect the validity of the parabolic dependency of the rms width on distance of pulse propagation. So, although we have assumed loss compensation, this method of dispersion analysis will still hold even if fiber loss is considered. We shall now use this method to find an analytical expression for the rms width of the pseudo-random optical signal after undergoing dispersion.

We start by doing a quick review of the method. Assume the wave envelope of the signal after traveling distance z is $u(t,z)$, we can write the Schröndinger equation describing it as

$$i\frac{\partial u}{\partial t} = Hu \tag{6.27}$$

where the operator H includes, in it's general form, dispersive effects to all orders and is given by

$$H = \sum_{n=2}^{\infty} \frac{i^n \beta_n}{n!} \frac{\partial^n}{\partial t^n} \tag{6.28}$$

and

$$\beta_n = \left(\frac{d^n \beta}{d\omega^n}\right)_{\omega=\omega_0} \tag{6.29}$$

w_0 is the carrier frequency and b is known as the propagation constant. We can write the moments of the signal as

$$I_n(x) \equiv \langle T^n \rangle = \int_{-\infty}^{+\infty} u^*(t,z)t^n u(t,z)\, dt \tag{6.30}$$

If we introduce the commutative operator, operator $[H, t^n]$ as

$$[H, t^n] = Ht^n - t^n H \tag{6.31}$$

The following lowest-order moments can then be inferred:

$$\left.\begin{aligned} I_0 &= \int_{-\infty}^{+\infty} u^*(t,z)\, u(t,z)\, dt = \int_{-\infty}^{+\infty} \left|u_0(t,z)\right|^2 dt\,, \\ I_1 &= \int_{-\infty}^{+\infty} u^*(t,z)\, t\, u(t,z)\, dt = a_0 + a_1 z\,, \\ I_2 &= \int_{-\infty}^{+\infty} u^*(t,z)\, t^2 u(t,z)\, dt = b_0 + b_1 z + b_2 z^2 \end{aligned}\right\} \tag{6.32}$$

Physically, I_0 signifies the conservation of pulse energy, I_1 governs asymmetry of pulse shape while I_2 is a measure of pulse broadening. Higher order moments I_3 and I_4 can also be calculated by this technique and govern the skewness and kurtosis of the intensity profile of the pulse, respectively (Agrawal, 2002). To calculate the rms width of the signal, it is then sufficient to find the moments of the signal upto I_2 only. The coefficients a_j and b_j of equation (6.32) are determined by

$$
\left.
\begin{aligned}
a_0 &= \int_{-\infty}^{+\infty} u_0^*(t)\, t\, u_0(t)\, dt, \\
a_1 &= i \int_{-\infty}^{+\infty} u_0^*(t)\big[H, t\big]\, u_0(t)\, dt, \\
b_0 &= \int_{-\infty}^{+\infty} u_0^*(t)\, t^2 u_0(t)\, dt, \\
b_1 &= i \int_{-\infty}^{+\infty} u_0^*(t)\big[H, t^2\big]\, u_0(t)\, dt, \\
b_2 &= -\frac{1}{2}\int_{-\infty}^{+\infty} u_0^*(t)\Big[H,\big[H, t^2\big]\Big]\, u_0(t)\, dt
\end{aligned}
\right\}.
\tag{6.33}
$$

Using equations (6.28) and (6.31) in (6.33) we can derive, to third dispersive order, the coefficients a_1, b_1, and b_2 as

$$
\left.
\begin{aligned}
a_1 &= \beta_2 \operatorname{Im} \int_{-\infty}^{+\infty} u_0 \frac{\partial u_0^*}{\partial t}\, dt + \frac{\beta_3}{2} \int_{-\infty}^{+\infty} \left|\frac{\partial u_0}{\partial t}\right|^2 dt, \\
b_1 &= 2\beta_2 \operatorname{Im} \int_{-\infty}^{+\infty} u_0\, t\, \frac{\partial u_0^*}{\partial t}\, dt + \beta_3 \int_{-\infty}^{+\infty} t \left|\frac{\partial u_0}{\partial t}\right|^2 dt, \\
b_2 &= \left(\beta_2\right)^2 \int_{-\infty}^{+\infty} \left|\frac{\partial u_0}{\partial t}\right|^2 dt - \frac{\beta_2 \beta_3}{2} \operatorname{Im} \int_{-\infty}^{+\infty} \frac{\partial u_0^*}{\partial t}\frac{\partial^2 u_0}{\partial t^2}\, dt + \left(\frac{\beta_3}{2}\right)^2 \int_{-\infty}^{+\infty} \left|\frac{\partial^2 u_0}{\partial t^2}\right|^2 dt
\end{aligned}
\right\}
\tag{6.34}
$$

We find that the derivative of the $Sa(\cdot)$ function produces an expression whose integral in the limits of interest ($-\yen,+\yen$) do not converge. This means that we will not be able to find the values of the coefficients in equation (6.34) if we keep to this function in $u_0(t)$. We need to make the following Gaussian function approximation in place of the $Sa(\cdot)$ function:

$$
Sa\left(\frac{\delta w}{2} t\right) \approx \exp\left(\frac{-(c\delta wt)^2}{2}\right)
\tag{6.35}
$$

We choose $c = 0.304$ so that the functions have the same widths at $1/e$ intensity. Recall that the statistical properties of $u_0(t)$ is dependent on the pseudonoise part of the signal only. It can then safely be said that replacing the $Sa(\cdot)$ in the real envelope function part of the signal will not change the prior analyses of the statistical properties.

Replacing the approximated function into (6.5) and using the modified u_0 in equations (6.33) and (6.34), we can now find all the coefficients (Chua, Abbou, Chuah, & Majumder, 2004):

$$
\left.
\begin{aligned}
a_0 &= 0 \\
a_1 &= \beta_2 \left(\frac{-F\sqrt{\pi}}{c} \right) + \frac{\beta_3}{2} \left(\frac{F^3}{12c} \sqrt{\pi}\delta w \right) \\
b_0 &= \frac{F\sqrt{\pi}}{2(c\delta w)^3} \\
b_1 &= 0 \\
b_2 &= \frac{(\beta_2)^2}{12} \left(\frac{F^3}{c} \sqrt{\pi}\delta w \right) + \frac{\beta_2\beta_3}{8} \left(\frac{F^3}{c} \sqrt{\pi}(\delta w)^2 \right) + \frac{(\beta_3)^2}{320} \left(\frac{F^5 \sqrt{\pi}(\delta w)^3}{c} \right)
\end{aligned}
\right\}
$$

(6.36)

The parameters b_2 and b_3 are related to the second order D and third order S dispersion parameters as (Agrawal, 1997):

$$
D = -\left(2\pi c / \lambda^2 \right) \beta_2
$$

(6.37)

$$
S = (2\pi c / \lambda^2)^2 \beta_3 + (4\pi c / \lambda^3) \beta_2
$$

(6.38)

and l is the operating wavelength of the lightsource for the pulse generator.

The coefficients a_0, b_0 and b_1 can be easily obtained. Substituting the coefficients obtained into equation (6.32) produced the following:

$$
\left.\begin{aligned}
I_0 &= \frac{F\sqrt{\pi}}{c\delta w} \\[2mm]
I_1 &= \left[\beta_2\left(\frac{-F\sqrt{\pi}}{c}\right) + \frac{\beta_3}{24}\left(\frac{F^3}{c}\sqrt{\pi}\delta w\right)\right]z \\[2mm]
I_2 &= \frac{F\sqrt{\pi}}{2(c\delta w)^3} + \left[\frac{(\beta_2)^2}{12c}F^3\sqrt{\pi}\delta w + \frac{\beta_2\beta_3}{8c}F^3\sqrt{\pi}(\delta w)^2 + \frac{(\beta_3)^2}{320c}F^5\sqrt{\pi}(\delta w)^3\right]z^2
\end{aligned}\right\}
$$

$$(6.39)$$

We observe that generally $I_1 \,^1\, 0$, so the encoded signal is expected to lose its symmetry as it propagates in the fiber link. However we are not so concerned with this as we are not interested in the actual shape of the signal in this analysis and merely assume that it remains a pseudorandom signal with low intensity. We now find the rms width of the initial phase encoded signal, using the modified $u_0(t)$. This will also give us verification if our approximation of the function in equation (6.35) is acceptable.

$$
T_\sigma(0) = \left\{\frac{b_0 - a_0^2}{I_0}\right\}^{1/2} = \frac{1}{\sqrt{2}(c\delta w)} = \frac{T_0 F}{4c}
$$

$$(6.40)$$

This approximates quite closely the rms width of the phase encoded optical signal obtained in (6.13) which has the original $Sa(\cdot)$ function. Next, we will obtain the moments and rms width $T_s(z)$ of the optical signal at the receiver end located at a distance of z.

$$
\langle T \rangle = \frac{I_1}{I_0} = \left[\beta_2(-\delta w) + \frac{\beta_3}{24}F^2(\delta w)^2\right]z
$$

$$(6.41)$$

$$
\langle T^2 \rangle = \frac{I_2}{I_0} = \frac{1}{2(c\delta w)^2} + \left[\frac{(\beta_2)^2}{12}F^2(\delta w)^2 + \frac{\beta_2\beta_3}{8}F^2(\delta w)^3 + \frac{(\beta_3)^2}{320}F^4(\delta w)^4\right]z
$$

$$(6.42)$$

Figure 2. Peak power, RMS width pair of optical signals propagating along system (Chua, Abbou, Chuah, & Majumder, 2004)

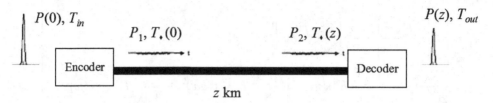

$$T_\sigma(z) = \left[\left\langle T^2 \right\rangle - \left\langle T \right\rangle^2 \right]^{1/2}$$

$$= T_\sigma(0) \left[1 + \frac{32c^2}{3} \left(\frac{\beta_2 z}{T_0^2 F} \right)^2 + \frac{320c^2}{3\sqrt{2}} \left(\frac{\beta_2 \beta_3 z^2}{T_0^5 F^3} \right) + \frac{64c^2}{45} \left(\frac{\beta_3 z}{T_0^3 F} \right)^2 \right]^{1/2} \tag{6.43}$$

Since we have assumed loss compensation, we can use the principle of conservation of pulse energy to find the peak optical power $P(z)$ of the distorted optical pulse recovered in the case of matched decoder (Chua, Abbou, Chuah, & Majumder, 2004). We use Figure 2 as an illustration of how this is achieved.

We show the original input pulse, the initial pseudorandom signal, the pseudorandom signal at the receiver and the decoded pulse. The associated [peak power, rms width] pairs for the different signals are $[P(0), T_{in}]$, $[P_1, T_s(0)]$, $[P_2, T_s(z)]$ and $[P(z), T_{out}]$ respectively. We can assume that the signal energy is conserved completely throughout the system. By using conservation of signal energy at encoder, we obtain

$$P(0)T_\sigma(0) = P_1 T_\sigma(0) \frac{T_\sigma(0)}{T_{in}} \tag{6.44}$$

By doing the same at the decoder, we obtain

$$P(z)T_\sigma(z) = P_2 T_\sigma(z) \frac{T_\sigma(z)}{T_{out}} \tag{6.45}$$

We know that $T_s(0)$ is function of code length and T_{in} only. At the decoder, we use the reverse of the argument, i.e. T_{out} is function of code length and $T_s(z)$ only.

Since code length obviously does not change, we can infer that $T_s(0)/T_{in} = T_s(z)/T_{out}$. Then, by using conservation of signal energy along the fibre, i.e. $P_1 T_s(0) = P_2 T_s(z)$, and comparing equations (6.44) and (6.45), we find that

$$P(0)T_\sigma(0) = P(z)T_\sigma(z) \qquad (6.46)$$

In our case here, we have $P(0) = 1$. For the case of unmatched decoder, since we assume random spectral codes, the recovered pulse will remain as a low-intensity pseudorandom signal. Using the techniques outlined above, we can now calculate the rms width and peak optical power of correctly decoded optical pulses at the receiver.

BIT ERROR RATE

This analysis has been carried out by Ma, Zuo, Pu, and Lin (2002) and we will repeat the steps here for completeness. In the course of doing so, we also investigate the effects of shot and thermal noise, at the receiver, in the calculation of the BER. To begin with, we will assume always that $T_\sigma \leq T_b$, where T_b is the bit duration. Physically, this implies that the encoded pseudorandom optical signal will always fit within the bit slot of the data transmitted. For n users in the system, the interference effect can be seen as the sum of statistically independent multiple random processes and can be modeled as a stationary random process whose pdf is given by the $(n-1)$ convolution of the single user pdf (Peebles, 2001). Since the single-user pdf is given by (6.23), we find the pdf for the multiple access interference (MAI) noise to be given by

$$p_n(x) = \frac{x^{n-1}}{\sigma^{2n}(n-1)!}e^{-(x/\sigma^2)} \qquad (6.47)$$

In order to calculate the BER (for the case of no dispersion and ignore noise at the receiver), we assume that the receiver detects a "1" if the decoded intensity exceeds a threshold value and a "0" otherwise. If we further assume that on-off keying occurs with equal probability (each with probability ½), then the average probability of error is $\frac{1}{2}(P_{FA} + P_{MD})$ where P_{FA} is the probability that the multiple access interference (MAI) alone crosses the threshold during any sampling instant (false alarm) and P_{MD} is the probability that the combination of a transmitted "1" and MAI do not cross the threshold (missed detection) (Salehi et al., 1990).

Let the photocounts detected by receiver photo detector be denoted by random variable Y^1, and θ is the threshold of decoder. The BER P_b for the system with N users is then given by:

$$P_b = \frac{1}{2}\left[\Pr(Y^1 > \theta \mid b_i^1 = 0) + \Pr(Y^1 \leq \theta \mid b_i^1 = 1)\right] \tag{6.48}$$

where

$$\Pr(Y^1 > \theta \mid b_i^1 = 0)$$

$$= \sum_{i=1}^{N-1} \binom{N-1}{i} p^i (1-p)^{N-1-i} \int_\theta^\infty \frac{x^{i-1}}{\sigma^{2i}(i-1)!} . e^{-\left(\frac{x}{\sigma^2}\right)} dx \tag{6.49}$$

$$= \sum_{i=1}^{N-1} \binom{N-1}{i} p^i (1-p)^{N-1-i} e^{-a} \sum_{k=0}^{i-1} \frac{a^k}{k!}$$

where $a = q/s^2$ and

$$p = \frac{1}{2} . \frac{T_\sigma}{T_b} \tag{6.50}$$

In (6.50), the ratio T_σ / T_b represents the duty cycle and T_σ is found from equation (6.43). Further, the second term in equation (6.48) is given by:

$$\Pr(Y^1 \leq \theta \mid b_i^1 = 1)$$

$$= \sum_{i=1}^{N-1} \binom{N-1}{i} p^i (1-p)^{N-1-i} \int_1^\theta \frac{(x-1)^{i-1}}{\sigma^{2i}(i-1)!} . e^{-\left(\frac{(x-1)}{\sigma^2}\right)} dx \tag{6.51}$$

$$= \sum_{i=1}^{N-1} \binom{N-1}{i} p^i (1-p)^{N-1-i} \left(1 - e^{-b} \sum_{k=0}^{i-1} \frac{b^k}{k!}\right)$$

where $b = (q-1)/s^2$

We have not accounted for degradation of peak power (due to dispersion effect) of correctly decoded signal and also receiver noise in our derivation of the BER. So equations (6.49) and (6.51) represent BER calculation in the ideal case, where the only performance impairment effect is due to MAI. In order to include dispersion effect and receiver noise, we need to make Gaussian approximations for the pdf of the various noise sources. We do this first by noticing that when the number of interfering users n becomes large, the probability distribution function of the multiple access noise at the receiver reaches a Gauss distribution with mean of ns^2 and variance ns^4. This can be denoted by the notation $N(ns^2, ns^4)$. We reach this conclusion by invoking the central limit theorem (Peebles, 2001). Shot noise for the receiver is usually a Poisson random process, and its expectation and variance can be denoted by σ_{sh}^2. But in order to simplify our analysis, we will assume that it is a Gaussian random process. Thermal noise of receiver is always a Gaussian distribution $N(0, \sigma_{th}^2)$.

We can now use a Gaussian approximation in deriving the BER of the system. So, we can rewrite (6.49) as

$$
\begin{aligned}
&\Pr(Y^1 > \theta \mid b_i^1 = 0) \\
&= \sum_{i=1}^{N-1} \binom{N-1}{i} p^i (1-p)^{N-1-i} \int_\theta^\infty \frac{1}{\sqrt{2\pi}\sigma_{i0}} e^{-((x-\mu_{i0})^2/2\sigma_{i0}^2)} \, dx \\
&= \sum_{i=1}^{N-1} \binom{N-1}{i} p^i (1-p)^{N-1-i} Q\left(\frac{\theta - \mu_{i0}}{\sigma_{i0}}\right)
\end{aligned}
\tag{6.52}
$$

where

$$
\left.\begin{aligned}
\mu_{i0} &= i\sigma^2 + \sigma_{sh}^2 \\
\sigma_{i0}^2 &= i\sigma^4 + \sigma_{sh}^2 + \sigma_{th}^2
\end{aligned}\right\}
\tag{6.53}
$$

Similarly, we can also rewrite (6.51) as

$$
\begin{aligned}
&\Pr(Y^1 \leq \theta \mid b_i^1 = 1) \\
&= \sum_{i=1}^{N-1} \binom{N-1}{i} p^i (1-p)^{N-1-i} \int_{-\infty}^\theta \frac{1}{\sqrt{2\pi}\sigma_{i1}} e^{-((x-\mu_{i1})^2/2\sigma_{i1}^2)} \, dx \\
&= \sum_{i=1}^{N-1} \binom{N-1}{i} p^i (1-p)^{N-1-i} Q\left(\frac{\mu_{i1} - \theta}{\sigma_{i1}}\right)
\end{aligned}
\tag{6.54}
$$

where

$$\left. \begin{aligned} \mu_{i1} &= i\sigma^2 + \sigma_{sh}^2 + P(z) \\ \sigma_{i1}^2 &= i\sigma^4 + \sigma_{sh}^2 + \sigma_{th}^2 \end{aligned} \right\} \tag{6.55}$$

Here, $P(z)$ is the peak optical power of correctly decoded pulse and can be calculated from equation (6.46). The noise sources at the receiver consist of shot noise, circuit thermal noise and phase induced intensity noise (Agrawal, 1997). It has been revealed, in various studies, that in OCDMA systems the noise effect is dependent on the type of code sequence used. One example of such a study is by Wei, Shalaby, and Ghafouri-Shiraz (2001) on the performance analysis of modified congruence codes for FBG based spectral amplitude coding OCDMA systems. In that study it was indicated that when the power of the transmitted optical pulse is sufficiently large, then intensity noise becomes the dominant noise factor. However, when the transmitted power is not sufficiently large, thermal and shot noise sources become dominant, and the effect of thermal noise is much larger than that of shot noise. To simplify our analysis, we will assume that shot and thermal noises are the dominant noise sources and will ignore intensity noise. We also do not consider the dependency of shot noise on code sequence used. Thermal noise is a function of the receiver operating parameters only and has no dependency on code sequence.

We can write the shot noise variance as (Agrawal, 1997)

$$\sigma_{sh}^2 = 2eI_p B \tag{6.56}$$

where e is the charge of electron, I_p is the average photocurrent and B is the noise equivalent bandwidth of the receiver. Similarly the thermal noise variance can be written as (Agrawal, 1997)

$$\sigma_{th}^2 = 4K_b T_n B / R_L \tag{6.57}$$

where K_b is Boltzmann's constant, T_n is the absolute receiver noise temperature and R_L the receiver load resistance. The average photocurrent I_p is given $I_p = RP_{in}$, where P_{in} is the received optical signal and R is the responsivity of the receiver given as

$$R = \eta e / h\upsilon_c \tag{6.58}$$

Here, h is the quantum efficiency, h is the Planck constant and n_c is the center frequency of the original optical pulse. The parameter n_c can be calculated from the operating wavelength l of the lightsource. Note that P_{in} is the power of incorrectly decoded pulses, which we can in our case approximate as $s^2/2$.

We will calculate the BER of the system operating at 1 Gb/s in three different fiber configurations - the case of normal SMF with $D=16$ps/km/nm and $S=0.08$ps/km/(nm)^2, DSF with with $D=3$ps/km/nm and $S=0.08$ps/km/(nm)^2 and a fully dispersion compensated fiber link.

We list in Table 1 the other parameters we used in our calculation. We conclude our analysis by noting that the Gaussian approximation method we have used above is a standard, but pessimistic, method to analyze system performance without having to know the exact structure of the code sequence (Yang, & Kwong, 2002). This will provide us with upper bound estimates of the BER. To obtain more accurate performance figures, the structure of the code sequence will need to be examined and a combinatorial method used to perform the calculations. The results of our analyses are then relative and provide us with means to gauge the impact of dispersion effects on the OCDMA system performance.

Influence of Optical Pulsewidth on System Performance

Figure 3 shows the curves of bit-error rate (BER) versus threshold q of the receiver for different settings of the initial optical pulsewidth T_0. We show the curves for cases of SMF, DSF and DCF at a distance of 150km for a system with 20 users and code length of 127.

From the curves in Figure 3, we can clearly see that the dispersive effect of the fiber on bit-error rate becomes more apparent as the value of T_0 becomes smaller. It is easy to understand this from a physical basis. When we make the initial Gauss pulse narrower, the effective rms width of the encoded optical signal becomes smaller which, in turn, accentuates pulse broadening. The received optical peak power then degrades. The effect is very evident in the case of SMF, not so much for DSF and especially true when T_0 is reduced to 3ps. We also observe that the

Table 1. Typical parameters used in the calculation

Parameter	Value
T_b	1000 ps
l	1550 nm
R	0.8
B	100 MHz
R_L	100Ω
T_n	300 K

Figure 3. Bit-error probability versus threshold q with different T_0 (Chua, Abbou, Chuah, & Majumder, 2004)

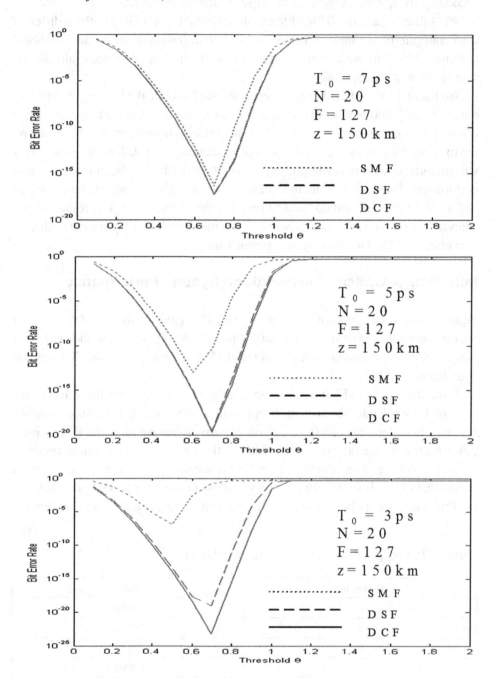

optimum threshold is around 0.7 on the average. However the narrower we make T_0, the smaller the optimum q becomes. This is especially severe for the case of SMF. Physically, this is due to degraded receiver sensitivity because of much reduced received optical peak power. We observe that in the case of DCF, making T_0 smaller improves system performance. This result is consistent with the findings in (Ma, Zuo, Pu, & Lin, 2002) and performance improvement can be attributed to the lower duty cycle. For the case of DSF, performance gain (by a factor of around 3) is seen when T_0 is reduced from 7ps to 5ps. However reducing T_0 further to 3ps does not help in achieving any more performance gain; in fact, the effect of dispersion becomes accentuated in this case. We can therefore come to the conclusion that although the performance of the system should improve as T_0 becomes narrower, for the case of SMF and DSF, this is countered by the effect of dispersion, which becomes worse.

Influence of Code Length on System Performance

Figure 4 shows the curves of BER versus threshold q when we change the code length F. We change code length from $F=127$ to $F=63$, and $F=255$, while keeping T_0 constant at 3ps. In the case of SMF, we can see the system performance deteriorate very steeply and the system can be considered as quite impractical at the distance we are considering. In the case of DSF also, the system performance drops sharply (by a factor of almost 12) and the effect of dispersion is accentuated. For DCF, as consistent with the findings in (Ma, Zuo, Pu, & Lin, 2002), system performance is also reduced. The increased dispersion effect is due to the smaller rms width of the encoded optical signal while performance reduction is attributable to the larger variance (more MAI). On the reverse, when we increase the code length from $F=127$ to $F=255$, we immediately see an increase in system performance and lessening of dispersion effect. Increasing code length then increases both system performance and reduces the effect of dispersion. Recall that increasing code length also results in more unique signature sequences, thereby potentially increasing the number of users that can be supported. But of course having longer codes translates into the need for complex encoder-decoder that could raise the cost of implementation.

Comparison of Transmission Distances

Figure 5 shows the curves of BER versus transmission distance for different pulse-width of the initial optical pulse. We plot the results for the cases when SMF and DSF are used, and set $T_0 = 3, 5$ and 7 ps. We set $F = 127, N = 20$ and the threshold value q = 0.7. It is clearly seen that making the pulsewidth narrower increases

Figure 4. Bit-error probability versus threshold q with different F (Chua, Abbou, Chuah, & Majumder, 2004)

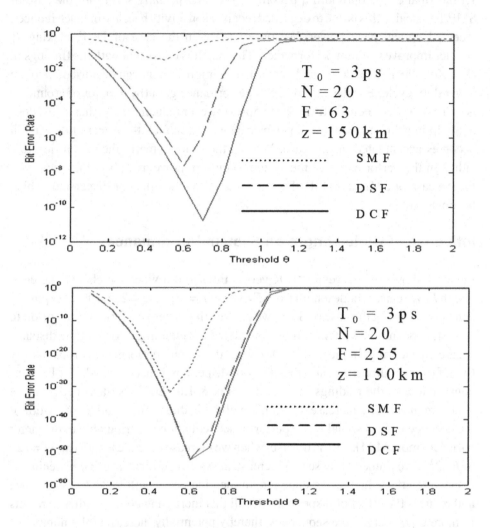

performance of the system initially at short distances but becomes a problem when distance becomes longer. If we look at the case when T_0=3ps, the BER becomes 10^{-10} at distance of z=60km for SMF, while for the case of DSF the same BER is reached when z=300km. Similarly for the case when T_0=5ps, BER of 10^{-10} is reached at z=160km for SMF and z=800km for DSF. We can then conclude that, for the same BER, the DSF link achieves on average about five times longer transmission distance compared to SMF link.

Figure 5. Bit-error probability versus distance for a) SMF b) DSF (Chua, Abbou, Chuah, & Majumder, 2004)

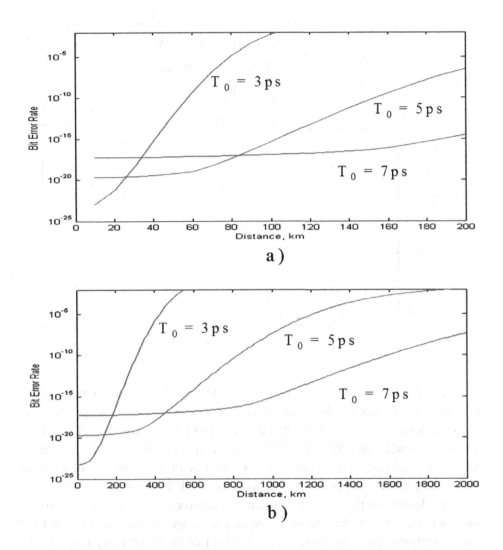

a)

b)

Accuracy of Gaussian Approximation and Influence of Noise

We conclude our results analysis by comparing the accuracy of the Gaussian approximation for the pdf of the MAI compared to the calculations for the BER using the exact (N-1) convolution of the single user pdf. We also look at the effect of including shot and receiver noise in the final BER figures. Figure 6 shows the curves for BER versus number of users for the cases of calculation using exact pdf, the Gaussian approximated pdf and Gaussian approximated pdf with receiver noise. We set T_0

Figure 6. Bit-error probability versus number of users

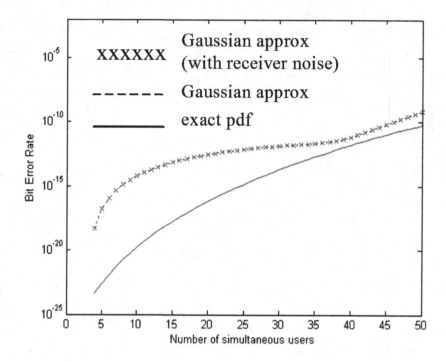

= 5ps and $F = 127$ for the exact pdf and both the Gaussian approximated cases. If we compare the BER results obtained using exact versus Gaussian approximated pdf's, we notice that for small number of users the Gaussian approximated calculation overestimates the BER. As we increase the number of users, the two sets of results become closer. This is only to be expected as for larger number of users, the Gaussian approximation becomes even more justified. When we add receiver noise into the calculations, the curve obtained almost completely overlaps with the results without noise. The result is the same even if we change the parameters T_0 and F in our calculations. This leads us to the conclusion that for OCDMA systems, MAI is the dominant noise factor, not shot and thermal noise.

SUMMARY

Longer code length is desirable to support more users, which in turn imposes a requirement for wider spectral bandwidth for the case of a coherent system. This translates into the need for use of ultrashort pulses as the input optical signal. Short pulses are more susceptible to fiber dispersion which in turn causes pulse spreading and degradation of received optical peak power. System performance will suffer as a result. In order to study the effects of dispersion on the performance of a phase encoded OCDMA system, an analytical approach based on the method of moments is developed. Further, the rms width and received optical peak power of the pseudo-random optical signal as it propagates along a fiber transmission link were derived and system performance was evaluated for different operating parameters and fiber configurations, using a Gaussian approximation for the pdf for all the signal and noise sources at the receiver.

REFERENCES

Agrawal, G. P. (Ed.). (1997). *Fiber Optic Communication Systems*. New York: Wiley.

Agrawal, G. P. (Ed.). (2002). *Nonlinear Fiber Optics*. Boston: Academic Press.

Anderson, D. (1983, June). Variational Approach to Nonlinear Pulse Propagation in Optical Fibers. *Physical Review A.*, *27*(6), 3135–3145. doi:10.1103/PhysRevA.27.3135

Anderson, D., & Lisak, M. (1987). Analytic Study of Pulse Broadening in Dispersive Optical Fibers. *Physical Review A.*, *35*(1), 184–187. doi:10.1103/PhysRevA.35.184 PMID:9897942

Capmany, J., & Mallea, G. (1999). Autocorrelation Pulse Distortion in Optical Fiber cdma Systems Employing Ladder Networks. *Journal of Lightwave Technology*, *17*(4), 570–578. doi:10.1109/50.754786

Chua, C. H., Abbou, F. M., Chuah, H. T., & Majumder, S. P. (2004, February). Performance Analysis on Phase-encoded ocdma Communication System in Dispersive Fiber Medium. *IEEE Photonics Technology Letters*, *16*(2), 668–670. doi:10.1109/LPT.2003.821240

Chung, F. R. K., Salehi, J. A., & Wei, V. K. (1989). Optical Orthogonal Codes: Design, Analysis, and Applications. *IEEE Transactions on Information Theory*, *35*(3), 595–604. doi:10.1109/18.30982

Fatallah, H., & Rusch, L. A. (1999). Robust Optical FFH-CDMA Communications: Coding in Place of Frequency and Temperature Controls. *Journal of Lightwave Technology*, *17*(8), 1284–1293. doi:10.1109/50.779148

Fatallah, H., Rusch, L. A., & LaRochelle, S. (1999). Passive Optical Fast Frequency-hop CDMA Communication System. *Journal of Lightwave Technology, 17*(3), 397–405. doi:10.1109/50.749379

Goodman, J. W. (2000). *Statistical Optics.* New York: Wiley.

Grunnet-Jepsen, A., Johnson, A. E., Maniloff, E. S., Mossberg, T. W., Munroe, M. J., & Sweetser, J. N. (1999, June). Fiber Bragg Grating Based Spectral Encoder/Decoder for Lightwave CDMA. *Electronics Letters, 35*(13), 1096–1097. doi:10.1049/el:19990722

Igarashi, Y., & Yashima, H. (2001). Performance of Dispersion Compensation for Ultrashort Light Pulse cdma. In *Proceedings of IEEE Region 10 Conference on Electrical and Electronic Technology*, (vol. 2, pp. 769-775). IEEE. doi:10.1109/TENCON.2001.949697

Kwong, W. C., & Prucnal, P. R. (1990). Synchronous cdma Demonstration for Fiber Optic Networks with Optical Processing. *Electronics Letters, 26*(24), 1990–1992. doi:10.1049/el:19901287

Ma, W., Zuo, C., Pu, H., & Lin, J. (2002, May). Performance Analysis on Phase-encoded ocdma Communication System. *Journal of Lightwave Technology, 20*(5), 798–803. doi:10.1109/JLT.2002.1007932

Marhic, M. E. (1993). Coherent Optical cdma Networks. *Journal of Lightwave Technology, 11*(5), 854–864. doi:10.1109/50.233249

Marhic, M. E., & Chang, Y. L. (1989, October). Pulse Coding and Coherent Decoding in Fiber Optic Ladder Networks. *Electronics Letters, 25*(22), 1535–1536. doi:10.1049/el:19891032

Peebles, P. Z. (2001). *Probability, Random Variables and Random Signal Processes.* New York: McGraw-Hill.

Peterson, R. L., Ziemer, R. E., & Borth, D. E. (1995). *Introduction to Spread Spectrum Communications.* Upper Saddle River, NJ: Prentice Hall.

Prucnal, P. R., Santoro, M. A., & Fan, T. R. (1986). Spread Spectrum Fiber Optic Local Area Network Using Optical Processing. *Journal of Lightwave Technology, 4*(5), 547–554. doi:10.1109/JLT.1986.1074754

Prucnal, P. R., Santoro, M. A., & Seghal, S. K. (1986). Ultrafast All-optical Synchronous Multiple Access Fiber Networks. *IEEE Journal on Selected Areas in Communications, 4*(9), 1484–1493. doi:10.1109/JSAC.1986.1146484

Razavi, M., & Salehi, J. A. (2002). Statistical Analysis of Fiber-optic cdma Communication Systems-Part I: Device Modeling. *Journal of Lightwave Technology*, *20*(8), 1304–1316. doi:10.1109/JLT.2002.800298

Razavi, M., & Salehi, J. A. (2002). Statistical Analysis of Fiber-optic cdma Communication Systems-Part II: Incorporating Multiple Optical Amplifiers. *Journal of Lightwave Technology*, *20*(8), 1317–1328. doi:10.1109/JLT.2002.800299

Salehi, J. A. (1989). Code Division Multiple-access Techniques in Optical Fiber Networks-Part I: Fundamental Principles. *IEEE Transactions on Communications*, *37*(8), 824–833. doi:10.1109/26.31181

Salehi, J. A. (1989). Emerging Optical Code-division Multiple Access Communication Systems. *IEEE Network*, *1*(2), 31–39. doi:10.1109/65.21908

Salehi, J. A., & Brackett, C. A. (1989). Code Division Multiple-access Techniques in Optical Fiber Networks-Part II: Systems Performance Analysis. *IEEE Transactions on Communications*, *37*(8), 834–842. doi:10.1109/26.31182

Salehi, J. A., Weiner, A. M., & Heritage, J. P. (1990, March). Coherent Ultrashort Light Pulse Code Division Multiple Access Communication Systems. *Journal of Lightwave Technology*, *8*(3), 478–491. doi:10.1109/50.50743

Sampson, D. D., & Jackson, D. A. (1990). Coherent Optical Fiber Communication System Using all-optical Correlation Processing. *Optics Letters*, *15*(10), 585–587. doi:10.1364/OL.15.000585 PMID:19768016

Sampson, D. D., & Jackson, D. A. (1990). Spread-spectrum Optical Fiber Network Based on Pulsed Coherent Correlation. *Electronics Letters*, *26*(19), 1550–1552. doi:10.1049/el:19900995

Sardesai, H. P., Chang, C. C., & Weiner, A. M. (1998). A femtosecond Code-division Multiple-Access Communication System Test Bed. *Journal of Lightwave Technology*, *167*, 211–224.

Shah, J. (2003). Optical CDMA. *Optics and Photonics News*, 42-47.

Shalaby, H. M. H. (1998). Direct Detection Optical Overlapping PPM-CDMA Communication Systems with Double Optical Hardlimiters. *Journal of Lightwave Technology*, *17*(7), 1158–1165. doi:10.1109/50.774248

Stok, A., & Sargent, E. H. (2000). Lighting the Local Area: Optical Code-division Multiple Access and Quality of Service Provisioning. *IEEE Network*, *14*(6), 42–46. doi:10.1109/65.885669

Tamura, S., Nakano, S., & Akazaki, K. (1985). Optical Code-multiplex Transmission by Gold Sequences. *Journal of Lightwave Technology*, *3*(1), 121–127. doi:10.1109/JLT.1985.1074148

Tsuda, H., Takenouchi, H., Ishii, T., Okamoto, K., Goh, T., & Sato, K. et al. (1999). Spectral Encoding and Decoding of 10Gbit/s Femtosecond Pulses Using High Resolution Arrayed-waveguide Grating. *Electronics Letters*, *35*(14), 1186–1188. doi:10.1049/el:19990783

Vannucci, G., & Yang, S. (1989). Experimental Spreading and Despreading of the Optical Spectrum. *IEEE Transactions on Communications*, *37*(7), 770–780. doi:10.1109/26.31171

Wei, Z., Shalaby, H. M. H., & Ghafouri-Shiraz, H. (2001). Modified Quadratic Congruence Codes for Fiber Bragg-grating-based Spectral-amplitude-coding Optical CDMA Systems. *Journal of Lightwave Technology*, *19*(9), 1274–1281. doi:10.1109/50.948274

Weiner, A. M., Heritage, J. P., & Salehi, J. A. (1988). Encoding and Decoding of Femtosecond Pulse. *Optics Letters*, *10*(4), 300–302. doi:10.1364/OL.13.000300 PMID:19745879

Yang, G. C., & Kwong, W. C. (1997). Performance Comparison of Multiwavelength cdma and wdma+cdma for Fiber-optic Networks. *IEEE Transactions on Communications*, *45*(11), 1426–1434. doi:10.1109/26.649764

Yang, G. C., & Kwong, W. C. (2002). *Prime Codes with Applications to CDMA Optical and Wireless Networks*. Norwood, MA: Artech House.

Yao, X. S., Feinberg, J., Logan, R., & Maleki, L. (1993). Limitations on Peak Pulse Power, Pulse Width, and Coding Mask Misalignment in a Fiber-optic Code Division Multiple-access System. *Journal of Lightwave Technology*, *11*(5), 836–846. doi:10.1109/50.233247

Zuo, C., Ma, W., Pu, H., & Lin, J. (2001). The Impact of Group Velocity on Frequency-hopping Optical Code Division Multiple Access System. *Journal of Lightwave Technology*, *19*(10), 1416–1419. doi:10.1109/50.956128

KEY TERMS AND DEFINITIONS

Bit-Error Rate (BER): Refers to the number of received bits that have been altered due to noise, interference, distortion or bit synchronization errors. Fiber optic communication systems normally have a BER value of 10^{-9}.

Cross-Correlation: Defines a measure of similarity of two different signal waveforms.

Dispersion-Shifted Fiber (DSF): A type of fiber that provides low attenuation and dispersion at 1550 nm.

M-Sequence Code: A maximal length sequence code generated and characterized by a polynomial sequence code using linear feedback shift register (LFSR) circuits.

Multiple Access Interference (MAI): Interference due to overlapping of spectral components from other network users. It severely degrades the system capacity and the signal quality as the number of users increases.

Optical Code Division Multiple Access (OCDMA): A multiple access technique in which several users can send information simultaneously over a single communication channel sharing a band of frequencies without undue interference between them. Orthogonal codes are assigned to different users and the receiver uses the appropriate code to extract the desired signal.

Single-Mode Fiber (SMF): An optical fiber that has a small core diameter and designed to support only one mode of light propagation above the cutoff wavelength.

Section 3

Chapter 7
OTDM–WDM:
Operation Principle

ABSTRACT

The purpose of this chapter is to discuss the operation principle of an OTDM-WDM transmission system. It provides a clear picture about all building blocks of the OTDM-WDM transmission system. It also contains descriptions of various techniques that can be used to generate ultra short optical pulses for OTDM system. The basic principles of multiplexing and demultiplexing and filtering processes are explained by a discussion of several practical scenarios related to OTDM-WDM transmission system.

INTRODUCTION

OTDM-WDM is attractive from two opposing perspectives. Firstly, the integration of WDM in OTDM systems is required to maximize the bandwidth utilization as a pure OTDM system cannot achieve bit rates high enough to fully cover the potentially available bandwidth. Secondly, the integration of OTDM in WDM systems is required to increase the bit rate per WDM channel to reduce the number of WDM channels for reasons mentioned earlier. Thus, the solution looks to combine both OTDM and WDM such that WDM provides the higher hierarchy (high capacity) multiplexing while OTDM takes care of the lower hierarchy tributaries.

DOI: 10.4018/978-1-4666-6575-0.ch007

OTDM: OPERATING PRINCIPLE

Time Division Multiplexing (TDM) in the optical domain is often called optical time domain multiplexing (OTDM) to differentiate it from electrical time domain multiplexing (ETDM) where the same process is performed in the electrical domain. The basic operating principle of OTDM is shown in Figure 1.

In this scheme, the optical transmitters are separately modulated by the signals from different channels where each transmitted laser signal has the same wavelength and operates at the same bit rate, $B_{R,ch}$. The optical pulses from the transmitters are time multiplexed by sending clock signals with different phase shifts to the transmitters. Alternatively, the phase shifts can be induced through the use of time delay lines. The timing of the clock signals is such that the pulse generated from each transmitter (channel) occupies a different, allocated bit slot within each time period, $T = 1 / B_{R,ch}$. The overall bit rate is then given by $B_R = N \times B_{R,ch}$, where N is the number of individual channels. Thus, the bit slot allocated to each channel has the same time length T and the bit slot allocation pattern is repeated throughout the multiplexed OTDM signal. The time multiplexed optical pulses are then transmitted through the optical fiber. Figure 2 shows an example of Intensity Modulated (IM), Return-to-Zero (RZ) pulses undergoing the OTDM process. At the receiving end, the optical pulses have to be demultiplexed by an OTDM demultiplexer. The outputs of the demultiplexer correspond to the output of each time-multiplexed channel. Each of these outputs would then have to be received by separate detectors. The demultiplexing process is shown in Figure 3.

The OTDM process can result in very high speed multiplexed signals with bit rates that can go above 1 Tb/s in some cases (Nakazawa, 2000). The overall speed depends on the number of channels or tributaries that are multiplexed together. Each channel is obtained from the modulation of laser signals using an individual data stream or through ETDM of multiple data streams. Nowadays, the speed of each individual OTDM channel is normally in the range of 10 to 40 Gb/s. This is because

Figure 1. OTDM system block diagram (Hiew, Abbou, & Chuah, 2006)

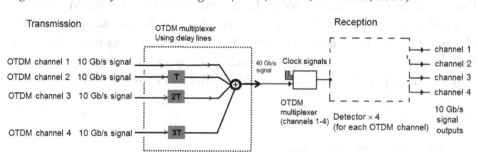

Figure 2. OTDM multiplexing process (4 x 10 Gb/s, 8 ps FWHM Gaussian pulses) (Hiew, Abbou, & Chuah, 2006)

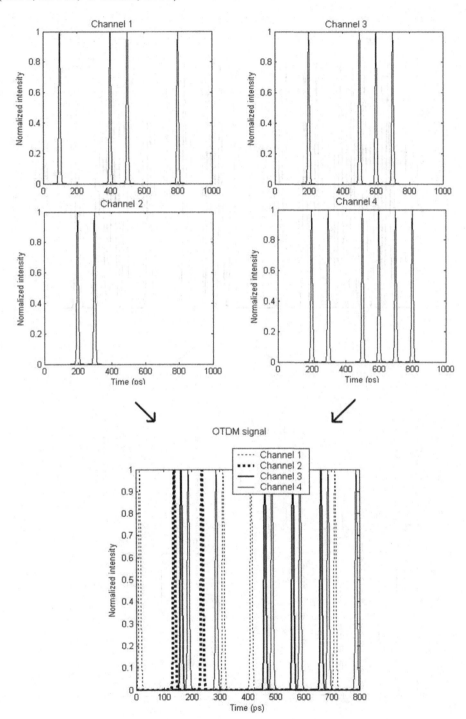

Figure 3. OTDM demultiplexing process (4 x 10 Gb/s, 8 ps FWHM Gaussian pulses)
(Hiew, Abbou, & Chuah, 2006)

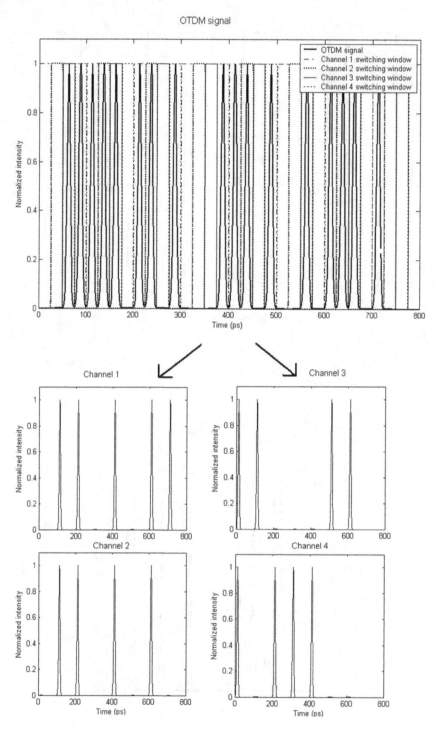

the maximum speed of ETDM is limited to about 40 Gb/s due to the limitations of electronic circuits. At present, 10 Gb/s channels are more common since the electronic equipment used to generate such signals are more cheaply available. Therefore, to increase the data rate, there is no choice but to perform the multiplexing in the optical domain. Ultimately, the capacity of the OTDM system is determined by the total speed of the multiplexed signal, which in turn is limited to the speed that we can reliably transmit through the optical fiber, receive and process.

OTDM DEVICES AND TECHNIQUES

To accomplish OTDM, some specialized devices would be required to perform the multiplexing and demultiplexing. All other devices such as transmitters and receivers are similar to the ones used for single-channel (non-multiplexed) systems except that the demands for TDM devices naturally possess stricter criteria for timing jitter and pulse width of transmission pulses. The high speeds of OTDM signals which require all optical signal processing technologies as conventional electron based technologies are not capable of attaining such speeds. To achieve OTDM using high speed photonic technologies, the key technologies include ultra short optical pulse generation and modulation, all-optical multiplexing and demultiplexing as well as optical timing extraction (Saruwatari, 2000). Some other technologies that are only occasionally used in OTDM, such as all-optical repeating, optical sampling and all-optical signal regeneration, will not be discussed in detail (Vlachos, 2003).

ULTRA SHORT OPTICAL PULSE GENERATION

In order to achieve very high speed OTDM transmission, it naturally follows that the pulse width of the transmitted pulses must be very narrow to accommodate the short bit period. Thus, it is essential for optical sources to generate picosecond transform-limited (TL) chirpless pulses at repetition rates ranging from 10 to 40 GHz. In addition, the repetition rate should be tunable and controllable to permit synchronization with other signals, and oscillation wavelength should be tunable to optimize picosecond pulse transmission. Table 1 summarizes and compares various ultra short optical pulse generation techniques that have been used.

The first method listed in Table 1 is gain switching of distributed feedback laser diodes (DFB-LD) that can generate 5-7 ps nearly TL pulses by applying a down-chirp compensation technique using normal dispersion of dispersion shifted fibers (Takada, Sugie, & Saruwatari, 1987). Due to the ease in tuning its frequency, gain switching has been used in many early experiments. Further reduction to pulses <

Table 1. Ultra short optical pulse generation techniques

Method	Repetition Frequency	$\Delta\tau$ (ps)	$\Delta\tau . \Delta\nu$	Comment
Gain switching of DFB-LD	arbitrary	~ 20 (6) (0.8)	> TL (~ TL) (~ TL)	down-chirping (with chirp compensation: CC) (with CC + adiabatic soliton compression)
CW + EA modulator	arbitrary	~ 15 (2.5)	~ TL (~ TL)	relatively large pulse width (with adiabatic soliton compression)
Mode-locking of LD	Fixed	~ 10 (< 1)	> TL (~ TL)	conventional type (CPM-type or EA modelocker)
Harmonic mode-locking of EDF laser	Tunable	~ 3	TL	wavelength tunable, ~ 20 nm
SC generation in DSF	Tunable	< 1	~ TL	wavelength tunable, > 200 nm

3ps can be achieved using nonlinear pulse compression techniques such as an adiabatic soliton compression technique incorporated together with the linear chirp compensation technique.

The second method is gating of continuous wave (CW) light with sinusoidally driven electro-absorption (EA) modulators (Suzuki, 1992). This is based on the nonlinear transmittance of EA modulators and can generate nearly TL pulses with relatively large pulse widths. To improve this, adiabatic soliton compression can be used.

The third method is mode-locking of Laser Diode (LD) (Chen, 1991), which is capable of producing very narrow optical pulse widths. Utilizing a new type of LD capable of colliding-pulse mode-locking (CPM), pulses less than 1 ps duration has been demonstrated. The main drawback of this method is non-tunability of repetition frequency and a relatively large spectral width as compared with the TL condition. To improve the operation characteristics, various new mode-locked LDs have been studied such as sub-picosecond pulse generation from an active mode-locked monolithic multi-quantum well (MQW) LD integrated with MQW-EA modulators, repetition-rate tunable lasers using passive mode-locking of micro-mechanically tunable LDs and femtosecond optical pulse generation from an active mode-locked LD.

The fourth method is harmonic mode-locking of erbium-doped fiber (EDF) laser (Takada, & Miyazawa, 1990), which can generate purely TL pulses without requiring any chirp compensation or pulse compression. EDF lasers are normally tens of meters long as it consists of a length of fiber. However, such lasers are difficult to stabilize and various methods have been developed to try to overcome this, including using a high-finesse Fabry-Perot (FP) etalon, dithering the cavity length and using a polarization maintaining cavity.

The fifth method is supercontinuum (SC) generation in a dispersion shifted fiber (DSF) pumped with an intense picosecond pulse. When an intense optical pulse transits over a low dispersion fiber, an SC pulse, which has a wide spectral range, is induced through the combined effects of various optical nonlinear processes (Mori, 1997). For example, 1542 nm, 3 ps TL pulses from a 6.3GHz mode-locked EDF laser transmitted over 3 km of dispersion shifted fiber can generate an SC pulse with a 200 nm wide spectrum ranging from 1450 nm to 1650 nm. The SC spectrum exhibits continuous, flat-top broadening as well as some coherency. It has been shown that the desired flatly broadened SC spectrum can be generated from a dispersion decreasing fiber. SC generation is capable of producing very short pulse widths up to the femtosecond range. However, its main advantage is its wide, flatly-broadened spectrum, which is extremely suitable to use in generating WDM signals.

ALL-OPTICAL TDM MULTIPLEXER/DEMULTIPLEXER

The function of the multiplexer is to combine individual tributaries into the higher hierarchy signal while the demultipexer is used to reverse the process and they are both crucial to OTDM systems. The operational speed of conventional, electronics-based TDM techniques is limited to around 40 Gb/s. Thus, all-optical multiplexing/demultiplexing (MUX/DEMUX) is a critical issue, which requires special devices.

To realize high speed OTDM systems, a stable optical MUX is required. A compact MUX using planar lightwave circuits called PLCs are commonly used. The PLC-MUX is based on the principle of multistage interferometer-type multiplexing using delay lines. These devices are not real MUXs that serve to combine different channels, but they are very efficient for generating high speed OTDM test signals from an original low speed signal. Actual all-optical modulation applied for TDM MUX operation was reported using four wave mixing (FWM) in a traveling-wave semiconductor amplifier (TW-SOA) (Kawanishi & Kamatani, 1994) where a higher repetition rate optical pulse train is all-optically modulated by full sets of lower speed optical signals. Another method for TDM MUX demonstrated utilizes an ultra short optical pulse source and highly dispersive fibers to cause linearly chirped pulse broadening.

All-optical DEMUXs are key devices for developing high speed OTDM systems. Various all-optical DEMUX techniques are listed below:

1. Optical Kerr switch,
2. **Four Wave Mixing (FWM) Switch:** Fiber, semiconductor optical amplifier (SOA),
3. Cross phase modulation (XPM) switch,
4. **Loop Mirror:** NOLM, SLALOM, TOAD.

The first DEMUX operation at 2Gb/s was demonstrated with an optical Kerr switch. However, this device is highly polarization-sensitive and requires complete birefringence compensation for higher speed operation (Morioka, Saruwatari, & Takada, 1987). It is difficult for the Kerr switch to operate without polarization dependence.

The second method uses the FWM process that occurs in silica fiber or SOAs. This method is capable of very stable, polarization-insensitive operation when using polarization maintaining fibers called PANDA fibers. All-optical demultiplexing at very high speeds such as 500 Gb/s (Morioka, 1996) have been demonstrated with this technique using PANDA fibers as a nonlinear media. However, it is expected that FWM in SOAs is a more realistic DEMUX because of the SOAs compact size and no wavelength limitation as compared to FWM in fibers. Results have been demonstrated at high speeds and the performance is highly dependent on the characteristics of the SOA used.

The third method is the XPM switch (Patrick & Ellis, 1993), which utilizes the XPM effect that occurs in fibers or SOAs. The process induces frequency shifts that are capable of creating simple DEMUXs because interferometry is not required. This method can also provide multiple, simultaneous outputs from a single DEMUX operation on the OTDM signal.

The fourth method is a promising DEMUX configuration that uses the concept of loop mirrors. Most of these systems use the concept of induced phase shift from effects such as the nonlinear XPM as its underlying operating principle. Signals are propagated through loops of nonlinear media suitably tailored to achieve the desired DEMUX operation. A commonly used loop mirror is the nonlinear optical loop mirror (NOLM) based on the Sagnac interferometer (Doran & Wood, 1988). It utilizes the interference between two counter-propagating optical signals propagating through the same fiber loop. The NOLM switch has low required power and can use small nonlinearity media such as silica fibers because it can be of very long lengths. Multiple channel output has been performed and 640 Gb/s DEMUX operation has been demonstrated using dispersion flattened fibers. Other loop mirror configurations include the semiconductor laser amplifier in a loop mirror configuration called SLALOM and the terahertz optical asymmetric demultiplexer called TOAD. The underlying principle behind the different loop mirror configurations are generally the same. However, in the case of SLALOM or TOAD, the XPM effect occurs in SOAs inside hybrid arrangements of fiber loop mirrors with SOAs.

Recently, interferometric devices such as the Mach-Zehnder interferometer with integrated SOAs have also been used as switching elements (Pieper, 1997). The MZI is a general interferometer configuration commonly used in optical communication systems for a variety of purposes, including filtering, wavelength conversion, signal modulation, signal demodulation, mutiplexing and demultiplexing. The block diagram of the MZI is shown in Figure 4.

As can be seen, the MZI is a very simple device consisting of an input with its coupler, two separate arms and an output with its coupler. The idea is to propagate the input through two separate arms that possess different characteristics such as different lengths that would induce a different propagation delay on either arm. The signals from the two arms are then mixed together again in the output to obtain the sum of the signals in one arm and the difference in the other. By adjusting the characteristics of both arms including properties such as gain and using the outputs of either arm accordingly, many different uses can be found for the MZI. The MZI can be constructed simply by connecting the two output ports of a 3 dB coupler to the two input ports of another 3 dB coupler. There are other constructions but the underlying configuration is the same. For OTDM demultiplexing, the received OTDM signal will be fed through one arm while a reference clock signal is fed through the other arm.

Optical Timing Extraction

Optical timing extraction is the process of extracting the timed clock from the received optical signals. Normally, for non-TDM optical signal transmission, clock extraction is required to time the sampling instances of the decision level circuit in the receiver. For OTDM systems, the optical timing is also essential for the operation of a variety of devices such as demultiplexers, repeaters and optical signal processing

Figure 4. MZI block diagram (Hiew, Abbou, & Chuah, 2006)

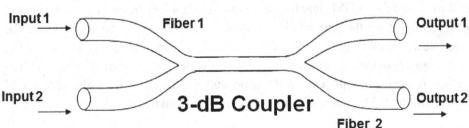

devices. Most importantly, the clock signal is required for OTDM demultiplexing to function properly. Requirements for optical timing extraction include ultra-fast operation, low phase noise, high sensitivity and phase insensitivity. Once again, the highest operating speed of current electrical timing circuits is about 40 GHz determined by the microwave mixer used as a phase detector in a phase-lock loop (PLL) circuit. Thus, optical timing extraction techniques are required. Various techniques are listed below:

1.   **Optical Tank Circuit:** Fabry-Perot etalon, Brillouin gain in fiber.
2.   **Injection Locking:** Self pulsating DFB-LD, mode-locked LD, mode-locked fiber laser.
3.   **Phase Lock Loop (PLL):** Electrical PLL, $LiNbO_3$ modulator, gain modulation in TW-SOA, FWM in SOA, FWM in fiber.

An optical tank circuit is a passive structure that extracts the carrier spectral component and line spectral components from the received signal in the frequency domain through the use of a filter such as the FP resonator (Jinno & Matsumoto, 1992) or using the narrow bandwidth Brillouin gain in an optical fiber. The configuration is simple but attainable speeds of operation have also been low.

Injection locking utilizes self-pulsating LDs such as multielectrode LDs, optical inverters and self-pulsating DFB-LDs or mode-locked fiber lasers, whose output repetition frequency is locked to that of an injected optical pulse train (Sartorius, 1998). Using these techniques, 5 GHz and 10 GHz clocks can be generated all-optically. However, so far these techniques have not been good enough in terms of root mean square (rms) timing jitter and relative phase error, to be used for very high speed operation.

A PLL in principle has no phase error and results in complete retiming. In practice, this is limited by how fast the PLL can operate. As mentioned before, the operational speed of electrical PLL circuits is limited by the response of the phase comparators used; thus, photonics based cross-correlation techniques have been developed. Early methods utilized the recovery of a residual low speed, single channel frequency component from the overall high bit rate received signal. This process was demonstrated using a TW-SOA as an all-optical phase correlator. However, in real multiplexed OTDM signals, there is no residual low frequency clock component and to extract the retimed clock, the phase detection must be performed at the multiplexed clock frequency. Some of the methods used include a PLC multiplier utilizing gain modulation in the SOA or a prescaler PLL circuit utilizing the harmonic frequency components of the short optical clock and the high-speed FWM process in the SOA (Kamatani, Kawanishi, & Saruwatari, 1994).

WDM: OPERATING PRINCIPLE

The basic operating principle is shown in Figure 5. In this scheme, different signals from different channels are used to modulate the laser sources separately where each laser source is operated on a different center frequency or wavelength. Note that the wavelength and frequency of electromagnetic wave are inter-related through the well-known formula of $\nu = f\lambda$, where ν is the velocity of the electromagnetic (EM) wave, f is the frequency and λ is the wavelength. The output signals from the different sources are then combined in the frequency or wavelength domain by a WDM multiplexer.

As each laser source would have a different center frequency, the signals for each channel would occupy a different, allocated space in the frequency spectrum. The combined signal is passed through the fiber. The process is shown in Figure 6.

At the receiving end, a WDM demultiplexer separates the different channels occupying different spectral locations, which are then detected by separate receivers. The WDM demultiplexer performs functionally as a set of bandpass optical filters, each with a different center frequency that corresponds to the center frequency of the target channel, and the output of each filter is sent to separate detectors. The process is shown in Figure 7.

Using WDM, we can allocate many channels at different spectral locations to effectively 'fill up' the amount of bandwidth available for transmission in the optical fiber. In this case, the limit to total WDM system capacity is determined by the total bandwidth available and the efficiency in which we utilize this bandwidth.

Figure 5. WDM system block diagram (Hiew, Abbou, & Chuah, 2006)

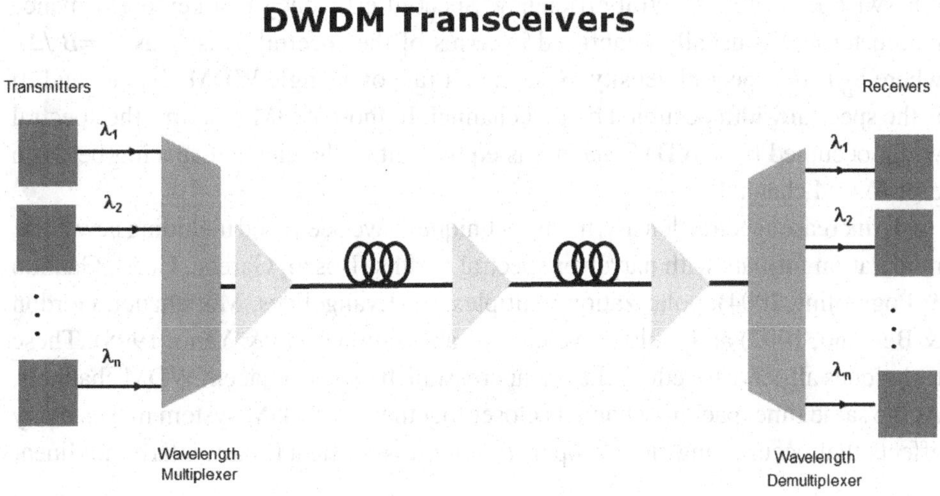

DWDM Transceivers

Transmitters — λ_1, λ_2, λ_n — Wavelength Multiplexer

Receivers — λ_1, λ_2, λ_n — Wavelength Demultiplexer

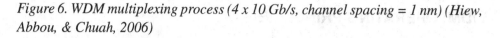

Figure 6. WDM multiplexing process (4 x 10 Gb/s, channel spacing = 1 nm) (Hiew, Abbou, & Chuah, 2006)

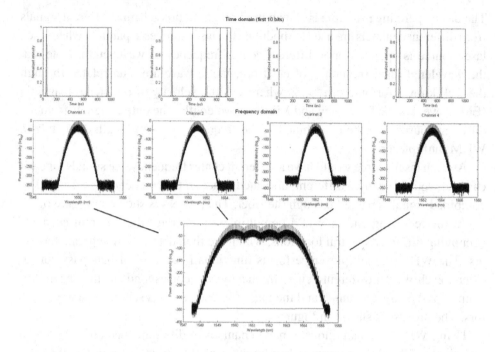

Nowadays, the total bandwidth available in the silica optical fiber for use in optical communication is limited by the bandwidth of the amplifiers used to overcome propagation loss along the system, thus there is a specified limit to the spectral width available for use in communication. Therefore, to increase the system capacity, we have to §increase the amount of information transmitted per unit of spectral width, otherwise known as spectral efficiency. Spectral efficiency is a key performance parameter and is usually quantified in terms of the spectral density as $S_D = B_R / \Delta f$, where S_D is the spectral density, B_R is the bit rate of a single WDM channel and Δf is the spectral width occupied by that channel. In most WDM systems, the spectral width occupied by a WDM channel is equivalent to the channel spacing between each WDM channel.

To increase spectral density, many techniques have been used including new pulse modulation formats with narrower spectral widths (Bosco, Garena, Curri, Gaundo & Poggiolini, 2004), polarization multiplexing (Evangelides, Mollenauer, Gordon & Bergano, 1992) and multi-wavelength stabilization (Ono & Yano, 1998). These techniques all serve to reduce the linear crosstalk between adjacent WDM channels. At the same time, packing channels closer together in a WDM system makes many effects that occur along fiber propagation more significant, particularly nonlinear

Figure 7. WDM demultiplexing process (4 x 10 Gb/s, channel spacing = 1 nm) (Hiew, Abbou, & Chuah, 2006)

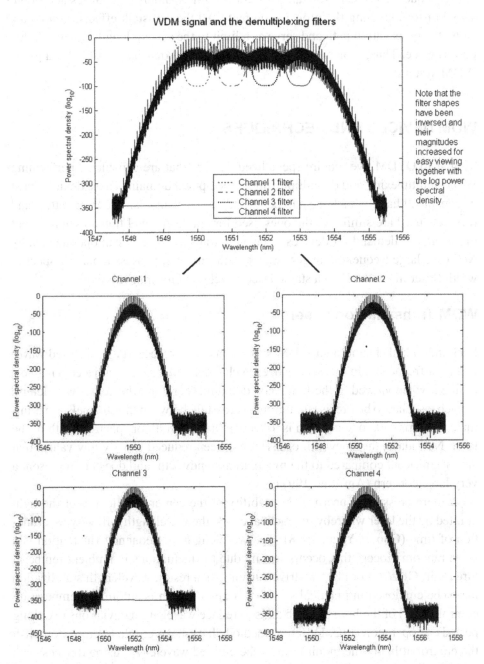

effects such as cross phase modulation (XPM) and four wave mixing (FWM). These effects induce nonlinear crosstalk between WDM channels that causes additional signal distortion along the propagation path. All the crosstalk effects accumulate along the propagation path and serve as a limit to the system length and to reliable performance. Thus, it also puts a limit to the spectral density possible for a given WDM system.

WDM DEVICES AND TECHNIQUES

Similar to OTDM, we require specialized devices that are capable of performing WDM multiplexing and demultiplexing in the optical domain. These devices must be capable of handling a large number of individual channels. The transmitters and receivers used are similar to the ones used for single channel transmission except that there is a demand for devices, especially transmitters that can operate equally well over large frequency ranges (wavelength tunable), possess a narrow spectral width (laser linewidth) and a stable laser wavelength for transmission.

WDM Transmission Lasers

Each individual channel in a WDM system has to be placed at a designated wavelength or frequency. In this scenario, each channel will have two adjacent channels beside it when viewed in the frequency domain. Therefore, the center wavelength of each laser has to be precise to minimize crosstalk between the channels. To minimize this crosstalk, one concern is to reduce the linewidth or spectral width of the laser. Nowadays, the linewidth of lasers has been reduced to very low values that are insignificant compared to the modulation bandwidth, and does not represent a very large concern (Agrawal, 1997).

A more pressing concern is the stability of the center wavelength of the light emitted by the laser whereby in practical cases, the wavelength will vary as a function of time (Ono & Yano, 1998). The wavelength or frequency fluctuation is a slow, random process that occurs mainly due to fluctuations in ambient temperature (unit: GHz/°C) or electric drive current. As a result, wavelength stabilization has to be employed in practical systems. A key concern is automatic temperature control (ATC) of the lasers, which aims to reduce wavelength deviations over long periods of operation time. Different methods have been employed to accomplish the control utilizing the monitoring of the emitted wavelength using devices such as a FP cavity, an arrayed waveguide grating (AWG) and a Fourier spectroscopic multiwavelength meter.

Another area of interest is the generation of the carrier laser signal itself. Many systems still use DFB or distributed Bragg reflector (DBR) semiconductor lasers as a laser source. Each WDM channel is generated with its own laser. However to maintain flexibility, these laser sources need to be independently wavelength tunable. The wavelength of the transmitted light can be tuned by methods such as Bragg gratings (Agrawal, 1997). Nowadays, monolithically integrated WDM transmitters are often used, whereby light emission and multiplexing is carried out together in an integrated device.

Tunable Optical Filter

Before we look into practical, large-scale multiplexers and demultiplexers for WDM systems, we will first look into the basic device that provides the functionality of frequency/wavelength selection, which is the optical filter shown in Figure 8. Let us first clarify that the optical filter is used in practically all optical communication systems, not just in WDM systems. In fact, it is generally used as well in single channel and OTDM systems that employ optical amplification. This helps crucially reduce amplifier noise. This is dealt with in detail in a later section. In the case of any frequency multiplexed signals such as the WDM system, an optical filter can be used to filter out any particular channel out of the overall WDM signal spectra.

For practical systems, tunable optical filters, which can filter out one channel at a specific wavelength that can be changed by tuning the passband of the optical filter, are needed. This filter needs to be placed just before the receiver. Optimiza-

Figure 8. Optical filter shape examples (Bandwidth = 120 GHz) (Hiew, Abbou, & Chuah, 2006)

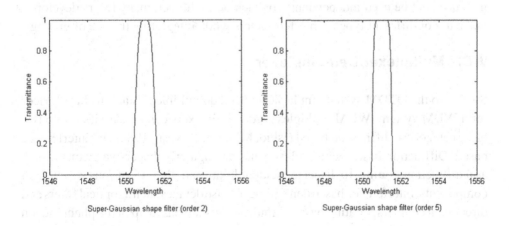

Super-Gaussian shape filter (order 2)   Super-Gaussian shape filter (order 5)

tion of the filter bandwidth is normally required as there are two important factors that react oppositely to changes in the filter bandwidth. A small bandwidth would cut off high frequency portions of the signal causing the signal pulses to broaden in the time domain, inducing a phenomenon known as intersymbol interference (ISI). On the other hand, a large bandwidth might overlap into the spectrum of adjacent WDM channels, thus causing linear crosstalk between channels.

The desirable properties in a tunable optical filter include wide tuning range to maximize a range of channels that can be selected, sharp filter roll-off rate to reduce adjacent channel crosstalk, fast tuning speed to minimize access time, small insertion loss, polarization insensitivity, stability against environmental changes and low cost.

Three common tunable optical filters used are the Fabry-Perot (FP) filter (Keiser, 2000), the Mach-Zehnder (MZ) filter and grating based filters. The FP filter is based on the FP interferometer that consists of a cavity formed by two highly reflecting mirrors. This configuration is in fact the one used for semiconductor lasers. It can be made tunable by techniques such as controlling the length of the cavity by using a piezoelectric transducer or changing the refractive index of a liquid crystal cavity FP filter.

A Mach Zehnder tunable optical filter consists of a chain of MZIs. The first coupler shifts the input signal into two equal parts, which acquire different phase shifts if the arm lengths are made different, before they interfere again at the next coupler. This is repeated along the chain. Since the relative phase shift is wavelength dependent, the transmitivity is also wavelength dependent, thus it can function as a filter. By adjusting the arm lengths of the chain suitably, we can tune the filter accordingly.

Another class of filters is grating-based filters that make use of the wavelength selectivity provided by gratings such as the Bragg grating (Born & Wolf, 1980). There are many ways to construct such gratings including fiber Bragg gratings (Bennion, Williams, Zhang, & Sugden, 1996). On the whole, the class of filters presented here need not be used independently of each other. In fact, many filters developed make use of different type of interferometers while integrating the use of gratings.

WDM Multiplexer/Demultiplexer

Similar to the OTDM system, multiplexers and demultiplexers are the key devices for a WDM system. WDM multiplexers/demultiplexers can be classified into two basic categories: diffraction based (Ishio, Minowa, & Nosu, 1984) and interference based. Diffraction based demultiplexers use an angularly dispersive element, such as a diffraction grating, to disperse incident light spatially into various wavelength components. Interference based demultiplexers use devices such as optical filters and directional couplers. Grating based demultiplexers are based upon the phenomenon of Bragg diffraction from an optical grating. The underlying principle is that the input WDM signal is focused onto a reflection grating that splits various wavelength components spatially, and these separate components are then focused onto individual fibers using a lens. If the components are split and separated properly, the resultant output of the various individual fibers would be the demultiplexed channels.

Filter based demultiplexers are based on the phenomenon of optical interference. The most popular filter used to make the demultiplexers is the MZ filter. The chain of MZIs can create a WDM demultiplexer when properly constructed. The advantage of the MZI structure is that it can be fabricated on compact semiconductor slabs or PLCs. An integrated approach to demultiplexing makes use of a phased array of optical waveguides that acts as a grating. These devices are commonly called arrayed waveguide gratings (AWG) and are widely used nowadays (Hibino, 2002; Uetsuka, 2004). They can be fabricated using semiconductor substrate technology (InGaAsP/InP technology), thus permitting the integration of the demultiplexer with photodiodes to produce integrated WDM receivers. The basic idea is similar to the grating based filters. The incoming WDM signal is coupled into an array of planar waveguides after a coupling section. The signal propagating within each waveguide experiences a different phase shift due to the different lengths of the waveguides. The phase shifts are wavelength dependent because of the frequency dependence of the mode propagation constant. At the output, the different channels focus onto different spatial spots through another coupling section.

The efficiency of the AWG can be close to 100% (Dragone, 1989) and proper design can lead to polarization insensitivity (Spiekman, 1996). AWGs have become the most popular option due to its advantages of low insertion loss (improved by spot size converters), capability of handling vast number of channels in a WDM signal (up to 400 nowadays) and integrability into a compact module as a PLC. Recent advances in AWG technology is discussed in (Uetsuka, 2004; Dragone, 1989).

So far, we have focused on WDM demultiplexers only. This is because WDM multiplexers use the same devices as the demultiplexers. This can be done because the functionality of the device depends on the direction of propagation because of the inherent reciprocity of optical waves in a dielectric media. For example, we can use the AWG as a multiplexer by inputting the various individual channels into the output end of the demultiplexer. The reciprocal process would multiplex all the channels together into one WDM signal at the other end. For this reason, AWGs can be integrated together with semiconductor laser sources to produce integrated WDM transmitters.

WDM Transmitters and Receivers

Integrated transmitters mean fully operational WDM transmitters that include the tunable laser sources of the different channels and the multiplexer (normally AWG), all connected together within a compact module. Sometimes, other devices may be included within such as built-in amplifiers and electro-absorption (EA) modulators. Integrated WDM receivers consist of the demultiplexer along with the photodiode array used for optical detection. Electronic amplifiers can also be integrated.

Within the integrated module, the devices are connected together through silica paths or waveguides. Using the InP-based optoelectronic integrated circuit (OEIC) technology, monolithically integrated WDM transmitters and receivers have been developed. Hybrid integrated transmitters and receivers have also been developed using PLCs fabricated with silica-on-silicon technology (Uetsuka, 2004). These devices are compact, have low power consumption and eliminate the need for many individual devices that have to be separately controlled.

As mentioned earlier, another method fast attracting attention is supercontinuum generation (SC). This method can produce ultra short optical pulses for high bit rate systems but this is not a major WDM concern as the bit rate of each individual channel is low unlike the OTDM signal. The advantage lies in the wide, flatly broadened SC spectra, whereby many WDM channels can be produced at arbitrary wavelengths from a single SC spectra by merely filtering out the desired wavelengths (Agrawal, 2001) using devices such as the AWG WDM demultiplexer. This reduces the need for many separate DFB-LDs for each WDM channel and the associated ATC for each laser diode. At the same time, this method can generate ultra short pulses for each individual WDM channel, clearing the way for future systems employing high bit rates per individual WDM channel. Furthermore, the output WDM pulses feature a very low jitter (<0.3 ps for 15 ps pulses) and good frequency stability (1.26 GHz/°C) (Morioka, 1995).

OTDM-WDM SYSTEM

The general OTDM-WDM system diagram is shown in Figure 9. OTDM is used to multiplex lower rate bit streams and the resultant high bit rate OTDM signal is treated as a WDM channel. Multiple WDM channels are then multiplexed together to create a high capacity WDM signal that maximizes transmission capacity over the fiber length.

Before we look further into the operation of the system, first let us explore why this system has been proposed as a possible solution to future high capacity, multi-terabit/s optical transmission systems. The basic driving force for the implementa-

Figure 9. OTDM-WDM system block diagram (Hiew, Abbou, & Chuah, 2006)

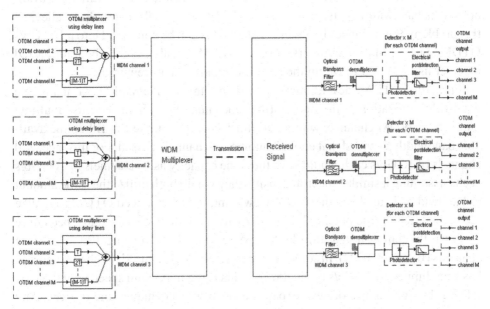

tion of multiplexed systems is to push towards ever increasing capacities of optical transmission systems. To this end, we first examine the future prospects of OTDM and WDM technologies separately as we aim for increased capacity.

From the OTDM development viewpoint, we can expect that it will be very difficult for a purely OTDM system to fully utilize the potential capacity of the optical fiber. As mentioned earlier, the total bandwidth available for use in transmission through the optical fiber is limited by the gain bandwidth of the optical amplifiers used. Depending on how these amplifiers are pumped, their operation can be separated into different bands such as the C or L (Srivastave, 2000) bands that cover different frequency ranges. Assuming an available bandwidth of about 100 nm, this roughly converts in terms of frequency to about 12500 GHz or 12.5 THz. Even if we assume a modest spectral density value of 1 b/s/Hz, this means that the combined OTDM signal would need to attain a bit rate of 12.5 Tb/s to fully utilize the bandwidth. This translates to a bit period of 80 fs, a pulse width too short to be attained by any means currently available. More importantly, such a short bit period makes the signal extremely vulnerable to timing jitter that occurs either in devices or through fiber propagation. Increasing the spectral density to increase system capacity, would further increase the required bit rate and reduce the bit period.

It can be seen that a single OTDM signal is not feasible to fully utilize the available fiber bandwidth. Thus, combining OTDM with WDM can help to alleviate this problem. For instance, 16 channels of 10 Gb/s can be combined into a 160 Gb/s OTDM signal. Multiple numbers of these OTDM signals can then be multiplexed together using WDM to fill up the available bandwidth as required.

From the OTDM development viewpoint, the problem of maximizing the bandwidth utilization in the optical fiber does not exist. This is because multiple numbers of WDM channels with an arbitrary channel bit rate can fill up the available bandwidth provided that enough number of channels is used. For instance, 240 channels of 10 Gb/s each would have the same capacity as 15 channels of 160 Gb/s each. Assuming a similar spectral density, they would both utilize the same amount of bandwidth. Thus, from the WDM viewpoint, it does not need OTDM to realize the optical fiber's true potential. Indeed, many modern systems and test beds have successfully demonstrated ultra high capacity transmission using 10 Gb/s WDM channels (Bergano, 2002). In some other cases, the individual WDM channel bit rate has been limited to 40 Gb/s (Cai, 2002) as this is the maximum speed attainable by ETDM through the use of new, expensive electronic techniques and devices. Any further increase would necessitate the use of OTDM.

Further, the integration of OTDM into purely WDM would greatly assist in the creation of all-optical networks (Castanon, Tonguz, & Bononi, 1997; Varvarigos, 1998). The idea is to create seamless integrated high speed communication networks that reside purely in the optical domain without the need for optoelectronic conversion that can become a potential bottleneck when there is a need to upgrade the network speed.

SUMMARY

By using OTDM to increase the individual channel rate, the number of WDM channels required would be decreased. This is an advantage because the number of WDM channels in the main high capacity trunk lines can become very large. For instance, the aforementioned 12.5 THz bandwidth would require 1250 WDM channels of 10 Gb/s per channel at a spectral density of 1 b/s/Hz. The problem with utilizing large numbers of WDM channels is a matter of cost. This is because each WDM channel would need its own laser source and its associated ATC. Also, the number of detectors and filters would also need to be increased. As reliable, high-speed laser sources are very expensive to purchase and maintain, any reductions in the number of WDM channels used in a system are helpful. By utilizing OTDM to generate high bit rate WDM channels, we can reduce the number of WDM channels required to fill up a specified amount of transmission bandwidth.

Further, utilizing OTDM allows for the use of different multiplexing techniques at lower capacity distribution lines depending on suitability and previously installed hardware. The reduction of WDM channels also distributes the load of channel management to distributed nodes. The main line no longer needs to manage large amounts of channels in small distribution packages but only the high speed OTDM signals. The task of breaking down the high speed signals gradually to its lower speed tributaries can be distributed to nodes that lie along the distribution line to the end user. In this sense, OTDM is easier to use in the lower end distribution line to split the high bit rate signal down into lower bit rate tributaries.

REFERENCES

Agrawal, G. P. (Ed.). (1997). *Fiber-Optic Communication Systems*. Wiley-Interscience.

Agrawal, G. P. (Ed.). (2001). *Nonlinear Fiber Optics*. Academic Press.

Bennion, I., Williams, J. A. R., Zhang, L., Sugden, K., & Doran, N. J. (1996). Uv-written in-fibre Bragg gratings. *Optical and Quantum Electronics*, 28(2), 93. doi:10.1007/BF00278281

Bergano, N. S. (2002). *640 gb/s Transmission of Sixty-four 10 gb/s wdm Channels over 7200 km with 0.33 (bits/s)/hz Spectral Efficiency*. Academic Press.

Born, M., & Wolf, E. (1980). *Principles of Optics*. Oxford, UK: Pergamon Press.

Borne, D. V. D., Sandel, N. E., Khoe, G. D., & Waardt, H. D. (2004). Pmd and Nonlinearity-induced Penalties on Polarization-multiplexed Transmission. *IEEE Photonics Technology Letters*, 16(9), 2174–2176. doi:10.1109/LPT.2004.833079

Bosco, G., Carena, A., Curri, V., Gaudino, R., & Poggiolini, P. (2002). On the Use of nrz, rz and csrz Modulation at 40 gb/s with Narrow dwdm Channel Spacing. *Journal of Lightwave Technology*, 20(9), 1694–1704. doi:10.1109/JLT.2002.806309

Bosco, G., Carena, A., Curri, V., Gaudino, R., & Poggiolini, P. (2004). Modulation Formats Suitable for Ultrahigh Spectral Efficient wdm Systems. *IEEE Journal of Selected Topics in Quantum Electronics*, 10(2), 321–328. doi:10.1109/JSTQE.2004.827830

Cai, J. X. (2002). Long-haul 40 gb/s dwdm Transmission with Aggregate Capacities Exceeding 1 tb/s. *Journal of Lightwave Technology*, 20(12), 2247–2257. doi:10.1109/JLT.2002.806770

Cartaxo, A. V. T. (1999). Cross-phase Modulation in Intensity Modulation – Direct Detection wdm Systems with Multiple optical Amplifiers and Dispersion Compensators. *Journal of Lightwave Technology, 17*(2), 178–190. doi:10.1109/50.744218

Castanon, G. A., Tonguz, O. K., & Bononi, A. (1997). Ber Performance of Multiwavelength Optical Cross-connected Networks with Deflection Routing. *IEEE Proc-Communicaions, 144,* 114-120

Chen, M., Wu, M. C., Tanbun-Ek, T., Logan, R. A., & Chin, M. A. (1991). Subpicosecond Monolithic Colliding-pulse Mode-locked Multiple Quantum-well Lasers. *Applied Physics Letters, 58*(12), 1253–1258. doi:10.1063/1.104327

Chiang, T. K., Kagi, N., Marhic, M. E., & Kazovsky, L. G. (1996). Cross-phase Modulation in Fiber Links with Multiple Optical Amplifiers and Dispersion Compensators. *Journal of Lightwave Technology, 14*(3), 249–260. doi:10.1109/50.485582

Desurvire, E. (1994). *Erbium-doped fiber amplifiers: Principles and Applications.* New York: Wiley-Interscience.

Doran, N. J., & Wood, D. (1988). Nonlinear-optical Loop Mirror. *Optics Letters, 13*(1), 56–58. doi:10.1364/OL.13.000056 PMID:19741979

Dragone, C. (1989). Efficient N*N star couplers using Fourier optics. *Journal of Lightwave Technology, 7*(3), 479–489. doi:10.1109/50.16884

Duce, A. D., Killey, R. I., & Bayvel, P. (2004). Comparison of Nonlinear Pulse Interactions in 160-gb/s Quasi-Linear and Dispersion Managed Soliton Systems. *Journal of Lightwave Technology, 22,* 1483–1498.

Evangelides, S. G., Mollenauer, L. F., Gordon, J. P., & Bergano, N. S. (1992). Polarization Multiplexing with Solitons. *Journal of Lightwave Technology, 10*(1), 28–35. doi:10.1109/50.108732

Gnauck, A. H., Raybon, G., Bernasconi, P. G., Leuthold, J., Doerr, C. R., & Stulz, L. W. (2003). 1-tb/s (6 x 170.6 gb/s) Transmission over 2000-km nzdf Using otdm and rz-dpsk Format. *IEEE Photonics Technol, 15*(11), 1618–1620. doi:10.1109/LPT.2003.818634

Hibino, H. (2002). Recent Advances in High-density and Large-scale awg Multi/Demultiplexers with Higher Index-contrast Silica-based plcs. *IEEE Journal of Selected Topics in Quantum Electronics,* 8.

Hiew, C. C., Abbou, F. M., & Chuah, H. T. (2006). *Performance Analysis and Design of an Optical TDM-WDM Transmission System and Network* (Tech. Rep. No. 1). Malaysia: Multimedia University and Alcatel Network Systems.

Ishio, H., Minowa, J., & Nosu, K. (1984). Review and status of wavelength-division-multiplexing technology and its application. *Journal of Lightwave Technology, 2*(4), 448–463. doi:10.1109/JLT.1984.1073653

Jinno, M., & Matsumoto, T. (1992). Optical Tank Circuits Used for All-optical Timing Recovery. *IEEE Journal of Selected Topics in Quantum Electronics, 28*(4), 895–900. doi:10.1109/3.135207

Kahn, J. M., & Ho, K. P. (2004). Spectral Efficiency Limits and Modulation/Detection Techniques for dwdm Systems. *IEEE Journal of Selected Topics in Quantum Electronics, 10*(2), 259–272. doi:10.1109/JSTQE.2004.826575

Kamatani, O., Kawanishi, S., & Saruwatari, M. (1994). Prescaled 6.3 ghz Clock Recovery from 50 gbit/s tdm Optical Signal with 50 ghz pll Using Four-wave Mixing in a Traveling-wave Laser Diode Optical Amplifier. *Electronics Letters, 30*(10), 807–809. doi:10.1049/el:19940546

Kawanishi, S., & Kamatani, O. (1994). All-optical Time Division Multiplexing Using Four-wave Mixing. *Electronics Letters, 30*(20), 1697–1698. doi:10.1049/el:19941153

Keiser, G. (2000). *Optical Fiber Communications*. McGraw-Hill.

Kumar, S., Mauro, J. C., Raghavan, S., & Chowdhury, D. Q. (2002). Intrachannel Nonlinear Penalties in Dispersion-managed Transmission Systems. *IEEE Journal of Selected Topics in Quantum Electronics, 8*(3), 626–631. doi:10.1109/JSTQE.2002.1016366

Lichtman, E. (1995). Limitations Imposed by Polarization-dependent Gain and Loss on All-Optical Ultralong Communication Systems. *Journal of Lightwave Technology, 13*(5), 906–913. doi:10.1109/50.387808

Liu, X., Xie, C., & van Wijngaarden, A. J. (2004). Multichannel pmd Mitigation and Outage Reduction through fec with Sub-burst-error-correction Period pmd Scrambling. *IEEE Photonics Technology Letters, 16*(9), 2183–2185. doi:10.1109/LPT.2004.833088

Marcuse, D., Chraplyvy, A. R., & Tkach, E. W. (1994). Dependence of Cross-phase Modulation on Channel Number in Fiber wdm Systems. *Journal of Lightwave Technology, 12*(5), 885–889. doi:10.1109/50.293982

Mecozzi, A., & Shtaif, M. (2004). Signal-to-noise-ratio Degradation Caused by Polarization-dependent Loss and the Effect of Dynamic Gain Equalization. *Journal of Lightwave Technology, 22*(8), 1856–1871. doi:10.1109/JLT.2004.832424

Menyuk, C. R. (1987). Nonlinear Pulse Propagation in Birefringent Optical Fibers. *IEEE Journal of Selected Topics in Quantum Electronics, 23*(2), 174–176. doi:10.1109/JQE.1987.1073308

Mori, K., Takara, H., Kawanishi, S., Saruwatari, M., & Morioka, T. (1997). Flatly Broadened Supercontinuum Spectrum Generated in a Dispersion Decreasing Dibre with Convex Dispersion Profile. *Electronics Letters, 33*(21), 1806–1808. doi:10.1049/el:19971184

Morioka, T. (1995). Multiwavelength Picosecond Pulse Source with Low Jitter and High Optical Frequency Stability Based on 200-nm Supercontinuum Filtering. *Electronics Letters, 31*(13), 1164–1166. doi:10.1049/el:19950759

Morioka, T., Saruwatari, M., & Takada, A. (1987). Ultrafast Optical Multi/Demultiplexer Utilizing Optical kerr Effect in Polarization-maintaining Single-mode Fibres. *Electronics Letters, 23*(9), 453–454. doi:10.1049/el:19870326

Morioka, T., Takara, H., Kawanishi, S., Kitoh, T., & Saruwatari, M. (1996). Error-free 500 gbit/s All-optical Demultiplexing Using Low-noise, Low-jitter Supercontinuum Short Pulses. *Electronics Letters, 32*(9), 833–834. doi:10.1049/el:19960559

Nakazawa, M. (2000). Solitons for Breaking Barriers to Terabit/second wdm and otdm Transmission in the Next Millenium. *IEEE Journal of Selected Topics in Quantum Electronics, 6*(6), 1332–1343. doi:10.1109/2944.902187

Noe, R., Sandel, D., & Mirvoda, V. (2004). Pmd in High-bit-rate Transmission and Means for its Mitigation. *IEEE Journal of Selected Topics in Quantum Electronics, 10*(2), 341–355. doi:10.1109/JSTQE.2004.827842

Ono, T., & Yano, Y. (1998). Key Technologies for Terabit/second wdm Systems with High Spectral Efficiency of over 1 bit/s/hz. *IEEE Journal of Selected Topics in Quantum Electronics, 34.*

Pachnicke, S., Man, E. D., Spalter, S., & Voges, E. (2005). Impact of the In-line Dispersion-compensation Map on Four-wave Mixing (fwm) – Impaired Optical Networks. *IEEE Photonics Technology Letters, 17*(1), 235–237. doi:10.1109/LPT.2004.838629

Patrick, D. M., & Ellis, A. D. (1993). Demultiplexing Using Crossphase Modulation-induced Spectral Shifts and kerr Polarization Rotation in Optical Fibre. *Electronics Letters, 29*(2), 227–229. doi:10.1049/el:19930156

Sartorius, B., Bornholdt, C., Brox, O., Ehrke, H. J., Hoffmann, D., Ludwig, R., & Möhrle, M. (1998). optical Clock Recovery Module Based on Self-pulsating dfb Laser. *Electronics Letters*, *34*(17), 1664–1665. doi:10.1049/el:19981152

Saruwatari, M. (2000). All-optical Signal Processing for Terabit/second Optical Transmission. *IEEE Journal of Selected Topics in Quantum Electronics*, *6*(6), 1363–1374. doi:10.1109/2944.902190

Spiekman, L. H., Amersfoort, M. R., De Vreede, A. H., van Ham, F. P. G. M., Kuntze, A., & Pedersen, J. W. et al. (1996). Design and realization of polarization independent phased array wavelength demultiplexers using different array orders for TE and TM. *Journal of Lightwave Technology*, *14*(6), 991–995. doi:10.1109/50.511599

Srivastava, A. K., Radic, S., Wolf, C., Centanni, J. C., Sulhoff, J. W., Kantor, K., & Sun, Y. (2000). Ultradense wdm Transmission in l-band. *IEEE Photonics Technology Letters*, *12*(11), 1570–1572. doi:10.1109/68.887758

Suzuki, M. (1992). Transform-limited Optical Pulse Generation up to 20 ghz Repetition Rate by Sinusoidally Driven Ingaasp Electroabsorption Modulator. In *Proceedings of Lasers and Electro-optics* (cleo'92). CLEO.

Takada, A., & Miyazawa, H. (1990). 30 ghz Picosecond Pulse Generation from Actively Mode-locked Erbium-doped Fiber Laser. *Electronics Letters*, *26*(3), 216–217. doi:10.1049/el:19900145

Takada, A., Sugie, T., & Saruwatari, M. (1987). High-speed Picosecond Optical Pulse Compression from Gain-switched 1.3μm Distributed Feedback-laser Diode (dfb-ld) Through Highly Dispersive Single-mode fiber. *Journal of Lightwave Technology*, *5*(10), 1525–1533. doi:10.1109/JLT.1987.1075418

Tkach, R. W., Chraplyvy, A. R., Forghieri, F., Gnauck, A. H., & Derosier, R. M. (1995). Four-photon Mixing and High-speed wdm Systems. *Journal of Lightwave Technology*, *13*(5), 841–849. doi:10.1109/50.387800

Uetsuka, H. (2004). Awg Technologies for Dense wdm Applications. *IEEE Journal of Selected Topics in Quantum Electronics*, *10*(2), 393–402. doi:10.1109/JSTQE.2004.827841

Varvarigos, E. M. (1998). The 'Packing' and the 'Scheduling Packet' Switch Architecture for Almost All-optical Lossless Networks. *Journal of Lightwave Technology*, *16*(10), 1757–1767. doi:10.1109/50.721062

Vlachos, K., Pleros, N., Bintjas, C., Theophilopoulos, G., & Avramopoulos, H. (2003). Ultrafast Time-domain Technology and its Application in All-optical Signal Processing. *Journal of Lightwave Technology, 21*(9), 2895–2915. doi:10.1109/JLT.2003.816826

Wang, D., & Menyuk, C. R. (1999). Polarization Evolution due to the kerr Nonlinearity and Chromatic Dispersion. *Journal of Lightwave Technology, 17*(12), 2520–2529. doi:10.1109/50.809672

Weinert, C. M., Ludwig, R., Pieper, W., Weber, H. G., Breuer, D., Petermann, K., & Kuppers, F. (1999). 40 gb/s and 4 x 40 gb/s tdm/wdm Standard Fiber Transmission. *Journal of Lightwave Technology, 17*(11), 2276–2284. doi:10.1109/50.803020

Wu, M., & Way, W. I. (2004). Fiber Nonlinearity Limitations in Ultra-dense wdm Systems. *Journal of Lightwave Technology, 22*(6), 1483–1498. doi:10.1109/JLT.2004.829222

Yamamoto, Y., & Inoue, K. (2003). Noise in Amplifiers. *Journal of Lightwave Technology, 21*(11), 2895–2915. doi:10.1109/JLT.2003.816887

Zhu, B. (2002). *Transmission of 3.2 tb/s (80 x 42.7 gb/s) over 5200 km of Ultrawave Fiber with 100-km Dispersion-managed Spans Using rz-dpsk Format.* Academic Press.

KEY TERMS AND DEFINITIONS

Arrayed Waveguide Grating (AWG): Refers to an optical device that is commonly used in WDM based optical network as multiplexer/demultiplexer to multiplex several wavelengths channels onto a single optical fiber at the transmission end and to retrieve individual channels of different wavelengths at the receiving end.

Distributed Feedback Laser Diodes (DFB-LD): A type of laser diode having the gain medium of the device periodically structured as a diffraction grating.

Electro-Absorption Modulators (EAM): A semiconductor device that can be used to modulate the intensity of a laser beam via an electric voltage.

Intensity Modulated (IM): Refers to a modulation technique in which the optical power output of a source is varied in accordance with some characteristic of the information signal.

Mach-Zehnder Modulator: An optical device used as modulator to electrically controlling the output amplitude or the phase of the light wave signal passing through it.

Nonlinear Optical Loop Mirror (NOLM): An optical device used in optical switching and demultiplexing. It is constructed using a fiber loop whose ends are connected to two output ports of a 3-dB fiber coupler.

Phase-Locked Loop (PLL): A control system that generates an output signal whose phase is related to the phase of an input signal.

Chapter 8
OTDM–WDM:
Propagation Impairments Analysis

ABSTRACT

OTDM-WDM Intensity Modulation (IM) systems employing optical amplification and Dispersion Management (DM) are analyzed. Interchannel nonlinear effects present the input power limit to system performance. Therefore, a lumped DM system performed better than a fully inline DM system through reduction of coherent channel interaction. With proper channel spacing, all demultiplexed OTDM channels and the multiplexed signal show the same performance.

INTRODUCTION

The effects that impair OTDM-WDM propagation, particularly the nonlinear effects are analysed. In order to observe these impairments clearly, some basic optimization of the system is performed beforehand. These are only simple optimizations; a more comprehensive optimization process will be dealt with in the next chapters. Also, we need to make sure the propagation step sizes are chosen properly, striking a balance between processing time and accuracy. The systems under study are long distance, IM systems employing periodic optical amplification and DM. Generally, the systems consist of N OTDM channels of 10 Gb/s bit rates multiplexed to form an OTDM signal. Each of these OTDM signals are separate WDM channels that are multiplexed as required. The resultant WDM signal is propagated through

DOI: 10.4018/978-1-4666-6575-0.ch008

the optical system and demultiplexed at the receiver. BER or Q-factor analysis is performed on both the WDM and OTDM channels. From the analysis, techniques to improve the performance of the OTDM-WDM system are proposed.

SYSTEM BLOCK DIAGRAM AND OPERATION MODEL

The system block diagram is shown in Figure 1. Each transmitted channel employs RZ modulation, which consists of Gaussian pulses with full wave half maximum (FWHM) width of 8 ps. The OTDM channel bit rate is 10 Gb/s, which are multiplexed to form 40 Gb/s WDM channels. Both the OTDM and WDM multiplexing processes are assumed ideal. We simulate five adjacent WDM channels with equal channel spacing of Δf GHz, and the results are obtained from the middle channel (centered at 1550 nm). This is sufficient as almost all effects on a WDM channel are caused by its first two spectrally adjacent neighbors (Yu, Reimer, Grigoryan, & Menyuk, 2000). Each OTDM channel is encoded using different pseudo-random bit sequences (PRBS) of length 2^9-1 bits so that they are uncorrelated. The signal is transmitted across 18 spans of nonzero dispersion shifted fiber (NZ-DSF) of length 50 km each with dispersion $D = 4$ ps/nm/km, dispersion slope $Sl = 0.1$ ps/nm²/km, effective area $A_{eff} = 55$ μm² and attenuation $\alpha = 0.2$ dB/km. The dispersion compensating fiber (DCF) has $D = -100$ ps/nm/km, $Sl = -2.5$ ps/nm²/km, $A_{eff} = 30$ μm² and $\alpha = 0.55$ dB/km. The DCF is either used as periodic (inline) dispersion compensation placed after each NZ-DSF span (specified in terms of length, L_{inl}) or as pre-dispersion compensation (length, L_{pre}) and post-dispersion compensation (length, L_{post}).

The DM scheme is ideal so that second and third order dispersion cancels out for all channels at the receiver. A second order, super-Gaussian optical bandpass filter with bandwidth BW_{wdm}, is used for WDM demultiplexing as this is the shape of many common demultiplexers. OTDM demultiplexing is performed using an

Figure 1. System block diagram for OTDM-WDM propagation impairments study (Hiew, Abbou, Chuah, Majumder, & Hairul, 2004)

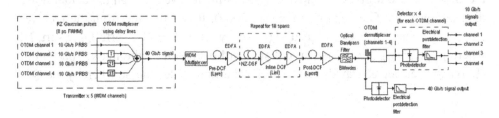

ideally square switching window with 92% duty cycle. All receivers are assumed ideal with no shot and electrical thermal noise, considering that the dominant noise in long-range systems is accumulated ASE. A five-pole, Bessel postdetection low-pass electric filter is used with single sided bandwidth BW_{ele}. Erbium doped fiber amplifiers (EDFA), with a population inversion factor n_{sp} of 2, are placed after each fiber span. The ASE is modeled as circular complex additive white Gaussian noise (AWGN) with uniform random phase distribution and added onto the WDM signal after each amplifier along the transmission link. The signal and noise are propagated together by solving the nonlinear Schrödinger equation (NLSE) using the split-step Fourier method (SSFM). Single polarization is assumed for all signals and noise. Multiple runs are performed until the results converge.

Generally, the multiplexed WDM signal is treated as a single signal and propagated through the transmission link. In this work, we refer to this method as the lumped channel SSFM (LC-SSFM). This method accounts for all linear effects (such as dispersion, linear crosstalk) and most nonlinear effects (such as self-phase modulation (SPM), cross-phase modulation (XPM) and four-wave mixing (FWM)). It also accounts for the interaction between these effects and between signal and noise (such as parametric gain). We neglect the effect of delayed nonlinear response, also called the Raman effect, in this chapter. To account for SPM and XPM alone, while neglecting parametric effects like FWM, a modification of the SSFM is discussed in (Leibrich & Rosenkranz, 2003). We refer to this technique as the separated channel SSFM (SC-SSFM), where each WDM channel is propagated separately and interactions between the channels are limited to a summation term on the right hand side of the NLSE accounting for XPM between all the channels (Leibrich & Rosenkranz, 2003). This technique gives an accurate simulation of the signal propagation when FWM is insignificant. In this work, we use the SC-SSFM for special cases where we intend to analyze the effect of SPM+XPM alone so as to determine the exact nature of the impairment on the system.

PERFORMANCE ESTIMATION MODELS

For IM systems, the Gaussian approximated Q factor is commonly used to estimate the BER because it gives a relatively good estimate, even though the actual noise distribution is not Gaussian (Kim & Yu, 2002). It is estimated from the receiver current eye diagram as $Q_{IM} = |\mu_1 - \mu_0| / (\sigma_1 + \sigma_0)$ with BER $= (1/2)$ erfc$[Q_{IM} / \text{sqrt}(2)]$ where $\mu_{1,0}$ and $\sigma_{1,0}$ are the mean and standard deviation of the marks/spaces rail (Bergano, Kerfoot, & Davidson, 1993). Furthermore, a technique whereby the Q is conditioned to the received patterns of 3 bits can more accurately account for ISI (Anderson & Lyle, 1994) and is used here. When expressed in decibels, we use the common convention of Q(dB) = 20 $\log_{10}$(Q).

Optimization of Filter Bandwidths

First, we optimize the bandwidth of the optical filter BW_{wdm} in Figure 2 and Figure 3. There are two windows of optimal performance at 40 GHz and 65 GHz. The 40 GHz filter results in a signal distorted by significant ISI but it reduces the amplitude jitter induced by noise and distortion, as well as the linear crosstalk between WDM channels. The 65 GHz filtered signal has little ISI but it allows more linear crosstalk and does not effectively reduce the amplitude jitter. As such, the 65 GHz filter results in good performance for back-to-back signals while the 40 GHz filter results in better performance for the signal after propagation through the transmission link as propagation effects induce significant amplitude jitter. For the electrical filter bandwidth BW_{ele}, optimal performance is achieved as long as $BW_{ele} \geq BW_{wdm}$ when BW_{wdm} is optimal. We use BW_{wdm} = 40 GHz and BW_{ele} = 50 GHz for the simulations.

Figure 2. Optimization of optical filter bandwidth, BWwdm for 40 Gb/s signal: back-to-back signal (-10 dBm optical noise added just before receiver) (Hiew, Abbou, Chuah, Majumder, & Hairul, 2004)

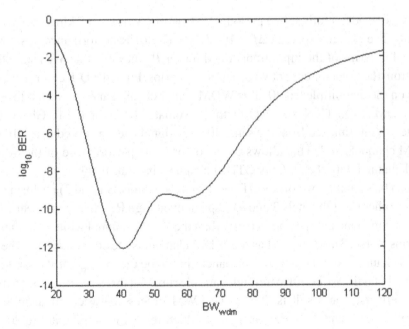

Figure 3. Optimization of optical filter bandwidth, BWwdm for 40 Gb/s signal: received signal after transmission link (Hiew, Abbou, Chuah, Majumder, & Hairul, 2004)

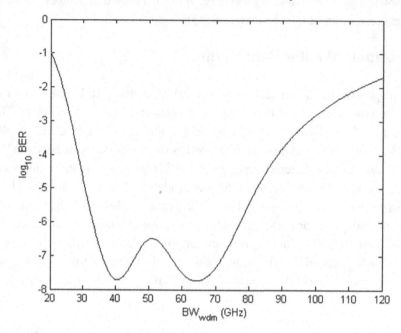

Effect of Channel Spacing

First, we consider a fully inline periodic DM system with $L_{inl} = 2$ km and $L_{pre} = L_{post} = 0$ km. The channel spacing Δf is 100 GHz. The BER performance is shown in Figure 4 in terms of the input transmitted power P_{in} into the link. We estimate the BER from the Q-factor under two different scenarios. First, the Q-factor is evaluated based on the demultiplexed 40 Gb/s WDM center channel and is referred to as "40 Gb/s WDM channel". Next, the Q-factor is evaluated based on the 10 Gb/s OTDM channels demultiplexed from the same 40 Gb/s signal and is referred to as "10 Gb/s OTDM channels 1-4". This allows us to compare the performance of the 40 Gb/s WDM channel with the 10 Gb/s OTDM channels in a fair manner.

It can be seen that two of the OTDM channels (channels 1 and 3) perform better than the other two (channels 2 and 4), especially at high P_{in} where nonlinear effects are dominant. One pair performs better than the WDM channel while the other pair performs worse. This is logical as the WDM channel is the combination of the four OTDM channels and its BER performance should be the average of its constituent OTDM channels. We confirm through multiple runs that this is not due to bit pattern-related effects. The result is due to the FWM process between adjacent WDM channels' center and 40 GHz harmonics, which results in a spike at the 20 GHz

Figure 4. BER vs. input transmitted power, Pin for the 40 Gb/s WDM channel and its four OTDM channel tributaries using Δf = 100 GHz (Hiew, Abbou, Chuah, Majumder, & Hairul, 2004)

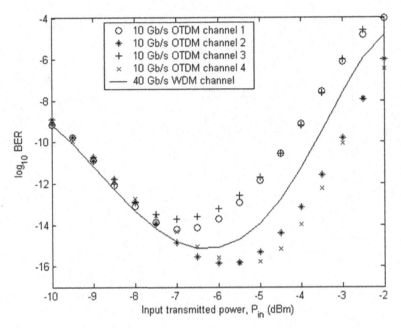

harmonic of the center channel as seen in Figure 6. The spike at 20 GHz results in a 20 GHz crosstalk noise. As this is exactly half of the WDM channel bit rate of 40 Gb/s, it affects two of the channels coherently while skipping the other two. Practically, we want all the OTDM channels to have the same performance. To do this, it is best to use a channel spacing that does not share the same factors as the WDM channel bit rate. Throughout this work, we set Δf as 97 GHz, which is close to the 100 GHz originally intended and does not lead to any FWM products at frequencies that repeat coherently for particular OTDM channels. The result is shown in Figure 5 where all the OTDM channels and the WDM channel share relatively the same BER performance except for small pattern related deviations.

Analysis of Propagation Effects

The "U" shape of the BER-P_{in} curves suggests the influence of nonlinear effects that limits the performance of the system. This is examined in Figure 7 and Figure 8 with Δf = 97 GHz. Note that since all the OTDM channels have the same performance, only one is shown in the figure for clarity. The same performance is seen in both the 40 Gb/s WDM channel and its resultant 10 Gb/s OTDM channels. This is

Figure 5. BER vs. input transmitted power, Pin for the 40 Gb/s WDM channel and its four OTDM channel tributaries using Δf = 97 GHz for a fully inline DM system (Hiew, Abbou, Chuah, Majumder, & Hairul, 2004)

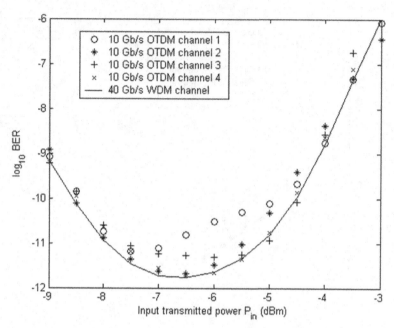

Figure 6. Power spectral density of received WDM signal after transmission link (focus on center WDM channel) (Hiew, Abbou, Chuah, Majumder, & Hairul, 2004)

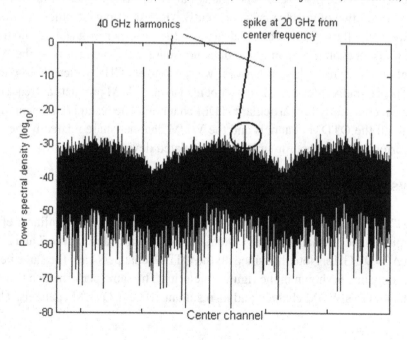

Figure 7. BER vs. Pin for transmission under different combinations of linear and nonlinear effects. Solid line is for the 40 Gb/s WDM channel while dotted line is for the 10 Gb/s OTDM channel: five scenarios (Abbou, Wong, Hiew, Abid, & Chuah, 2007)

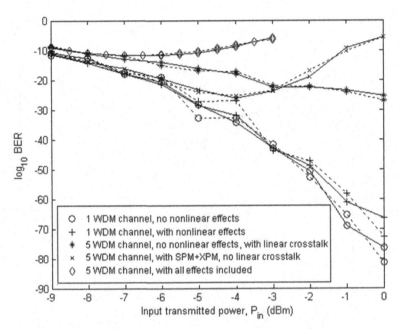

expected as the OTDM demultiplexing here uses ideal square pulses with high duty cycles that would not induce added distortion. Thus, the performance of the separate OTDM channels would be similar to the multiplexed signal it originated from. Five different propagation scenarios are explored: a) 1 WDM channel without nonlinear effects; b) 1 WDM channel with nonlinear effects; c) 5 WDM channels without nonlinear effects but with linear crosstalk; d) 5 WDM channels with SPM+XPM but no linear crosstalk (obtained using SC-SSFM) and e) 5 WDM channels with all effects included (linear crosstalk, FWM, XPM, SPM).

It can be seen that without nonlinear effects the "U" shape is not present, and increasing the transmitted power would continuously improve the BER performance as a higher transmitted power leads to higher signal to noise (SNR) ratio at the receiver. The noise is caused by the ASE induced by the EDFAs used for signal amplification. Both second and third order dispersion are not significant impairments as they have been fully compensated for in the ideal DM scheme employed here. The introduction of more than one WDM channel causes linear crosstalk that induces some distortion that is quite significant. However, the effect is linear and does not give rise to the "U" shape.

Figure 8. BER vs. Pin for transmission under different combinations of linear and nonlinear effects. Solid line is for the 40 Gb/s WDM channel while dotted line is for the 10 Gb/s OTDM channel: three scenarios (Abbou, Wong, Hiew, Abid, & Chuah, 2007)

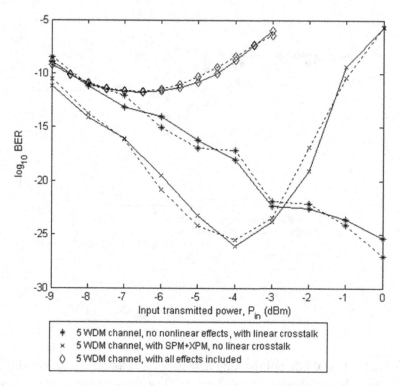

On the other hand, nonlinear effects increase in significance as P_{in} increases and these effects induce distortion and crosstalk. Thus, a limit to P_{in} is reached when the nonlinear effects induced distortion overcomes the improvement obtained by a higher SNR. To examine the effect of SPM alone, we include the nonlinear effects but propagate only one WDM channel. As seen, the presence of SPM alone does not cause significant impairment to the signal over the range of transmitted powers considered. By including XPM through the propagation of five WDM channels using the SC-SSFM, the "U" shape is produced with the P_{in} limit at -4 dBm. Due to the use of the SC-SSFM, linear crosstalk is not considered for the SPM+XPM case. This explains why the optimum BER here is better than the case of 5 WDM channels with linear crosstalk but no nonlinear effects. Including parametric effects (FWM) and linear crosstalk by using the LC-SSFM for five WDM channels, the limit decreases to -6.5 dBm with much increased BER. This means that the most significant impairment, which presents a limit at higher input powers, is FWM, while

XPM plays a smaller but still significant role. This is logical as the channel spacing used here is small and both XPM and FWM effects increase with smaller channel spacing (Tkach, Chraplyvy, Gnauck, & Derosier, 1995; Chiang, Kagi, Marhic, & Kazovsky, 1996). The results here show that FWM plays a bigger role in the high bit rate, dense WDM environment with periodic DM.

Pre- and Post-Dispersion Compensation

Noticing that the main sources of distortion are the interchannel nonlinear effects of XPM and FWM, we remove the periodic dispersion compensation by setting $L_{inl} = 0$ and place all the burden of dispersion compensation on the pre- and post-dispersion compensation spans by setting $L_{pre} = L_{post} = 18$ km (dispersion split ratio = 50%). We expect this to reduce the influence of XPM and FWM, as both these effects depend on the coherent interaction between co-propagating WDM channels within the optical fiber (Tkach, Chraplyvy, Gnauck, & Derosier; Chiang, Kagi, Marhic, & Kazovsky, 1996). Generally, the relatively high local dispersion of the fiber ($D = 4$ ps/nm/km) used here results in a relatively strong walk-off between the channels that would reduce both XPM and FWM. However, this is undermined by the periodic DM scheme, which supports coherent interaction, because the WDM channels are realigned back to their original states by the DCF just before it is amplified. After amplification, the interchannel nonlinear effects are strongest as the channel powers are high. Thus, most of the nonlinear interaction occurs during this time before the channels walk-off again due to the local dispersion. This process is repeated at every DM span and the nonlinear effects accumulate. By relying on pre- and post-dispersion compensation, the channels within the transmission link are always dispersed and walked-off from one another. Thus coherent interaction is reduced, and we hope to reduce the nonlinear distortion caused by high input powers. The BER performance is shown in Figure 9. The lumped DM scheme attains better performance with the P_{in} limit increased to -5 dBm and a lower optimum BER compared to the fully inline DM scheme. This means that interchannel nonlinear effects have been reduced due to the reduction of coherency between WDM channels.

However, it is interesting to note that SPM effects have increased as demonstrated by the "U" shape of the "1 WDM channel with nonlinear effects" scenario. This is because the high residual dispersion throughout the transmission link increases the effect of SPM, specifically the class of effects known as the *intrachannel* nonlinear effects such as *intrachannel* XPM and *intrachannel* FWM (Kumar, 1998). The increased intrachannel nonlinear effects reduce some of the performance gain obtained by the reduction of interchannel effects. However, interchannel nonlinear effects are still dominant as the 5-channel system still shows a lower transmission power limit.

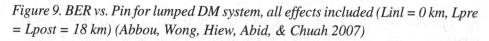

Figure 9. BER vs. Pin for lumped DM system, all effects included (Linl = 0 km, Lpre = Lpost = 18 km) (Abbou, Wong, Hiew, Abid, & Chuah 2007)

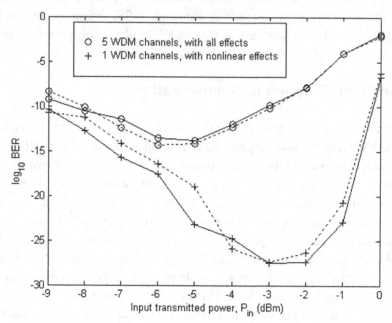

Using a Post-OTDM Demultiplexing Optical Filter

In order to improve the performance of the OTDM-WDM system, we use an additional optical filter, referred to as the OTDM filter, and placed after OTDM demultiplexing but before photodetection as in Figure 10.

The OTDM filter used is a second order, super-Gaussian bandpass filter with bandwidth BW_{otdm}. The reason for the use of the OTDM filter is shown in Figure 11. The OTDM demultiplexing process is basically a multiplication in the time

Figure 10. Using a post-OTDM demultiplexing optical filter (OTDM filter)

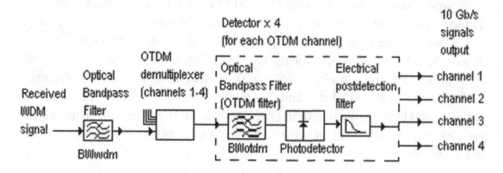

Figure 11. Power spectral density plots of the received 40 Gb/s WDM channel and the 10 Gb/s demultiplexed OTDM channel (Hiew, Abbou, & Chuah, 2006)

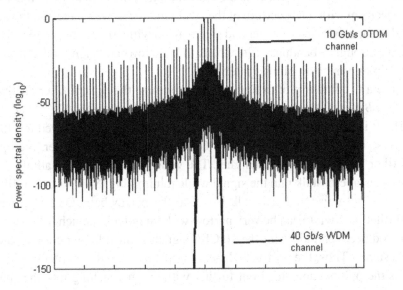

Figure 12. Optimization of optical filter bandwidths BWwdm and BWotdm (Δf = 97 GHz, Linl = 2 km, Lpre = Lpost = 0 km, Pin = -6.5 dBm) (Hiew, Abbou, & Chuah, 2006)

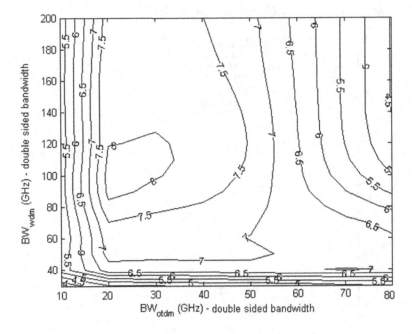

domain. Thus, it is a convolution in the frequency domain. The resulting 10 Gb/s demultiplexed channel spectrum is the convolution of the optically filtered 40 Gb/s signal spectrum with the spectrum of the switching window. As a result, the demultiplexed channel becomes a wideband signal again with 10 GHz harmonics. Putting the signal through a bandpass filter leads to a narrowband signal once again that would help minimize amplitude jitter.

We use a Q contour plot in Figure 12 to optimize the optical filter bandwidths BW_{wdm} and BW_{otdm}. The electrical filter bandwidth BW_{ele} is set at $BW_{ele} = (BW_{otdm} + 10)$ GHz. It is interesting to note that optimal performance is achieved for 90 GHz $< BW_{wdm} < 120$ GHz and $BW_{otdm} \approx 30$ GHz. With the OTDM filter, the optimal WDM filter bandwidth is much higher. The wideband WDM filter allows a lot of noise and linear crosstalk into the signal while minimizing ISI. The task of filtering out the residual noise and crosstalk is left to the narrowband OTDM filter. The OTDM filter bandwidth can be very narrow without inducing much ISI because the time period between pulses for the 10 Gb/s signal is much longer compared to the 40 Gb/s signal. Thus, the post-OTDM-demultiplexed signal can tolerate ISI much better as the pulses can spread out further without encroaching into the space of

Figure 13. BER vs. input transmitted power, Pin for the 40 Gb/s WDM channel and its four OTDM channel tributaries while using the OTDM filter (Δf = 97 GHz, BWwdm = 110 GHz, BWotdm = 15 GHz); Fully inline DM: Linl = 2 km, Lpre = Lpost = 0 km (Hiew, Abbou, Chuah, & Hairul, 2005)

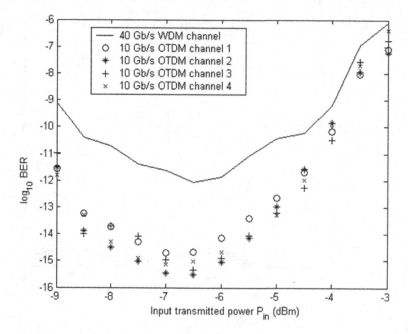

neighboring pulses. The filter bandwidth values are set to BW_{wdm} = 110 GHz and BW_{otdm} = 30 GHz to obtain the results in Figure 13. We checked that these are also the optimal bandwidth values for the lumped DM system. Compared with Figure 14 and Figure 6 there is significant improvement in the performance of the 10 Gb/s demultiplexed channels with the use of the OTDM filter. In fact, their performance surpasses that of the 40 Gb/s signal they originate from due to the use of the very narrow OTDM filter that helps to reduce amplitude jitter without causing high ISI. This improvement occurs for both lumped and periodic DM with better overall performance achieved for lumped DM once again.

We test the distance limit of the OTDM-WDM system in Figure 15 by propagating the signal through N spans of NZ-DSF using a fully inline DM scheme (L_{inl} = 2 km). The system shows good performance up to N = 38 (total link length = 1976 km) with the use of the OTDM filter providing a Q gain of 0.7 – 1.1 dB. Notice that the optimum P_{in} decreases as transmission distance increases indicating that non-linear effects increases in significance compared to ASE noise for longer links.

Next, we reduce the channel spacing for higher spectral efficiency in Figure 16 using a hybrid DM scheme (Linl = 1 km, Lpre = Lpost = 9 km, total link length =

Figure 14. BER vs. input transmitted power, Pin for the 40 Gb/s WDM channel and its four OTDM channel tributaries while using the OTDM filter (Δf = 97 GHz, BWwdm = 110 GHz, BWotdm = 15 GHz); Fully lumped DM: Linl = 0 km, Lpre = Lpost = 18 km (Hiew, Abbou, Chuah, & Hairul, 2005)

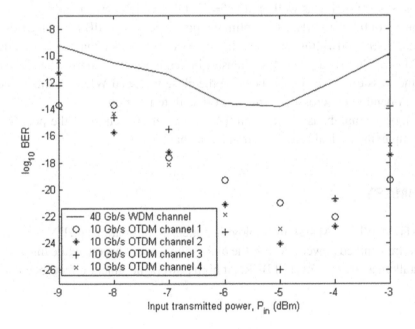

Figure 15. Optimal Q (dB) vs. number of spans, N for receiver with or without the OTDM filter (optimum Pin indicated and Linl = 2 km, Lpre = Lpost = 0 km, Δf = 97 GHz) (Hiew, Abbou, Chuah, & Hairul, 2005)

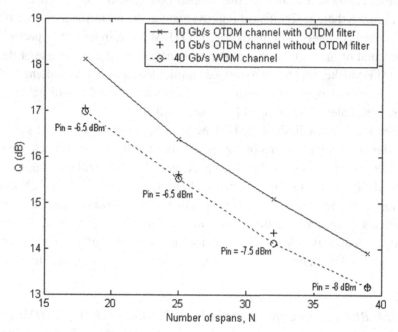

900 km). The hybrid scheme shows improved performance over the inline scheme and the system performs well up to $\Delta f = 77$ GHz which corresponds to a spectral efficiency of 0.52 bits/s/Hz. The optimal input power was -5 dBm for all cases. The optimal filter bandwidths remained the same as well. Notice that the Q gain due to the OTDM filter reduces as Δf decreases, indicating that the narrowband filtering becomes less effective. This is because the closely spaced WDM channels induce more in-band linear crosstalk, which is difficult to filter out.

A more comprehensive study on the use and effectiveness of the post OTDM demultiplexing optical filter is examined in chapter 14.

SUMMARY

An OTDM-WDM, IM system employing optical amplification and DM is analyzed. At low transmitted powers, ASE is the main source of distortion, while linear WDM crosstalk increases the overall BER. At high powers, nonlinear effects become sig-

Figure 16. Optimal Q (dB) vs. channel spacing, Δf for receiver with or without the OTDM filter (Linl = 1 km, Lpre = Lpost = 9 km, total link length = 900 km) (Hiew, Abbou, Chuah, & Hairul, 2005)

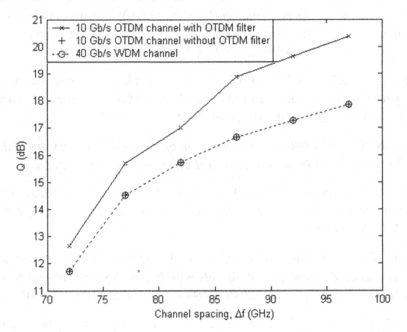

nificant, especially interchannel effects where FWM is the main source of distortion while XPM is also significant. Therefore, a lumped DM system performed better than a fully inline DM system due to the reduction of coherent channel interaction though the performance gain is limited by a corresponding gain in intrachannel nonlinear effects. Choosing the channel spacing properly, the OTDM multiplexed signal (WDM channel) and all its constituent OTDM channels show the same BER performance. Introducing an optical narrowband bandpass filter after OTDM demultiplexing improves the BER performance of the OTDM channels significantly by reducing amplitude jitter while possessing high tolerance towards ISI due to the wider time period between pulses. The OTDM-WDM link shows good performance up to 2000 km with the OTDM filter providing a Q gain of 0.7 – 1.1 dB. The optimal input power reduces for longer distances due to increased significance of nonlinear effects. A 900-km link showed good performance for spectral efficiencies as low as 0.52 bits/s/Hz, though the Q gain provided by the OTDM filter reduces as channel spacing decreases.

REFERENCES

Abbou, F. M., Wong, H. Y., Hiew, C. C., Abid, A., & Chuah, H. T. (2007). Performance evaluation of dispersion managed optical TDM-WDM transmission system in the presence of SPM, XPM, and FWM. *Journal of Optical Communications*, *28*(3), 221–224. doi:10.1515/JOC.2007.28.3.221

Anderson, C. J., & Lyle, J. A. (1994). Technique for Evaluating System Performance Using q in Numerical Simulations Exhibiting Intersymbol Interference. *Electronics Letters*, *30*(1), 71–72. doi:10.1049/el:19940045

Bergano, N. S. (2002). *640 gb/s Transmission of Sixty-four 10 gb/s wdm Channels over 7200 km with 0.33 (bits/s)/hz Spectral Efficiency*. Academic Press.

Bergano, N. S., Kerfoot, F. W., & Davidson, C. R. (1993). Margin Measurements in Optical Amplifier Systems. *IEEE Photonics Technology Letters*, *5*(3), 304–306. doi:10.1109/68.205619

Bosco, G., Carena, A., Curri, V., Gaudino, R., & Poggiolini, P. (2002). On the Use of nrz, rz and csrz Modulation at 40 gb/s with Narrow dwdm Channel Spacing. *Journal of Lightwave Technology*, *20*(9), 1694–1704. doi:10.1109/JLT.2002.806309

Bosco, G., Carena, A., Curri, V., Gaudino, R., Poggiolini, P., & Benedetto, S. (2000). Suppression of Spurious Tones Induced by the Split-step Method in Fiber Systems Simulation. *IEEE Photonics Technology Letters*, *12*(5), 489–491. doi:10.1109/68.841262

Cai, J. X. (2002). Long-haul 40 gb/s dwdm Transmission with Aggregate Capacities Exceeding 1 tb/s. *Journal of Lightwave Technology*, *20*(12), 2247–2257. doi:10.1109/JLT.2002.806770

Chiang, T. K., Kagi, N., Marhic, M. E., & Kazovsky, L. G. (1996). Cross-phase Modulation in Fiber Links with Multiple Optical Amplifiers and Dispersion Compensators. *Journal of Lightwave Technology*, *14*(3), 249–260. doi:10.1109/50.485582

Gnauck, A. H., Raybon, G., Bernasconi, P. G., Leuthold, J., Doerr, C. R., & Stulz, L. W. (2003). 1-tb/s (6 x 170.6 gb/s) Transmission over 2000-km nzdf Using otdm and rz-dpsk Format. *IEEE Photonics Technology Letters*, *15*(11), 1618–1620. doi:10.1109/LPT.2003.818634

Hiew, C.C., Abbou, F.M., Chuah, H.T., and Majumder, & Hairul, A. A. R. (2004). OTDM-WDM Propagation Impairments and Techniques to Improve Performance. In *Proceedings of the IASTED International 13/16/16 Conference on Communication Systems and Networks (csn)*. Marbella, Spain: IASTED.

Hiew, C. C., Abbou, F. M., & Chuah, H. T. (2006). *Performance Analysis and Design of an Optical TDM-WDM Transmission System and Network* (Tech. Rep. No. 1). Malaysia: Multimedia University and Alcatel Network Systems.

Hiew, C. C., Abbou, F. M., Chuah, H. T., & Hairul, A. A. R. (2005). A Technique to Improve Optical Time Division Multiplexing-Wavelength Division Multiplexing Performance. *IEICE Electronics Express, 2*(24), 1–6. doi:10.1587/elex.2.589

Hiew, C. C., Abbou, F. M., Chuah, H. T., Majumder, S. P., & Hairul, A. A. R. (2004). Ber Estimation of Optical wdm rz-dpsk Systems Through the Differential Phase Q. *IEEE Photonics Technology Letters, 16*(12), 2619–2621. doi:10.1109/LPT.2004.836759

Humblet Azizoglu, P. A., & Azizoglu, M. (1991). On the Bit Error Rate of Lightwave Systems with Optical Amplifiers. *Journal of Lightwave Technology, 9*(11), 1576–1582. doi:10.1109/50.97649

Kim, H., & Yu, C. X. (2002). Optical Duobinary Transmission System Featuring Improved Receiver Sensitivity and Reduced Optical Bandwidth. *IEEE Photonics Technology Letters, 14*(8), 1205–1207. doi:10.1109/LPT.2002.1022019

Kumar, S., Mauro, J. C., Raghavan, S., & Chowdhury, D. Q. (2002). Intrachannel Nonlinear Penalties in Dispersion-managed Transmission Systems. *IEEE Journal of Selected Topics in Quantum Electronics, 8*(3), 626–631. doi:10.1109/JSTQE.2002.1016366

Leibrich, J., & Rosenkranz, W. (2003). Efficient Numerical Simulation of Multichannel wdm Transmission Systems Limited by xpm. *IEEE Photonics Technology Letters, 15*(3), 395–397. doi:10.1109/LPT.2003.807901

Nakazawa, M. (2000). Ultrahigh-speed Long-distance tdm and wdm Soliton Transmission Technologies. *IEEE Journal of Selected Topics in Quantum Electronics*, 6.

Norimatsu, S., & Maruoka, M. (2002). Accurate q-factor Estimation of Optically Amplified Systems in the Presence of Waveform Distortions. *Journal of Lightwave Technology, 20*(1), 19–27. doi:10.1109/50.974814

Sinkin, O. V., Holzlohner, V., Zweck, J., & Menyuk, C. R. (2003). Optimization of the Split-step Fourier Method in Modeling Optical-fiber Communications Systems. *Journal of Lightwave Technology, 21*(1), 61–68. doi:10.1109/JLT.2003.808628

Tkach, R. W., Chraplyvy, A. R., Forghieri, F., Gnauck, A. H., & Derosier, R. M. (1995). Four-photon Mixing and High-speed wdm Systems. *Journal of Lightwave Technology, 13*(5), 841–849. doi:10.1109/50.387800

Weinert, C. M., Ludwig, R., Pieper, W., Weber, H. G., Breuer, D., Petermann, K., & Kuppers, F. (1999). 40 gb/s and 4 x 40 gb/s tdm/wdm Standard Fiber Transmission. *Journal of Lightwave Technology, 17*(11), 2276–2284. doi:10.1109/50.803020

Yu, T., Reimer, W. M., Grigoryan, V. S., & Menyuk, C. R. (2000). *A Mean Field Approach for Simulating Wavelength-division Multiplexed Systems.* Academic Press.

KEY TERMS AND DEFINITIONS

Additive White Gaussian Noise: A basic noise model used in telecommunication to study the effect of many random processes that occur in nature.

Non Zero-Dispersion-Shifted Fiber (NZ-DSF): A type of single-mode fiber having zero-dispersion wavelength near the 1550 nm window.

Optical Time Division Multiplexing (OTDM): Refers to the optical multiplexing of signals in time domain. OTDM allows transmitting and receiving independent signals over a common transmission path by means of synchronized switches at each end of the transmission link so that each signal appears on the transmission path only a fraction of time in an alternating pattern.

Post-Dispersion Compensation: A piece of dispersion compensation fiber is added at the transmitter.

Pre-Dispersion Compensation: A process that changes the spectral amplitude of the input pulse in such a way that dispersion induced degradation is eliminated or reduced.

Q-Contour Plot: A contour plot is a graphic representation of the relationships among three design parameters (variables) in two dimensions.

Split-Step Fourier Method (SSFM): Refers to a pseudo-spectral numerical method used to solve the nonlinear Schrödinger equation. SSFM relies on computing the solution in small steps, and treating the linear and the nonlinear steps separately.

Chapter 9
OTDM–WDM System Components Modeling

ABSTRACT

The purpose of this chapter is to discuss OTDM-WDM system components modeling. Any attempt to model the OTDM-WDM system components would need to take into account a number of key issues that have to be decided upon before a particular system setup can be implemented. Among the key issues are signal modulation format, OTDM channel bit rate, WDM channel bit rate, spectral density, length of transmission, amplification scheme, dispersion management scheme, and optical devices. Further, throughout the chapter, examples are used to demonstrate how OTDM-WDM devices, such as the transmitter, multiplexer, optical fiber, filter, amplifier, demultiplexer, and receiver, are modeled.

INTRODUCTION

The optical fiber link can be composed of a combination of different fiber types with varying properties. These fiber links may be separated by EDF. As that serves to amplify the attenuated signal. A combination of fiber types and amplifiers may repeat along a transmission link and these are known as fiber spans. If the spans are repeated due to the amplification scheme, they are also known as amplifier spans. If the span configurations are determined from the DM scheme, they are also known as DM spans. Besides the repeated spans, notice that in the diagram, single lengths of DCF are also placed at the beginning and end of the transmission link. These lengths known as the pre-compensation and post-compensation fiber lengths are quite commonly used in modern DM schemes.

DOI: 10.4018/978-1-4666-6575-0.ch009

At the receiving end, the received signal is first filtered using an optical filter to remove excess noise. In simulations, the optical filter can also generally be used as the WDM demultiplexer as it can effectively isolate a single WDM channel from the full spectrum WDM signal. In practice, an AWG is used to demultiplex all the WDM channels at once, producing a different WDM channel at each of its outputs. The AWG is in effect just a linear combination of optical filters with different center frequencies. In the case of simulations, only 1 or 2 WDM channels are normally required as samples. Therefore, individual optical filters can effectively be used as the WDM demultiplexer in these scenarios. After WDM demultiplexing, OTDM demultiplexing is performed to obtain the constituent OTDM channels, which are the received samples of the initial input signals. These signals can then be detected using the optical receivers (detectors) that generally consist of a front photodetector used to convert the received optical signal to an electrical signal, followed by an electrical post-detection low-pass filter. The electrical signals from each detector are the outputs of the OTDM-WDM system.

From the system model, we can see that the system consists of a number of components that have to be modeled separately. These components can be lumped into categories or blocks. The blocks required for the OTDM-WDM system here include the transmitter, multiplexer, optical fiber, filter, amplifier, demultiplexer and receiver.

OTDM-WDM SYSTEM MODEL

With reference to the block diagram of the OTDM-WDM system shown in Figure 1, optical signals with similar laser center frequencies modulated using different sets of pseudo-random bit sequences (PRBS) are referred to as OTDM channels and are multiplexed together using OTDM to form higher bit rate OTDM signals. These OTDM signals act as the WDM channels. The WDM channels are then multiplexed together using a WDM multiplexer to form the overall WDM signal that is to be transmitted. For system modeling using simulations, the signal can then be transmitted through one of two different configurations, back-to-back and point-to-point. In back-to-back transmission, the signal is sent straight to the receiver without passing through any fiber links. Optical noise is often added directly using an optical noise generator placed right before the receiver in order to specify the received optical signal to noise ratio (OSNR). In point-to-point transmission, the signal is propagated through a fiber link that consists of a variety of fiber types and amplifiers (EDFA) that are joined together end to end.

Figure 1. OTDM-WDM system block diagram

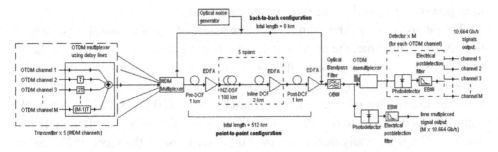

Transmitters

The basic transmitting device is assumed to be an optical laser source. Ideally, this generates a continuous wave (CW) signal with a discrete frequency or wavelength (impulse function in the frequency domain) given by (Agrawal, 2001)

$$L\left(\lambda_l, t\right) = \cos\left(\omega_l t\right) \tag{9.1}$$

where ω_l is the laser angular frequency and λ_l is the associated wavelength.

In reality, the laser frequency is not an ideal impulse function but possesses a finite linewidth or bandwidth. For cases where the linewidth is comparable to the modulation bandwidth, research has been carried out to study its impact on fiber systems. However, for modern lasers, the linewidth is small and for high bit rate systems such as the OTDM-WDM system, the linewidth is relatively insignificant as compared to the signal modulation bandwidth. As such, the linewidth can be safely assumed to be zero in most cases, resulting in equation (9.1). In practice, the laser used for transmission is also a source of noise as it produces spontaneous emission in addition to the desired stimulated emission. The spontaneous emission results in random noise in both the intensity and the phase. Laser intensity noise is commonly represented by the relative intensity noise (RIN) parameter specified in terms of dB/Hz and relative to the laser output power (Agrawal, 1997).

$$RIN = \frac{1}{B_N}\left(\frac{\mathrm{E}\left\{\left|P\left(t\right) - P_o\right|^2\right\}}{P_o^2}\right) \tag{9.2}$$

where P_o is the noiseless (mean) laser power, $P(t)$ is the time-variant noise distorted laser power and B_N is the noise equivalent bandwidth.

The intensity noise is random and is often assumed to have a Gaussian distribution. At the same time, the noise also has a random phase too, known as the laser phase noise. The phase noise is often assumed to have a uniform distribution. In this study, we normally ignore the effects of laser noise and assume the use of ideal, noiseless lasers. This is because a typical laser RIN is -150 dB/Hz, which is a small value when compared to the effects of ASE noise in optically amplified systems. Thus, ASE noise usually dominates over the laser noise at the receiver (Mecozzi & Shtaif, 2001). For short-range systems without amplification, RIN can become significant and this has been studied elsewhere (Agrawal, 1997).

The CW signal has to be modulated with information before it is useful for transmission. Modulating the optical carrier wave generates optical signals by superimposing the information signal onto the source. Basically, the modulators can be divided into two: internal or external. In an internal modulator, the laser source itself is directly modified by the information signal to produce a modulated optical field. This type of modulation is generally limited by the linear range of the laser's power characteristic. Nowadays, the external modulator is generally used, especially for high capacity systems as it has higher performance. In external modulation, the source light is focused through an external device, whose propagation characteristics are altered by the modulating signal. Modulation is achieved via the electro-optic or acoustic effect of the material, in which external currents can modify the transmission properties of the inserted light (carrier wave). These effects can produce delay variations (phase modulation) or intensity changes (intensity modulation) on the excited beam. In this way, the information on the electrical signal would be imprinted onto the optical carrier wave creating the optical signal or pulse stream.

Modulation is defined as the process by which some characteristics of the carrier are varied in accordance with a modulating wave. Thus, we can decide how to encode the information normally carried in binary form onto the carrier. In digital communication, the modulating wave consists of binary data or an M-ary encoded version of it. Digital modulation is generally used as it provides more information capacity, compatibility with digital data services, higher data security and also better quality communication. Modulation formats for optical communication systems are similar to their counterparts in radio and microwave communication. Three basic modulation formats can be considered for optical transmission: phase, amplitude or frequency modulation in modulating the optical carrier. The digital representatives of these modulations are phase shift keying (PSK), amplitude shift keying (ASK), and frequency shift keying (FSK).

In phase shift keying (Linke & Gnauck, 1998), the phase is modulated while keeping the amplitude and the frequency constant. For 2-level encoding, the phase generally takes two values, 0 and π depending on whether a '1' or a '0' is transmitted. In frequency shift keying, the information is encoded on the optical carrier by shifting the carrier frequency itself. For 2-level encoding, the carrier frequency takes 2 values depending on whether a '1' or a '0' is transmitted. FSK modulation can also be viewed as a kind of PSK modulation such that the carrier's phase increases or decreases linearly over the bit duration.

Amplitude shift keying (ASK) is also called intensity modulation (IM) or on-off keying (OOK). It consists of the carrier sinusoid or the pulse-shaped carrier that can be shaped on and off with a unipolar binary signal. ASK was among the first modulation techniques to be used and precedes analog communication systems. In ASK format, the amplitude is modulated while keeping the frequency and the phase constant. For 2-level encoding, the amplitude takes one of two fixed values during each bit period, depending on whether a '1' or '0' is being transmitted. In most practical cases, the amplitude will be set to zero during the transmission of the '0' bit.

Amplitude modulation is still the most often used modulation format in optical systems. For the OOK system, the general optical signal is given by

$$U\left(t\right) = \left\{ \sum_{n=0}^{N-1} a_n p\left(t - nT\right) \right\} L\left(\lambda_l, t\right) \qquad (9.3)$$

where a_n is the PRBS of length $N = (2^{15})/M$ bits and M is the number of OTDM channels, T is the single OTDM channel signal bit period and $p(t)$ is the signal pulse shape.

$L(t)$ represents the CW laser and this function can normally be ignored in system simulations. This is because the slowly varying envelope approximation is often used to reduce simulation time. In this approximation, the signal modulation rate is assumed to be significantly slower than the laser frequency. When this is assumed, the effects of the laser frequency can be safely ignored and the CW function may be removed resulting in

$$U\left(t\right) = \sum_{n=0}^{N-1} a_n p\left(t - nT\right) \qquad (9.4)$$

In effect, the approximation translates the center of the signal frequency domain from zero to ω_l. The resultant simulated signal is the outer trace (envelope) of the modulated CW signal. This approximation holds true even for modern day high bit rate optical systems as the laser frequency in the 1550 nm transmission window is around 193.55 THz; still significantly higher than the signal modulation rate or bit rate.

From equation (9.4), we can see that the optical pulse stream is modulated using the bit sequence, a_n and a specified signal pulse shape, $p(t)$. The bit sequence can be any random (or even non-random) sequence of 1's and 0's. On the other hand, the pulse shape is an important parameter that can be specified by the system engineer and determines the modulation format. Pulse shapes can be categorized into the return-to-zero (RZ) or non-return-to-zero (NRZ) modulating formats. The NRZ format consists ideally of basic square pulses as shown in Figure 2(a), where the signal pulse is in its 'on' state over the entire bit period for a 1 bit. The expression of the ideal NRZ pulse is given by

$$p(t) = \text{rect}(t(M/T)) \tag{9.5}$$

where rect() is the rectangular function. In practice, the ideal instantaneous shift of the rectangular function is impossible and the NRZ looks more like Figure 2(b) where there is a small gradient (slope) at the shift. On the other hand, the RZ format consists of signal pulses that are only in their 'on' state over a portion of the bit period. The key attribute that differentiates the RZ and NRZ format is the amount of the bit period that represents the encoded information. For NRZ, the entire bit period is used to encode the information while for RZ only a portion of the bit period is used. The duration of time in which the pulses stay at its 'on' state is measured by the duty cycle

$$DC = t_{FWHM,} / T_R \tag{9.6}$$

where $t_{FWHM,}$ is the full wave half maximum (FWHM) width of the RZ pulse and $T_R = T/M$ Thus, the NRZ format would ideally have DC = 1 or 100% duty cycle, while RZ formats normally use 33%, 50% or 67% duty cycles.

There are many types of RZ formats and these are classified based on the particular pulse shape used. Some of the pulse shapes used in RZ formats include the hyperbolic-secant pulse (used in solitons), the Gaussian pulse or the raised-cosine pulse (Agrawal, 2001).

Hyperbolic-secant:

$$p\left(t\right) = \sec h\left(\frac{t}{t_0}\right)\exp\left(-\frac{iCt^2}{2t_0^2}\right) \tag{9.7}$$

$$t_0 = t_{FWHM} / 1.763 \tag{9.8}$$

Figure 2. Signal consisting of (a) NRZ pulses (ideal) (b) NRZ pulses (practical) and (c) RZ pulses (Gaussian shaped) (Hiew, Abbou, & Chuah, 2006)

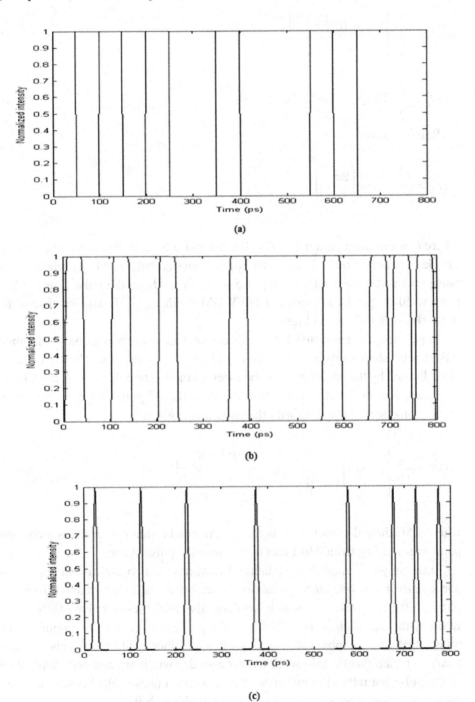

(a)

(b)

(c)

Gaussian or Super-Gaussian:

$$p(t) = \exp\left(-\frac{1+iC}{2}\left(\frac{t}{t_0}\right)^{2m}\right)$$

(9.9)

$$t_0 = t_{FWHM} / (2 \exp(-0.366512921/(2m)))$$

(9.10)

Raised-cosine:

$$p(t) = \frac{1}{2}\left(1 - \cos\left(\frac{2\pi}{T_R}t\right)\right)$$

(9.11)

where C is the chirp parameter ($C = 0$ if the pulse is chirp-free), m is the order of the Gaussian pulse ($m > 1$ denotes a Super-Gaussian pulse) and t_0 is related to the pulse width (the exact relation to pulse width depends on the pulse shape, where pulse width is specified in terms of its FWHM width, t_{FWHM}). Examples of some RZ pulse shapes are shown in Figure 3.

In practice, the generated RZ pulses are kept as close as possible to the theoretical pulse shapes given in equations (9.7) – (9.11) as required. However, we are often limited by the capabilities of the external modulation devices. A model used in (Pauer, Winzer, & Leeb, 2001) tries to follow the RZ pulse shape generally seen in most practical modulators with the pulse shape given by

$$p(t) = \frac{E_b}{2T_p}\left[1 - \sin\left(\frac{\pi}{\alpha T_p}\left(\left|t - (1+\alpha)\frac{T_p}{2}\right| - \frac{T_p}{2}\right)\right)\right]$$

(9.12)

where E_b is the pulse energy, T_p is the effective pulse duration and α is a constant parameter ranging from 0 to 1 that determines the pulse shape.

In recent years, another modulation format has seen an increase in popularity, particularly in new breakthrough laboratory experiments. This format is differential phase shift keying (DPSK), which is a derivative of the regular phase shift keying whereby the signal phase is shifted by π if a particular symbol (for example, 0) is transmitted while no phase shift occurs when the other symbol (e.g. 1) is transmitted. This means that the information is not encoded within the absolute phase of the signal pulse but rather the presence or absence of a phase shift between adjacent pulses, which in other words is the differential phase shift.

Figure 3. Examples of RZ pulse shapes (Hiew, Abbou, & Chuah, 2006)

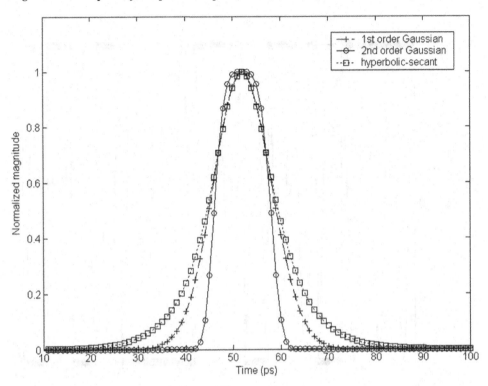

The advantage of this method over conventional phase shift keying is that the receiver need not have a reference clock that is in phase with the transmitter clock. This allows for the use of a direct detection receiver. Recently, this modulation format, called RZ-DPSK when used with RZ pulses, has attracted a lot of interest due to published findings that show its ability to suppress nonlinear effects (Xu, 2003; Wang & Kahn, 2004). This is in addition to its well-known advantage of having a 3-dB improvement in receiver sensitivity over OOK formats when used with a balanced detector (Spellmeyer, Gottschalk, Caplan, & Stevens, 2004; Humblet Azizoglu, & Azizoglu, 1991). The DPSK signal shown in in Figure 4 is given by

$$U(t) = \sum_{n=0}^{N-1} p(t - nT) \exp\left(jb_n d(t - nT)\right) \tag{9.13}$$

Figure 4. DPSK modulated carrier (Hiew, Abbou, & Chuah, 2006)

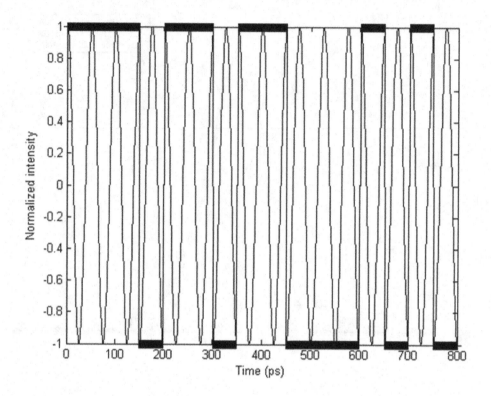

where $d(t)$ is the differential phase pulse shape generally given by the ideal rectangular function and b_n is the differential phase sequence related to the bit sequence. For the common binary DPSK (BDPSK) format with 1 bit/symbol and if a phase shift occurs when $a_n = 0$ and no phase shift occurs when $a_n = 1$, b_n is given by

$$b_n = | \pi(1-a_n) - b_{n-1} | \qquad (9.14)$$

where the first (initial) value of b_n is arbitrarily 0 or π.

Lately, the issue of the type of modulation to be used for WDM systems has attracted much attention. Previously, most systems employed NRZ OOK with direct detection due to its simplicity, small spectral width and the complications of coherent detection. However, further studies into propagation effects that occur within the fiber have revealed that RZ pulse modulation can attain better transmission performance (Linke & Gnauck, 1998). This has also led to the development of soliton transmission. The increased performance of RZ modulation lies in its ability to withstand nonlinear effects and residual dispersion in the fiber despite its inherently wider spectral width compared to the NRZ modulation. Some systems have also employed frequency chirping to the RZ pulses to help increase performance (Mu, Yu, Grigoryan, & Menyuk, 2002).

The search for better modulation techniques has led back to increased interest into RZ-DPSK modulation as discussed earlier. Another modulation technique developed is the optical duobinary modulation, a fundamental correlative coding in partial response signaling which is RZ in nature. It requires an additional coding and encoding processes, but it can be recovered using conventional direct detection type optical receivers. The duobinary transmission technique was studied by Lender in the 60's as a means of transmitting binary data into an electrical cable with high frequency cut-off characteristics. Recently, it has been applied to optical systems due to its narrower spectrum that promises to reduce the effects of linear crosstalk and increase tolerance towards dispersion (Kim & Yu, 2002). This enables the reduction of WDM channel spacing, thus increasing the spectral density. A later study clarified that the optical duobinary modulation offers no advantage over ordinary binary modulation in terms of the average high frequency spectral content as long as the same basic pulse shapes are used, but an improvement in spectral efficiency is achievable by using narrow band pulses in the duobinary case (Shtaif & Gnauck, 1999). Another modulation technique also currently under study is the pulse position modulation (PPM) where the intensity of the RZ pulse is constant, but its position changes according to the bit logic (Leeson, 2004).

A new area that has also generated interest is to increase the bit rate per symbol in an effort to increase the spectral density. Previously, all the optical modulation techniques discussed used 1 bit per symbol or 1 bit per baud. It is widely known that current electronic communication systems generally use multiple bits per symbol to increase transmission capacity. Research is underway to look at the prospect of bringing this to optical communication by adopting modulation techniques with multiple bits per symbol, such as multiple level OOK (Agrawal, 2001), differential quadrature phase shift keying (DQPSK) (Cho, 2004; Milivojevic, 2005), differential 8-PSK (D8PSK) (Han & Li, 2005) and multiple bits per symbol PPM (Leeson, 2004). The main concern with using these techniques is whether the overall capacity can be increased without sacrificing system reliability in terms of bit error rate (BER). This is because if the new modulation technique increases the bit rate per symbol, but requires an increase in WDM channel spacing to maintain reliable transmission over the required distance, then overall spectral density does not improve. It all comes down to approaching the limiting channel capacity of the optical channel (Kahn & Ho, 2004; Narimanov & Mitra, 2002).

OTDM Multiplexers

In an OTDM system, the optical signal is time multiplexed in the following manner

$$S_{OTDM}\left(\lambda,t\right) = \sum_{m=0}^{M-1} U_m\left(t - mT_R\right) \tag{9.15}$$

where $U_m(t)$ is the signal of the mth OTDM channel, M is the number of OTDM channels and $T_R = T/M$ where T is the bit period of the signals $U_m(t)$. Basically, in equation (9.15) each of the M OTDM channels are delayed till they arrive at their designated bit slots. The delayed forms are then summed together. The process is given in diagram form in Figure 5. For the OTDM system to function properly, the width of the pulses usually specified in terms of its full wave half maximum (FWHM) width has to be below a certain threshold to avoid overlapping between separate OTDM channels after time multiplexing. As a general rule of thumb,

$$t_{FWHM} < T_R \tag{9.16}$$

In practice, the optimum value of t_{FWHM} should be quite significantly smaller.

Notice that in equation (9.15), the time multiplexing occurs as an ideal addition of the respective time-delayed (phase-shifted) OTDM channels. In practice, the time delays induced may not be exact, and this could lead to jitter of the relative OTDM

Figure 5. Functional diagram of OTDM multiplexer (Hiew, Abbou, & Chuah, 2006)

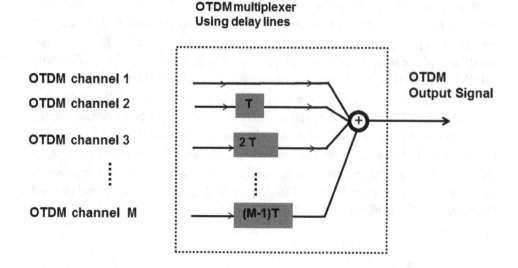

channel positions which could induce timing jitter errors and neighboring channel overlap as in Figure 6. Notice that the timing jitter leads also to amplitude jitter if the jitter is comparable to the bit period as in Figure 6. This is because the pulses can then move into the space of an adjacent pulse causing the addition of the pulses, and inducing amplitude jitter. The amplitude jitter is random since the timing jitter is random. In this study, we assume that the time delays of all the OTDM channels are exact and the subsequent addition of the channels are ideal. In effect, we assume ideal OTDM multiplexing.

Another factor that is important is the extinction ratio of the signal pulses. Extinction ratio is defined as

$$r_{ex} = P_0 / P_1 \qquad (9.17)$$

where P_0 is the off-state (logic 0) power while P_1 is the on-state (logic 1) power. The ideal extinction ratio should be zero. In practice, a finite extinction ratio caused by the tails of the pulses extending over to other bit slots would induce crosstalk between bit slots.

WDM Multiplexers

In an OTDM-WDM system, each multiplexed OTDM signal as specified in equation (9.15) is treated as a separate WDM channel and are multiplexed together using WDM multiplexers. The process is given by

$$A(t) = \sum_{w=1}^{W} \left(S_{OTDM,w}(t) L(\lambda_w, t) \right) \qquad (9.18)$$

Figure 6. OTDM signal with and without random timing jitter (16 x 10 Gb/s OTDM channels, Gaussian pulses with t_{FWHM} = 3 ps) (Hiew, Abbou, & Chuah, 2006)

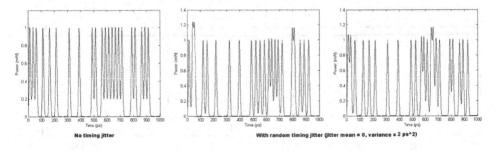

209

where $S_{OTDM,w}$ is the OTDM signal that forms the wth WDM channel and λ_w is the wth channel's center wavelength. In essence, equation (9.18) is just the addition of w OTDM signals where each one has a different center wavelength or frequency. The resulting process is as shown in Figure 7.

For the WDM system to properly function, the WDM channel spacing specified in terms of frequency separation, Δf or wavelength separation $\Delta \lambda$ are key parameters and are given by

$$\Delta \lambda = \lambda_k - \lambda_l \tag{9.19}$$

$$\frac{\Delta \lambda}{\lambda_0} = \frac{\Delta f}{f_0} \tag{9.20}$$

where λ_k and λ_l are the center wavelengths of adjacent WDM channels k and l respectively, while λ_0 and f_0 are the reference wavelength and frequency currently under consideration. To avoid excessive overlapping between adjacent WDM channels and the resultant linear crosstalk, as a general rule of thumb,

$$BW < \Delta f \tag{9.21}$$

where *BW* is the double-sided bandwidth of the WDM channel. However, to increase system capacity in modern day systems, it becomes necessary to reduce the WDM channel spacing to accommodate more channels within the limited amount of bandwidth available in the optical fiber transmission windows. Thus, an important parameter used to quantify system capacity is the spectral density or spectral efficiency given by

Figure 7. Concept diagram of SSFM partitioning process (Hiew, Abbou, & Chuah, 2006)

Fiber of Length, L

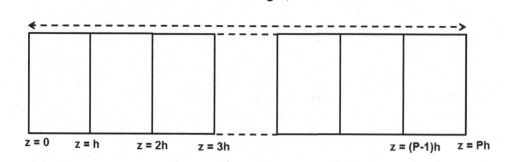

$$S_D = \frac{B_R}{\Delta f} \tag{9.22}$$

where S_D is the spectral density normally given in units of bits/s/Hz and B_R is the WDM channel bit rate. Thus, the limits to channel spacing are continuously pushed to increase system capacity for modern day dense WDM (DWDM) and ultra dense WDM (UDWDM) systems.

Nonlinear Schrodinger Equation (NLSE)

The transmitted signal then flows through the optical fiber link. The commonly used method to model the nonlinear propagation of light signals within an optical fiber cavity is the nonlinear Schrodinger equation (NLSE) given up to the second order dispersion as (Agrawal, 2001),

$$\frac{\partial A}{\partial z} + \beta_1 \frac{\partial A}{\partial t} + \frac{i}{2} \beta_2 \frac{\partial^2 A}{\partial t^2} + \frac{\alpha}{2} A = i\gamma |A|^2 A \tag{9.23}$$

where α is the attenuation parameter, β_1 with v_g being the group velocity, β_2 is the second order dispersion parameter and γ is the nonlinearity coefficient. The NLSE is derived from a simplification of the basic Maxwell's equations that govern the propagation of electromagnetic waves (including optical signals), whereby the optical fiber acts as the propagation medium and sets the boundary conditions (Agrawal, 2001).

For the sake of convenience, a frame of reference moving with the pulse at the group velocity v_g (called the retarded frame) is often used, with the transformation $T = t - z/v_g = t - \beta_1 z$. The result of the transformation of equation (9.23) is (Agrawal, 2001).

$$\frac{\partial A}{\partial z} + \frac{i}{2} \beta_2 \frac{\partial^2 A}{\partial T^2} + \frac{\alpha}{2} A = i\gamma |A|^2 A \tag{9.24}$$

Equation (9.24) is often referred to as the basic NLSE. The equation works to describe the propagation of a signal in a dispersive, nonlinear medium under the effect of attenuation. However, for ultrashort optical pulses (width < 100fs), where the spectral width of the pulses becomes comparable with the carrier frequency, other effects such as third order dispersion and intrapulse Raman scattering become important. Intrapulse Raman scattering originates from the retarded nature of nonlinear response and causes self-frequency shift (Agrawal, 2001). Inclusion of the delayed nonlinear response using the perturbative approach and the third order dispersion leads to

$$
\frac{\partial A}{\partial z} + \frac{i}{2}\beta_2 \frac{\partial^2 A}{\partial T^2} - \frac{1}{6}\beta_3 \frac{\partial^3 A}{\partial T^3} + \frac{\alpha}{2}A =
$$
$$
i\gamma \left[|A|^2 A - \frac{i}{\omega_0}\frac{\partial}{\partial T}\left(|A|^2 A \right) - R_T A \frac{\partial |A|^2}{\partial T} \right]
$$

(9.25)

where β_3 is the third order dispersion parameter, ω_0 is the optical carrier frequency and R_T is related to the slope of the Raman gain.

There are three new terms in equation (9.25) as compared to equation (9.24). The new term on the left hand side takes into account the third order dispersion parameter. Keep in mind that the order of the dispersion parameter can be taken to whatever number that we choose to use (including fourth, fifth, etc). Taking up to a higher order of dispersion would lead to a more accurate model of the dispersion curve with the cost of larger computational effort. Some simulation programs have used up to fifth order dispersion but third order dispersion is generally sufficient for most current applications. The second term on the right hand side is responsible for self-steepening and shock formation at a pulse edge (Agrawal, 2001), a phenomenon that has attracted some attention but is generally not too important in analyzing the performance of optical systems and may be ignored. The third term on the right has its origin in the delayed Raman response and is responsible for the self-frequency shift mentioned earlier.

Equation (9.25) is often referred to as the generalized NLSE and it is capable of accurately simulating the propagation of a lightwave within an optical fiber. However, there are still a number of assumptions implicit within this equation. Firstly, the equation assumes that the signal varies at a rate much slower than the carrier frequency (the so-called slowly varying envelope approximation or the paraxial approximation). This assumption is valid so long as the optical pulse width is much larger than the optical period. This approximation breaks down for pulses shorter than 10 fs. When this occurs, the Maxwell equations that govern the signal propagation need to be solved directly in the time domain using finite-difference methods (Agrawal, 2001). These methods are more accurate than the NLSE with fewer approximations made, but it comes with the cost of a vast increase in computational effort. Thus, the NLSE is generally used instead, as even today's most advanced systems still utilize pulses that are much wider than the optical period.

Another assumption in equation (9.25) is that the signal is traveling with a single polarization. In truth, the signal traveling in an optical fiber may have arbitrary polarization. To model arbitrary polarization, a few adjustments have to be made to the NLSE. Firstly, we split the signal to its two orthogonal polarizations and model both polarization modes. Modal birefringence may be represented by a mode-propagation constant β that is slightly different for the modes polarized in the two orthogonal directions, leading to polarization mode dispersion (PMD) (Noe, Sandel, Mirvoda, 2004; Liu, Zhang, & Guo, 2003). At the same time, the interaction between the two polarization modes through birefringence and nonlinearity has to be taken into account when modeling the propagation of the fiber. To simulate the effects of polarization, many methods have been used. Many of these methods are extensions of the NLSE and usually involve the simulation of the two polarization modes either as two separate NLSE equations linked through a few shared variables or as a two-member vector. A widely used method is the representation of the orthogonal polarizations of the signal as a two-member array in a single vector form of the NLSE, where the lightwave can be represented on a Poincare sphere (Menyuk, 1987). However, the effects of polarization and birefringence are ignored in this study where we assume that all lightwaves within the optical fiber are of a single polarization mode. This allows us to use the single polarization form of the NLSE as given in equation (9.25). We can do this as we have avoided the use of polarization multiplexing techniques and assumed the negligibility of polarization-related effects.

On the other hand, equation (9.25) also ignores the effects of SRS and SBS as the detailed study of both these effects is beyond the scope of this book. For the cases studied in this work, SRS effects can be safely ignored, as the SRS threshold power is very high and generally not attained. Furthermore, the SRS frequency shift is large and thus, the generated wave is normally out of the considered bandwidth. At the same time, we have also chosen not to explore the use of Raman fiber amplifiers. For systems employing Raman fiber amplifiers, adjustments have to be made to the NLSE to account for the effect of SRS by modeling the forward or backward propagating Raman wave and its interaction with the signal (Park, 2004; Liu, Zhang, & Guo, 2003). For SBS, the threshold power is lower and may be attained. However, this threshold power increases with higher bit rates, and most systems considered in this report are of very high bit rates. Furthermore, the main effect of SBS on the signals is limited to pump depletion as the spectral width of the Brillouin-gain spectrum is very small (~10MHz), and generated waves would normally fall outside the channels' bandwidths. Also, the generated waves are backward propagating and would not arrive at the receiver.

This brings us to another assumption present in equation (9.25), which is the assumption that the optical waves in the fiber only propagate in the forward direction. It ignores all waves that may be propagating backwards. Due to this, equation (9.25) is unsuitable to model systems where signals are propagated along both directions in a fiber. A commonly used system where waves propagate in both directions in a fiber is the backward-pumped Raman amplified optical fiber system (Bouteiller, Leng, & Headley, 2004; Zhou, 2004). To account for signals propagating in both directions, modifications can be made to the NLSE, using two interlinked equations that govern forward and backward propagation respectively (Park, 2004; Liu, Zhang, & Guo, 2003). For systems where signals are launched only in one direction, there may still be waves generated during propagation that move backwards. These waves could be generated due to SRS, SBS, Rayleigh or Mie scattering. They are normally small in magnitude and do not add up coherently, thereby not generating a significant interfering signal in the backward direction. The main effect of these phenomena would be pump depletion in the forward direction. However, the depletion occurs randomly and, taken on the average, it is represented in the attenuation factor of the fiber. In this study, we can safely assume single direction propagation since we do not use Raman fiber amplifiers.

Lastly, for the purposes of this study, we shall also ignore the effect of intrapulse Raman scattering (delayed nonlinear Raman response). This is done by neglecting the third term on the right hand side of equation (9.25). Though this term can become important in the study of high-speed optical communication systems and can occasionally be significant (Jiang & Fan, 2003; Peleg, 2004; Kumar, 1998), we have decided to focus on the generally more detrimental effects induced by the Kerr nonlinearity.

In applying the NLSE to OTDM-WDM systems, there are different ways to represent the multiple WDM channels. For WDM systems, each channel resides on different center frequencies, and we have to factor in the effects of interchannel XPM and FWM. There are generally two techniques used, which we call the distributed channel approach (Leibrich & Rosenkranz, 2003) and the lumped channel approach (Yu, Reimer, Grigoryan, & Menyuk, 2000). For the distributed channel approach, each WDM channel under study is modeled with its own separate NLSE that has to be solved. The XPM and FWM effects are included in additional terms on the right. For instance, the NLSE for a *W* channel WDM system would look like this

$$
\frac{\partial A_k}{\partial z} + \frac{\alpha_k}{2} A_k + \beta_1 \frac{\partial A_k}{\partial t} + \frac{i}{2} \beta_{2k} \frac{\partial^2 A_k}{\partial t^2} =
$$

$$
i\gamma_k \left[\left| A_k \right|^2 + 2\sum_{\substack{j=1 \\ j \neq k}}^{W} \left| A_j \right|^2 + \left[2 A_2^* A_3 A_4 e^{i\Delta\beta z} + \ldots \right] \right]
$$

(9.26)

where k denotes the kth channel. The first term on the right accounts for SPM, the second group of terms account for XPM and the third group of terms account for FWM. This technique has been proven effective in the calculation of XPM effects through the summation term on the right, where the contribution of each WDM channel other than the currently considered channel is summed up. However, it is impractical to be used when FWM is to be taken into account. This is because each new FWM mix requires a new term on the right hand side of equation (9.26), which has been abbreviated to only one term in the equation here to save space. Each new term represents a new FWM mix. The number of mixes increases greatly for increasing WDM channels, thus creating an impractical number of terms in equation (9.26) that has to be dealt with. Therefore, the distributed channel approach is often used only for the simulation of WDM systems when we want to ignore FWM and look at the effect of SPM or XPM alone. In this method, each channel has its own NLSE and these NLSEs are linked together by the XPM summation term. Thus, they have to be solved one by one through a particular distance step before we can progress to the next distance step.

The lumped channel approach is the more general approach that allows us to take into account all the effects at once. In this approach, all the WDM channels that we intend to simulate are multiplexed together as in equation (9.18) and considered as one signal. This signal is used as the input to equation (9.25). We just substitute the A in equation (9.25) with the OTDM-WDM signal given in equation (9.18). In this way, all interchannel effects such as XPM and FWM are automatically considered together with SPM within the nonlinear term on the right hand side of equation (9.25). This is because all the WDM channels' information is contained within A and any beating effects are automatically calculated when the nonlinear effects are considered. The lumped channel approach is thus more suitable for use in any general simulation of an optical system.

SPLIT-STEP FOURIER METHOD (SSFM)

The NLSE is a nonlinear partial differential equation that does not generally lead to analytical solutions except in some specific cases where the inverse scattering method can be employed (Agrawal, 2001). Thus, numerical approaches are often necessary to solve the equation and can be classified into two broad categories, namely, the finite-difference methods and the pseudospectral methods. Both methods have developed in parallel, though the more popular choice for modeling propagation through an optical fiber is the pseudospectral methods as they are generally faster by up to an order of magnitude for the same accuracy (Agrawal, 2001). Finite-difference methods have been applied for specific situations where the paraxial (slowly-varying envelope) approximations need to be relaxed or sometimes for the study of bidirectional beam propagation.

A pseudospectral method that has been extensively used to solve the pulse-propagation problem in nonlinear dispersive media is the split-step Fourier method (SSFM). This method is relatively fast and accurate in solving the NLSE. It can be readily applied to equation (9.25) by writing the equation in the form (Agrawal, 2001)

$$\frac{\partial A}{\partial z} = \left(D' + N'\right)A \tag{9.27}$$

where D' is a differential operator that accounts for linear effects and N' is a nonlinear operator that governs the effect of fiber nonlinearities given as

$$D' = -\frac{i}{2}\beta_2 \frac{\partial^2}{\partial T^2} + \frac{1}{6}\beta_3 \frac{\partial^3}{\partial T^3} - \frac{\alpha}{2}$$

$$N' = i\gamma\left[\left|A\right|^2 + \frac{2i}{\omega_0 A}\frac{\partial}{\partial T}\left(\left|A\right|^2 A\right) - R_T \frac{\partial\left|A\right|^2}{\partial T}\right] \tag{9.28}$$

For a short distance h, the solution of equation (9.27) may be approximated by

$$A\left(z+h,T\right) \approx \exp\left(hD'\right)\exp\left(hN'\right)A\left(z,T\right) \tag{9.29}$$

SSFM obtains an approximate solution by assuming that in propagating the optical field over a small distance h, the linear and nonlinear effects can be approximated to act independently. To do this, propagation from z to $(z + h)$ is carried out in two steps where in one part the nonlinear effects act alone while in the other part, the linear effects act alone. This method converges to the actual answer as h approaches zero. The execution of the linear operator over the distance h is carried out in the frequency domain using

$$\exp\left(hD'\right)A\left(z,T\right) = \left\{F^{-1}\exp\left[hD'\left(i\omega\right)\right]F\right\}A\left(z,T\right) \tag{9.30}$$

where F is the Fourier transform operator and F^{-1} is the inverse Fourier transform operator. On the other hand, the nonlinear operator is carried out in the time domain using

$$\exp\left(hN'\right)A\left(z,T\right) = \exp\left(hN'\left(t\right)\right)A\left(z,T\right) \qquad (9.31)$$

Notice that equation (9.29) obtains the signal at a distance of $(z + h)$ through computation of the known signal at distance z. To apply this to an actual fiber link of length L, we first divide the link into P equal portions of length Δz each, where $\Delta z = h$ and $L = P\Delta z = Ph$. If we know the nature of the transmitted signal at the beginning of the fiber link, $A(0,T)$, we can then use that as our starting point. Specifically, for the OTDM-WDM system, the initial transmitted signal is given by equation (9.18). Therefore, we can now use equation (9.29) to obtain the signal at distance h. Knowing the signal at distance h, we can then apply equation (9.29) again to obtain the signal at $2h$. This process is iterated until we obtain the signal at the end of the link at length L. In this way, the SSFM can be used to solve the NLSE step-by-step from the initial input signal to the final output at the end of the fiber. The length of Δz or h is known as the step size and a single portion is known as a step. A concept diagram is shown in Figure 7.

From equations (9.30) and (9.31), we can see that the linear effects are solved in the frequency domain while the nonlinear effects are solved in the time domain. Switching between the two domains is achieved using the fast Fourier transform (FFT). By assuming that linear and nonlinear effects are independent over the step size Δz, SSFM indirectly assumes that the nonlinear effects that arise within a single step occur instantaneously at a single position within the step, where in Figure 8(a) it is assumed to occur at the tail end of the portion. To improve the accuracy of the SSFM, it is common to assume that the nonlinear effects act at the center of the portion instead (Agrawal, 2001) so as to provide a more accurate balance. To do this, the linear operator is first simulated over the length $(1/2)\Delta z$, then the nonlinear operator with length of Δz is applied instantaneously at the center of the step size, and after that the linear operator is simulated over the remaining $(1/2)\Delta z$. The concept is shown in Figure 8(b).

The accuracy of the SSFM is largely dependent on the Δz parameter and the SSFM converges to absolute accuracy as Δz approaches zero. However, the smaller the step size is, the more number of steps has to be performed to fully simulate over the entire length of fiber under study. Absolute accuracy requires $\Delta z = 0$, which results in an infinite number of steps. Thus, absolute accuracy is impossible to achieve and in practice, we have to trade off accuracy with processing time, by assuming a short step size that can still maintain a required amount of accuracy. Even on the latest, fastest computers, the SSFM can be very time consuming, especially when simulating long distance systems or WDM systems where many channels have to be considered. Thus, many methods have been developed to increase the accuracy of the estimation using the same step sizes.

Figure 8. Location of effects using the SSFM process with (a) nonlinear effects at tail end of step size and (b) nonlinear effects at center of step size (Hiew, Abbou, & Chuah, 2006)

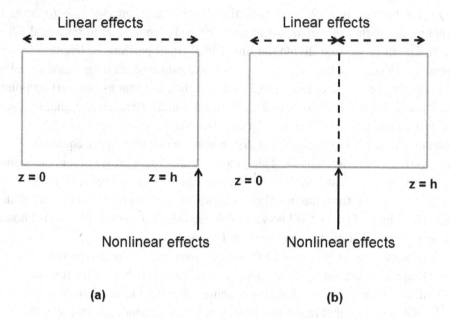

(a)   (b)

A simple method to improve the accuracy of estimation utilizes the trapezoidal approximation also known as the symmetrized SSFM (S-SSFM) where the SSFM for each step size is performed one and a half times. After obtaining the solution over one step size using equation (9.31) as the nonlinear operation, the output signal of the step, $A'(z+h,t)$ is obtained and this output signal is then used to re-estimate the nonlinear effects operator such that the nonlinear operator is now given by

$$\exp\left(hN'\right)A\left(z,T\right) = \exp\left(hN'\left(t\right)\right)\frac{A\left(z,T\right) + A\left(z+h,t\right)}{2} \tag{9.32}$$

This nonlinear operator is then reapplied onto the $(1/2)\Delta z$ linear signal and the result is linearly simulated over the final $(1/2)\Delta z$ again to obtain the more accurate output $A(z+h,t)$. The concept diagram is shown in Figure 9.

Using the trapezoidal approximation has led to better accuracies for the same step size (Agrawal, 2001). Thus, it can reduce simulation time even though it requires an additional iteration (1 additional FFT) as the increased accuracy allows us to increase the step size and reduce the number of steps required. The trapezoidal method can be categorized as a second-order predictor where the signal used to

Figure 9. Trapezoidal approximation algorithm for SSFM (Hiew, Abbou, & Chuah, 2006)

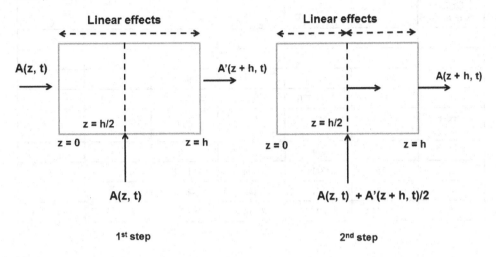

estimate the nonlinear effects is derived from the input signal to the current portion and the initially predicted output signal. This new signal is then used to obtain the new output, which can be called the corrected output.

Recently, another method expands upon this process, called the predictor-corrector SSFM (PC-SSFM) (Liu, Zhang, & Guo, 2003). The PC-SSFM method relies on the use of past data higher than the order of two to estimate the output. Instead of limiting ourselves to the input of the current portion, we actually have at our disposal the knowledge of the signal at the inputs of many past portions. This past knowledge of the signal can be used to better predict the signal at the current distance. This concept has been used before in other scientific fields. This work suggests the use of known inputs of past portions up to the fifth order. It provides the computed, optimal weights that should be multiplied to each past signal depending on its order. These weights are reproduced here in Table 1. As an example, the SSFM operation using the nth-order PC-SSFM can be given as

First:

$$\bar{U}\left(z_{j+1}, T\right) =$$
$$\exp\left(\frac{D'h}{2}\right)\exp\left[h\left(A_j N'_j + A_{j-1} N'_{j-1} + \ldots + A_{j-n+1} N'_{j-n+1}\right)\right]\exp\left(\frac{D'h}{2}\right)U\left(z_j, T\right)$$

Table 1. Weights for PC-SSFM

Order Number n	A_j	A_{j-1}	A_{j-2}	A_{j-3}	A_{j-4}	
2	3/2	-1/2				
3	23/12	-16/12	5/12			
4	55/24	-59/24	37/24	-9/24		
5	1901/720	-2774/720	2616/720	-1274/720	251/720	
Order Number n	C_{j+1}	C_j	C_{j-1}	C_{j-2}	C_{j-3}	C_{j-4}
2	1/4	2/4	1/4			
3	5/24	13/24	7/24	-1/24		
4	9/48	28/48	14/48	-4/48	1/48	
5	251/1440	897/1440	382/1440	-158/1440	87/1440	-19/1440

Then:

$$U\left(z_{j+1}, T\right) =$$
$$\exp\left(\frac{D'h}{2}\right)\exp\left[h\left(C_{j+1}\bar{N}'_{j+1} + C_j N'_j + \ldots + C_{j-n+1}N'_{j-n+1}\right)\right]\exp\left(\frac{D'h}{2}\right)U\left(z_j, T\right)$$

$$(9.33)$$

$\bar{N}'_{j+1}$ is obtained from $\bar{U}\left(z_{j+1}, T\right)$. Notice the similarity to S-SSFM except for the use of more than one previous point for the estimation and the emergence of the coefficients A_j and C_j as weights for the points. A_j and C_j are given in Table 1 for different values of order n.

The PC-SSFM has been shown to produce more accurate results compared to the regular and trapezoidal SSFM for the same value of step size, thus leading to potentially faster computational speeds (Liu, Zhang, & Guo, 2003). The trade-off is that the PC-SSFM increases the computational complexity per step size. However, this does not lead to much additional computational delay because the majority of the time consumed in SSFM calculations is in the FFT computation and the number of FFT computations required is proportional to the number of steps required. The number of FFTs performed in PC-SSFM is same as the trapezoidal method, thus the time taken per step is more or less the same. In this study, the PC-SSFM is used to solve the NLSE.

Time Domain Methods

Solving the NLSE through SSFM is called a pseudospectral method, as previously mentioned. This is because the process is performed while alternating between the time and frequency domains. As mentioned before, the FFT used to transform the signal to either domain is the main consumer of computational time. Therefore, an approach used to overcome this is to solve the propagation of the signal solely in the time domain. Some new methods solve the NLSE purely in the time domain by representing the linear effect of dispersion as a linear filter in the time domain (Carena, Curri, Gaudino, Poggiolini, & Benedetto, 1997). The characteristics of this filter are determined by the dispersion characteristics of the fiber. Thus, all effects are taken into account in the time domain without the need for the FFT. This saves on computational effort and time in the long run even though additional initial calculations have to be made to determine the linear filter characteristics. This method is beyond the scope of this book, but may constitute a subject matter for future work.

ANALYTICAL METHODS

Analytical methods refer to techniques that try to obtain the resulting signal from the initial transmitted signal and system parameters without requiring the use of simulation models such as the NLSE. Instead, the resultant signal can be obtained through the use of a closed-form expression or equation that can be calculated quickly. Ideally, this would be a better alternative. However, due to the large number of effects associated with the optical fiber system, the effects of the various devices and the sheer number of parameters that need to be optimized, derivation of analytical formulas is difficult. As such, it has been mainly limited to specific scenarios such as the inverse scattering method mentioned earlier.

In most other scenarios, non-stationary noise or effects that depend on the random bit sequences are present. In such cases, a fully analytical solution is not possible as we have to account for the randomness. Thus, stochastic methods have been derived that are able to estimate the statistical behavior of the received signal. However, the use of such methods are limited to particular scenarios and normally only certain performance parameters such as BER or amplitude jitter are obtained and not the full representation of the signal. One such method is the moment generating function discussed in Section IV.

Therefore, for the OTDM-WDM system, an analytical model has not been successfully derived. Thus, we still have to rely on simulation models to accurately predict the signal behavior along the fiber propagation. The simulation model accurately tracks the behavior of a specified signal from transmission to reception to bit decision and can be easily integrated with the device models used. To obtain more general results, multiple runs over the same sets of parameters but with random bit sequences and noise can be performed, and the average is taken. Such a technique is absolutely accurate as the number of runs approaches infinity. Therefore, though simulation techniques are accurate, they are very time-consuming. This drives the pursuit to derive time-saving analytical models that can account for more extensive scenarios.

Some promising analytical or semi-analytical techniques that have been suggested in recent years are the use of the Volterra series (Peddanarappagari& Brandt-Pearce, 1998) or the perturbation models, additive (Vannucci, Serena, & Bononi, 2002) and multiplicative (Ciaramella & Forestieri, 2005). These methods seem promising though they also have their share of limitations and assumptions. The study of these methods may be a subject of future work.

Global System Simulation Parameters

From the previous section, we have observed the importance of the distance step size, Δz in determining the computational time. In general, there are a number of global simulation parameters that have to be defined before we can model the optical system effectively. One of it is the previously mentioned step size that is integral to the propagation model of the optical fiber. Another essential parameter is time and, consequently, frequency. The time step, Δt is the resolution of time used to represent the signal. It is required because simulations are performed on computers that use a discrete representation of time. As such, Δt is the space in time between two represented points on a signal. In this way, a signal of bit period T would have $N_T = T/\Delta t$ represented points per bit period. The total number of points used to represent the signal of B bits is then given by

$$N_{total} = N_T \times B \tag{9.34}$$

Basically, the larger the number of points used to represent the signal, the larger the computational effort required to perform operations such as the FFT. To reduce the number of points, we can either reduce the number of bits simulated or N_T. The minimum number of bits required usually depends on the simulation scenario. To observe different effects, a different number of bits is required to obtain good and stable results. For example, reference (Francia, 1999) looks into the minimum number of bits required to obtain stable results in the presence of FWM. In general, results obtained using small numbers of bits tend to be volatile, with high variance between repeated simulations. As the number of simulated bits increase, the results are more stable and possess low variance between repeated simulations. Recently, a study has shown the necessity of high numbers of bits required to accurately simulate WDM signals in the presence of large intrachannel nonlinear effects (Wickham, Essiambre, Gnauck, Winzer, & Chraplyvy, 2004).

Another way to reduce N_{total} is to reduce N_T by increasing Δt. This results in a coarser time scale leading to a less fine representation of the signal. The limit to this is given by the required simulation bandwidth, BW_{sim}. For an OTDM-WDM signal, we have to make sure that

$$BW_{sim} > BW_{WDM},$$ (9.35)

where BW_{WDM} is the bandwidth of the total w-channel multiplexed WDM signal ($BW_{WDM} = wBW$), so that the signal is well represented over its entire spectrum. The time step is inversely related to the simulation bandwidth such that

$$BW_{sim} = 1/\Delta t$$ (9.36)

Thus, the time step can only be increased up to a certain point so that equation (9.35) is maintained. In the same vein, simulating more WDM channels will increase BW_{WDM}, increasing the requirement for the simulation bandwidth and putting more restraint on Δt.

At this point, it is worth mentioning that the inverse relation also exists between the frequency step, Δf and the overall simulation time, t_{total} where

$$t_{total} = N_{total} \times \Delta t$$ (9.37)

The relation is

$$\Delta f = 1/t_{total}$$ (9.38)

For WDM systems, using the lumped channel approach means that we have to simulate a wide bandwidth spectrum in order to fit all the channels in. A wide frequency spectrum corresponds to a short time step, Δt. A short time step means that we need large array sizes to represent a signal with large array sizes once again lead to long processing times. To overcome this, it would be advantageous to reduce the frequency spectrum required by reducing the number of WDM channels simulated. Due to the nature of linear and nonlinear crosstalk where their effects decrease with increasing spacing between the channels, adjacent channels have the most significant effect on any single channel. Therefore, a general approach is to only consider one channel and simulate that channel along with its adjacent channels to account for the crosstalk (Yu, Reimer, Grigoryan, & Menyuk, 2000). We assume that other channels would be similarly affected. The number of adjacent channels required depends on the accuracy desired, balanced with the computational time. It has been shown that taking up to the second or third neighbor is often sufficient to obtain very high accuracy (Yu, Reimer, Grigoryan, & Menyuk, 2000). Densely packed WDM systems would logically require more neighbors to be considered.

Amplifiers

The amplifiers used in this study are EDFAs. For an amplifier gain of G, the input to output signal relation within the amplifier is given by

$$P_{out} = G \times P_{in} \tag{9.39}$$

where P_{in} is the average power of the input signal into the amplifier and P_{out} is the average power of the output signal of the amplifier. This is a simple relation and is general to the operation of all amplifiers. For EDFAs, the amplifier gain is often given in units of decibels as well where

$$G_{dB} = 10 \log(G) \tag{9.40}$$

On the other hand, the ASE is modeled as zero mean, additive white Gaussian noise (AWGN) with variance equal to

$$\sigma_{sp}^2 = n_{sp}(G - 1)h\nu B_o \tag{9.41}$$

where n_{sp} is the population inversion factor (depends on the amplifier design), G is the gain of the amplifier, h is the Planck's constant, ν is the input signal reference frequency and B_o is the ASE noise bandwidth. Mathematically, the Gaussian or normal distribution is given by (Proakis, 1989)

$$f_G\left(x \mid \mu, \sigma\right) = \frac{1}{\sigma\sqrt{2\pi}} \exp\left[\frac{-\left(x - \mu\right)^2}{2\sigma^2}\right] \tag{9.42}$$

where μ and σ are the mean and standard deviation of the distribution respectively. With zero mean and variance given by equation (9.41), the ASE distribution is given by

$$f_{ASE}\left(x \mid \mu, \sigma\right) = \frac{1}{\sqrt{2\pi n_{sp}\left(G-1\right)h\nu B_0}} \exp\left(\frac{-x^2}{2n_{sp}\left(G-1\right)h\nu B_0}\right) \tag{9.43}$$

where x refers to the magnitude of the ASE noise field while the variance of the Gaussian distribution in equation (9.41) is the power of the ASE noise over a noise bandwidth B_0. Meanwhile, the power spectral density (psd) of the ASE white noise spectrum can then be given by

$$S_{ASE} = P_{ASE}/B_0 = \sigma_{sp}^2/B_0 = n_{sp}(G-1)h\nu \tag{9.44}$$

In our simulations, the ASE noise is added onto the signal in the time domain. This is done by building a random time domain representation of the AWGN ASE noise generated by each individual amplifier. We first obtain equation (9.41) with the noise bandwidth B_0 set to BW_{sim}. Using the obtained variance, we can generate a random sequence of the ASE field magnitude through

$$\left|E_{ASE}\right| = \sqrt{\sigma_{sp}^2} A\left[f_G\left(x \mid 0,1\right), N_{total}\right] \tag{9.45}$$

where E_{ASE} is the ASE noise field and $A[f_G(x|0,1),N_{total}]$ is a sequence of length N_{total} points generated by randomly sampling points from a Gaussian distribution given as in equation (9.42) with a mean of 0 and standard deviation of 1. Equation (9.45) generates a random time representation of the ASE field magnitude that is of the same length as the signal sequence. With this method, the ASE noise simulation becomes more accurate and similar to an ideal white noise distribution when the time spacing between the instantaneous time samples approaches zero ($\Delta t \rightarrow 0$). This of course, limited by the processing time as a smaller Δt, results in more sample points and longer processes.

Next, to correctly account for the phase influence of ASE, the ASE noise is modeled with a random phase as well. The model used is a uniform random phase distribution as the ASE emissions in practice can be of any arbitrary phase. The uniform random distribution is given by

$$f_U\left(x \mid a, b\right) = \frac{1}{b-a} I_{[a,b]}\left(x\right) \tag{9.46}$$

where a and b are the edge points and I is a constant line from a to b. A random time representation of the noise phase is built similar to the case of magnitude using

$$\angle E_{ASE} = B\left[f_U\left(x \mid -\pi, \pi\right), N_{total}\right] \tag{9.47}$$

where B is a sequence of length N_{total} points generated by randomly sampling points from a uniform distribution given as equation (9.46) with edge points $-\pi$ and π. The phase is multiplied onto the magnitude obtained in equation (9.45) to obtain the ASE noise field as

$$E_{ASE} = \left|E_{ASE}\right|\exp\left(j\angle E_{ASE}\right) \tag{9.48}$$

The ASE noise field is added onto the signal field after each amplifier along the transmission link such that

$$E_{out} = (E_{in}G) + E_{ASE} \tag{9.49}$$

where E_{in} and E_{out} are the input and output fields of the amplifier respectively.

The Gaussian distributed amplitude, uniform random phase ASE is also known as the complex circular AWGN. The random phase is required to accurately model ASE propagation effects and is especially significant in phase modulated systems, where detection is based on the phase and not the magnitude of the optical signal received. Even for intensity modulated systems, without the random phase, the results are inaccurate, particularly when optical filtering is used.

Filters

In the OTDM-WDM system, optical filters are essential for demultiplexing and noise reduction. It is commonly used for WDM demultiplexing or filtering out excess white noise (particularly ASE noise) both at the receiver and within the fiber link. Occasionally, it is also used right after the transmitter to filter the transmitted pulse into a desired shape. The filters used are classified based on the shape of the filter function. Some of the common filter shapes used are given below in terms of the filter transfer functions or transmitivity, $T(\nu)$ where ν is the frequency parameter.

Gaussian (or Super-Gaussian) filter:

$$T\left(\nu\right) = \exp\left[-\frac{1}{2}\left(\frac{\nu}{\nu_0}\right)^{2m}\right]^2 \tag{9.50}$$

where m is the Gaussian order ($m>1$, indicates a Super-Gaussian filter) and

$\nu_0 = BW/(2\,\exp(-0.366512921/(2m))$ where BW is the filter bandwidth.

Bessel filter:

$$T\left(\nu\right) = \frac{k}{\displaystyle\prod_{n=1}^{N}\left(\nu - p\left(n\right)\right)} \tag{9.51}$$

where k is the gain constant, N is the order of the filter and $p(n)$ are the poles determined by the order and cutoff frequency of the filter, which can be found using lookup tables.

Fabry-Perot filter:

$$T\left(\nu\right) = \frac{1}{1 + \left(\dfrac{2F}{\pi}\right)^2 \sin^2\left(\dfrac{\pi\nu}{FSR}\right)} \tag{9.52}$$

where

$$F = \frac{\pi\sqrt{R}}{1-R}$$

is the finesse, R is the facet power efficiency, and

$$FSR = \frac{c}{2L_{FP}}$$

is the free spectral range of the FP filter, c is the velocity of light in free space and L_{FP} is the effective length of the FP etalon.

Square (ideal) filter:

$$T(\nu) = rect\left(\frac{\nu}{BW}\right) \tag{9.53}$$

The Gaussian filter is commonly used on the optical signal while the Bessel filter is commonly used on the electrical signal after photodetection. In general, the filters are applied onto the signal using the expression

$$F_{out} = F_{in} \times T(\nu) \tag{9.54}$$

where F_{in} and F_{out} are the frequency representations of the input and output signal fields given by $F_{in} = F(E_{in})$ and $E_{out} = F^{-1}(F_{out})$ and F is the Fourier transform function. A comparison of filter shapes is shown in Figure 10.

Figure 10. A comparison of different filter shapes (Filter bandwidth is set to 10 GHz) (Hiew, Abbou, & Chuah, 2006)

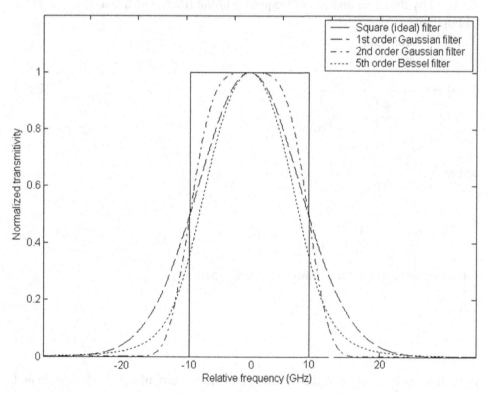

OTDM Demultiplexer

The demultiplexing process is the reverse of the multiplexing process. OTDM demultiplexing is performed in the following manner for m up to M OTDM channels

$$E_{REC,m}\left(t\right) = E_{REC,OTDM,w}\left(t\right)W_S\left(t - (m-1)T_R\right) \tag{9.55}$$

where $E_{REC,OTDM}$ is the received OTDM signal of the wth WDM channel, $U_{REC,m}(t)$ is the demultiplexed m^{th} OTDM channel and $W_S(t)$ is the switching window function given by

$$W_S\left(t\right) = \sum_{n=0}^{N} a_n k\left(t - nT\right) \tag{9.56}$$

where a_n is the bit sequence, N is the number of bits and $k(t)$ is the switching window shape. The switching window shape may be of any pulse shape such as Gaussian, Super-Gaussian, NRZ square or hyperbolic secant.

In practice, the clock timing is extracted from the received OTDM signal using devices such as the phase-locked loop (PLL). In terms of reception, errors can be induced during OTDM demultiplexing. This can occur through imperfect extinction ratio of the demultiplexer switching window or timing jitter of the clock signal caused by imperfect clock timing extraction. A switching window with imperfect extinction ratio for a particular slot may leak over to adjacent slots as in Figure 11 and cause power from adjacent slots to leak into the current slot. This may distort the pulse in the present slot or induces a noise floor if no pulse is present.

On the other hand, imperfect clock timing extraction leads to timing jitter in the position of the switching window with respect to the signal pulse. This effect is significant as a wrongly timed clock would lead to a wrongly positioned switching window as well as sampling at the wrong decision instances. Observe in Figure 12 that when the pulse peak does not coincide with the switching window center, the pulse peak is attenuated. Consequently, the timing jitter induces a corresponding amplitude jitter. This problem can be reduced through the use of windows with a more rectangular shape. Such windows make more allowances for timing jitter without resulting in pulse attenuation. Work is constantly in progress to obtain switching windows with more rectangular shapes (Lee, 2003) which can also be

Figure 11. Imperfect OTDM switching window extinction ratio (16 x 10 Gb/s channels, signal Gaussian pulse width = 3 ps, switching window FWHM width = 5 ps) (Hiew, Abbou, & Chuah, 2006)

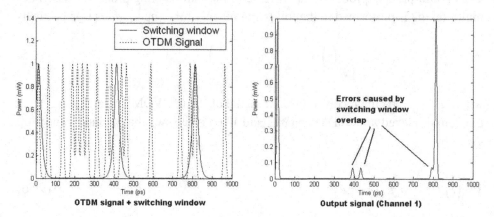

OTDM signal + switching window   Output signal (Channel 1)

modeled as higher-order Gaussian shapes. In our simulations, we assume ideal clock extraction at the center of the bit periods, such that no timing jitter is caused by the clock timing extraction. This simplifies the analysis and is valid for well-constructed clock extraction circuits.

WDM Demultiplexers

The WDM demultiplexing process is typically represented as a filtering function. In this method, the WDM demultiplexer is effectively a repetition of the basic filter function at the center frequency of each of the W WDM channels within the WDM signal given by

$$E_{REC,OTDM,w}\left(\nu\right) = E_{REC,WDM}\left(\nu\right) D_w\left(\nu, f_w\right) \tag{9.57}$$

where $E_{REC,WDM}(\nu)$ is the received WDM signal, $E_{REC,OTDM,w}(\nu)$ is the demultiplexed wth WDM channel and $T(\nu, fw)$ is the filter function of the demultiplexer centered at frequency f_w, which coincides with the center frequency of the wth WDM channel. The filter function may be of any shape. Normally, in our simulations, we choose one of the WDM channels as a target channel. From the perspective of the single target channel, WDM demultiplexing is just a basic filter function. Many commercial demultiplexers have a second-order Gaussian shape, and this is used frequently in this book.

Figure 12. Amplitude jitter induced by timing jitter of the switching window (16 x 10 Gb/s OTDM, signal Gaussian pulse width = 3 ps, switching window FWHM width = 5 ps) (Hiew, Abbou, & Chuah, 2006)

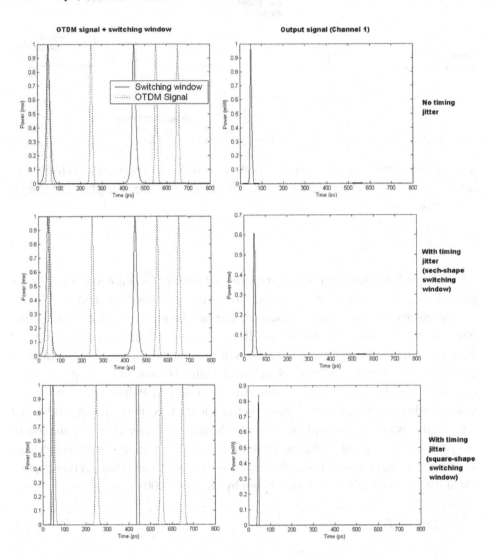

INTENSITY MODULATION: DIRECT DETECTION RECEIVER

The general model of the intensity modulation – direct detection (IM-DD) receivers used in this paper is shown in Figure 13.

The received signal shown is after both the WDM and OTDM demultiplexing process. Looking at Figure 13 closely, we see that the basic configuration is that of

Figure 13. General IM-DD receiver model (Hiew, Abbou, & Chuah, 2006)

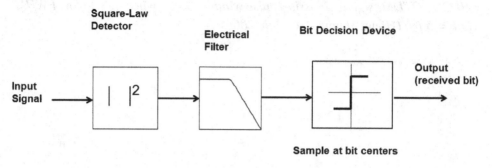

a square-law detector (photodiode), which converts optical power to electrical current, followed by an electrical filter and a bit decision device. The photodiode relation is given by

$$I_{PD}(t) = R_d \mid E_{PD}(t) \mid^2 \qquad (9.58)$$

where $E_{PD}(t)$ is the received optical intensity at the detector (photodiode), R_d is the photodiode responsivity and $I_{PD}(t)$ is the converted photodiode current.

The electrical filter is mainly used to filter out the receiver noises such as shot noise and thermal noise, but it can also filter out excess ASE noise in case the optical filter is not optimal. Shot noise arises from the statistical nature of the production and collection of photoelectrons when optical signal is incident on the photodiode, and these statistics have been demonstrated to follow a Poisson process. In our study, we have assumed a negligible photodiode dark current (Keiser, 2000) and ignored the avalanche multiplication noise (Keiser, 2000) by assuming the use of *pin* photodiodes and not avalanche photodiodes (APD). The shot noise is modeled as additive white Gaussian noise that occurs only when there is optical power present at the photodiode with variance given by (Keiser, 2000)

$$\sigma_{sh}^2 = 2eR_d P_{rec} B_e \qquad (9.59)$$

where e is the electron charge, P_{rec} is the average received optical power and B_e is the electrical filter bandwidth.

Another important noise source is the thermal noise that exists within the external circuitry of the receiver connected to the photodiode. Thermal noise refers to the current flow in the circuit caused by thermal excitation of the electrons. This thermal noise could come from any source, but the most common and unavoidable source would be the room temperature itself. Usually, the thermal noise of the receiver circuit is dominated by the noise from the amplifier that immediately follows the photodiode. This is because the small photocurrent immediately after detection is most vulnerable to the effects of spurious current induced by thermal excitation. The thermal noise is also modeled as white Gaussian noise with variance given by (Keiser, 2000)

$$\sigma^2{}_{th} = \frac{4kTB_e}{R_L} \tag{9.60}$$

where T is temperature in Kelvin, k is the Boltzmann's constant and R_L is the resistance of the load.

Both the shot and thermal noises are added in the time domain in the same manner as the ASE noise except that they are added onto the electrical signal, instead. Due to the presence of shot and thermal noise, a low-pass electrical filter is normally placed after the receiver to filter these noises out. The filter helps reduce the noise by eliminating the portions of the noise that lie outside the signal bandwidth. The shape and bandwidth of the electrical filter is a subject of optimization for each system. The electric filter used is a low-pass filter that can be of any shape, depending on the situation. However, most practical systems use a high order Bessel filter. Mostly, we use a fifth order Bessel filer in our simulations. In our study here, we mostly focus on long distance, periodically amplified systems. In such systems, ASE noise normally dominates over the shot and thermal noise (Bosco, Carena, Gaudino, & Poggiolini, 2002). As such, the shot and thermal noise may be neglected in such scenarios with hardly any loss of accuracy.

A decision device samples the received current at the output of the electrical filter at time instances and compares that value to a decision threshold to determine the bit logic. The sampling time is determined in practice by the clock extraction circuit but in our simulations, we assume ideal clock extraction and take the center of the bit period as the decision instant. Following that, the decision threshold has to be optimized depending on the signal received to obtain the optimal BER. The subject of obtaining the BER using numerical simulations is explored in detail in Section IV.

DPSK RECEIVER

The receiver model described here is based on the general IM system. For different modulation schemes, the receiver configuration is different, but the components used are often the same and the noise models used are similar. For instance, the DPSK receiver block diagram is shown in Figure 14.

The DPSK receiver shown here is based on direct detection with a balanced detection scheme (Gnauck & Winzer, 2005; Xu, Liu, & Wei, 2004; Winzer & Kim, 2003). This is the receiver configuration used in modern DSPK systems as it combines the convenience of direct detection with the sensitivity improvements of differential phase modulation. Phase demodulation is normally performed with a Mach-Zehnder interferometer (MZI) acting as an optical delay interferometer while square-law detection is performed with a photodiode, as described earlier. The output of the two arms of the MZI is the sum and difference respectively of the received signal with its delayed counterpart. The delay used is normally one bit period, T. For a DPSK signal, the sum and difference are the intensity modulated version of the signal and its inverse respectively. For single-port detection, only the signal from the sum arm is photodetected while the two signals are separately photodetected in the balanced detection configuration and compared using a subtractor. The detection and comparison of the signals on both arms creates the 3-dB receiver sensitivity gain when using the balanced detector for direct detection DPSK (Gnauck & Winzer, 2005). The process of balanced detection can be summarized in the following equations

$$E_{DEL}(t) = E_{REC}(t\text{-}T) \tag{9.61}$$

$$E_{SUM}(t) = E_{REC}(t) + E_{DEL}(t) \tag{9.62}$$

Figure 14. DPSK balanced detection receiver (Hiew, Abbou, & Chuah, 2006)

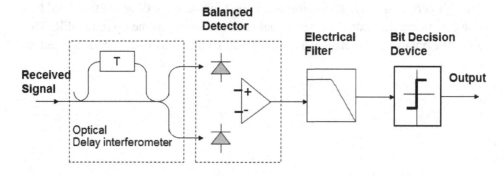

$$E_{DIFF}(t) = E_{REC}(t) - E_{DEL}(t) \tag{9.63}$$

$$E_{OUT}(t) = |E_{SUM}(t)|^2 - |E_{DIFF}(t)|^2 \tag{9.64}$$

where $E_{DEL}(t)$ is the delayed version of the received optical signal field, $E_{REC}(t)$. $E_{SUM}(t)$ and $E_{DIFF}(t)$ are the sum and difference fields that are the outputs of the two MZI arms and $E_{OUT}(t)$ is the output of the subtractor and thus, the output of the balanced detector. $E_{OUT}(t)$ is then fed into the electrical filter, followed by the bit decision device to obtain the received bit.

NETWORK MODELS

The simulation of the system is extended from the point-to-point system to an interconnected network of multiple nodes. Since there are many possible types of networks, the scope of this report has been limited to the modeling of the Manhattan Street Network (MSN) (Maxemchuk, 87). The MSN is an interconnected mesh network consisting of $N = 2^n$ nodes, where n is the dimensions of the network. The block diagram of an N = 16 nodes MSN, also known as MSN16, is shown in Figure 15 where G^O and G^I are the gains of the output or input amplifiers.

Some of the characteristics of the MSN are listed below

1. It is a packet based network that can incorporate WDM technology. Each packet is of the same length and is assumed to occupy the same amount of time, T such that T is a unit of time slot. At the same time, there can also be an arbitrary number of WDM channels. As such, there can be a packet present at each time slot T for each WDM channel.
2. The network consists of nodes and the interconnections between the nodes. Given the dimension of the network n, the number of nodes is N = 2n. A proper MSN can only exist for a number of nodes that correspond to the formula.
3. Each node has two input links and two output links, which are basically fiber connections. The directions of adjacent links are opposite of one another. When a packet moves across a link, it is said to have undergone a hop.
4. The nodes are all interconnected and the links loop back across the network. Thus, all nodes have relatively the same location within the network. Therefore, relative addressing may be used.
5. Each node can receive (absorb) or transmit a packet onto a time slot at each WDM channel if the slot is free. Since there are two inputs for each node, a generated packet may be transmitted only if one of the inputs is free.

Figure 15. Manhattan Street Network block diagram (16 nodes) (Hiew, Abbou, & Chuah, 2006)

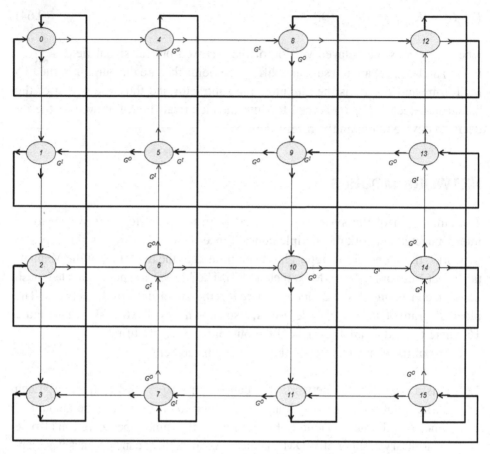

6. Each input can be switched onto either of the two outputs. The choice of output is based on its destination and is computed based on the shortest path algorithm. If both inputs want to be switched onto the same output, a clash occurs and this has to be solved by an appropriate routing algorithm.

To simplify the modeling of the network, a few assumptions are made (Forghieri, Bononi, & Prucnal, 1995).

1. All networks are a combination of nodes and interconnections only, and each propagation from one node to the next is called a hop.
2. Every node is a combination of devices, and each node has the same properties.
3. Each interconnection within the network has the same properties and distance.

4.   The bit times of all channels are aligned.

5.   All lasers transmit with the same power.

With these assumptions made, what remains to be done is to set the models used to represent the nodes and the interconnections between the nodes. Notice that in the method used here, the node and interconnection models used are modular, meaning that any models may be used and can be combined together as separate components. An example of a model of the interconnection is a fiber link. In this report, the interconnection link is typically a DM fiber link with an amplifier placed either at the front or end of the link.

On the other hand, the node may consist of any combination of devices. A typical example of a WDM, two-input, two-output network node is shown in Figure 16 (Castanon, Tonguz & Bononi, 1997).

In Figure 16, the block diagram shows one possible submodule that corresponds to a particular WDM channel. Note that there the number of submodules is equal to the number of WDM channels since each WDM channel is spatially demultiplexed onto each separate submodule. The channels are then combined together again at the output multiplexers. Also, note that each of the two inputs and outputs into a node are WDM multiplexed signals heading into and out from separate directions. At the same time, there are two receivers, but there is only one transmitter in each submodule. Having one transmitter only helps prevent overloading at the outputs.

Most of the devices shown in Figure 16 have already been explored in previous sections. However, one issue that has to be taken into account when modeling the network node is the loss within the node caused by the separate devices and the coupling between them. This is significant because the loss within the node (~12

Figure 16. Network node block diagram (Hiew, Abbou, & Chuah, 2006)

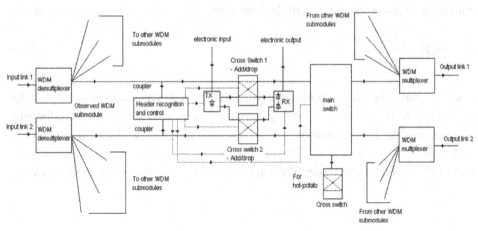

dB) is often much higher than the fiber loss within the interconnections. Thus, an amplifier is often included right after the output to compensate for the losses within the node.

There is also a new device included in Figure 16, which has not been shown before in this report, that is the cross switch. The cross switch can act as an add-drop multiplexer or just as a plain switch between two input signals to two output links. An ideal cross switch can switch the two input signals onto their designated output links without any crosstalk between the signals. However, in a practical cross switch, there is leakage, whereby some portion of an input signal is leaked onto the link that is not its designated output. This leakage, specified by the crosstalk leakage parameter α, induces a crosstalk on the actual signal that is designated for that output link Castanon, Tonguz & Bononi, 1997). This crosstalk is in-band crosstalk since both input signals into the cross switch are of the same wavelength channel. Though the crosstalk leakage is small (-30 dB), its accumulation can be significant. Furthermore, since the crosstalk is a function of the input signal power, it can place a limit to the signal power as well.

Effectively, each cross switch induces a crosstalk on a signal that passes through it. This crosstalk is modeled as an additive colored (band-limited) Gaussian noise with uniform random phase noise

$$PSD_{leak}\left(\nu\right) = S_{leak} rect\left(\frac{\nu}{BW_{eff}}\right) B\left[f_U\left(x \mid -\pi, \pi\right), N_{total}\right] \tag{9.65}$$

where rect is the rectangular function, ν is the frequency parameter and BW_{eff} is the effective noise bandwidth normally about 1-2 times the signal bandwidth. B determines the uniform random phase and is a sequence of length N_{total} points generated by randomly sampling points from a uniform distribution given as in equation (9.46) with edge points $-\pi$ and π. S_{leak} is the leakage crosstalk power spectral density given by

$$S_{leak} = P_{leak}\left(\alpha\right) BW_{eff} \tag{9.66}$$

where $P_{leak}(\alpha)$ is the leakage power that is dependent on the crosstalk leakage parameter α, which specifies the proportion of power that is leaked. A simple intuitive formula to determine the leakage power is $P_{leak}(\alpha) = \alpha P_{in}$ where P_{in} is the input power into each arm of the cross switch. However, in practical networks, $P_{leak}(\alpha)$ is also a function of the probabilistic nature of packet generation and absorption in the network.

When the nodes and interconnections have been modeled, the propagation of the signal over any number of hops until it is absorbed by the receiving node can be easily simulated using all the existing models for the devices and fiber propagation. Thus, the propagation of a signal in a network is effectively just a point-to-point simulation of the signal from transmitting node to receiving node, with the only difference being the interactions within the nodes and the variation in the number of hops. Therefore, we can easily predict that the received signal will differ depending on the number of hops it takes between its transmitting and receiving node. The focus then turns onto the problem of predicting the average number of hops a signal propagates through in order to obtain the average behavior of the signal.

SUMMARY

Various methods and techniques that can be used in OTDM-WDM system components modeling were discussed. Among the key issues that have to be decided upon early as they establish the system link that will be employed are the length of transmission, amplification scheme, and dispersion management scheme. Other key issues such as the signal modulation format, OTDM channel bit rate, WDM channel bit rate, spectral density can be optimized for a particular system setup through simulations to obtain the optimal performance that the system is capable of. After the system has been established, there is still a number of variables that have to be optimized in order to achieve optimal performance for a particular system configuration. Among these parameters are: signal pulse width, optical filter bandwidth, electrical postdetection filter bandwidth, and input power into the transmission link.

REFERENCES

Agrawal, G. P. (Ed.). (1997). *Fiber-optic Communication Systems*. Wiley-Interscience.

Agrawal, G. P. (Ed.). (2001). *Nonlinear Fiber Optics*. Academic Press.

Bosco, G., Carena, A., Curri, V., Gaudino, R., & Poggiolini, P. (2002). On the Use of nrz, rz and csrz Modulation at 40 gb/s with Narrow dwdm Channel Spacing. *Journal of Lightwave Technology, 20*(9), 1694–1704. doi:10.1109/JLT.2002.806309

Bouteiller, J. C., Leng, L., & Headley, C. (2004). Pump-pump Four-wave Mixing in Distributed raman Amplified Systems. *Journal of Lightwave Technology, 22*(3), 723–732. doi:10.1109/JLT.2004.824459

Carena, A., Curri, V., Gaudino, R., Poggiolini, P., & Benedetto, B. (1997). A time-domain Optical Transmission System Simulation Package Accounting for Nonlinear and Polarization-related Effects in Fiber. *IEEE Journal on Selected Areas in Communications, 15*(4), 751–765. doi:10.1109/49.585785

Castanon, G. A., Tonguz, O. K., & Bononi, A. (1997). Ber Performance of Multiwavelength Optical Cross-connected Networks with Deflection Routing. *IEE Proc-Communications., 144*, 114-120.

Cho, P. S., Harston, G., Kerr, C. J., Greenblatt, A. S., Kaplan, A., & Achiam, Y. et al. (2004). Investigation of 2-b/s/hz 40-gb/s dwdm Transmission over 4 x 100 km smf-28 Fiber Using rz-dqpsk and Polarization Multiplexing. *IEEE Photonics Technology Letters, 16*(2), 656–658. doi:10.1109/LPT.2003.821272

Ciaramella, E., & Forestieri, E. (2005). Analytical Approximation of Nonlinear Distortions. *IEEE Photonics Technology Letters, 17*(1), 91–93. doi:10.1109/LPT.2004.838152

Dragone, C. (1989). Efficient N*N star couplers using Fourier optics. *Journal of Lightwave Technology, 7*(3), 479–489. doi:10.1109/50.16884

Forghieri, F., Bononi, A., & Prucnal, P. R. (1995). Analysis and Comparison of Hot-potato and Single-buffer Deflection Routing in Very High Bit Rate Optical Mesh Networks. *IEEE Transactions on Communications, 43*(1), 88–98. doi:10.1109/26.385939

Francia, C. (1999). Constant Step-size Analysis in Numerical Simulation for Correct Four-wave-mixing Power Evaluation in Optical Fiber Transmission Systems. *IEEE Photonics Technology Letters, 11*(1), 69–71. doi:10.1109/68.736394

Gnauck, A. H., & Winzer, P. J. (2005). Optical Phase-shift Keyed Transmission. *Journal of Lightwave Technology, 23*(1), 115–130. doi:10.1109/JLT.2004.840357

Han, Y., & Li, G. (2005). Sensitivity Limits and Degradations in od8psk. *IEEE Photonics Technology Letters, 17*(3), 720–722. doi:10.1109/LPT.2004.842337

Hiew, C. C., Abbou, F. M., & Chuah, H. T. (2006). *Performance Analysis and Design of an Optical TDM-WDM Transmission System and Network* (Tech. Rep. No. 1). Malaysia: Multimedia University and Alcatel Network Systems.

Humblet Azizoglu, P. A., & Azizoglu, M. (1991). On the Bit Error Rate of Lightwave Systems with Optical Amplifiers. *Journal of Lightwave Technology, 9*(11), 1576–1582. doi:10.1109/50.97649

Jiang, Z., & Fan, C. (2003). A Comprehensive Study on xpm- and srs-induced Noise in Cascaded im-dd Optical Fiber Transmission Systems. *Journal of Lightwave Technology*, *21*(4), 953–960. doi:10.1109/JLT.2003.810076

Kahn, J. M., & Ho, K. P. (2004). Spectral Efficiency Limits and Modulation/Detection Techniques for dwdm Systems. *IEEE Journal of Selected Topics in Quantum Electronics*, *10*(2), 259–272. doi:10.1109/JSTQE.2004.826575

Keiser, G. (Ed.). (2000). *Optical Fiber Communications*. McGraw-Hill.

Kim, H., & Yu, C. X. (2002). Optical Duobinary Transmission System Featuring Improved Receiver Sensitivity and Reduced Optical Bandwidth. *IEEE Photonics Technology Letters*, *14*(8), 1205–1207. doi:10.1109/LPT.2002.1022019

Kumar, S. (1998). Influence of Raman Effects in Wavelength-division Multiplexed Soliton Systems. *Optics Letters*, *23*(18), 1450–1452. doi:10.1364/OL.23.001450 PMID:18091813

Lee, J. H. (2003). All-optical tdm Data Demultiplexing at 80 gb/s with Significant Timing Jitter Tolerance Using a Fiber Bragg Grating Based Rectangular Pulse Switching Technology. *Journal of Lightwave Technology*, *21*(11), 2518–2523. doi:10.1109/JLT.2003.819123

Leeson, M. L. (2004). Pulse Position Modulation for Spectrum-sliced Transmission. *IEEE Photonics Technology Letters*, *16*(4), 1191–1193. doi:10.1109/LPT.2004.824668

Leibrich, J., & Rosenkranz, W. (2003). Efficient Numerical Simulation of Multichannel wdm Transmission Systems Limited by xpm. *IEEE Photonics Technology Letters*, *15*(3), 395–397. doi:10.1109/LPT.2003.807901

Linke, R. A., & Gnauck, A. H. (1998). High-capacity Coherent Lightwave Systems. *Journal of Lightwave Technology*, *6*(11), 1750–1769. doi:10.1109/50.9992

Liu, X., & Lee, B. (2003). A Fast Method for Nonlinear Schrodinger Equation. *IEEE Photonics Technology Letters*, *15*(11), 1549–1551. doi:10.1109/LPT.2003.818679

Liu, X., Xie, C., & van Wijngaarden, A. J. (2004). Multichannel pmd Mitigation and Outage Reduction Through fec with Sub-burst-error-correction period pmd Scrambling. *IEEE Photonics Technology Letters*, *16*(9), 2183–2185. doi:10.1109/LPT.2004.833088

Liu, X., Zhang, H., & Guo, Y. (2003). A Novel Method for Raman Amplifier Propagation Equations. *IEEE Photonics Technology Letters*, *15*(3), 392–394. doi:10.1109/LPT.2002.807929

Maxemchuk, N. F. (87). Routing in the Manhattan Street Network. *IEEE Transanction on Communications, 35*, 503-512.

Mecozzi, A., & Shtaif, M. (2001). On the Capacity of Intensity Modulated Systems Using Optical Amplifiers. *IEEE Photonics Technology Letters, 13*(9), 1029–1031. doi:10.1109/68.942683

Menyuk, C. R. (1987). Nonlinear Pulse Propagation in Birefringent Optical Fibers. *IEEE Journal of Quantum Electronics, 23*(2), 174–176. doi:10.1109/JQE.1987.1073308

Milivojevic, B., Abas, A. F., Hidayat, A., Bhandare, S., Sandel, D., & Noe, R. et al. (2005). 1.6-b/s/hz 160-gb/s 230-km rz-dqpsk Polarization Multiplex Transmission with Tunable Dispersion Compensation. *IEEE Photonics Technology Letters, 17*(2), 495–497. doi:10.1109/LPT.2004.839372

Mu, R. M., Yu, T., Grigoryan, V. S., & Menyuk, C. R. (2002). Dynamics of the Chirped Return-to-zero Modulation Format. *Journal of Lightwave Technology, 20*, 608–617. doi:10.1109/50.996580

Narimanov, E. E., & Mitra, P. (2002). The Channel Capacity of a Fiber Optics Communication System: Perturbation Theory. *Journal of Lightwave Technology, 20*(3), 530–537. doi:10.1109/50.989004

Noe, R., Sandel, D., & Mirvoda, V. (2004). Pmd in high-bit-rate Transmission and Means for its Mitigation. *IEEE Journal of Selected Topics in Quantum Electronics, 10*(2), 341–355. doi:10.1109/JSTQE.2004.827842

Park, J., Kim, P., Park, J., Lee, H., & Park, N. (2004). Closed Integral Form Expansion of raman Equation for Efficient Gain Optimization Process. *IEEE Photonics Technology Letters, 16*(7), 1649–1651. doi:10.1109/LPT.2004.827968

Pauer, M., Winzer, P. J., & Leeb, W. R. (2001). Bit Error Probability Reduction in Direct Detection Optical Receivers Using rz Coding. *Journal of Lightwave Technology, 9*(9), 1255–1262. doi:10.1109/50.948272

Peddanarappagari, K. V., & Brandt-Pearce, M. (1998). Volterra Series Approach for Optimizing Fiber-optic Communications System Designs. *Journal of Lightwave Technology, 16*(11), 2046–2055. doi:10.1109/50.730369

Peleg, A. (2004). Log-normal Distribution of Pulse Amplitudes Due to raman Cross Talk in Wavelength Division Multiplexing Soliton Transmission. *Optics Letters, 29*(17), 1980–1982. doi:10.1364/OL.29.001980 PMID:15455753

Proakis, J. G. (Ed.). (1989). *Digital Communications*.

Shtaif, M., & Gnauck, A. H. (1999). The Relation Between Optical Duobinary Modulation and Spectral Efficiency in wdm Systems. *IEEE Photonics Technology Letters, 11*(6), 712–714. doi:10.1109/68.766794

Spellmeyer, N. W., Gottschalk, J. C., Caplan, D. O., & Stevens, M. L. (2004). High-sensitivity 40-gb/s rz-dpsk with Forward Error Correction. *IEEE Photonics Technology Letters, 16*(6), 1579–1581. doi:10.1109/LPT.2004.827417

Vannucci, A., Serena, P., & Bononi, A. (2002). The rp Method: A New tool for the Iterative Solution of the Nonlinear Schrodinger Equation. *Journal of Lightwave Technology, 20*(7), 1102–1112. doi:10.1109/JLT.2002.800376

Wang, J., & Kahn, K. (2004). Impact of Chromatic and Polarization-mode Dispersions on dpsk Systems Using Interferometric Demodulation and Direct Detection. *Journal of Lightwave Technology, 22*(2), 362–371. doi:10.1109/JLT.2003.822101

Wickham, L. K., Essiambre, R. J., Gnauck, A. H., Winzer, P. J., & Chraplyvy, A. R. (2004). Bit Pattern Length Dependence of Intrachannel Nonlinearities in Pseudolinear Transmission. *IEEE Photonics Technology Letters, 16*(6), 1591–1593. doi:10.1109/LPT.2004.826782

Winzer, P. J., & Kim, H. (2003). Degradations in Balanced dpsk Receivers. *Journal of Lightwave Technology, 15*, 1282–1284.

Xu, C., Liu, X., & Wei, X. (2004). Differential Phase-shift Keying for High Spectral Efficiency Optical Transmissions. *IEEE Photonics Technology Letters, 10*, 281–293.

Xu, C., Xiang Liu, , Mollenauer, L. F., & Xing Wei, . (2003). Comparison of Return-to-zero Differential Phase Shift Keying and on-off Keying in Long Haul Dispersion Managed Transmission. *IEEE Photonics Technology Letters, 15*(4), 617–619. doi:10.1109/LPT.2003.809317

Yu, T., Reimer, W. M., Grigoryan, V. S., & Menyuk, C. R. (2000). *A Mean Field Approach for Simulating Wavelength-division Multiplexed Systems*. Academic Press.

Zhou, X., & Birk, M. (2004). New Design Method for a wdm System Employing Broad-band raman Amplification. *IEEE Photonics Technology Letters, 16*(3), 912–914. doi:10.1109/LPT.2004.823726

KEY TERMS AND DEFINITIONS

Amplitude-Shift Keying (ASK): Refers to a modulation technique in which bit values assigned to discrete amplitude levels of an analog carrier waveform to transmit digital data.

Demultiplexer (Demux): Is an optical device that separates the optical stream back into its optical signal component (one-to-many) and directs them to their output lines.

Dispersion Compensation Fiber (DCF): The effects of chromatic dispersion can be mitigated by inserting a fiber segment called dispersion-compensating fiber (DCF) that cancel chromatic dispersion's effects as a light pulse passes through.

Dispersion Management (DM): Refers to the management schemes that not only compensate for the accumulated dispersion but simultaneously optimizes the interaction between non-linear Kerr processes and the optical signal.

Frequency Shift Keying (FSK): Refers to a modulation technique in which information bit values are represented by different frequencies. The binary bit "0" is represented by a wave at a specific frequency, and binary bit "1" is represented by a wave at a different frequency.

Manhattan Street (MS) Network: MSN is a directed regular two-input and two-output mesh connected packet communication network.

Multiplexer (Mux): Is an optical device that allows simultaneous transmission of multiple optical signals across a single fiber link.

Phase Shift Keying (PSK): PSK refers to a modulation technique in which the phase of a transmitted signal is varied to convey information.

Relative Intensity Noise (RIN): Describes the fluctuation of the amplitude and phase of light emitted by a laser diode.

Section 4

Chapter 10
Performance Analysis Models

ABSTRACT

Modeling and performance analysis are crucial components in the understanding and design of high-speed optical communication systems. The purpose of this chapter is to discuss methods and techniques that can be used in modeling and performance analysis. It provides descriptions of various techniques that can be used to efficiently model and evaluate OTDM-WDM systems. Throughout the chapter, examples are used to demonstrate how the techniques can be applied to model and to evaluate the performance of high-speed optical communication systems.

INTRODUCTION

Many methods have been developed to judge the performance of an optical system, some direct and some indirect. This chapter starts by discussing techniques such as the estimation of the eye penalty, calculation of signal to noise ratio (SNR), as well as estimation of amplitude and timing jitter, and Monte Carlo simulation. Further, in order to complete the modeling of the network environment begun in pervious sections, a direct method based BER estimation model for optical networks is discussed using tools that have been developed earlier.

DOI: 10.4018/978-1-4666-6575-0.ch010

EYE PENALTY ESTIMATION

The eye penalty is estimated from the receiver eye diagram, whereby we can use the optical eye diagram or the current eye diagram. The optical eye diagram is drawn based on the received optical signal while the current eye diagram is drawn based on the photodetected current. In order to draw the eye diagram, we plot over P bit periods where P is a small number and every multiple of P bit periods simulated is drawn back over the same axis as shown mathematically below

$$ED\left(t\right) = \sum_{n=0}^{N/P-1} U\left(nPt,\left(n+1\right)Pt\right) \tag{10.1}$$

where $ED(t)$ is the eye diagram, $U(nPt,(n+1)Pt)$ refers to the signal from time nPt to time $(n+1)Pt$ and N is the total number of bits. An eye diagram example is shown in Figure 1.

From the figure, the eye penalty is estimated by

$$\text{Eye penalty (dB)} = 10 \log_{10}(Upp\_thr \, / \, Low\_thr) \tag{10.2}$$

where Upp_thr and Low_thr are the upper and lower thresholds of the eye diagrams respectively obtained from the center of the bit period. A closed eye indicates a high presence of noise while an open eye indicates good system performance. The eye penalty gives a rough estimation of the performance of the system by quantifying the relative 'opening' of the eye.

Figure 1. Receiver current eye diagram with and without distortion (Hiew, Abbou, & Chuah, 2006)

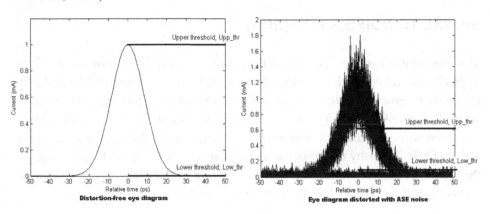

AMPLITUDE AND TIMING JITTER

Some methods attempt to calculate the timing or amplitude jitter induced on the system during propagation or at the receiver. There are again many methods to define the amplitude or timing jitters, depending on the normalization criteria. A simple amplitude jitter definition is given by

$$\text{Amplitude jitter (dB)} = 10 \log_{10}(E[\, |U_1 - E[U_1]| \,] / E[U_1]) \tag{10.3}$$

where $E[]$ is the expected (mean) function and U_1 is the amplitude of the 1's of the signal at the bit period center. In general, amplitude jitter refers to the deviation of the signal pulse amplitude from its mean or stable value. Normally, it is measured at the center of the bit period, which is the time instant used for bit decisions.

A simple timing jitter definition is given by

$$\text{Timing jitter} = E[|\text{Maxt}[U_1] - T|] \tag{10.4}$$

where $\text{Maxt}[]$ is a function that determines the time instant when a signal is maximum within a particular bit period. In general, timing jitter refers to the deviation of the peak of the signal pulse from the actual center of the bit period, which is the time instant used for bit decisions. If the peak deviates from the bit decision instance, the sampled signal will be lower than the peak and, thus, reduces the signal power detected.

The magnitude of the amplitude or timing jitters can be used to estimate the performance of the system. This estimation is useful as the amplitude or timing jitter can often be obtained in closed-form analytical expressions. At the same time, both parameters can be easily measured from signals obtained either through experiments or simulation.

SIGNAL TO NOISE RATIO (SNR)

This method involves the derivation of the signal to noise ratio at the optical receiver. Typically, the ratio calculated is the optical signal to noise ratio (OSNR) at the input of the receiver, although occasionally the SNR of the photodetected current is derived. The SNR is a valid performance indicator as it indicates the level of noise distortion while remaining independent of the absolute values of signal or noise power. There are many methods and derivations to obtain the SNR depending on the signal, noise and system configuration. Many of these methods are obtained from classical communication theory (Proakis, 1989).

In the case of practical OTDM-WDM studied here, the SNR is normally obtained from the resulting simulated signal at the receiver. This SNR is then used either as a performance indicator or as a system parameter. There are many ways to define SNR as given in communication literature (Proakis, 1989). For convenience, it is often useful to define the SNR used. In this study, we use either of the following two definitions

$$OSNR = \int_{B_N} S_S\left(f\right)df \left/ \int_{B_N} S_N\left(f\right)df \right. \tag{10.5}$$

or

$$OSNR = E_b/N_0 = (P_{rec}\, T_R)/(N_0) \tag{10.6}$$

where $S_S(f)$ is the signal power spectral density (psd) function, $S_N(f)$ is the noise psd function, B_N is the noise bandwidth, N_0 is the optical noise power spectral density (psd) with white noise approximation, E_b is the signal bit energy and P_{rec} is the average received signal power. The received OSNR of a signal distorted by accumulated ASE along a transmission link can also be approximated by

$$OSNR = E_b/N_0 = \left(P_{in}T_R\right)\left/\left(\sum_{a=1}^{7} N_a\right)\right. \tag{10.7}$$

where N_a is the noise psd of amplifier a and P_{in} is the average input transmission power per WDM channel into the link..

There is a simple method used to estimate the BER of a system directly from the SNR of the received signal. In this method, the BER is given by (Agrawal, 1997)

$$BER = \frac{1}{2}erfc\left(SNR\right) \tag{10.8}$$

However, this method is a simplistic one that makes many assumptions including a Gaussian distributed noise, negligible effects of waveform distortion and balanced noises at bits '1' and '0'. These assumptions are not generally true and thus, equation (10.6) is not a reliable measure of the BER.

In this study, the SNR is more often used as a system parameter. This means that we specify a range of SNRs for the received signal, and then the performance of the system is evaluated over this range using a more definitive performance estimator.

BIT ERROR RATE

The most direct method in determining the performance or reliability of a system is the bit error rate (BER) defined as (Proakis, 1989)

$$BER = \frac{BitErrors}{N} \qquad (10.9)$$

where *BitErrors* is the number of errors in *N* bits. The BER is the most important parameter as it informs us directly on the expected average performance of the system without any unnecessary intermediaries. Ultimately, the BER is the bottom line that determines the effectiveness and reliability of the system.

To design a reliable system, the commonly taken convention is that the BER must be lower than 10^{-9}. Sometimes, a requirement of 10^{-12} is desired. This requirement has been relaxed recently in some systems where forward error coding (FEC) is employed (Liu, Xie, & van Wijngaarden, 2004; Liu & Wei, 2003). In such systems, the BER requirement is around 10^{-5} because the FEC can be used to correct some of the bit errors, thereby reducing the actual BER after error correction. Still, the necessary requirement for BER is generally very low. In an experimental setup, we can obtain the BER by using an actual BER counter to count the bit errors that occur during transmission over a reasonable span of time. To obtain a good BER estimate, we average the bit errors obtained over a reasonable number of bits transmitted using equation (10.9). A general rule of thumb for a reasonable number of bits required is that N > 10(1/BER). This is easily obtained in experiments because we can simply average over a large number of transmitted bits by taking the bit error measurements over a long span of time.

In numerical simulations, the BER has to be estimated or approximated based on the system models and calculations. Generally, the techniques used for BER approximation can be classified into three broad categories. These are the simulation methods, the analytical methods and the semi-analytical methods. Simulation methods attempt to estimate the BER from the signal at the receiver obtained by simulating a bit sequence through the entire system model. This is time consuming but accurate. On the other hand, analytical methods aim to derive closed-form expressions or equations that can calculate the BER given a set of system parameters. This is ideally what is desired because with such equations, the BER can be calculated quickly for various different parameters without the need for lengthy simulations. However, as noted earlier, derivation of analytical formulas is difficult. As such, it has been mainly limited to specific scenarios, configurations and particular effects Marcuse, 1991; Wang & Kahn, 2004). A way to extend the scope of an analytical formula is to apply it to a signal obtained through simulation. This is called the semi-analytical method in which part of the results is obtained from simulation and the remaining part through an analytical formula.

MONTE-CARLO SIMULATION

A classic example of a simulation method to estimate the BER of a system is the Monte Carlo simulation (Proakis, 1989; Jeruchim, Balaban, & Shanmugam, 1992). This is perhaps the most generally applicable method to estimate BERs from simulations of communication systems. Generally, in numerical simulations, obtaining the BER is a difficult problem. This is because of the large number of bits required to correctly estimate low BERs which require us to simulate long bit sequences and model their propagation through the system to the receiver, where the bit decision is made on the received signal. Simulating and modeling the propagation of long bit sequences take a lot of processing power and consequently, long periods of time as explained earlier. This processing time can be incurred during the generation, filtering or reception of the signal, but most of the delay is incurred in the iterative methods necessary for the solution of the NLSE that models fiber propagation.

Generally, the bit stream used in a computer simulation is a pseudorandom bit sequence (PRBS) of a finite length, N bits. To obtain the BER at the low values required, we have to simulate a PRBS sequence that is long enough with the minimum length, $N_{min} = 1/(BER_{min})$, where BER_{min} is the minimum BER of the analyzed system. In practice, since the bit sequence and the propagation effects are random, to estimate an accurate BER, the bit sequence must be much longer than N_{min} or the simulation has to be performed many times to obtain a BER averaged over more bits until its value converges. The bit errors that occur in N simulated bits are counted and the BER is obtained using (108). This method of direct bit error counting is also called the Monte Carlo simulation. Formally speaking, the Monte Carlo simulation estimates the BER of a particular system by modeling the transmission of N bits through the system from generation to bit detection. The number of bit errors is counted by comparing the received bit sequence with the transmitted bit sequence, and the BER is calculated using equation (10.9). Mathematically, it can be represented by

$$BER_{MC} = \frac{\sum_{n=1}^{N} \left| BS_{REC}(n) - BS_{TR}(n) \right|}{N} \qquad (10.10)$$

where BER_{MC} is the BER estimated through Monte Carlo simulation, BS_{REC} is the received bit sequence after bit detection at the receiver and BS_{TR} is the transmitted bit sequence.

In our simulations, the bit errors are calculated from the current entering the bit decision device depicted in Figure 14 of Chapter-9. In the bit decision device, two things occur. First, the input signal is sampled at every bit period, T to obtain the sampling point for each bit. In practice, the position of the sampling within the bit period is determined by a clock signal derived from the input signal using devices such as a phase-locked loop (PLL). Ideally, this position should be at the center of the bit periods where the signal pulse is maximum. We assume ideal sampling in our model.

From the samples obtained, the received bit sequence is determined using a threshold. The optimum received bit sequence that corresponds to the minimum BER in equation (10.10) is obtained when the threshold, D is optimum, D_{opt}. In practice, the optimum threshold is determined through conditioning of the decision device. In our simulations, D_{opt} is determined by varying D until the minimum BER is obtained. To do this efficiently, we use a step algorithm where for each step D is either increased or decreased by half its previous step size depending on which result was minimal. This continues until the step size reaches a specified minimum. Note that the accuracy improves as the minimum step size decreases at the cost of increased computation time. In this method, the only difference between estimating the BER for IM/DD and DPSK systems is the initial D. For IM/DD, the initial D should be set approximately about $0.5 \max(I_{in})$ while for DPSK balanced detection, the initial D should be zero.

The Monte Carlo simulation is still the most accurate way to estimate the BER of a system in numerical simulations. This is because it is based on 'brute force' counting and averaging. The trade off is of course, the large processing power required, causing simple simulations to last for days or weeks even on the fastest processors. The long processing time makes extensive simulations using this technique difficult.

Q FACTOR MODEL

Thus, models have been developed to estimate the BER from a much shorter sequence of bits. These methods attempt to approximate the BER based on the behavior of a much shorter length of simulated bits. Some of these methods have been reasonably successful in particular situations, but no general method has been obtained that is applicable to all optical communication systems and different methods have to be applied for different system configurations.

A popular simulation method used to estimate the BER in intensity modulated (IM) systems is the Q factor model. The core of this model is based on certain assumptions made on the probability distribution function (pdf) of the noise. In effect, it assumes that the noise pdf at the input of the bit decision device for an IM system is Gaussian. The reasoning for this is that the noises that distort the optical signal such as ASE, thermal and shot noise are AWGN noises. Thus, the accumulated noise at the detection device is probably Gaussian as well. However, it has been shown that the noise at the input of the bit decision device for the general AWGN distorted optical IM signal after passing through the filter-photodetector-filter configuration at the receiver is not exactly Gaussian (Kumar, Mauro, Raghavan, & Chowdhury, 2002).

This fact alone would have invalidated the approximation, but it was also discovered that the Gaussian approximation of the noise is effective when the bit decision threshold or level is chosen such that the BER approaches minimum (Agrawal, 1997; Bergano, Kerfoot, & Davidson, 1993). Since the minimum BER of a system is normally the parameter of interest, the Gaussian approximation remains valid for most practical purposes. Generally, the BER, $P_e(D)$ for a decision level D can be given as

$$P_e(D) = \frac{1}{2}\left(P_e(1/0) + P_e(0/1)\right) \tag{10.11}$$

where $P_e(1/0)$ is the probability of detecting a '1' given a bit '0', while $P_e(0/1)$ is the probability of detecting a '0' given a bit '1'. They are given by

$$P_e(1/0) = \int_{D}^{\infty} PDF_0(A)\, dA$$
$$P_e(0/1) = \int_{-\infty}^{D} PDF_1(A)\, dA \tag{10.12}$$

where A is the decision variable and D is the decision threshold/level. If we assume that the noise is Gaussian, the BER can be written as [131]

$$P_e(D) = \frac{1}{4}\left(erfc\left(\frac{D - \mu_0}{\sqrt{2}\sigma_0}\right) + erfc\left(\frac{\mu_1 - D}{\sqrt{2}\sigma_1}\right)\right) \tag{10.13}$$

where μ_1, μ_0 are the means of bits 1 and 0 respectively while σ_1, σ_0 are the standard deviations of bits 1 and 0 respectively. The complementary error function, erfc(x) is defined as

$$erfc\left(x\right) = \frac{2}{\sqrt{\pi}} \int\limits_{x}^{\infty} e^{-t^2} dt \tag{10.14}$$

Close study of the noise pdf tails, which determine the BER, have shown that while the Gaussian approximation overestimates the initial part of the tail and then underestimates the latter part, the overall result averages out to produce a good estimation . The minimum BER is obtained from the BER as defined in equation (10.13) by varying D until an optimal decision level D_{opt} is obtained that minimizes the BER. The minimum BER, $P_e(D_{opt})$ is then related to the Q factor as (Norimatsu, Maruoka, & Maruoka, 2002)

$$P_e\left(D_{opt}\right) = \frac{1}{2} erfc\left(\frac{Q_{IM}}{\sqrt{2}}\right) \tag{10.15}$$

where we have written the Q factor as Q_{IM} because this model is only applicable for the IM system. This reason we specify this explicitly will become clearer when we deal with Q factors in DPSK systems in Section V. Also, note that the correspondence of the BER and Q is one-to-one. If we assume that the received signal consists of two rails corresponding to bit logics '1' and '0' and the optimum threshold is a value located between them that minimizes the total BER, the Q factor can be more simply expressed as (; Bergano, Kerfoot, & Davidson, 1993)

$$Q_{IM} = \frac{\mu_1 - \mu_0}{\sigma_1 + \sigma_0} \tag{10.16}$$

where it is solely in terms of μ_1, μ_0, σ_1 and σ_0. Note that the Q_{IM} is defined for $P_e(D_{opt})$, the optimum BER.

Using the Gaussian noise Q model approximation, to obtain the BER for a system, we still have to run the full system simulations to obtain the received signal current at the input of the bit decision device. This signal is sampled at the decision instances (normally the center of the bit periods) to obtain a set of sampled data. From this set of sampled data from the signal, we can obtain μ_1, μ_0, σ_1 and σ_0. We can do this because for numerical simulations, we know the transmitted bit sequence, which naturally becomes the expected received bit sequence. Thus, we can sort the sampled data set into two pools depending on whether the expected received bit is '0' or '1'. From here, we can easily obtain the means and standard deviations of the signal corresponding to received bits '1' and '0' respectively. Knowing this, we can compute the Q factor using equqtion (10.16). and the corresponding minimum BER using equqtion (10.15). Figure 2 shows how the means and standard deviations may be obtained from the current eye diagram whereby the decision instance sampling of bit rails '1' and '0' each forms a Gaussian distribution with a calculable mean and standard deviation.

If the transmitted bit sequence is not known, estimating the Q factor becomes much more problematic. Experimentally, $P_e(D_{opt})$ can be measured by changing D until the minimum BER is achieved. Once again, this is not realistic when the Q factor is high (BER is low) due to the long time required to measure the bit errors. A quicker solution is proposed in (; Bergano, Kerfoot, & Davidson, 1993), which utilizes a data set of decision levels (D) and corresponding BERs ($P_e(D)$) from 10^{-5} to 10^{-10} that can be measured in relatively shorter times. A quadratic function is then fitted onto the data set and is used to estimate μ_1, μ_0, σ_1 and σ_0. These parameters are then used to obtain the Q using equation (10.16). An improved version of this method was recently proposed in ((Norimatsu, Maruoka, & Maruoka, 2002). These methods have actually been developed for application in experiments where the Q factor model is used to shorten the time it takes to physically measure the BER for low BER systems. This is possible as we only need to gather a data set of measurements at higher BER values and fit this data onto the quadratic equation to estimate the minimum BER. The specific details regarding the quadratic function is not examined in this report because we deal with numerical simulations. Thus, we have knowledge of the transmitted bit sequence and need not resort to the more time-consuming methods involving data sets and BER measurements.

The Q factor model has become very popular in IM system simulation and the estimated Q from the Gaussian approximation is fundamentally accurate when

Figure 2. Q factor estimation from the current eye diagram (Hiew, Abbou, & Chuah, 2006)

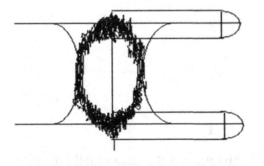

Bit "1" rail
Obtain mean and std. dev.

Bit "0" rail
Obtain mean and std. dev.

Decision sampling instance
- Center of bit period -

dealing with signals distorted chiefly by AWGN such as ASE. Using the Q factor, the number of simulated bits required is vastly reduced as even 10^4 bits are sufficient to estimate BERs of up to 10^{-12}. This represents a significant reduction in processing time over the Monte Carlo simulation. However, one area of concern is the applicability of the Q factor when the signal is also significantly distorted by other factors, such as dispersion, ISI, WDM linear crosstalk and nonlinear effects. These other factors can also be generally called waveform distortions as opposed to noise distortions caused by AWGN. In the presence of waveform distortions, the accuracy of the Q factor model may not be maintained, particularly if the Gaussian approximation fails. Research has shown that the accuracy of the Q factor model is reduced when waveform distortions are significant (Anderson & Lyle, 1994; (Norimatsu, Maruoka, & Maruoka, 2002). Fortunately however, the Gaussian approximation often still holds for BER close to minimum, and the Q factor model is relatively accurate even in the presence of waveform distortions ((Norimatsu, Maruoka, & Maruoka, 2002).

Furthermore, to account for waveform distortions, some modifications can be made to the Q factor model to reduce the loss of accuracy. Generally, these methods are based on the concept of multiple rails in the receiver current eye diagram. Basically, this concept proposes that in the presence of waveform distortions, both the '0's and '1's does not consist of a single rail, but each of them splits into multiple rails. This concept is shown in Figure 3.

The diagram is noiseless so that the effect of waveform distortion can be clearly seen in isolation. The '1's split into N_1 rails while the '0's split into N_0 rails. Each of these rails possesses a separate Gaussian distribution. Thus, the BER of each of the '0' rails may be calculated using ((Norimatsu, Maruoka, & Maruoka, 2002)

$$P_{0,j}\left(D\right) = \frac{p_{0,j}}{2}\,erfc\left(\frac{D - \mu_{0,j}}{\sqrt{2}\sigma_{0,j}}\right)$$ (10.17)

and the '1' rails using

$$P_{1,j}\left(D\right) = \frac{p_{1,j}}{2}\,erfc\left(\frac{\mu_{1,j} - D}{\sqrt{2}\sigma_{1,j}}\right)$$ (10.18)

where $P_{n,j}(D)$ is the BER caused by rail j of bit n; $\mu_{n,j}$ is the mean of rail j of bit n; $\sigma_{n,j}$ is the standard deviation of rail j of bit n; and $p_{n,j}$ is the probability of occurrence of rail j of bit n. The probability of occurrences satisfy

Figure 3. Multiple rails of the noiseless eye diagram in the presence of waveform distortions (Hiew, Abbou, & Chuah, 2006)

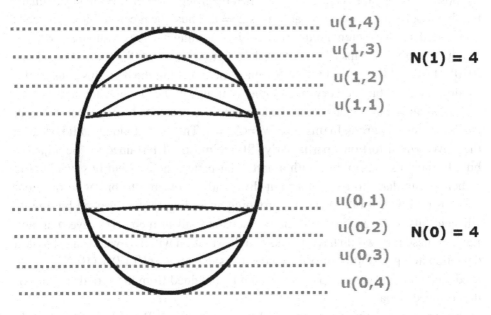

$$\sum_{j=0}^{N_0-1} p_{0,j} + \sum_{j=0}^{N_1-1} p_{1,j} = 1 \tag{10.19}$$

The average BER over all the rails is thus given by

$$P_e\left(D\right) = \sum_{j=0}^{N_0-1} P_{0,j}\left(D\right) + \sum_{j=0}^{N_1-1} P_{1,j}\left(D\right) \tag{10.20}$$

Once again, D is varied to obtain the optimum decision level D_{opt} that minimizes the BER in equation (10.20). The minimum BER, $P_e(D_{opt})$ is then related to the Q factor through equation (10.15).

To use the multiple rails method, we have to use a model to determine the number of rails and their individual properties of mean, standard deviation and probability of occurrence. One method involves the assignment of probability distributions to the occurrences of the rails and their means ((Norimatsu, Maruoka, & Maruoka, 2002). In this book, we use a simple and effective method to determine the number of rails and their properties, which we call bit patterning or pattern conditioning, and is based on reference (Anderson & Lyle, 1994). This method involves the classification of the known expected bit sequence into the 2^N possible bit sequence patterns, which can be formed by a group of N bits. For example, in 3-bit patterning, we consider the possible but patterns that can be formed by groups of 3 bits. From basic binary number theory, the number of patterns is $2^3 = 8$. Thus, the received bit sequence is now sorted into 8 different groups with 3-bit patterning whereas without bit patterning, it was only 2 groups ('0' and '1'). The 8 groups are: '000', '100', '001', '101', '010', '110', '011', '111'. If the center bit is the target bit, the 8 groups consist of 4 groups in the '0' bit category and another 4 groups in the '1' bit category.

The assumption is that each of the 8 groups is expected to form a separate rail in the current eye diagram. In this case, $N_0 = N_1 = 4$. This assumption is valid because the waveform distortions, particularly ISI, are mostly determined by the adjacent bits. In such a scenario, bits with a particular pattern of adjacent bits would tend to behave similarly to each other but differently compared to bits with different patterns of adjacent bits. Thus, by grouping according to the received bit and its adjacent bits, each group would have a separate rail in the current eye diagram. Each of these rails would have a Gaussian distribution with its own mean, standard deviation and probability of occurrence. Thus, equations (10.17) – (10.20) can be used, and all the necessary parameters can be obtained from the sorted samples of the received signal.

Pattern conditioning has been found to estimate the BER much more accurately in the presence of waveform distortions (Anderson & Lyle, 1994). In this study, we generally use the Q factor model with 3-bit patterning. Note however that the pattern conditioning can be extended to the received pattern of 4, 5 or more bits as required for higher accuracy by considering the effect of more adjacent bits. The drawback is, of course, increased computation time and the reduction of samples per group. In most cases, the nearest adjacent bits are much more significant than the others and thus, 3-bit patterning is usually sufficient. For OTDM-WDM systems, note that the bit sequence used for pattern conditioning should be the sequence during its most significant filtering process, which is normally the WDM demultiplexing process, since the main optimization between ISI and crosstalk occurs here. Thus, in this situation, the bit sequence used for pattern conditioning is the OTDM multiplexed sequence and not the individual OTDM channel sequences.

Besides the Q factor and the BER, the results obtained using the Q model are also often presented in other ways. One is the Q contour plot, which is basically a 3D graphical representation of results whereby two parameters under study are plotted against the X and Y axis respectively, while the Q obtained for a particular set of parameters is plotted as the Z-axis point for the parameters' corresponding coordinates. The set of Q values over the range of the parameters forms a contour that clearly indicates the pattern of behavior with respect to the two varying parameters. The Q contour plot is often used for optimization in our studies. Another alternate representation of the Q is the Q factor in decibels defined as $Q(dB) = 20 \log_{10}(Q)$.

DIFFERENTIAL PHASE Q (DP-Q)

DPSK systems can be modeled using the same approaches as the IM system to obtain the signal behavior in the OTDM-WDM system. The only change is to the transmitter whereby DPSK modulation has to be performed on the signal. However, the same BER estimation models cannot be used. Previously, there have been attempts to use the IM Q factor model to estimate the BER of DPSK systems employing balanced detectors. This has proven to be inaccurate by a number of studies and is not recommended for use (Bosco & Poggiolini, 2004). This is because the noise at the input of the bit decision device after DPSK balanced detection is not Gaussian Kumar, Mauro, Raghavan, & Chowdhury, 2002; Zhang, 2004). Unlike the case for IM, the noise does not approach a Gaussian approximation when the BER approaches minimum. Thus, the IM Q factor model fails. The pdf of the noise after DPSK balanced detection has been looked into (Zhang, 2004) and it is investigated in this book too.

Recently a modified version of the Q factor has been proposed and shows good promise to be used in estimating the BER of DPSK systems (Xu, Liu, & Wei, 2004; Wei, Liu, & Xu, 2003). We refer to this method here as the differential phase Q (DP-Q). Proposed specifically for use in direct-detection RZ-DPSK modulated systems employing balanced detection receivers, the DP-Q is based on the Gaussian approximation of the noise at the center of each rail of the differential phase eye diagram. The differential phase is the phase difference between two sampling points separated by one bit period mapped from [-π/2, 3π/2]. Mathematically, the differential phase is obtained by

$$\Delta\varphi = \angle E_{REC}\left(t\right) - \angle E_{REC}\left(t - T_R\right) \tag{10.21}$$

Then, all differential phase that falls outside the range [-π/2, 3π/2] is normalized to within those boundaries (note that phase repeats at intervals of 2π). The differential phase eye diagram is analogous to the current eye diagram except that it is in terms of differential phase and is generated from the optical signal. An example of the differential phase eye diagram is shown in Figure 4. As the phase information of the signal is only available in the optical domain, the differential phase eye diagram has to be built from the optical signal and not the current signal by necessity. Note that for DPSK, a differential phase of π indicates a bit '0' and zero differential phase indicates a bit '1'. Thus, these are the two rails in the differential phase eye diagram.

From the differential phase eye diagram, we can sample the differential phases at the sampling instances (center of bit periods). In the DP-Q model, the assumption is that the distribution of the differential phase samples is Gaussian, and though the

Figure 4. Differential phase eye diagram (Hiew, Abbou, & Chuah, 2006)

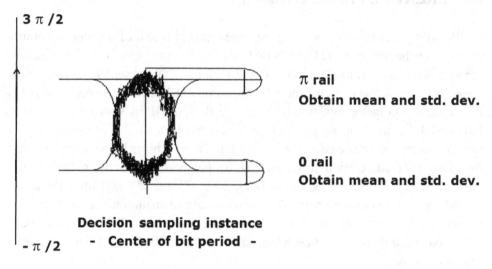

π rail
Obtain mean and std. dev.

0 rail
Obtain mean and std. dev.

Decision sampling instance
- Center of bit period -

actual pdf may not actually be Gaussian, it seems to provide an approximately ac-curate fit (Mecozzi, 2004). Thus, the same derivation process following the IM Q factor model can be performed and the DP-Q is thus obtained as

$$Q_{\Delta\varphi} = \frac{\pi}{\sigma_{\Delta\varphi,0} + \sigma_{\Delta\varphi,\pi}} \qquad (10.22)$$

where $\sigma_{\Delta\phi,0}$ and $\sigma_{\Delta\phi,\pi}$ are the standard deviations of the 0 or π rails. Note that this is analogous to the IM Q factor, Q_{IM} but is different in one aspect. That is the mean terms are absent and are instead replaced by a factor of π. This is in fact, just a simplification because $\mu_{\Delta\phi,\pi} - \mu_{\Delta\phi,0} = \pi$.

The BER is then estimated using

$$P_e\left(D_{opt}\right) = erfc\left(\frac{Q_{\Delta\varphi}}{\sqrt{2}}\right) \qquad (10.23)$$

This is analogous to the IM Q factor model again except for the absence of the (1/2) factor. This factor is absent because phase is circular and continuous across 2π and the tails of the Gaussian distributions may overlap with each other causing bit errors on both sides. Thus, the error probability is two times the IM case where the Gaussian distributions can only overlap with each other on one side. On the whole, the DP-Q is applied the same way as the IM Q factor except that the DP-Q operates in the optical domain on the differential phase. The DP-Q is simple to obtain from simulations as it only requires the differential phase eye diagram obtained from the received optical field envelope. The sorting of the expected received bits into '0' or '1' can be done with the known transmitted bit sequence and this corresponds to sorting the differential phase into groups of 'π' and '0' respectively. With the sorting done, the standard deviation can be easily calculated and applied in equation (10.22) with the BER obtained using equation (10.23).

The results in (Wei, Liu, & Xu, 2003) showed that the DP-Q gave qualitatively good results that followed the trend of the results obtained from Monte Carlo simulation (Note that Monte Carlo simulation is still applicable to DPSK systems and is in fact generally regarded as the most accurate but is time-consuming). Thus, DP-Q could correctly predict trends and optimization points. This was true even for DPSK signals influenced by waveform distortions such as ISI, linear crosstalk and nonlinear effects. This was a very encouraging sign and showed that the DP-Q could potentially be used over the same broad range of applicability as the IM Q factor. However, the results in (Wei, Liu, & Xu, 2003) showed that even though the DP-Q was qualitatively accurate, it was not quantitatively correct. The DP-Q regularly underestimated the BER when compared to the Monte Carlo simulation. This underestimation was systemic and occurred over broad ranges. Thus, it demonstrated that the DP-Q still has serious accuracy issues.

In this book, a modification to the originally proposed DP-Q, which is called the modified DP-Q is used Hiew, Abbou, & Chuah, 2006) and is given by

$$Q_{\Delta\varphi,\mathrm{mod}} = Q_{\Delta\varphi} = \frac{0.87\pi}{\sigma_{\Delta\varphi,0} + \sigma_{\Delta\varphi,\pi}} \tag{10.24}$$

The BER is then obtained using equation (10.23) again. Note that in equations (10.22) and (10.24), the only difference between the DP-Q and the modified DP-Q is the factor of 0.87, which is called the correction factor.

NETWORK BER MODEL

In this section, we look at BER estimation in networks using the tools we have developed earlier. This section also completes the modeling of the network environment begun in pervious section. Firstly, as initially explained earlier, the performance or BER of a network is not fixed but is a function of the number of hops taken before it is absorbed. We refer to this BER curve as *BER(n)* where n is the number of hops traversed. Thus, there is no such thing as a fixed BER for a network. However, we can obtain an expected BER that can predict the average BER of a typical packet traversing through the network from random and arbitrary transmitting and receiving nodes. We can do this if we know the probability density function (pdf) of the number of hops taken by a regular packet to reach its destination. This pdf is known as the hop distribution, $P(n)$ and is unique for a particular network configuration. In this way, the average BER can be specified as (Castanon, Tonguz, & Bononi, 1997)

$$BER_{av} = BER(n)P(n) \tag{10.25}$$

$P(n)$ is unique for any particular network configuration. In this report, we look specifically at the MSN16 network with two-input, two-output network nodes. Still this is insufficient since obtaining the hop distribution; we also need to know the routing strategy, especially in the event of routing clashes. Here, we use the routing strategy known as deflection routing (Forghieri, Bononi, & Prucnal, 1995). In deflection routing, there is the possibility of using buffers (implanted using optical delay lines) or wavelength converters to ease congestion and improve throughput.

Next, we look briefly at the concept of deflection routing. This routing algorithm deals with the scenario when there is a routing clash. This occurs when the two packets in a node is addressed to the same output link at the same time, where the decision on the output link is made based on the shortest path algorithm. In deflection routing, when this clash occurs, one of the packets gets to use the desired output link while the other is 'deflected' onto the other output link whereby it needs to use a longer path to get to its destination. The probability that a packet has to be deflected is denoted as p. There are only two input signals into each node. Therefore, there is no risk of there being a third packet that has to be dropped.

On the issue of packet generation, we know that at each node, there is a possibility that a packet can be generated at the transmitter. Since there can only be two signals at a time in the node, the packet can only be generated when one of the links within the node is empty. In other words, this means that there were less than two inputs into the node. When this occurs, a packet may be placed onto the empty slot at the node. In this way, the limit of two signals in the node is maintained. Packets to be transmitted are automatically placed on an electronic transmitter queue waiting to be transmitted. Thus, the probability that a new packet is generated and placed on that queue at a node is the key determining parameter and is denoted by g.

Knowing p and g, we can obtain the link utilization u, which is the probability of finding a packet at the input links of a node at each time slot. In our model, each submodule has two receivers and one transmitter, thus the link utilization is

$$u = \frac{\sqrt{a^2 + g^2\left(1-a\right)^2} - a}{g\left(1-a\right)^2} \qquad (10.26)$$

where a is the probability of packet absorption given by

$$a = 1 \,/\, H \qquad (10.27)$$

H is the average number of hops that packets experience before absorption. It is our aim to obtain the average number of hops as a function of p. To do that, we first have to obtain a formula that relates the transition of the packets across the network.

To observe this transition, we use the method of tracking the progress of a test packet through the MSN employing deflection routing. Let Π be the N x N transition matrix whose elements π_{ij} represent the probability that the test packet will move to node i at its $(k+1)^{\text{th}}$ hop, being at node j at its kth hop. The state transition diagram for the MSN16 network given in Figure 15 of chapter-9 is obtained by setting node 0 as the destination node and noting the probabilities of the shortest path to the destination. The new diagram is shown in Figure 5 and the corresponding transition matrix is given by

$\Pi(p) = [1\ 0\ 0\ 1\text{-}p\ 0\ 0\ 0\ 0\ 0\ 0\ 0\ 1\text{-}p\ 0\ 0\ 0$

$0\ 0\ 0\ 0\ 0\ 1/2\ 0\ 0\ 0\ 0\ 0\ 0\ 0\ 0\ 0\ 0$

$0\ 1/2\ 0\ 0\ 0\ 0\ 0\ 0\ 0\ 0\ 0\ 0\ 0\ 0\ 1/2\ 0$

$0\ 0\ 1\text{-}p\ 0\ 0\ 0\ 0\ 1\text{-}p\ 0\ 0\ 0\ 0\ 0\ 0\ 0\ 0$

$0\ 0\ 0\ 0\ 0\ 1/2\ 0\ 0\ 0\ 0\ 0\ 0\ 0\ 0\ 0\ 0$

$0\ 0\ 0\ 0\ 0\ 0\ 1/2\ 0\ 0\ 1/2\ 0\ 0\ 0\ 0\ 0\ 0$

$0\ 0\ p\ 0\ 0\ 0\ 0\ p\ 0\ 0\ 0\ 0\ 0\ 0\ 0\ 0$

$0\ 0\ 0\ 0\ 1/2\ 0\ 0\ 0\ 0\ 0\ 0\ 1/2\ 0\ 0\ 0\ 0$

$0\ 0\ 0\ 0\ 1/2\ 0\ 0\ 0\ 0\ 0\ 0\ 1/2\ 0\ 0\ 0\ 0$

$0\ 0\ 0\ 0\ 0\ 0\ 0\ 0\ p\ 0\ 0\ 0\ 0\ p\ 0\ 0$

0 0 0 0 0 0 1/2 0 0 1/2 0 0 0 0 0 0

0 0 0 0 0 0 0 0 0 0 1/2 0 0 0 0 1 1/2

0 0 0 0 0 0 0 0 1-p 0 0 0 0 1-p 0 0

0 1/2 0 0 0 0 0 0 0 0 0 0 0 0 0 1/2 0

0 0 0 0 0 0 0 0 0 0 1/2 0 0 0 0 1 1/2

0 0 0 p 0 0 0 0 0 0 0 0 p 0 0 0] $\qquad$ (10.28)

Let $B(k)$ be the state vector at time k, whose elements $b_i(k)$ represent the probability that the test packet will arrive node i at its kth hop. Given the distribution $B(k)$ at time k, the state at time $k+1$ is

$$B(k+1) = \Pi(p)\, B(k) \qquad (10.29)$$

This equation can fully specify the progress of the packet through the network as long as we know the transition matrix and the initial state of the network. The state $[1\ 0 \ldots 0]^{\text{T}}$ is the solution to which the chain converges as $k \rightarrow \infty$. The transition matrix is fully specified according to equation (10.28) as long as we know the deflection probability p. On the other hand, the initial state vector is well approximated by

$$B(0) = [0\ 1/(N\text{-}1), \ldots, 1/(N\text{-}1)]^{\text{T}} \qquad (10.30)$$

Therefore, the only thing remaining is to find the deflection probability p. This involves a number of steps. First, we obtain the average number of hops of the test packet, H as

$$H = \sum_{k=1}^{\infty} k\left[b_o\left(k\right) - b_0\left(k-1\right)\right] \qquad (10.31)$$

Note that $b_0(k)$ is seen to be the cumulative distribution function (cdf) of the number of hops taken by the test packet to arrive at the destination node 0. With H obtained, we can easily obtain a using equation (10.27). Next, we have to derive a new property known as the don't-care probability, P_{dc}. To clarify this property, first note that in the state transition diagram in Figure 5, there are many nodes whereby the probability of exiting at either output is equal to 1/2. This means that taking either one of the two outputs will lead to a shortest path. In other words, the shortest

Figure 5. State transition diagram for MSN16 network with deflection routing (Hiew, Abbou, & Chuah, 2006)

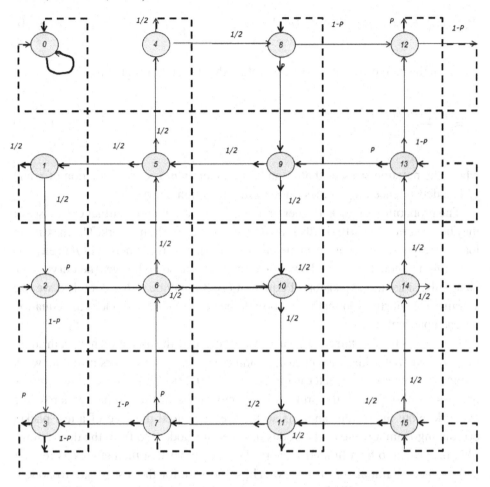

hop length required to reach the destination node does not change no matter which output is taken from that current node. Such a node is known as a don't-care node. Hence, the don't-care probability P_{dc} is defined as the long-run fraction of time that the test packet is at a don't-care node and is given by

$$P_{dc} = \frac{\sum_{k=0}^{\infty} \sum_{i \in DC} b_i(k)}{H} \qquad (10.32)$$

where DC is the set of don't care nodes. For the case in Figure 5, the don't care nodes are i = 1, 4, 5, 6, 9, 10, 11, 14, 15.

Next, we define the care probability as

$$P_c = \left[u\left(1-a\right) + uag + \left(1-u\right)g \right]\left(1 - P_{dc}\right)$$

(10.33)

From the care probability, we can obtain the deflection probability as

$$p = \frac{1}{2}\frac{P_c\left(p,g\right)}{2}$$

(10.34)

where the notation stresses that P_c and consequently p, is only a function of p and g. The dependence on p comes through the transition matrix.

The probability of packet generation g is a network parameter that can be set or may be dynamic, and is basically linked to the loading of the network. The maximum load corresponds to a g of 1. On the other hand, since p is a function of p itself, this is an implicit equation in p. Thus, it can possibly be solved to get the curve $p(g)$. Generally, since the expansion of equation (10.34) can be rather complex, we use a numerical substitution method to obtain the correct p that balances the equation for each particular g.

Once p has been obtained, we can use it to complete the transition matrix in equation (10.28). With this, we can easily compute all the state vectors of the network for any k number of hops later using equation (10.29). With this done, we already possess a full picture of the probability of movement of the test packet across the network. Note that in our analysis so far, we have used the case of a test packet originating from anyone of the nodes destined for node 0 to form the derivations. This may seem to be a limited scenario but remember that the network is regular and balanced (similar for all nodes). Thus, the case for the test packet to node 0 can be generalized to all other packets with any other destination nodes. Therefore, the hop distribution P(n) used in equation (10.25), which is the probability density function (pdf) of the number of hops taken by a regular packet to reach its destination can simply be given by

$$P(n) = b_0(n) - b_0(n\text{-}1)$$

(10.35)

Now that we have obtained the $P(n)$, we need to know $BER(n)$ as well to obtain the BER_{av} in equation (10.35). Remember that is easy to simulate the propagation of the signal across any number of hops n as long as a complete model of the nodes and the interconnecting fiber links is provided. Simulations of the fiber links are easily done using models for the point-to-point system, and we know the models for most of the devices in the nodes. The only device with properties still unknown to us is the cross switch, specifically the cross switch induced leakage crosstalk. Equation (9.66) specifies the power spectral density of the leakage crosstalk where the only unknown quantity is the leakage power, $P_{leak}(\alpha)$ that is dependent on the crosstalk leakage parameter α. The reason this was not specified earlier is that $P_{leak}(\alpha)$ is also dependent on the link utilization, absorption and packet generation probabilities of the network. This is because there is no leakage caused by the cross switch if there is only one or zero signals at the input of the switch. Only when there are two signals at the input of the main cross switch can there be leakage between the signals. Thus, the leakage power becomes a function of the network probabilities (Castanon, Tonguz, & Bononi, 1997)

$$P_{leak} = u\left(1-a\right)P_{xt} \text{ if } i = 1$$

$$= u\left(1-a\right)P_{xt} + \left[uag + \left(1-u\right)g\right]P_{T}\alpha \text{ otherwise} \tag{10.36}$$

where i is the current node, P_{xt} is the signal power at the input of the cross switch and P_{T} is the transmitted laser power after the loss of the add-drop multiplexer.

With all devices and fiber links known, the simulation can be easily done across any number of n hops. We simply choose the limit to the range of number of hops n_{limit}, usually determined by the limit $P(n) \rightarrow 0$, and then simulate the propagation from $n = 0$ to $n = n_{limit}$, while determining the BER for each n along the way. The specific transmitting and receiving nodes are unimportant since all nodes and interconnections are similar. The BER can be obtained using the appropriate BER estimation method. The $BER(n)$ curve alone can tell a lot about the network, while together with $P(n)$, we can obtain the average BER from equation (10.25).

SUMMARY

Methods and techniques that can be used to model evaluate the performance of high speed optical communication systems were discussed. The eye penalty gives a rough estimation of the performance of the system by quantifying the relative 'opening' of the eye. However, the amplitude and timing jitters estimation is useful as the amplitude or timing jitter can often be obtained in closed-form analytical expressions. At the same time, both parameters can be easily measured from signals obtained either through experiments or simulation. The SNR is more often used as a system parameter. However, this method is a simplistic one that makes many assumptions including a Gaussian distributed noise, negligible effects of waveform distortion and balanced noises at bits '1' and '0'. These assumptions are not generally true and thus, SNR is not a reliable measure of the BER. A way to extend the scope of an analytical formula is to apply it to a signal obtained through simulation. This is called the semi-analytical method in which part of the results is obtained from simulation and the remaining part through an analytical formula. The Monte Carlo simulation is hence the most accurate way to estimate the BER of a system in numerical simulations. This is because it is based on 'brute force' counting and averaging. The trade off is of course, the large processing power required, causing simple simulations to last for days or weeks even on the fastest processors. The long processing time makes extensive simulations using this technique difficult.

REFERENCES

Agrawal, G. P. (Ed.). (1997). *Fiber-Optic Communication Systems*. Wiley-Interscience.

Anderson, C. J., & Lyle, J. A. (1994). Technique for Evaluating System Performance Using q in Numerical Simulations Exhibiting Intersymbol Interference. *Electronics Letters*, *30*(1), 71–72. doi:10.1049/el:19940045

Bergano, N. S., Kerfoot, F. W., & Davidson, C. R. (1993). Margin Measurements in Optical Amplifier Systems. *IEEE Photonics Technology Letters*, *5*(3), 304–306. doi:10.1109/68.205619

Bosco, G., & Poggiolini, P. (2004). On the q Factor Inaccuracy in the Performance Analysis of Optical Direct-detection dpsk Systems. *IEEE Photonics Technology Letters*, *16*(2), 665–667. doi:10.1109/LPT.2003.820475

Castanon, G. A., Tonguz, O. K., & Bononi, A. (1997). Ber Performance of Multiwavelength Optical Cross-connected Networks with Deflection Routing. *IEE Proc-Communications, 144*, 114-120.

Forestieri, E. (2000). Evaluating the Error Probability in Lightwave Systems with Chromatic Dispersion, Arbitrary Pulse Shape and Pre- and Post-detection filtering. *Journal of Lightwave Technology*, *18*(11), 1493–1503. doi:10.1109/50.896209

Forestieri, E. (2003). Correction to evaluating the Error Probability in Lightwave Systems with Chromatic Dispersion, Arbitrary Pulse Shape and Pre- and Post-detection Filtering. *Journal of Lightwave Technology*, *21*(6), 1957. doi:10.1109/JLT.2003.812719

Forghieri, F., Bononi, A., & Prucnal, P. R. (1995). Analysis and comparison of hot-potato and single-buffer deflection routing in very high bit rate optical mesh networks. *IEEE Transactions on Communications, 43*(1), 88–98. doi:10.1109/26.385939

Hiew, C. C., Abbou, F. M., & Chuah, H. T. (2006). *Performance Analysis and Design of an Optical TDM-WDM Transmission System and Network* (Tech. Rep. No. 1). Malaysia: Multimedia University and Alcatel Network Systems.

Hiew, C. C., Abbou, F. M., Chuah, H. T., Majumder, S. P., & Hairul, A. A. R. (2004). Ber Estimation of Optical wdm rz-dpsk Systems Through the Differential Phase q. *IEEE Photonics Technology Letters, 16*(12), 2619–2621. doi:10.1109/LPT.2004.836759

Humblet Azizoglu, P. A., & Azizoglu, M. (1991). On the Bit Error Rate of Lightwave Systems with Optical Amplifiers. *Journal of Lightwave Technology, 9*(11), 1576–1582. doi:10.1109/50.97649

Jeruchim, M. C., Balaban, P., & Shanmugam, K. S. (1992). *Simulation of Communication Systems*. New York: Plenum Press. doi:10.1007/978-1-4615-3298-9

Kumar, S., Mauro, J. C., Raghavan, S., & Chowdhury, D. Q. (2002). Intrachannel Nonlinear Penalties in Dispersion-managed Transmission Systems. *IEEE Journal of Selected Topics in Quantum Electronics, 8*(3), 626–631. doi:10.1109/JSTQE.2002.1016366

Liu, X., & Wei, X. (2003). Increased osnr Gains of Forward-error Correction in Nonlinear Optical Transmissions. *IEEE Photonics Technology Letters, 15*(7), 999–1001. doi:10.1109/LPT.2003.813443

Liu, X., Xie, C., & van Wijngaarden, A. J. (2004). Multichannel pmd Mitigation and Outage Reduction Through fec with Sub-burst-error-correction Period pmd Scrambling. *IEEE Photonics Technology Letters, 16*(9), 2183–2185. doi:10.1109/LPT.2004.833088

Marcuse, D. (1991). Calculation of Bit-error Probability for a Lightwave System with Optical Amplifiers and Post-detection Gaussian Noise. *Journal of Lightwave Technology, 9*(4), 505–513. doi:10.1109/50.76665

Mecozzi, A. (2004). Probability Density Functions of the Nonlinear Phase Noise. *Optics Letters, 29*. PMID:15072354

Nakazawa, M. (2000). Ultrahigh-speed Long-distance tdm and wdm Soliton Transmission Technologies. *IEEE Journal of Selected Topics in Quantum Electronics, 6*.

Norimatsu, M., & Maruoka, M. (2002). Accurate q-factor Estimation of Optically Amplified Systems in the Presence of Waveform Distortions. *Journal of Lightwave Technology*, 20(1), 19–27. doi:10.1109/50.974814

Proakis, J. G. (Ed.). (1989). *Digital Communications*.

Tu, K. Y., Forestieri, E., Kaneda, N., Secondini, M., Leven, A., Koc, U.-V., & Hocke, R. (2004). Modeling Accuracy of a Fiber-optics Test Bed Using mgf Method. *IEEE Photonics Technology Letters*, 16(12), 2646–2648. doi:10.1109/LPT.2004.836771

Wang, J., & Kahn, J. M. (2004). Accurate Bit-error-ratio Computation in Nonlinear crz-ook and crz-dpsk Systems. *IEEE Photonics Technology Letters*, 16(9), 2165–2167. doi:10.1109/LPT.2004.833033

Wang, J., & Kahn, K. (2004). Impact of Chromatic and Polarization-mode Dispersions on dpsk Systems Using Interferometric Demodulation and Direct Detection. *Journal of Lightwave Technology*, 22(2), 362–371. doi:10.1109/JLT.2003.822101

Wei, X., Liu, X., & Xu, C. (2003). Numerical Simulation of the spm Penalty in a 10-gb/s rz-dpsk System. *IEEE Photonics Technology Letters*, 15(11), 1636–1638. doi:10.1109/LPT.2003.818664

Xu, C. (2003). Comparison of Return-to-zero Differential Phase Shift Keying and On-off Keying in Long Haul Dispersion Managed Transmission. *IEEE Journal of Selected Topics in Quantum Electronics*, 15, 617–619.

Xu, C., Liu, X., & Wei, X. (2004). Differential Phase-shift Keying for High Spectral Efficiency Optical Transmissions. *IEEE Journal of Selected Topics in Quantum Electronics*, 10(2), 281–293. doi:10.1109/JSTQE.2004.827835

Zhang, J. (2000). Bit Error Rate Analysis of otdm System Based on Moment Generation Function. *Journal of Lightwave Technology*, 18(11), 1513–1518. doi:10.1109/50.896211

Zhang, X. (2004). Noise Statistics in Optically Preamplified Differential Phase-shift Keying Receivers with Mach-zehnder Interferometer Demodulation. *Optics Letters*, 29. PMID:14971745

Zhou, Y. R., & Watkins, L. R. (1995). Rigorous approach to performance modeling of nonlinear, optically amplified im/dd systems. *IEE Proc-Optoelctron.*, 142, 271-278.

KEY TERMS AND DEFINITIONS

Amplitude Jitter: Refers to optical signal level variations, which cause optical energy fluctuations that result in amplitude margins degradations leading to errors.

Deflection Routing: A routing strategy used in packet switched networks to reduce the need of buffering packets. It is also known as hot potato routing.

Eye Diagram: Overlaying the optical waveforms of many bits produces an eye pattern, which can be used as an indicator of the quality of signals in high-speed optical transmission systems.

Forward Error Correction (FEC): An error control system used to enhance data reliability. The channel code is used to determine the most likely transmitted sequence of information symbols.

Power Spectral Density (PSD): Describes the signal power distribution over the frequency.

Pseudorandom Sequence: A deterministic sequence that is referred to as a noiselike or pseudonoise signal.

Timing Jitter: Refers to temporal fluctuations induced by variation of optical pulses arrival times.

Chapter 11
Optimization of Parameters for Optimal Performance

ABSTRACT

The impact of the signal pulse width and the optical filter bandwidth on the perfor-mance of both RZ and NRZ On-Off Keying (OOK) Optical Time Division Multiplexing (OTDM)-Wavelength Division Multiplexing (WDM) systems are studied in this chapter. Using polynomial fitting, an approximated expression for the optimal signal pulse duty cycle as a function of the spectral density S_D and Optical Signal to Noise Ratio (OSNR) is provided. Further, it is found that the bit rate per WDM channel does not affect the optimum signal pulse duty cycle. As the spectral density S_D increases, DC_{opt} increases, reducing the signal spectral width to compensate for the reduced the WDM channel frequency spacing Δf. For increasing OSNR, DC_{opt} increases slightly, especially at higher S_D. The authors found that ideal NRZ per-forms better than optimized RZ at high S_D but worse at low S_D.

INTRODUCTION

The current trend in WDM systems is the pursuit of higher spectral densities in dense WDM (DWDM) and ultra-dense WDM (UDWDM) systems (Cai, 2002; Gnauck, 2003), and (Weinert, 1999). This is because increasing spectral efficiency is a convenient way to increase transmission capacity. Many of these dense OTDM-WDM systems still use the on-off keying (OOK) format with either return-to-zero

DOI: 10.4018/978-1-4666-6575-0.ch011

(RZ) or non-return-to-zero (NRZ) modulation (Weinert, 1999). For regular WDM, the optimization of optical filter bandwidths has been studied extensively 4 (Bosco, Carena, Curri, Gaudino, & Poggiolini, 2002). However, in dense OTDM-WDM, the optimization has to be performed over high spectral densities using higher bit rates. Also, the optimization of signal pulse width relative to filter bandwidth and signal bit rate is often omitted. In this chapter, we use rigorous simulation to optimize dense OOK OTDM-WDM systems for both RZ and NRZ modulation with signal bit rate, signal pulse width, optical filter bandwidth and signal to noise ratio as parameters. Further, using polynomial fitting, we provide an approximated expression for the optimal signal pulse duty cycle as a function of spectral density and *OSNR*.

PERFORMANCE ESTIMATION MODEL

The system block diagram for both back-to-back and point-to-point configuration is shown in Figure 1. Each OTDM channel consists of a 9.953 Gb/s OOK signal, with assumed forward error coding (FEC) overhead of 7%, yielding a total bit rate of 10.664 Gb/s and is given by

$$U\left(t\right) = \sum_{n=0}^{N-1} a_n p\left(t - nT\right) \tag{11.1}$$

where a_n is the pseudorandom bit sequence (PRBS) of length $N = (2^{15})/M$ bits and M is the number of OTDM channels, T is the 10.664 Gb/s signal bit period and $p(t)$ is the pulse shape. The total time multiplexed signal bit period $T_R = T/M$ while the bit rate $B_R = 1/T_R = M/T$. For RZ modulation, the pulse shape is chirp-free Gaussian: $p(t) = \exp(-0.5(t/T_0)^2)$ where $T_0 = t_{FWHM}/1.665$ and t_{FWHM} is the full wave half maximum (FWHM) pulse width. For NRZ modulation, the pulse shape is ideally

Figure 1. System block diagram for OOK parameter optimization

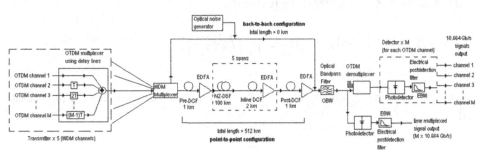

square: $p(t) = rect(t(M/T))$. Five time-multiplexed (M x 10.664 Gb/s) signals are WDM multiplexed with frequency spacing Δf and centered at 1549 nm. Results are obtained from the centre channel where WDM crosstalk is balanced (Yu, Reimer, Grigoryan, & Menyuk, 2000).

The optical filter is second-order Gaussian and the electrical filter is fifth-order Bessel. Shot and electrical thermal noise are neglected since optical noise is dominant. The OTDM demultiplexing window is almost ideal (square): fifth-order Gaussian with a width of $0.6(T/M)$. The electrical filter bandwidth, $EBW = 2OBW$, where OBW is the optical filter bandwidth, because high EBWs are optimal when shot and thermal noises are neglected (Bosco, Carena, Curri, Gaudino, & Poggiolini, 2002).

For back-to-back configuration, the transmitted WDM signal is added with optical noise and fed straight into the receiver. For point-to-point configuration, the WDM signal is transmitted across the link shown in Figure 1. The nonzero dispersion shifted fiber (NZ-DSF) has dispersion $D = 2.16$ ps/nm/km, dispersion slope $Sl = 0.06$ ps/nm²/km, effective area $A_{eff} = 55$ µm² and attenuation $\alpha = 0.2$ dB/km. The dispersion compensating fiber (DCF) has $D = -90$ ps/nm/km, $Sl = -2.5$ ps/nm²/km, $A_{eff} = 30$ µm² and $\alpha = 0.55$ dB/km. Dispersion management (DM) is ideal such that all dispersion is fully compensated for at the receiver. Each erbium doped fiber amplifier (EDFA) compensates for all attenuation suffered in its preceding span but generates ASE, which is added onto the signal after each amplifier. ASE and optical noise are modeled as circular complex additive white Gaussian noise (AWGN) with uniform random phase distribution. Signal and noise are propagated together by solving the nonlinear Schrödinger equation (NLSE) using the split-step Fourier method (SSFM) (Yu, Reimer, Grigoryan, & Menyuk, 2000) with single polarization assumed. To more accurately compare system capacity across varying bit rates, we use spectral density, S_D as the quantifier defined as

$$S_D = B_R/\Delta f \tag{11.2}$$

For intensity modulated systems, the Gaussian approximated Q is commonly used to estimate the BER where various techniques can be used to obtain it (Bergano, 2002; Anderson & Lyle, 1994). Here, we use

$$BER_{k,j}\left(D_{opt}\right) = \left(p_{k,j}/2\right)erfc\left(\left|D_{opt} - \mu_{k,j}\right|/\sqrt{2}\sigma_{k,j}\right) \tag{11.3}$$

for bit k, rail j where $\mu_{k,j}$ and $\sigma_{k,j}$ are the mean and standard deviation of the particular rail,

$$\sum_k \sum_j p_{k,j} = 1$$

and D_{opt} is the optimized receiver threshold (Norimatsu & Maruoka, 2002). The values of $\mu_{k,j}$ and $\sigma_{k,j}$ are easily obtained in our case since the initial PRBS is known and can be used, following the technique in (Anderson & Lyle, 1994), to classify according to each possible received pattern of 3 bits where each pattern is assumed to possess a separate rail. This technique is more accurate in the presence of waveform distortions (Norimatsu & Maruoka, 2002; Anderson & Lyle, 1994) compared to the conventional method in (Bergano, 2002). The *BER* is related to the *Q* through (Norimatsu & Maruoka, 2002)

$$BER = (1/2)\text{erfc}[Q / \text{sqrt}(2)] \tag{11.4}$$

To obtain the average performance over all OTDM channels, we define the average *BER* as

$$BER_{av} = \sum_{p=1}^{M} BER_p \Big/ M \tag{11.5}$$

where BER_p is the *BER* of OTDM channel *p*. Optimal parameters and performance are extracted from BER_{av} contour plots, similar to the Q-contour plots in (Bosco, Carena, Curri, Gaudino, & Poggiolini, 2002) where the parameters to be optimized are placed on the X and Y axes while the Z-axis gives the BER_{av}.

RESULTS AND DISUCUSSION

First, we verified that the *BER* of a directly detected, (*M* x 10.664) Gb/s OTDM signal is the same as the BER_{av} obtained from its 10.664 Gb/s OTDM demultiplexed constituents as long as we use the same bit sequence for the pattern conditioning.

Back-to-Back Configuration

Back-to-back system is optimized to obtain the optimal pulse width $t_{FWHM,opt}$ and optimal filter bandwidth OBW_{opt}. The optimization is performed based on the normalized parameters, which are defined as follows

$$BW_{norm,opt} = OBW_{opt} / B_R \tag{11.6}$$

$$DC_{opt} = t_{FWHM,opt} / T_R \tag{11.7}$$

where $BW_{norm,opt}$ is the optimum normalized optical filter bandwidth and DC_{opt} is the optimal signal pulse duty cycle. The received optical signal to noise ratio (OSNR) for back-to-back configuration used is defined as

$$OSNR = E_b/N_0 = (P_{rec} T_R)/(N_0) \tag{11.8}$$

$$SdB = 10 \log_{10}(OSNR) \tag{11.9}$$

where N_0 is the optical noise power spectral density (psd), P_{rec} is the received signal power per WDM channel and SdB is the $OSNR$ in units of decibels. The optimized signal pulse duty cycle for RZ modulation is shown in Figure 2 as a function of spectral density S_D for three total bit rates, $B_R = 42.656$ Gb/s (4-OTDM), 85.312 Gb/s (8-OTDM) and 170.624 Gb/s (16-OTDM), as well as for three values of $OSNR$ (14, 17, 20 dB). The pulse width for NRZ is by definition fixed and thus, not optimizable.

From the curves in Figure 2, we can conclude that the relationship between DC_{opt} and S_D is equal for all values of B_R. In other words, the bit rate per WDM channel does not affect the optimum signal pulse duty cycle. Keep in mind though that the actual signal pulse width has to change to maintain a specified duty cycle when the bit rate changes, as given in equation (11.7). On the other hand, as S_D increases, DC_{opt} increases, reducing the signal spectral width to compensate for the reduced Δf. Also, the $DC_{opt} - S_D$ curve changes slightly when the $OSNR$ is varied. For increasing $OSNR$, DC_{opt} increases slightly, especially at higher S_D. Thus, using polynomial fitting, we may approximate the optimal signal pulse duty cycle as a function of S_D and $OSNR$

$$DC_{opt} = -\left(1.333 + \frac{(SdB - 17)}{5.5}\right)S_D^2 +$$
$$\left(2.362 + \frac{(SdB - 17)}{4}\right)S_D - \left(0.350 + \frac{(SdB - 17)}{12.5}\right)$$

for $0.5 < S_D < 0.8$ \hfill (11.10)

$$DC_{opt} \approx 0.5 \text{ for } S_D < 0.5 \tag{11.11}$$

Equation (11.11) is simple enough and was found to be approximately true over the range of $OSNR$ considered and up to very low values of S_D. The value is constant

Figure 2. Back-to-back system for 4, 8 or 16 OTDM channels per WDM channel and OSNR = 14, 17 or 20 dB: Optimum signal pulse duty cycle, DCopt (%) versus spectral density, SD (RZ modulation) (Abbou)

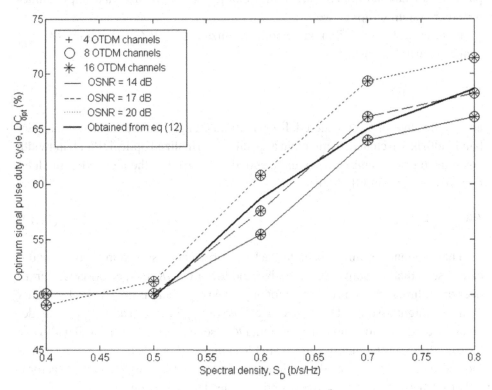

since for $S_D < 0.5$, linear crosstalk becomes insignificant and further separation of the WDM channels does not greatly impact the performance. On the other hand, equation (11.10) is a bit more complex since it relies on two parameters. As the dependence on OSNR does not generally lead to very significant changes, a simplified form of equation (11.10) where DC_{opt} is assumed to be independent of *OSNR* can be written as

$$DC_{opt} = -1.333S_D^2 + 2.362S_D - 0.350$$

for $0.5 < S_D < 0.8$ 						(11.12)

This equation is very useful since in most practical systems, the signal pulse duty cycle (pulse width) has to be decided upon first without prior knowledge of the received *OSNR*. This equation was found to be reasonably accurate in predicting the optimal signal duty pulse cycle over the range of *OSNR* tested (11-23dB). Though equations (11.10)-(11.12) are obtained from the specific setup of Gaussian pulses and Gaussian optical filters, they can potentially be used as simple guides for other system setups as well.

In the case of optical filter bandwidth optimization, for RZ modulation, $BW_{norm,opt}$ is approximately constant,

$$BW_{norm,opt} \approx 1.05 \tag{11.13}$$

across all values of S_D considered. Keep in mind though that the actual optical filter bandwidth has to change to maintain a specified normalized optical filter bandwidth when the bit rate changes, as given in equation (11.6). For the ideal NRZ modulation, $BW_{norm,opt}$ is slightly higher

$$BW_{norm,opt} \approx 1.25 \tag{11.14}$$

The resultant optimized back-to-back performance is shown in Figure 3 and it can be seen that for both cases of higher and lower *OSNR*, the performance curves over the entire S_D range is the same for any given B_R. There is no penalty for higher B_R as we might assume. This is because, when t_{FWHM} is optimizable, t_{FWHM} can decrease accordingly to maintain a constant DC_{opt} so that the signal spectral width can 'fill up' the extra channel spacing available at higher B_R while the optimum *OBW* is located. Thus, S_D is the key determining parameter and B_R only becomes a factor if either *OBW* or t_{FWHM} are not freely optimizable. This can occur in practice if t_{FWHM} is restricted to broad specifications by hardware restrictions, especially when the $t_{FWHM,opt}$ required is too narrow. On the whole, the results show that if signal pulse width is freely tunable, the bit rate per WDM channel can be increased continuously in back-to-back configuration without inducing any additional penalties.

Comparing between ideal NRZ and RZ modulation, it can be seen that ideal NRZ performs better at high S_D but worse at low S_D (cutoff at $S_D \approx 0.6$). The NRZ pulse is essentially similar to a wide t_{FWHM} RZ pulse. Thus, it performs worse than t_{FWHM}–optmized RZ at low S_D but better at high S_D. The improvement over RZ at high S_D is due to our use of ideal square NRZ pulses that have no pulse tails and thus, do not suffer from neighboring pulse overlap. The ideal NRZ pulses are, of course, not achievable in practice, and a practical NRZ pulse would have much stronger pulse tails and would, thus, have markedly reduced performance.

Figure 3. Back-to-back system for 4, 8 or 16 OTDM channels per WDM channel and OSNR = 17 or 20 dB: Bit error rate, BER versus spectral density, SD using optimized parameters obtained from Figure 2 (Abbou)

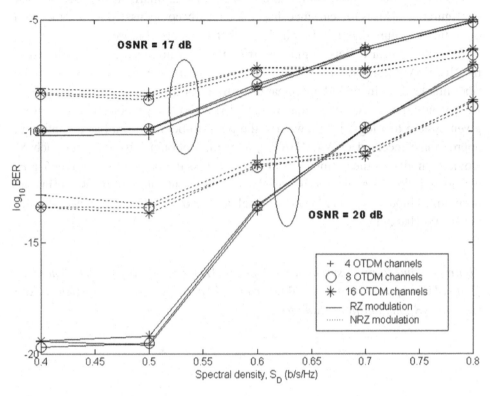

Point-to-Point Configuration

The received *OSNR* for point-to-point transmission distorted by accumulated ASE can be approximated by

$$OSNR = E_b/N_0 = \left(P_{in}T_R\right)\Big/\left(\sum_{a=1}^{7}N_a\right) \tag{11.15}$$

where N_a is the noise psd of amplifier a and P_{in} is the input transmission power per WDM channel into the link. First, we study point-to-point performance without nonlinear effects, where the received *OSNR* is set to 20 dB by using the appropriate P_{in} obtainable from equation (11.15). As seen from the dashed lines in Figure 5, this is similar to the back-to-back performance with *OSNR* = 20 dB in Figure 3.

This proves two things: firstly, equation (11.15) can accurately predict the received *OSNR* distorted solely by accumulated ASE; secondly, point-to-point transmission across a fiber link without nonlinear effects behaves similarly as the back-to-back configuration. This is logical since dispersion is fully compensated for and the main distortion is accumulated ASE, which is effectively optical noise.

When nonlinear effects originating from the Kerr nonlinearity are included in the NLSE (Yu, Reimer, Grigoryan, & Menyuk, 2000), increased power within the fiber link leads to increased nonlinear distortion. As such, an optimal input power, $P_{in,opt}$ would then exist. Since equation (11.15) is directly proportional to P_{in} for a given system topology, it follows that the point-to-point system has an optimum approximate received *OSNR*, $OSNR_{opt}$, as well. Obtaining the $P_{in,opt}$ for each S_D would then give us the optimal power region across the range of spectral densities considered. To give a fairer comparison across different values of B_R, we define the normalized input power per WDM channel, also known as the input power density per WDM channel

Figure 4. Point-to-point system for 4, 8 or 16 OTDM channels per WDM channel: Optimal input power density per WDM channel Sin,opt, versus spectral density, SD (RZ and NRZ modulation) (Abbou)

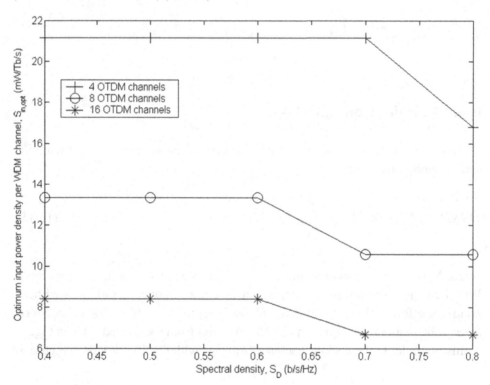

$$S_{in,opt} = P_{in,opt} / B_R \tag{11.16}$$

Setting DC_{opt} and $BW_{norm,opt}$, the optimum input power density per WDM channel is shown in Figure 4. It was found that $S_{in,opt}$ decreases slightly with increasing S_D. This is logical since decreasing Δf increases nonlinear effects. More importantly, we see that $S_{in,opt}$ decreases for increasing B_R indicating that nonlinear effects become more significant with increased B_R as the $P_{in,opt}$ does not increase proportionally with the bit rate per WDM channel. Note that the optimum power obtained here is based on our system configuration in Figure 1. Thus, the exact values of $S_{in,opt}$ shown here is not applicable to other general configurations though the general trends with respect to S_D and B_R can likely be extended across to other system configurations.

The resultant optimal performances are shown in Figure 5 which indicates that increased bit rate per WDM channel (B_R) induces higher performance penalties in the presence of nonlinear effects. The main reason for this is that we are using a dispersion managed system with high cumulative dispersion within the link, leading

Figure 5. Point-to-point system for 4, 8 or 16 OTDM channels per WDM channel: Bit error rate BER versus spectral density SD using optimized parameters (RZ and NRZ modulation). With nonlinear effects unless explicitly stated (Abbou).

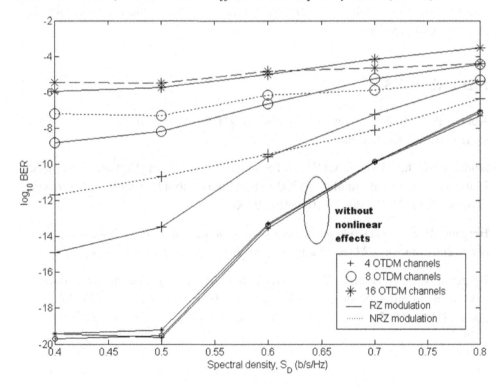

to significant intrachannel nonlinear effects. It is well known that intrachannel nonlinear effects cause increased distortion with increased bit rate (Kumar, Mauro, Raghavan, & Chowdhury, 2002). On the other hand, once again, it can be seen that ideal NRZ performs better than RZ at high S_D and worse at low S_D for the same reasons given earlier.

SUMMARY

The signal pulse width and the optical filter bandwidth for both RZ and NRZ modulation are optimized and equations to approximate the parameters are provided. With optimized pulse widths corresponding to a constant signal pulse duty cycle for a given spectral density (S_D), increasing the number of OTDM channels or bit rate (B_R) per WDM channel does not induce any additional performance penalties in back-to-back configuration. On the other hand, increased B_R causes increased performance penalties when nonlinear effects are taken into account in point-to-point transmission after signal power optimization. Thus, given specific system capacities (S_D) and performance criteria (*BER*), the upper limit to B_R is imposed strictly by nonlinear effects when dispersion is compensated for. Furthermore, it is found that ideal NRZ performs better than optimized RZ at high S_D but worse at low S_D, although it is worth pointing out that the ideal NRZ pulses are not normally achievable in practice.

REFERENCES

Abbou, F. M. (n.d.). *RZ and NRZ OOK OTDM-WDM Transmission System Optimizations*. Academic Press.

Anderson, C. J., & Lyle, J. A. (1994). Technique for Evaluating System Performance Using q in Numerical Simulations Exhibiting Intersymbol Interference. *Electronics Letters, 30*(1), 71–72. doi:10.1049/el:19940045

Bergano, N. S. (2002). *640 gb/s Transmission of Sixty-four 10 gb/s wdm Channels over 7200 km with 0.33 (bits/s)/hz Spectral Efficiency*. Academic Press.

Bergano, N. S., Kerfoot, F. W., & Davidson, C. R. (1993). Margin Measurements in Optical Amplifier Systems. *IEEE Photonics Technology Letters, 5*(3), 304–306. doi:10.1109/68.205619

Bosco, G., Carena, A., Curri, V., Gaudino, R., & Poggiolini, P. (2002). On the Use of nrz, rz and csrz Modulation at 40 gb/s with Narrow dwdm Channel Spacing. *Journal of Lightwave Technology, 20*(9), 1694–1704. doi:10.1109/JLT.2002.806309

Bosco, G., Carena, A., Curri, V., Gaudino, R., Poggiolini, P., & Benedetto, S. (2000). Suppression of Spurious Tones Induced by the Split-step Method in Fiber Systems Simulation. *IEEE Photonics Technology Letters, 12*(5), 489–491. doi:10.1109/68.841262

Cai, J. X. (2002). Long-haul 40 gb/s dwdm Transmission with Aggregate Capacities Exceeding 1 tb/s. *Journal of Lightwave Technology, 20*(12), 2247–2257. doi:10.1109/JLT.2002.806770

Chiang, T. K., Kagi, N., Marhic, M. E., & Kazovsky, L. G. (1996). Cross-phase Modulation in Fiber Links with Multiple Optical Amplifiers and Dispersion Compensators. *Lightwave Technol, 14*(3), 249–260. doi:10.1109/50.485582

Gnauck, A. H., Raybon, G., Bernasconi, P. G., Leuthold, J., Doerr, C. R., & Stulz, L. W. (2003). 1-tb/s (6 x 170.6 gb/s) Transmission over 2000-km nzdf using otdm and rz-dpsk Format. *IEEE Photonics Technology, 15*(11), 1618–1620. doi:10.1109/LPT.2003.818634

Hiew, C. C., Abbou, F. M., Chuah, H. T., Majumder, S. P., & Hairul, A. A. R. (2004). Ber Estimation of Optical wdm RZ-DPSK Systems Through the Differential Phase Q. *IEEE Photonics Technology Letters, 16*(12), 2619–2621. doi:10.1109/LPT.2004.836759

Humblet Azizoglu, P. A., & Azizoglu, M. (1991). On the Bit Error Rate of Lightwave Systems with Optical Amplifiers. *Journal of Lightwave Technology, 9*(11), 1576–1582. doi:10.1109/50.97649

Kim, H., & Yu, C. X. (2002). Optical Duobinary Transmission System Featuring Improved Receiver Sensitivity and Reduced Optical Bandwidth. *IEEE Photonics Technology Letters, 14*(8), 1205–1207. doi:10.1109/LPT.2002.1022019

Kumar, S., Mauro, J. C., Raghavan, S., & Chowdhury, D. Q. (2002). Intrachannel Nonlinear Penalties in Dispersion-managed Transmission Systems. *IEEE Journal of Selected Topics in Quantum Electronics, 8*(3), 626–631. doi:10.1109/JSTQE.2002.1016366

Leibrich, J., & Rosenkranz, W. (2003). Efficient Numerical Simulation of Multichannel wdm Transmission Systems Limited by xpm. *IEEE Photonics Technology Letters, 15*(3), 395–397. doi:10.1109/LPT.2003.807901

Nakazawa, M. (2000). Ultrahigh-speed Long-distance tdm and wdm Soliton Transmission Technologies. *IEEE Journal of Selected Topics in Quantum Electronics*, 6.

Norimatsu, S., & Maruoka, M. (2002). Accurate q-factor Estimation of Optically Amplified Systems in the Presence of Waveform Distortions. *Journal of Lightwave Technology*, *20*(1), 19–27. doi:10.1109/50.974814

Sinkin, O. V., Holzlohner, V., Zweck, J., & Menyuk, C. R. (2003). Optimization of the Split-step Fourier Method in Modeling Optical-fiber Communications Systems. *Journal of Lightwave Technology*, *21*(1), 61–68. doi:10.1109/JLT.2003.808628

Tkach, R. W., Chraplyvy, A. R., Forghieri, F., Gnauck, A. H., & Derosier, R. M. (1995). Four-photon Mixing and High-speed wdm Systems. *Journal of Lightwave Technology*, *13*(5), 841–849. doi:10.1109/50.387800

Weinert, C. M., Ludwig, R., Pieper, W., Weber, H. G., Breuer, D., Petermann, K., & Kuppers, F. (1999). 40 gb/s and 4 x 40 gb/s tdm/wdm Standard Fiber Transmission. *Journal of Lightwave Technology*, *17*(11), 2276–2284. doi:10.1109/50.803020

Yu, T., Reimer, W. M., Grigoryan, V. S., & Menyuk, C. R. (2000). *A mean Field Approach for Simulating Wavelength-division Multiplexed Systems*. Academic Press.

KEY TERMS AND DEFINITIONS

Back-to-Back System: A performance testing measurement in which the WDM signal is added with optical noise and fed straight into the receiver without passing through any fiber link.

Bandwidth: Determines the rate at which information can be transmitted across the fiber transmission medium.

Channel Frequency Spacing: Defines spacing between center frequencies (or wavelengths) of adjacent channels in an optical transmission system.

Point-to-Point System: A performance testing measurement in which the WDM signal is transmitted across the fiber link.

Polynomial Fitting: A technique that is used to find an approximating polynom of known degree for a given data.

Spectral Density: Describes how the energy of an optical signal is distributed over the frequency.

Chapter 12
Modified DP–Q and MGF BER

ABSTRACT

The optical return-to-zero differential phase shift keying system is analyzed in this chapter to determine the accuracy of the recently proposed differential phase Q method in estimating the bit error rate. It is found that this method consistently underestimates the bit error rate though it successfully predicts the qualitative behavior of single channel and wavelength division multiplexed systems for back-to-back and point-to-point configurations. A simple modification reduced the underestimation and produced highly accurate estimation.

INTRODUCTION

Lately, the return-to-zero differential phase shift keying (RZ-DPSK) format has been a matter of concern due to its suppression of nonlinear effects in wavelength division multiplexing (WDM) systems (Xu, 2003), in addition to its 3-dB receiver sensitivity improvement over intensity modulation (IM) formats (Humblet, Azizoglu, & Azizoglu, 1991). Experiments up to 40-Gb/s (Nakazawa, 2000) have been performed. However, for numerical simulation, there is still a search for a simple and reliable method to estimate the bit error rate (BER) of DPSK systems. Recently, three methods have been proposed: an analytical formula for pre-amplified receivers (Zhang, 2004), a semi-analytical method based on the Karhunen-Loéve (KL) expansion (Wang & Kahn, 2004; Bosco& Poggiolini, 2004) and the differential

DOI: 10.4018/978-1-4666-6575-0.ch012

phase Q (called DP-Q henceforth) (Wei, Liu, & Xu, 2003). In this chapter, we look at the process in which we arrive at the modified DP-Q in equation (10.24) and the tests used to validate its accuracy. Further, we will look at some of the tests we ran using the MGF BER estimation technique detailed earlier to gauge its accuracy and reliability.

Q FACTOR MODELS

For RZ-DPSK modulation, a new Q method based on the Gaussian approximation of the noise at the center of each rail of the "differential phase" eye diagram (Humblet, Azizoglu, & Azizoglu, 1991) where the differential phase is the phase difference between two sampling points separated by one bit period mapped from [-π/2, 3π/2]. It is defined as $Q_{\Delta\phi} = \pi / (\sigma_{\Delta\phi,0} + \sigma_{\Delta\phi,\pi})$ with $BER = \mathrm{erfc}[Q_{\Delta\phi} / \mathrm{sqrt}(2)]$ where $\sigma_{\Delta\phi,0}$ and $\sigma_{\Delta\phi,\pi}$ are the standard deviations of the 0/π rails. Analogous to the pattern conditioning used for IM, a similar modification to the DP-Q is proposed to accurately account for ISI. For each possible pattern of 3 bits, the probability of error is

$$BER_{p,left/right} = \frac{1}{2} erfc\left(\frac{\left| D_{left/right} - \mu_p \right|}{\sigma_p \sqrt{2}} \right)$$

(12.1)

where μ_p and σ_p are the mean and standard deviation of pattern p. $BER_{p,left/right}$ and $D_{left/right}$ refers to the BER and decision threshold of pattern p on either side of μ_p. We evaluate on two sides due to the circular nature of phase. The total BER is

$$BER = \sum_{p=1}^{8} \frac{n_p}{N} \left(BER_{p,left} + BER_{p,right} \right)$$

(12.2)

where n_p is the number of occurrences of pattern p and $N = \Sigma n_p$ provided $n_p > 1$. The DP-Q is simple to obtain from simulations as it only requires the "differential phase" eye diagram obtained from the received optical field envelope.

SIMULATION DETAILS

The system model is shown in Figure 1. Each transmitted channel uses 33% duty cycle RZ pulses that are ideally phase modulated by a Mach-Zehnder modulator

Modified DP-Q and MGF BER

Figure 1. System block diagram for modified DP-Q study (Hiew, Abbou, Chuah, Majumder, & Hairul, 2004)

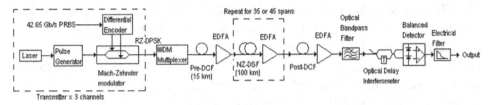

for RZ-DPSK. The channel bit rate is 40-Gb/s with assumed forward error coding (FEC) overhead of 6.7% yielding a total bit rate of 42.65-Gb/s. For back-to-back configuration, the multiplexed signal is sent directly to the receiver. A second order, super-Gaussian optical bandpass filter is used for WDM demultiplexing. All receivers are ideal with no shot and electrical thermal noise since the dominant noise in long-range systems is accumulated amplified spontaneous emission (ASE). A five-pole, Bessel postdetection electric filter is used with optimal bandwidth of 100 GHz. Three channels centered at 1550, 1551 and 1552 nm are simulated with results obtained from the center channel. Each channel is encoded by pseudo-random bit sequences of length 2^{16}-1 bits.

For point-to-point configuration, the signal is transmitted across 35 or 45 spans of nonzero dispersion shifted fiber (NZ-DSF) of length 100 km each with dispersion $D = 1$ ps/nm/km, dispersion slope $Sl = 0.05$ ps/nm^2/km, effective area $A_{eff} = 55$ µm^2 and attenuation $\alpha = 0.2$ dB/km. Dispersion compensating fiber (DCF) is placed at the beginning and end of transmission ($D = -100$ ps/nm/km, $Sl = -5$ ps/nm^2/km, $A_{eff} = 30$ µm^2, $\alpha = 0.55$ dB/km). Pre-dispersion compensation length is 15 km and post-dispersion compensation length is 20 or 30 km so that second and third order dispersion cancels out for all channels at the receiver. Erbium doped fiber amplifiers (EDFA) placed after each fiber span have a high Noise Figure of 7.78-dB, to increase the BER quickly for direct error counting. For back-to-back, optical noise is added to the WDM signal just before the receiver. For point-to-point, ASE is added onto the WDM signal after each amplifier along the transmission link and signal and noise are propagated together by solving the nonlinear Schrödinger equation (NLSE) using the split-step Fourier method (SSFM). Single polarization is assumed for all signals and noise. The ASE or optical noise is modeled as complex circular additive white Gaussian noise (AWGN), with uniform random phase. Multiple runs are performed until the results converge. In addition, optical signal to noise ratio (OSNR) is often used as a parameter and is defined as according to equation (10.5). Integration is performed over the noise bandwidth B_N, taken as 400 GHz.

RESULTS AND DISCUSSION

The BER obtained from direct error counting of the simulated output signal is always used as reference. We verified that RZ-DPSK BER counted from either the received optical differential phase or the output current is similar, provided the DPSK receiver is ideal. Next, using the vector addition of signal and noise fields, we obtain the differential phase of the back-to-back, single-channel signal distorted by complex circular AWGN *without* the optical filter.

$$
\Delta\varphi_0\left(t\right) = \tan^{-1}\left(\frac{X\left(t\right)\sin\theta\left(t\right)}{-A\left(t\right)+X\left(t\right)\cos\theta\left(t\right)}\right) +
$$
$$
\pi - \tan^{-1}\left(\frac{X\left(t-T\right)\sin\theta\left(t-T\right)}{A\left(t-T\right)+X\left(t-T\right)\cos\theta\left(t-T\right)}\right)
$$

for logic '0' (π phase shift)

$$
\Delta\varphi_1\left(t\right) = \tan^{-1}\left(\frac{X\left(t\right)\sin\theta\left(t\right)}{A\left(t\right)+X\left(t\right)\cos\theta\left(t\right)}\right) -
$$
$$
\tan^{-1}\left(\frac{X\left(t-T\right)\sin\theta\left(t-T\right)}{A\left(t-T\right)+X\left(t-T\right)\cos\theta\left(t-T\right)}\right)
$$

for logic '1' (zero phase shift)   (12.3)

where $0 \leq \Delta\phi_0(t) \leq 2\pi$ and $-\pi \leq \Delta\phi_1(t) \leq \pi$, while T is the bit period. $A(t)$ is the amplitude of the signal field and $X(t)$ is the zero mean, Gaussian distributed noise field whose variance is the noise power over B_N, while $\theta(t)$ is the uniform random distributed noise field phase at time t. Sampling t at the bit centers, we find that the $\Delta\phi_0(t)$ and $\Delta\phi_1(t)$ distributions are similar, suggesting that noise distribution of logic '1' and '0' are alike as in (Zhang, 2004).

In Figure 2, we see that BER counted from equation (12.3) exactly coincides with BER counted from back-to-back simulation without the optical and electrical filters. With an optical filter, the BER improves, especially at high received OSNR. This is due to the filter response, as the OSNR used for comparison is measured just before balanced detection for both scenarios. The optical filter bandwidth, $OBW =$ 120 GHz where $OBW > 2/T$ so that the filtered noise is approximately white. The reason for the improved performance is shown in Figure 3. Before optical filtering,

Modified DP-Q and MGF BER

Figure 2. Back-to-back, single-channel configuration: BER (direct count) vs. received OSNR with/without the optical filter (OBW = 120 GHz, no electrical filter) (Hiew, Abbou, Chuah, Majumder, & Hairul, 2004)

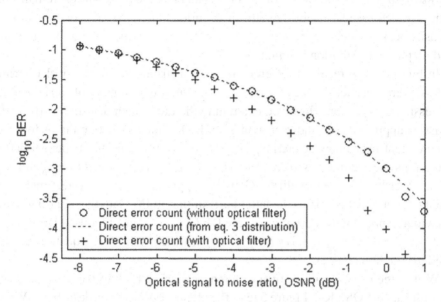

Figure 3. Back-to-back, single-channel configuration: Distribution of AWGN intensity before/after the optical filter, inset: log_{10} scale (OSNR = -4 dB) (Hiew, Abbou, Chuah, Majumder, & Hairul, 2004)

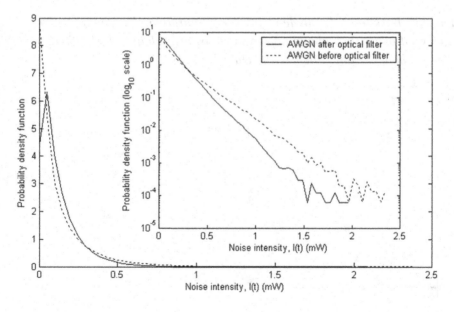

the AWGN intensity distribution, $I(t) = |X(t)|^2$ is a Chi-square distribution. After optical filtering, it is no longer a Chi-square distribution, such that the variance of the distribution has decreased although its mean (average noise power) remains the same. The decreased probability in the distribution tail means the reduction of high intensity peaks, which are the main source of bit errors in high OSNR. The uniform random phase distribution is retained.

In Figure 4, the received differential phase distribution after optical filtering, obtained through back-to-back sampling, is shown. It is symmetrical and resembles a Gaussian distribution. However, examining the tail, which determines BER, the Gaussian approximation shows a significant BER underestimation that is found to be consistent over many scenarios, suggesting that reducing the underestimation would improve accuracy. A correction factor of 1.15 is multiplied to $\sigma_{\Delta\phi,0}$ and $\sigma_{\Delta\phi,\pi}$ or σ_p, which we call the modified Gaussian approximation. It overestimates the initial tail but underestimates the latter part, similar to IM Gaussian approximation behaviour. Applying the correction to the DP-Q, we obtain a modified DP-Q equal to $Q_{\Delta\phi,modified} = 0.87 \, Q_{\Delta\phi} = 0.87\pi \, / \, (\sigma_{\Delta\phi,0} + \sigma_{\Delta\phi,\pi})$, which is the final equation as indicated in equation (10.24).

We test the DP-Q accuracy over different scenarios: back-to-back, single-channel with varying OSNR in Figure 5 tests the effect of AWGN; back-to-back, WDM with varying OBW in Figure 6 tests the effects of ISI and WDM linear crosstalk; and point-to-point WDM propagation with varying transmitted power per channel in Figure 7 tests the nonlinear and signal-ASE propagation effects. As expected,

Figure 4. Back-to-back, single-channel configuration: Distribution of received differential phase; actual and approximations, inset: $\log_{10}$ scale (OSNR = -4 dB) (Hiew, Abbou, Chuah, Majumder, & Hairul, 2004)

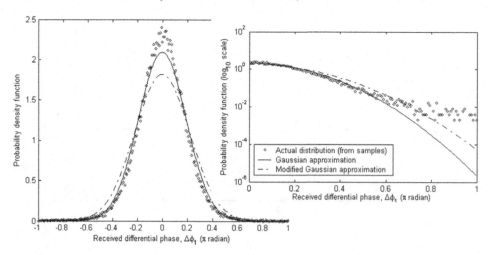

Figure 5. BER from different estimation models for back-to-back, single-channel vs. received OSNR (OBW = 120 GHz) (Hiew, Abbou, Chuah, Majumder, & Hairul, 2004)

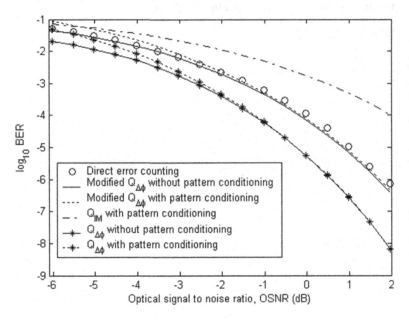

Figure 6. BER from different estimation models for back-to-back, WDM vs. OBW (OSNR = 0.71 dB or OSNR = -1.8 dB) (Hiew, Abbou, Chuah, Majumder, & Hairul, 2004)

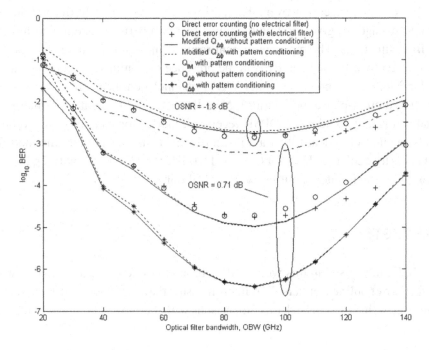

Figure 7. BER from different estimation models for point-to-point WDM propagation vs. transmitted power per channel (OBW = 90 GHz, across 35 spans or 45 spans) (Hiew, Abbou, Chuah, Majumder, & Hairul, 2004)

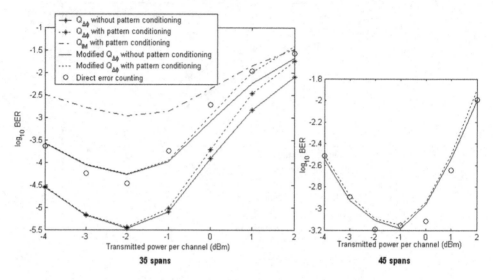

Q_{IM} does not provide a good BER estimation. On the other hand, it is found that while the DP-Q is qualitatively accurate in estimating the BER, it still has a consistent and significant underestimation. Pattern conditioning gives slightly better accuracy at low OSNR and high ISI. However, in Figure 5 to Figure 7, the modified DP-Q reveals good accuracy over all scenarios with or without pattern conditioning. Thus, it manages to give good predictions of system performance under high and low BER situations. The most significant result is in Figure 7 where the modified DP-Q correctly estimates the BER in the presence of nonlinear effects such as the Gordon-Mollenauer noise and inter-WDM channel nonlinear effects (four-wave mixing and cross-phase modulation). Note that the DP-Q operates on the optical signal and is only valid when DPSK receiver imperfections and electrical domain effects, such as electrical filters are insignificant. Thus, in Figure 6, the modified DP-Q fails to predict the BER for OBW > 110 GHz with an electrical filter, because the excess noise is filtered out in the electrical domain.

MGF TESTS

The MGF model used in this work will be limited to intensity modulated systems unaffected by nonlinear effects. To reliably measure the accuracy of a BER estimation technique, we have to fall back on comparisons with the slowest but most fundamentally accurate technique, the Monte Carlo technique. In Figure 8, the MGF model is compared with the Monte Carlo estimation and the Q factor model detailed earlier.

The comparison in Figure 8 indicates that the Q factor as expected gives a good estimate of the BER (remember that the Monte Carlo estimate is the reference). However, it is surprising that the MGF model significantly underestimates the BER. Also, the underestimation occurs systemically across the entire OSNR range even at very high BERs where errors are normally small.

Thus, comparisons are made once again using a simulated environment similar to that used in Forestieri (2003), so that we may compare our results with the results obtained there to make sure that the accuracy errors seen here are not due to errors in our simulation program. The results are shown in Figure 9.

Figure 8. Comparison between BER estimated from Monte Carlo, Q factor and MGF models (RZ Gaussian signal, 2nd order Gaussian optical filter, 5th order Bessel postdetection filter, back-to-back system) (Hiew, Abbou, & Chuah, 2006)

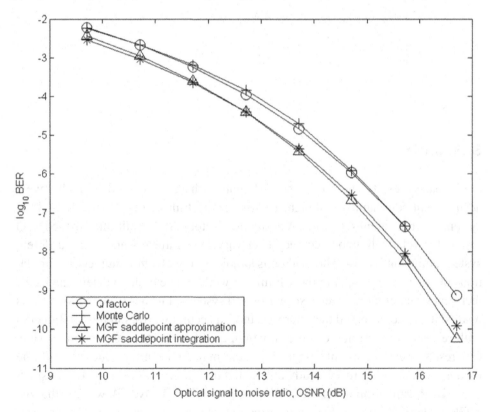

Figure 9. Comparison between BER estimated from Monte Carlo, Q factor, MGF model and from reference (Tu, 2004) (NRZ signal, Gaussian optical and postdetection filters with B0T = 8 and BRT = 0.7 respectively, back-to-back system) (Hiew, Abbou, & Chuah, 2006)

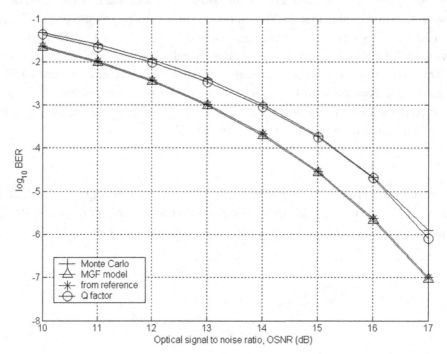

SUMMARY

Performance results show that the differential phase Q method is qualitatively accurate but consistently and significantly underestimates the BER of RZ-DPSK systems over different scenarios. A correction factor of 0.87 multiplied to the DP-Q resulted in relatively good accuracy over varying parameters and under different system dominant effects. The method is simple to implement in numerical simulations of any arbitrary system though further work can be done to determine its effectiveness under more diverse scenarios and systems. Further from the MGF tests results, it can be observed that there are indeed accuracy errors in the MGF model with respect to the Monte Carlo estimation, and these errors can be quite severe. Our results were consistent, suggesting there may be accuracy concerns with the model itself. Another recent study also found that there may be some errors small in the BER estimation using the MGF model (Tu, 2004). Overall, we find that the MGF model in its present form has systemic problems in its accuracy, which raises reliability issues.

REFERENCES

Bosco, G., & Poggiolini, P. (2004). On the q Factor Inaccuracy in the Performance Analysis of Optical Direct-detection dpsk Systems. *IEEE Photonics Technology Letters, 16*(2), 665–667. doi:10.1109/LPT.2003.820475

Castanon, G. A., Tonguz, O. K., & Bononi, A. (1997). Ber Performance of Multiwavelength Optical Cross-connected Networks with Deflection Routing. *IEE Proc-Communications, 144*, 114-120.

Forestieri, E. (2003). Correction to Evaluating the Error Probability in Lightwave Systems with Chromatic Dispersion, Arbitrary Pulse Shape and Pre- and Post-detection Filtering. *Journal of Lightwave Technology, 21*(6), 1957. doi:10.1109/JLT.2003.812719

Forghieri, F., Bononi, A., & Prucnal, P. R. (1995). Analysis and Comparison of Hot-potato and Single-buffer Deflection Routing in Very High Bit Rate Optical Mesh Networks. *IEEE Transactions on Communications, 43*(1), 88–98. doi:10.1109/26.385939

Hiew, C. C., Abbou, F. M., & Chuah, H. T. (2006). *Performance Analysis and Design of an Optical TDM-WDM Transmission System and Network* (Tech. Rep. No. 1). Malaysia: Multimedia University and Alcatel Network Systems.

Hiew, C. C., Abbou, F. M., Chuah, H. T., Majumder, S. P., & Hairul, A. A. R. (2004). Ber Estimation of Optical wdm rz-dpsk Systems Through the Differential Phase q. *IEEE Photonics Technology Letters, 16*(12), 2619–2621. doi:10.1109/LPT.2004.836759

Humblet Azizoglu, P. A., & Azizoglu, M. (1991). On the Bit Error Rate of Lightwave Systems with Optical Amplifiers. *Journal of Lightwave Technology, 9*(11), 1576–1582. doi:10.1109/50.97649

Nakazawa, M. (2000). Ultrahigh-speed Long-distance tdm and wdm Soliton Transmission Technologies. *IEEE J. of Sel. Top. in Quant. Elec., 6*.

Tu, K. Y., Forestieri, E., Kaneda, N., Secondini, M., Leven, A., Koc, U.-V., & Hocke, R. (2004). Modeling Accuracy of a Fiber-optics Test Bed Using mgf Method. *IEEE Photonics Technology Letters, 16*(12), 2646–2648. doi:10.1109/LPT.2004.836771

Wang, J., & Kahn, K. (2004). Impact of Chromatic and Polarization-mode Dispersions on dpsk Systems Using Interferometric Demodulation and Direct Detection. *Journal of Lightwave Technology, 22*(2), 362–371. doi:10.1109/JLT.2003.822101

Wei, X., Liu, X., & Xu, C. (2003). Numerical Simulation of the spm Penalty in a 10-gb/s rz-dpsk System. *IEEE Photonics Technology Letters*, *15*(11), 1636–1638. doi:10.1109/LPT.2003.818664

Xu, C., Xiang Liu, , Mollenauer, L. F., & Xing Wei, . (2003). Comparison of Return-to-zero Differential Phase Shift Keying and on-off Keying in Long Haul Dispersion Managed Transmission. *IEEE Photonics Technology Letters*, *15*(4), 617–619. doi:10.1109/LPT.2003.809317

Zhang, X. (2004). Noise Statistics in Optically Preamplified Differential Phase-shift Keying Receivers with Mach-zehnder Interferometer Demodulation. *Optics Letters*, 29. PMID:14971745

KEY TERMS AND DEFINITIONS

Differential Phase Q (DP-Q): Refers to the phase difference between two sampling points separated by one bit period. DP-Q method provides a good estimate for penalty due to nonlinear phase-shift.

Inter-Symbol Interference (ISI): Refers to a form of distortion of a signal in which one symbol interferes with subsequent symbols.

Moment-Generating Function (MGF): An alternative specification of the random variable probability distribution function.

Monte Carlo Estimation: A computerized mathematical technique that considers risks in quantitative analysis. The technique translates the uncertainty in the various aspects of a system to the predicted performance.

Optical Signal-to-Noise Ratio (OSNR): Refers to the ratio of the average optical power of the information signal component to the average power of the noise component in a signal. It is used in optical communications to compare the level of a desired signal to the level of noise.

Section 5

Chapter 13

Comparison of RZ–OOK and RZ–DPSK Optimal Performance

ABSTRACT

Using the Differential Phase Q (DP-Q) and the traditional Q factor, performance comparison of RZ-OOK and RZ-DPSK in dense OTDM-WDM systems is obtained in this chapter. When signal pulse widths and optical filter bandwidths are optimized, there is no upper limit to WDM channel bit rate (B_R) in the purely linear back-to-back configuration. Here, RZ-DPSK performed increasingly better than RZ-OOK in higher spectral density with Q gain increasing from 3 dB to 5 dB. In the nonlinear point-to-point configuration, higher B_R leads to increased performance penalties for both RZ-DPSK and RZ-OOK, while RZ-DPSK still outperforms RZ-OOK by up to 4 dB. The results obtained correlate with conventional results, indicating the potential of the DP-Q as a performance evaluation tool in numerical simulations.

INTRODUCTION

The analysis of RZ-DPSK systems from purely numerical simulations has been difficult due to a lack of a simple method for bit error rate (BER) estimation. However, recently, the differential phase Q (DP-Q) was proposed in (Wei, Liu, & Xu, 2003) and a modification to it was made in (Hiew, Abbou, Chuah, Majumder, & Hairul, 2004) to increase its accuracy and demonstrate its relative reliability for BER estimation.

DOI: 10.4018/978-1-4666-6575-0.ch013

Using the DP-Q and the traditional Q factor for OOK systems (Bergano, Kerfoot, & Davidson, 1993), performance comparison of RZ-OOK and RZ-DPSK in dense OTDM-WDM systems is obtained with varying spectral densities, WDM channel bit rates and signal to noise ratios while optimizing the signal pulse widths and optical filter bandwidths. Based on known conventional results (Gnauck, 2003), the effectiveness of using the DP-Q as a performance estimation tool is tested and verified to compare the performance of RZ-OOK and RZ-DPSK modulation in dense OTDM-WDM systems with optimization of parameters (Hiew, Abbou, Chuah, Majumder, & Hairul, 2004).

SYSTEM MODEL

The system block diagram for both back-to-back and point-to-point configuration is shown in Figure 1. Each OTDM channel consists of a 9.953 Gb/s signal, with assumed forward error coding (FEC) overhead of 7%, yielding a total bit rate of 10.664 Gb/s. It is given by

$$U(t) = \sum_{n=0}^{N-1} a_n p(t - nT) \tag{13.1}$$

where $a_n \in \{0,1\}$ for RZ-OOK or $a_n \in \{e^{j0}, e^{j\pi}\}$ for RZ-DPSK, $N = (2^{15})/M$ bits and M is the number of OTDM channels, T is the 10.664 Gb/s signal bit period and $p(t)$ is the pulse shape assumed to be chirp-free Gaussian: $p(t) = \exp(-0.5(t/T_0)^2)$ where $T_0 = t_{FWHM}/1.665$ and t_{FWHM} is the full wave half maximum (FWHM) pulse width. The total time multiplexed signal bit period $T_R = T/M$ while the bit rate $B_R = 1/T_R = M/T$.

Figure 1. System block diagram for comparisons between RZ-OOK and RZ-DPSK (Abbou, Chuah, Hiew, & Abid, 2008)

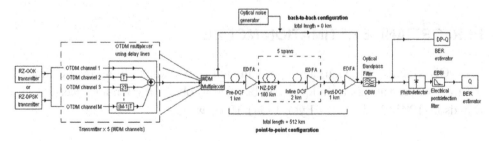

Five time-multiplexed (M x 10.664 Gb/s) signals are WDM multiplexed with frequency spacing Δf and centered at 1549 nm. Results are obtained from the centre channel where WDM crosstalk is balanced (Yu, Reimer, Grigoryan, & Menyuk, 2000). The optical filter used is a second-order Gaussian bandpass filter with bandwidth, *OBW*. Shot and electrical thermal noise are neglected since optical noise is dominant. The postdetection electrical filter is a fifth-order Bessel lowpass filter with bandwidth, $EBW = 2OBW$, because high *EBW*s are optimal when shot and thermal noises are neglected (Bosco, Carena, Curri, Gaudino, & Poggiolini, 2002). For RZ-OOK, BER estimation is carried out after the postdetection filter while for RZ-DPSK it is performed right after the optical filter with no balanced detection performed. This is because the DP-Q operates on the optical signal and implicitly assumes that it is followed by an ideal balanced detector Hiew, Abbou, Chuah, Majumder, & Hairul, 2004).

For back-to-back configuration, the transmitted WDM signal is added with optical noise and fed straight into the receiver without passing through any fiber link. For point-to-point configuration, the WDM signal is transmitted across the fiber link shown in Figure 1. The nonzero dispersion shifted fiber (NZ-DSF) has dispersion $D = 2.16$ ps/nm/km, dispersion slope $Sl = 0.06$ ps/nm²/km, effective area $A_{eff} = 55$ μm² and attenuation $\alpha = 0.2$ dB/km. The dispersion compensating fiber (DCF) has $D = -90$ ps/nm/km, $Sl = -2.5$ ps/nm²/km, $A_{eff} = 30$ μm² and $\alpha = 0.55$ dB/km. Dispersion management (DM) is ideal in such a way that all dispersion is fully compensated for at the receiver. Each erbium doped fiber amplifier (EDFA) compensates for all attenuation suffered in its preceding span but generates ASE, which is added onto the signal after each amplifier. ASE and optical noise are modeled as circular complex additive white Gaussian noise (AWGN) with uniform random phase distribution. Signal and noise are propagated together by solving the nonlinear Schrödinger equation (NLSE) using the split-step Fourier method (SSFM) (Yu, Reimer, Grigoryan, & Menyuk, 2000) with single polarization assumed. To more accurately compare system capacity across varying bit rates, we use spectral density, S_D as the quantifier defined as

$$S_D = B_R/\Delta f \tag{13.2}$$

PERFORMANCE ESTIMATION MODEL

For OOK systems, the Gaussian approximated Q is commonly used to estimate the *BER* where various techniques can be used to obtain it (Bergano, Kerfoot, & Davidson, 1993; Anderson & Lyle, 1994). Here, we use

$$BER_{k,j}\left(D_{opt}\right) = \left(p_{k,j}/2\right)erfc\left(\left|D_{opt} - \mu_{k,j}\right|/\sqrt{2}\sigma_{k,j}\right)$$

for bit k, rail j where $\mu_{k,j}$ and $\sigma_{k,j}$ are the mean and standard deviation of the particular rail,

$$\sum_{k}\sum_{j}p_{k,j} = 1$$

and D_{opt} is the optimized receiver threshold (Norimatsu & Maruoka, 2002). $\mu_{k,j}$ and $\sigma_{k,j}$ are easily obtained in our case since the initial PRBS is known and can be used, following the technique in (Anderson & Lyle, 1994), to classify each possible received pattern of 3 bits where each pattern is assumed to possess a separate rail. This technique is more accurate in the presence of waveform distortions (Norimatsu & Maruoka, 2002; Anderson & Lyle, 1994) compared to the conventional method in (Bergano, Kerfoot, & Davidson, 1993). The *BER* is related to the Q through *BER* = (1/2) erfc[Q_{OOK} / sqrt(2)].

For RZ-DPSK systems, the DP-Q is used, which is based on the Gaussian approximation of the noise at the center of each rail of the "differential phase" eye diagram (Wei, Liu, & Xu, 2003) where the differential phase is the phase difference between two sampling points separated by one bit period mapped from [-π/2, 3π/2]. The modified DP-Q obtained in (Hiew, Abbou, Chuah, Majumder, & Hairul, 2004) is defined as $Q_{DPSK} = 0.87\pi$ / ($\sigma_{\Delta\phi,0} + \sigma_{\Delta\phi,\pi}$) where $\sigma_{\Delta\phi,0}$ and $\sigma_{\Delta\phi,\pi}$ are the standard deviations of the 0 or π rails. The BER is obtained by $BER = erfc[Q_{DPSK}$ / sqrt(2)].

Optimal parameters and performance are extracted from Q or BER contour plots (Bosco, Carena, Curri, Gaudino, & Poggiolini, 2002), where the parameters to be optimized are on the X and Y axes while the Z axis gives the Q or BER. The Q factor in decibels for both OOK and DPSK is defined as $Q^{dB} = 20 \log_{10}(Q)$.

RESULTS AND DISCUSSION

First, back-to-back system is optimized to obtain the optimal signal pulse width $t_{FWHM,opt}$ and optimal filter bandwidth OBW_{opt}. These parameters are normalized using

$$BW_{norm,opt} = OBW_{opt} / B_R \tag{13.3}$$

$$DC_{opt} = t_{FWHM,opt} / T_R \tag{13.4}$$

Figure 2. Back-to-back system for 4, 8 or 16 OTDM channels per WDM channel and SdB = 14, 17 or 20 dB: Optimum signal pulse duty cycle, DCopt (%) versus spectral density, SD (RZ-OOK and RZ-DPSK modulation) (Abbou, Chuah, Hiew, & Abid, 2008)

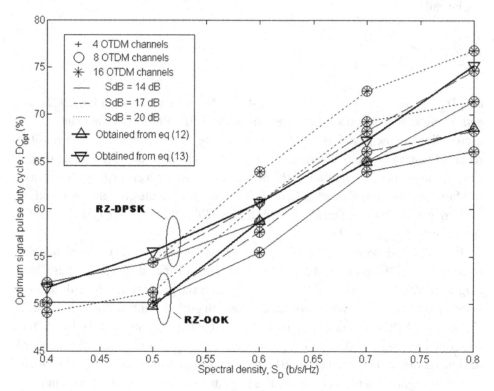

where $BW_{norm,opt}$ is the optimum normalized optical filter bandwidth and DC_{opt} is the optimum signal pulse duty cycle. The variation of DC_{opt} for both RZ-OOK and RZ-DPSK modulation are shown in Figure 2 as a function of spectral density S_D using three total bit rates, $B_R = 42.656$ Gb/s (4-OTDM), 85.312 Gb/s (8-OTDM) and 170.624 Gb/s (16-OTDM). Note that the variation of DC_{opt} in our simulations was assumed to be totally free (ideal) and not subject to the behavioral characteristics of practical pulse carvers. The received optical signal to noise ratio (OSNR) for back-to-back configuration used here is defined as

$$OSNR = E_b/N_0 = (P_{rec}\,T_R)/(N_0) \tag{13.5}$$

$$SdB = 10\log_{10}(OSNR) \tag{13.6}$$

where N_0 is the optical noise power spectral density (psd), P_{rec} is the received signal power per WDM channel and SdB is the $OSNR$ in units of decibels.

From Figure 2, we can conclude that for both RZ-OOK and RZ-DPSK, the relationship between DC_{opt} and S_D is equal for all values of B_R. In other words, the bit rate per WDM channel (B_R) does not affect the optimum signal pulse duty cycle (DC_{opt}). Keep in mind though that the actual signal pulse width (t_{FWHM}) has to change to maintain a specified duty cycle when the bit rate changes, as given in equation (13.6). On the other hand, as S_D increases, DC_{opt} increases, reducing the signal spectral width to compensate for the reduced Δf. Also, for increasing $OSNR$, DC_{opt} increases slightly, especially at higher S_D. Thus, using polynomial fitting, we can approximate DC_{opt} as a function of S_D and $OSNR$. However, in practical systems, the signal pulse duty cycle (pulse width) has to be decided upon first without prior knowledge of the received $OSNR$. Since, as seen from Figure 2, the $OSNR$ dependence does not lead to significant changes, simplified forms where DC_{opt} is assumed to be independent of $OSNR$ can be written as

For RZ-OOK,

$$DC_{opt} \approx -1.333 S_D^2 + 2.362 S_D - 0.350 \text{ for } 0.5 < S_D < 0.8$$

$$DC_{opt} \approx 0.5 \text{ for } 0.4 < S_D < 0.5 \tag{13.7}$$

For RZ-DPSK,

$$DC_{opt} \approx 0.6885 S_D^2 - 0.2361 S_D + 0.5018 \text{ for } 0.4 < S_D < 0.8 \tag{13.8}$$

Equations (13.7)-(13.8) are relatively accurate over the range of $OSNR$ considered (11-23 dB) and are shown in Fig 2. The value is approximately constant for $S_D < 0.5$ because linear crosstalk becomes insignificant and further separation of the WDM channels does not greatly impact the performance. Observe that DC_{opt} for RZ-DPSK is generally larger than that for RZ-OOk. This is consistent with the known property of RZ-DPSK being more tolerant to intersymbol interference (ISI) compared to RZ-OOK (Yamamoto & Inoue, 2003). Also, though (208)-(209) are obtained from the specific setup of Gaussian pulses and Gaussian optical filters, they can be used as simple guides for other setups as well.

In the case of optical filter bandwidth optimization, for RZ-OOK modulation, $BW_{norm,opt}$ is approximately constant, ($BW_{norm,opt} \approx 1.05$) across all values of S_D considered. Keep in mind though that the actual optical filter bandwidth has to change to maintain a specified normalized optical filter bandwidth when the bit rate changes, as given in equation (13.3). For RZ-DPSK modulation, $BW_{norm,opt}$ is dependent on

S_D, ($BW_{norm,opt} \approx -0.61 S_D + 1.42$). Once again, due to the increased tolerance towards ISI, RZ-DPSK has narrower $BW_{norm,opt}$ at high S_D.

From the resultant optimized back-to-back performance, we observe that for all given *OSNR*, the performance curves over the entire S_D range are the same for any given B_R. There is no penalty for higher B_R and this is true for both RZ-OOK and RZ-DPSK. This is because, when t_{FWHM} is optimizable, t_{FWHM} can decrease accordingly so that the signal spectral width can 'fill up' the extra channel spacing available at higher B_R to maintain a constant DC_{opt} while the optimum *OBW* is located. Thus, S_D is the key determining parameter and B_R only becomes a factor if either *OBW* or t_{FWHM} are not freely tunable. The results show that if signal pulse width is freely tunable, the bit rate per WDM channel can be increased continuously in back-to-back configuration (linear environment) without inducing additional penalties.

Next, the back-to-back performances of RZ-OOK and RZ-DPSK are compared in Figure 3. Since the performances are the same for 4, 8 or 16 OTDM channels, only one line is shown to represent all three in Figure 3 for clarity. Also, to assist in the comparisons, we define new parameters, referred to as Q gains.

$$Q_{OOK-OOK}\left(x, y\right) = Q_{OOK}^{dB}\left(SdB = y\right) - Q_{OOK}^{dB}\left(SdB = x\right) \tag{13.9}$$

$$Q_{DPSK-DPSK}\left(x, y\right) = Q_{DPSK}^{dB}\left(SdB = y\right) - Q_{DPSK}^{dB}\left(SdB = x\right) \tag{13.10}$$

$$Q_{OOK-DPSK}\left(x\right) = Q_{DPSK}^{dB}\left(SdB = x\right) - Q_{OOK}^{dB}\left(SdB = x\right) \tag{13.11}$$

From Figure 3, we can see that for both RZ-OOK and RZ-DPSK, an increase in *OSNR* leads to a proportional increase in Q when S_D is small. As S_D increases, the Q gain diminishes due to increased WDM linear crosstalk. Also, the higher DC_{opt} at high S_D used to reduce WDM crosstalk leads to increased intersymbol interference (ISI). It is clear in Figure 3 that RZ-DPSK suffers less penalty for increasing S_D compared to RZ-OOK, mainly due to its increased tolerance towards ISI. This can be clearly seen with the $Q_{OOK-DPSK}$ curves, which are around 3.5 dB at low S_D (higher optical bandwidths) and increases to up to 5 dB at high S_D (lower optical bandwidths), consistent with results in (Gnauck & Winzer, 2005). Note that the increase of Q gain in the $Q_{OOK-DPSK}$ curves with respect to increasing *OSNR* is due to the accumulated penalties incurred by RZ-OOK at high S_D.

Figure 3. Back-to-back system for 4, 8 or 16 OTDM channels per WDM channel and SdB = 14, 17 or 20 dB: Q gains (refer eqs. (210)-(212)) versus spectral density, SD using optimized t_{FWHM} and OBW (RZ-OOK and RZ-DPSK modulation) (Abbou, Chuah, Hiew, & Abid, 2008)

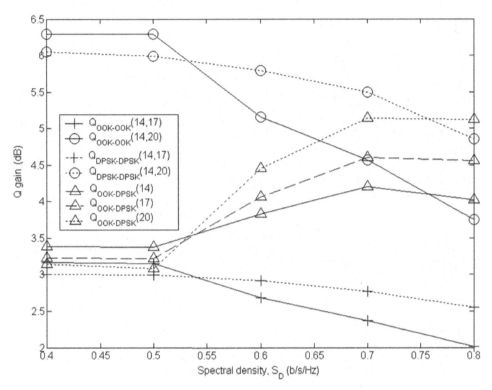

Point-to-Point Configuration

When nonlinear effects originating from the Kerr nonlinearity are included in the NLSE (Yu, Reimer, Grigoryan, & Menyuk, 2000), increased power leads to increased nonlinear distortion. As such, an optimal input power, $P_{in,opt}$ would then exist, which is equivalent to the launched power per span in our system setup. Setting DC_{opt} and $BW_{norm,opt}$, $P_{in,opt}$ and its associated optimum point-to-point performance for each S_D was obtained by observing the minima of the *BER* versus $P_{in,opt}$ curves. Since the optimum powers obtained are applicable only for this particular system setup (non-general results), the values are not shown here for brevity.

Instead, we focus on the behavioral trends of the optimized point-to-point performance shown in Figure 4 for both RZ-OOK and RZ-DPSK. It uses new Q differences (either gains or penalties) defined as

Figure 4. Point-to-point system for 4, 8 or 16 OTDM channels per WDM channel with optimized Pin, tFWHM and OBW: Q differences (refer eqs. (13.12)-(13.14)) versus spectral density, SD (RZ-OOK and RZ-DPSK modulation) (Abbou, Chuah, Hiew, & Abid, 2008)

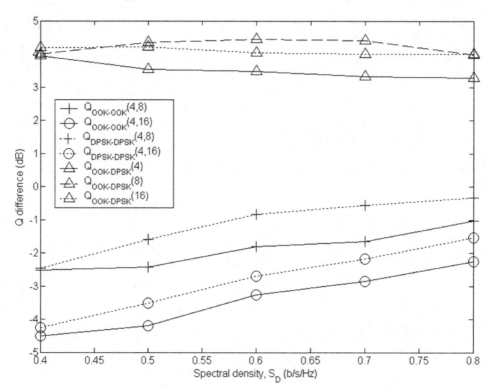

$$Q_{OOK-OOK}\left(x,y\right) = Q_{OOK}^{dB}\left(M=y\right) - Q_{OOK}^{dB}\left(M=x\right) \tag{13.12}$$

$$Q_{DPSK-DPSK}\left(x,y\right) = Q_{DPSK}^{dB}\left(M=y\right) - Q_{DPSK}^{dB}\left(M=x\right) \tag{13.13}$$

$$Q_{OOK-DPSK}\left(x\right) = Q_{DPSK}^{dB}\left(M=x\right) - Q_{OOK}^{dB}\left(M=x\right) \tag{13.14}$$

From Figure 4, we observe that performance for both RZ-OOK and RZ-DPSK deteriorates with increased B_R indicating clearly that nonlinear effects (caused by the nonlinear fiber refractive index) are the cause of the performance penalty since the performance was independent of B_R in the back-to-back case. Since our setup is basically a high bit-rate dispersion managed OTDM-WDM system, we expect the most significant nonlinear distortion to be intrachannel nonlinear effects (Yamamoto & Inoue, 2003; Pachnicke, Man, Spalter, 2005). The Q penalty with increasing B_R was slightly higher for RZ-OOK than for RZ-DPSK as expected, since RZ-OOK is more susceptible to intrachannel nonlinear effects (Yamamoto & Inoue, 2003). From the $Q_{DPSK\text{-}DPSK}$ curves, it can be seen that the Q gain obtained from using RZ-DPSK is approximately 3.5 dB across all S_D for 4 OTDM channels. The Q gain increases for higher B_R to approximately 4 to 4.5 dB. Considering our use of NZ-DSF fibers, this is consistent with the results reported in (Gnauck, 2003).

SUMMARY

Using the DP-Q for DPSK systems and the traditional Q factor for OOK systems, performance comparison of RZ-OOK and RZ-DPSK in dense OTDM-WDM systems is obtained. When signal pulse widths and optical filter bandwidths are optimized, there is no upper limit to WDM channel bit rate in the purely linear back-to-back configuration with dispersion fully compensated for. RZ-DPSK was found to possess higher optimum pulse widths since it is more tolerant to ISI. Thus, RZ-DPSK performed increasingly better than RZ-OOK in higher spectral density using narrower optical filter bandwidths with Q gain increasing from 3 dB to 5 dB. In the nonlinear point-to-point configuration, higher WDM channel bit rates led to increased performance penalties for both RZ-DPSK and RZ-OOK, due to the growing significance of intrachannel nonlinear effects. Here, RZ-DPSK outperformed RZ-OOK by up to 4 dB for all bit rates, demonstrating its robustness in the nonlinear environment. All the results obtained correlate with known conventional results, indicating the reliability of the DP-Q for estimating the performance of DPSK systems and its potential as a performance evaluation tool in numerical simulations.

REFERENCES

Abbou, F. M., Chuah, H. T., Hiew, C. C., & Abid, A. (2008). Comparisons of RZ-OOK and RZ-DPSK in Dense OTDM-WDM Systems Using Q-Factor Models. *J. R. Laser Research. Springer New York, 29*(2), 133–141.

Anderson, C. J., & Lyle, J. A. (1994). Technique for Evaluating System Performance Using q in Numerical Simulations Exhibiting Intersymbol Interference. *Electronics Letters, 30*(1), 71–72. doi:10.1049/el:19940045

Bergano, N. S., Kerfoot, F. W., & Davidson, C. R. (1993). Margin Measurements in Optical Amplifier Systems. *IEEE Photonics Technology Letters, 5*(3), 304–306. doi:10.1109/68.205619

Bosco, G., Carena, A., Curri, V., Gaudino, R., & Poggiolini, P. (2002). On the Use of nrz, rz and csrz Modulation at 40 gb/s with Narrow dwdm Channel Spacing. *Journal of Lightwave Technology, 20*(9), 1694–1704. doi:10.1109/JLT.2002.806309

Cai, J. X. (2002). Long-haul 40 gb/s dwdm Transmission with Aggregate Capacities Exceeding 1 tb/s. *Journal of Lightwave Technology, 20*(12), 2247–2257. doi:10.1109/JLT.2002.806770

Gnauck, A. H., Raybon, G., Bernasconi, P. G., Leuthold, J., Doerr, C. R., & Stulz, L. W. (2003). 1-tb/s (6 x 170.6 gb/s) Transmission over 2000-km nzdf Using otdm and rz-dpsk Format. *IEEE Photonics Technology, 15*(11), 1618–1620. doi:10.1109/LPT.2003.818634

Gnauck, A. H., & Winzer, P. J. (2005). Optical Phase-shift Keyed Transmission. *Journal of Lightwave Technology, 23*(1), 115–130. doi:10.1109/JLT.2004.840357

Hiew, C. C., Abbou, F. M., Chuah, H. T., Majumder, S. P., & Hairul, A. A. R. (2004). Ber Estimation of Optical WDM RZ-DPSK Systems through the Differential Phase Q. *IEEE Photonics Technology Letters, 16*(12), 2619–2621. doi:10.1109/LPT.2004.836759

Hiew, C. C., Abbou, F. M., Chuah, H. T., Majumder, S. P., & Hairul, A. A. R. (2005). Impact of a Post-OTDM-Demultiplexing Optical Filter on Dense OOK OTDM-WDM Transmission. *Fiber and Integrated Optics, 24*(5), 457–470. doi:10.1080/01468030590966562

Humblet Azizoglu, P. A., & Azizoglu, M. (1991). On the Bit Error Rate of Lightwave Systems with Optical Amplifiers. *Journal of Lightwave Technology, 9*(11), 1576–1582. doi:10.1109/50.97649

Norimatsu, S., & Maruoka, M. (2002). Accurate q-Factor Estimation of Optically Amplified Systems in the Presence of Waveform Distortions. *Journal of Lightwave Technology, 20*(1), 19–27. doi:10.1109/50.974814

Wei, X., Liu, X., & Xu, C. (2003). Numerical Simulation of the spm Penalty in a 10-gb/s rz-dpsk System. *IEEE Photonics Technology Letters, 15*(11), 1636–1638. doi:10.1109/LPT.2003.818664

Weiner, C. M. (1999). 40 gb/s and 4 x 40 gb/s tdm/wdm Standard Fiber Transmission. *Journal of Lightwave Technology, 17*(11), 2276–2284. doi:10.1109/50.803020

Xu, C., Liu, X., & Wei, X. (2004). Differential Phase-shift Keying for High Spectral Efficiency Optical Transmissions. *IEEE Photonics Technology Letters, 10*, 281–293.

Yamamoto, Y., & Inoue, K. (2003). Noise in Amplifiers. *Journal of Lightwave Technology, 21*(11), 2895–2915. doi:10.1109/JLT.2003.816887

Yu, T., Reimer, W. M., Grigoryan, V. S., & Menyuk, C. R. (2000). *A mean field approach for simulating wavelength-division multiplexed systems*. Academic Press.

KEY TERMS AND DEFINITIONS

Crosstalk: Refers to an undesired coupling of other optical signals/channels on the desired optical signal/channel. It includes both intrachannel crosstalk and interchannel crosstalk.

Optimization: A process of making a system fully functional and effective as possible ujsing mathematical methods.

Q-Factor: The performance of an optical communication system is often characterized using the Q-factor, which adopts the concept of the signal to noise ratio and assumes in general Gaussian noise distribution.

RZ-DPSK: Refers to a modulation technique based on differential phase shift keying using return-to-zero (RZ) as a line coding technique.

RZ-OOK: Refers to a modulation technique based on On-Off keying using return-to-zero (RZ) as a line coding technique.

Chapter 14
Impact of a Post–OTDM–Demux Optical Filter

ABSTRACT

The impact of a post-OTDM-demultiplexing optical filter on the performance of dense On-Off Keying (OOK) Optical Time Division Multiplexing (OTDM)-Wavelength Division Multiplexing (WDM) systems is studied in this chapter. For Return-to-Zero (RZ) modulation, it was found that the additional filter working in a double-tier filter configuration did not offer any significant improvements to performance when the signal pulse width is optimized. Improvements generally increase only when the signal pulse width deviates from its optimal value and only for low spectral densities. For ideal Non-Return-to-Zero (NRZ) modulation, however, significant improvements of around 1 dB are obtained using the double-tier configuration over a large range of spectral densities.

INTRODUCTION

Quite often in practice, an optical filter is placed after OTDM demultiplexing (Gnauck, 2003; Diez & Ludwig, 1998). This post-OTDM-demultiplexing filter is generally used to filter out high frequency noise induced by the OTDM demultiplexing process. However, for an OTDM-WDM system, this would become an additional optical filter as another optical filter is used as the WDM demultiplexer (Gnauck, 2003). The two filters combined can act as a double-tier filter configuration that may have different optimal bandwidths as compared to a regular single-tier filter

DOI: 10.4018/978-1-4666-6575-0.ch014

configuration and thus, may have an impact on the system performance (Diez & Ludwig, 1998). In this chapter (Hiew, Abbou, Chuah, Majumder, & Hairul, 2005), rigorous simulation is used to optimize the double-tier filter configuration and find out the conditions in which it provides performance improvement over the single-tier filter configuration.

SYSTEM MODEL

The system block diagram for both back-to-back and point-to-point configuration is shown in Figure 1. Each OTDM channel consists of a 9.953 Gb/s OOK signal, with assumed forward error coding (FEC) overhead of 7%, yielding a total bit rate of 10.664 Gb/s and is given by

$$U(t) = \sum_{n=0}^{N} a_n p(t - nT) \qquad (14.1)$$

where a_n is the pseudorandom bit sequence (PRBS) of length $N = (2^{15})/M$ bits and M is the number of OTDM channels, T is the 10.664 Gb/s signal bit period and $p(t)$ is the pulse shape. The total time multiplexed signal bit rate $B_R = M$ x 10.664 Gb/s $= M/T$. For RZ modulation, the pulse shape is chirp-free Gaussian ($m=1$)

$$p(t) = \exp[-0.5(t/T_0)^{2m}] \qquad (14.2)$$

where $T_0 = t_{FWHM}/k$, t_{FWHM} is the full wave half maximum (FWHM) pulse width and $k = 2(\exp[-0.3665/(2m)])$. For NRZ modulation, the pulse shape is ideally square

Figure 1. System block diagram for studying post-OTDM-demultiplexing filter (Hiew, Abbou, Chuah, Majumder, & Hairul, 2005)

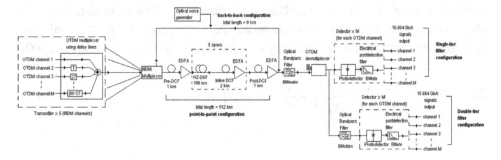

$$p(t) = \text{rect}[t(M/T)] \tag{14.3}$$

where rect[] is the rectangular function. Five time-multiplexed (M x 10.664 Gb/s) signals are WDM multiplexed with frequency spacing Δf and centered at 1549 nm. Results are obtained from the centre channel where WDM crosstalk is balanced (Yu, Reimer, Grigoryan, & Menyuk, 2000).

For back-to-back configuration, the transmitted WDM signal is added with optical noise and fed straight into the receiver. The received optical signal to noise ratio (OSNR) is defined as

$$OSNR = E_b/N_0 = (P_{rec}T)/(MN_0) \tag{14.4}$$

where N_0 is the optical noise power spectral density (psd) and P_{rec} is the received signal power per WDM channel. Shot and electrical thermal noises are neglected since optical noise is dominant. The WDM demultiplexer filter has a bandwidth of BW_{WDM} while the post-OTDM-demultiplexing filter has a bandwidth of BW_{OTDM}. Both optical filters have a second-order Gaussian shape. The electrical filter bandwidth $BW_{ele} = 2$ x min[BW_{WDM}, BW_{OTDM}] where min[] is the minimum function and its shape is fifth-order Bessel. The electrical filter bandwidth is purposely set high so that it does not become a contributing factor to system performance and it has been shown before that a high BW_{ele} is optimal when shot and thermal noises are neglected (Bosco, Carena, Curri, Gaudino, & Poggiolini, 2002). The OTDM demultiplexing window used is almost ideal (square): fifth-order Gaussian with a width of 0.6(T/M). For point-to-point configuration, the WDM signal is transmitted across the link shown in Figure 1. The nonzero dispersion shifted fiber (NZ-DSF) has dispersion $D = 2.16$ ps/nm/km, dispersion slope $Sl = 0.06$ ps/nm²/km, effective area $A_{eff} = 55$ μm² and attenuation $\alpha = 0.2$ dB/km. The dispersion compensating fiber (DCF) has $D = -90$ ps/nm/km, $Sl = -2.5$ ps/nm²/km, $A_{eff} = 30$ μm² and $\alpha = 0.55$ dB/km. Dispersion management (DM) is ideal in such a way that all dispersion is fully compensated for at the receiver. Each erbium doped fiber amplifier (EDFA) compensates for all attenuation suffered in its preceding span but generates ASE, which is added onto the signal after each amplifier. ASE and optical noise are modeled as circular complex additive white Gaussian noise (AWGN) with uniform random phase distribution. Signal and noise are propagated together by solving the nonlinear Schrödinger equation (NLSE) given by (Yu, Reimer, Grigoryan, & Menyuk, 2000)

$$\frac{\partial A}{\partial z} + \frac{i}{2}\beta_2 \frac{\partial^2 A}{\partial T_R^2} - \frac{1}{6}\beta_3 \frac{\partial^3 A}{\partial T_R^3} + \frac{\alpha}{2}A = i\gamma|A|^2 A \tag{14.5}$$

where A is the signal and noise combination, T_R is the retarded time frame, β_2 is the second-order dispersion parameter, β_3 is the third order dispersion parameter, α is the attenuation coefficient and γ is the nonlinear coefficient. The NLSE is solved using the split-step Fourier method (SSFM) with single polarization assumed.

The received OSNR for point-to-point transmission distorted by accumulated ASE can be approximated by

$$OSNR = E_b / N_0 = \left(P_{in} T \right) \Big/ \left(M \sum_{a=1}^{7} N_a \right) \qquad (14.6)$$

where N_a is the noise psd of amplifier a and P_{in} is the input transmission power per WDM channel into the link. To more accurately compare system capacity across varying bit rates, we use spectral density as the quantifier defined as $S_D = B_R / \Delta f$.

PERFORMANCE ESTIMATION MODEL

For OOK systems, the Gaussian approximated Q is commonly used to estimate the Bit Error Rate (BER) even though the exact distribution is not exactly Gaussian (Humblet, Azizoglu, & Azizoglu, 1991). Various methods can be used to obtain this Q (Bergano, Kerfoot, & Davidson, 1993; Anderson & Lyle, 1994). Here, we use

$$BER_{k,j}\left(D_{opt} \right) = \left(p_{k,j} / 4 \right) erfc \left(\left| D_{opt} - \mu_{k,j} \right| \Big/ \sqrt{2} \sigma_{k,j} \right) \qquad (14.7)$$

for bit k, rail j where $\mu_{k,j}$ and $\sigma_{k,j}$ are the mean and standard deviation of the particular rail and D_{opt} is the optimized receiver threshold (Norimatsu & Maruoka, 2002). The values of $\mu_{k,j}$ and $\sigma_{k,j}$ are easily obtained in our case since the initial PRBS is known and can be used, following the technique in (Anderson & Lyle, 1994), to classify each possible received pattern of 3 bits where each pattern is assumed to possess a separate rail. This technique is more accurate in the presence of waveform distortions (Norimatsu & Maruoka, 2002; Anderson & Lyle, 1994) compared to the conventional method in (Bergano, Kerfoot, & Davidson, 1993). The *BER* is related to the Q through (Norimatsu & Maruoka, 2002)

$$BER = (1/2)erfc[Q / sqrt(2)] \qquad (14.8)$$

To obtain the average performance over all OTDM channels, we define the average *BER* as

$$BER_{av} = \sum_{p=1}^{M} BER_p \bigg/ M \qquad (14.9)$$

where BER_p is the BER of OTDM channel p. Optimal parameters and performance are extracted from BER_{av} contour plots where the parameters to be optimized are placed on the X and Y axes while the Z-axis gives the BER_{av}. Consequently, we can then obtain the average Q, Q_{av} through equation (14.8). In this chapter, we often compare between the performance of a system using either a double-tier or a single-tier filter configuration. To better facilitate this comparison, we define a parameter referred to as the Q gain defined by

$$Q_{gain} \text{ (dB)} = 20 \log_{10}[Q_{av}'] - 20 \log_{10}[Q_{av}] \qquad (14.10)$$

where Q_{gain} is in units of decibels, Q_{av}' refers to the average Q using the double-tier filter configuration and Q_{av} refers to the average Q using a single-tier configuration. Thus, Q_{gain} is positive when the double-tier filter configuration improves the system performance.

Return-to-Zero (RZ) Results

First, we verified that the BER of a directly detected, (M x 10.664) Gb/s OTDM signal is the same as the BER_{av} obtained from its 10.664 Gb/s OTDM demultiplexed constituents. This is to make sure that the OTDM demultiplexer is ideal and does not induce any additional performance penalties. Next, we run tests on the back-to-back system using either 4 or 8 OTDM channels per WDM channel where the optimal signal pulse width, $t_{FWHM,opt}$ for each corresponding spectral density, S_D was found in and is reproduced in Table 1 (a) and (b) for convenience. Using these optimal parameters, the bandwidths of the optical filters for both the single-tier and double-tier filter configurations are optimized and shown in Table 1 (a) and (b).

For the double-tier configuration, the optimal bandwidths generally fall into one of two categories

$$BW_{WDM,opt} \approx BW_{WDM,opt}', BW_{OTDM,opt} > 40 \text{ GHz} \qquad (14.11)$$

$$BW_{WDM,opt} \approx 1.4 \ BW_{WDM,opt}', BW_{OTDM,opt} \approx 20 \text{ GHz} \qquad (14.12)$$

where $BW_{WDM,opt}'$ here indicates the optimal WDM demultiplexer bandwidth obtained from the single-tier configuration. A comparison of the performance (Q_{gain}) between the single and double tier configurations from $S_D = 0.3 - 0.8$ and for $OSNR = 17$ or

Table 1. RZ modulation optimal filter and pulse width parameters for single or double tier filter configuration over a range of spectral densities, SD using (a) 4 OTDM channels or (b) 8 OTDM channels per WDM channel

Spectral Density, S_D (b/s/Hz)	Optimal Signal Pulse Width, $t_{FWHM,opt}$ (ps)	Optimal Single-Tier Filter Configuration, $BW_{WDM,opt}$ (GHz)	Optimal Double-Tier Filter Configuration ($BW_{WDM,opt}$ I $BW_{OTDM,opt}$) (GHz)
(a)			
0.3	8.0	85	(120 I 20)
0.4	11.0	50	(70 I 20)
0.5	11.0	50	(55 I 40)
0.6	14.0	50	(55 I 40)
0.7	15.0	50	(55 I 40)
0.8	15.0	50	(50 I 40)
(b)			
0.3	4.0	170	(240 I 20)
0.4	5.5	95	(140 I 20)
0.5	6.0	95	(105 I 40)
0.6	7.0	95	(105 I 40)
0.7	7.5	95	(100 I 40)
0.8	7.5	95	(100 I 40)

20 dB with either 4 or 8 OTDM channels is shown in Figure 2. First, we note that the results are similar for the cases of both 4 and 8 OTDM channels indicating that any performance gain or loss due to the double-tier configuration works equally for both cases. This was found to be true throughout the tests run in this chapter.

In Figure 2, the shaded area represents the portion where the optimal double-tier filter configuration is given by equation (14.12) while the clear area is given by equation (14.11). It can be seen that for the case of the optimal filter bandwidths given as in equation (14.11), the double-tier configuration does not provide any significant benefits over the single-tier configuration. In fact, for this case, the double-tier configuration results in a performance penalty even though its $BW_{WDM,opt}$ is the same as that for the single-tier configuration. This occurs because we limited the optimization range of BW_{OTDM} in our tests to 40 GHz. Thus, the additional filter only serves to chop off the high frequency portions of the OTDM demultiplexed signal resulting in a loss of signal quality. To confirm this, we tested the system with $BW_{OTDM} \to \infty$ (similar to the single-tier configuration) and found that the $Q_{gain} \to 0$.

Figure 2. RZ modulation, back-to-back system: Performance improvement in terms of Qgain versus the spectral density SD for 4 or 8 OTDM channels per WDM channel and OSNR = 17 dB or 20 dB (Hiew, Abbou, Chuah, Majumder, & Hairul, 2005)

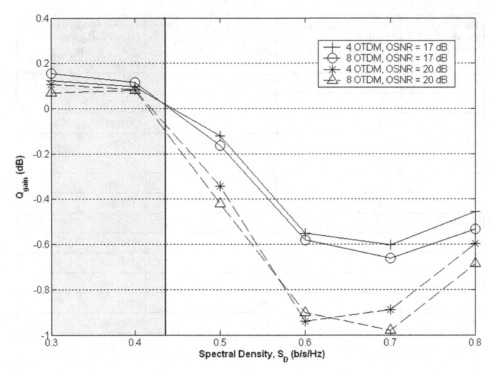

However, in the shaded region where the optimal double-tier filter bandwidths are given by equation (14.12), there is a performance improvement over the single-tier configuration. This is because there is a new optimal region here provided by the double-tier configuration where $BW_{WDM,opt}$ is significantly larger while $BW_{OTDM,opt}$ is about 20 GHz, which is approximately twice the OTDM demultiplexed signal bit rate. This new optimal region is made possible through the use of the double filters. The performance improves because a wider $BW_{WDM,opt}$ allows for larger spectral portions of the initial pre-OTDM-demultiplexing signal or WDM channel to pass through while the additional noise that is also allowed through at the same time can be filtered out by the narrow $BW_{OTDM,opt}$ after OTDM demultiplexing.

However, there are two important things to note. First of all, the improvement only occurs when S_D is low. The cutoff here is at $S_D \approx 0.4$. This is because at high S_D, the WDM channels are packed tightly together and increasing $BW_{WDM,opt}$ significantly would only lead to significant increases of WDM crosstalk. This sets a restriction to $BW_{WDM,opt}$ and hampers the potential of the double filter configuration. This restriction is less significant at low S_D. Secondly, even at low S_D, the performance improvements are very small. A Q_{gain} of around 0.2 dB seen here is in practice negligible. For both higher and lower *OSNR* (17 or 20 dB), the same conclusions apply with the only difference being that the penalties are even larger with higher OSNR for the regions that operate under equation (14.11), as the low noise discourages the use of the narrow BW_{OTDM}. This is true for all subsequent tests in this chapter as well.

For the point-to-point system, the same tests were run but with the *OSNR* set to the optimum values obtained in (Hiew, Abbou, Chuah, Majumder, & Hairul, 2004) and the results are shown in Figure 3. The point-to-point system here is affected by nonlinear effects, which causes performance penalties (Hiew, Abbou, Chuah, Majumder, & Hairul, 2004). However, the goal here is not to observe those penalties but to see if the double-tier configuration reacts any differently to the nonlinear effects compared to the single-tier configuration. The graph in Figure 4 is almost similar to that in Figure 3 indicating that the results conclusions obtained from the back-to-back system can be extended to the point-to-point system as well. This is true throughout this chapter as well.

Figure 3. RZ modulation, point-to-point system: Performance improvement in terms of Qgain versus the spectral density SD for 4 or 8 OTDM channels per WDM channel and optimized OSNR (Hiew, Abbou, Chuah, Majumder, & Hairul, 2005)

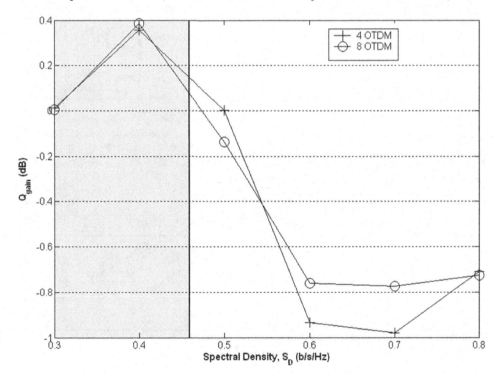

So far, we have seen that the double-tier configuration does not bring significant benefit to RZ system performance. To explore this further, we varied the signal pulse width around its optimum value with the varied $t_{FWHM} = t_{FWHM,opt} + t_{FWHM,shift}$ and compared the two different filter configurations and the results are shown in Figure 4. The results here are interesting as it indicates significant performance improvements (Q_{gain} up to 1 dB) of the double-tier configuration over the single-tier configuration when the signal pulse width deviates further from its optimum point. Once again, this only applies for $S_D = 0.4$ and below. For $S_D = 0.4$, there are performance improvements for $t_{FWHM} < t_{FWHM,opt}$ and performance penalties for $t_{FWHM} > t_{FWHM,opt}$. This is logical since a low signal pulse width increases the signal spectral width, thus making it more suitable for a wide BW_{WDM}, which can be provided by the double-tier configuration. For $S_D = 0.3$ though, the performance also improves for $t_{FWHM} > t_{FWHM,opt}$. This occurs because there are actually two optimal regions for

Figure 4. RZ modulation: Performance improvement in terms of Qgain versus the ratio of the signal pulse width variation from optimal point (t_{FWHM}, shift / t_{FWHM}, opt) for spectral densities of SD = 0.3 – 0.5 and for 4 or 8 OTDM channels per WDM channel (OSNR = 17 dB) (Hiew, Abbou, Chuah, Majumder, & Hairul, 2005)

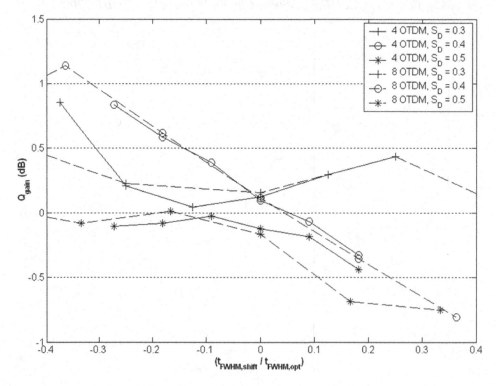

t_{FWHM} at $S_D = 0.3$ even for the single-tier configuration. The lower t_{FWHM} provides slightly better performance and thus the $t_{FWHM,opt}$ for $S_D = 0.3$ is lower than that for other S_D (refer to Table 1). When t_{FWHM} increases past $t_{FWHM,opt}$ in this case, it merely approaches the next optimal region from the *negative* direction. Thus, it also provides a performance improvement. The results in Figure 4 clearly indicate that significant performance improvement for the RZ modulated signal occurs when t_{FWHM} is below an optimal region and S_D is low.

Consequently, $t_{FWHM,opt}$ for the double-tier configuration could be different from that in Table 1, which is basically obtained using a single-tier configuration in (Hiew, Abbou, Chuah, Majumder, & Hairul, 2004). Our tests show that there are small shifts towards lower t_{FWHM} but they are not really significant. More importantly, the performance comparison between the two filter configurations using re-optimized t_{FWHM} shown in Figure 5 is similar to that in Figure 4. Therefore, we can conclude that when the RZ modulated signal pulse width is optimized; the double-tier filter configuration does not offer any significant performance improvements over the

Figure 5. RZ modulation: Performance improvement in terms of Qgain versus the spectral density SD for 4 or 8 OTDM channels per WDM channel with the signal pulse width, t_{FWHM} re-optimized for double-tier configuration (OSNR = 17 dB) (Hiew, Abbou, Chuah, Majumder, & Hairul, 2005)

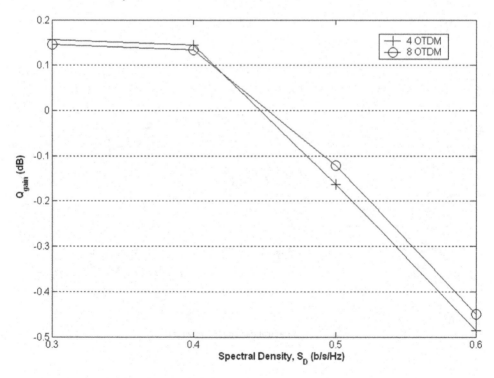

single-tier configuration. Thus, the post-OTDM-demultiplexing filter in this case is quite unnecessary unless it is required to filter out excessive noise induced by demultiplexing devices.

Non-Return-to-Zero (NRZ) Results

Next, the same tests are performed using ideal NRZ modulated signals. Note that there is no optimization of the NRZ signal pulse width as it is set by definition. The results for the back-to-back system are shown in Figure 6 while the results for the point-to-point system are in Figure 7. The corresponding filter bandwidths are shown in Table 2. Interestingly, for NRZ modulation, the double-tier configuration shows much larger performance improvements (Q_{gain} up to 1.7 dB) over the single tier configuration, in stark contrast to the RZ case. The improvements here are much larger and increases for increasing OSNR, and approaches levels that make it

Figure 6. NRZ modulation, back-to-back system: Performance improvement in terms of Qgain versus the spectral density SD for 4 or 8 OTDM channels per WDM channel and OSNR = 17 dB or 20 dB (Hiew, Abbou, Chuah, Majumder, & Hairul, 2005)

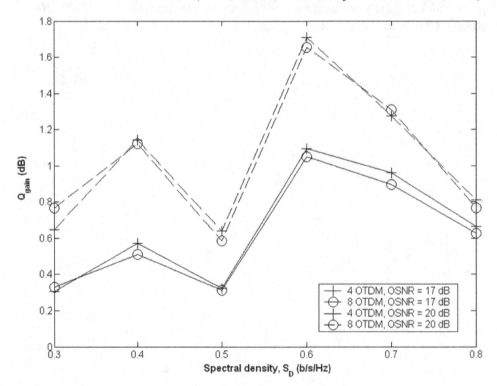

Figure 7. NRZ modulation, point-to-point system: Performance improvement in terms of Qgain versus the spectral density S_D for 4 or 8 OTDM channels per WDM channel and optimized OSNR (Hiew, Abbou, Chuah, Majumder, & Hairul, 2005)

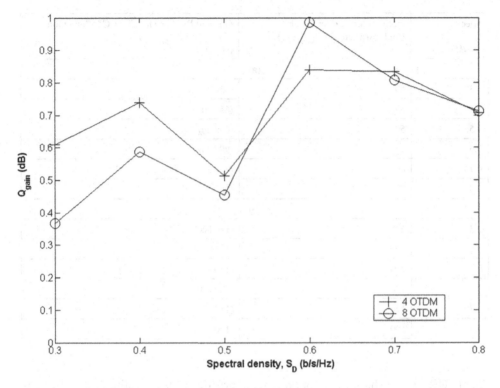

significant in practice. In addition, it can also be seen that significant performance improvements are obtained over the entire range of S_D from 0.3 to 0.8, unlike the RZ case. As such, the optimized double-tier filter configuration bandwidths for NRZ modulation falls under the category in (Eq. 14.12) over the entire range of S_D as seen in Table 2. For the point-to-point system with optimized *OSNR*, the double-tier configuration continues to show significant improvement with Q_{gain} up to 1 dB.

The difference compared to RZ is caused by our choice of the pulse shape modulation. Specifically, it is the ideal square NRZ pulse shape. The improved performance across a wide range of S_D suggests that the NRZ signal spectrum after OTDM demultiplexing becomes better matched to the Gaussian optical filter and thus, narrow filtering is better performed post-OTDM-demultiplexing. The results indicate that an optimized double-tier filter configuration can provide significant improvements for the NRZ signal. However, it is important to note that the ideal

Table 2. NRZ modulation optimal filter parameters for single or double tier filter configuration over a range of spectral densities, S_D using (a) 4 OTDM channels or (b) 8 OTDM channels per WDM channel

Spectral Density, S_D (b/s/Hz)	Optimal Single-Tier Filter Configuration, $BW_{WDM,opt}$ (GHz)	Optimal Double-Tier Filter Configuration $(BW_{WDM,opt} \mid BW_{OTDM,opt})$ (GHz)
(a)		
0.3	50	(65 | 20)
0.4	50	(65 | 20)
0.5	50	(65 | 20)
0.6	65	(90 | 20)
0.7	60	(75 | 20)
0.8	50	(60 | 20)
(b)		
0.3	100	(130 | 20)
0.4	100	(130 | 20)
0.5	100	(130 | 20)
0.6	130	(180 | 20)
0.7	120	(150 | 20)
0.8	100	(120 | 20)

square NRZ pulse shape is not obtainable in practice as the infinite drop-off rate is impossible to achieve. A practical NRZ pulse would have a finite drop-off rate and thus, would look more like a higher order super-Gaussian pulse. As such, its performance improvements would also be smaller. Still, the results here indicate that the double-tier configuration is useful when used in tandem with NRZ signals.

SUMMARY

The use of a post-OTDM-demultiplexing filter leads to the possibility of using a double-tier filter configuration in the optical domain. Successfully, the optimization of the double-tier filter configuration for dense OOK OTDM-WDM systems operating with either 4 or 8 OTDM channels per WDM channel over a wide range of spectral densities is achieved. Further, it is found that the optimal double-tier filter configuration for both back-to-back and point-to-point systems fall within one of two cases; where performance improvement over the optimized single-tier configuration are obtained for only one of these cases. For RZ modulation, the improvement in performance is small and only occurs at low spectral densities, but it increases when the signal pulse width deviates from its optimal value. With optimized signal pulse width, the performance improvements are insignificant indicating that the double-tier configuration does not help improve optimized RZ modulated systems. However, for ideal NRZ modulation, the double-tier configuration provides a substantial performance boost over the single-tier configuration over a large range of spectral densities.

REFERENCES

Abbou, F. M., Chuah, H. T., Hiew, C. C., & Abid, A. (2008). Comparisons of RZ-OOK and RZ-DPSK in Dense OTDM-WDM Systems Using Q-Factor Models. *J. R. Laser Research. Springer New York*, *29*(2), 133–141.

Anderson, C. J., & Lyle, J. A. (1994). Technique for Evaluating System Performance Using q in Numerical Simulations Exhibiting Intersymbol Interference. *Electronics Letters*, *30*(1), 71–72. doi:10.1049/el:19940045

Bergano, N. S., Kerfoot, F. W., & Davidson, C. R. (1993). Margin Measurements in Optical Amplifier Systems. *IEEE Photonics Technology Letters*, *5*(3), 304–306. doi:10.1109/68.205619

Bosco, G., Carena, A., Curri, V., Gaudino, R., & Poggiolini, P. (2002). On the Use of nrz, rz and csrz Modulation at 40 gb/s with Narrow dwdm Channel Spacing. *Journal of Lightwave Technology*, *20*(9), 1694–1704. doi:10.1109/JLT.2002.806309

Cai, J. X. (2002). Long-haul 40 gb/s dwdm Transmission with Aggregate Capacities Exceeding 1 tb/s. *Journal of Lightwave Technology*, *20*(12), 2247–2257. doi:10.1109/JLT.2002.806770

Gnauck, A. H., Raybon, G., Bernasconi, P. G., Leuthold, J., Doerr, C. R., & Stulz, L. W. (2003). 1-tb/s (6 x 170.6 gb/s) Transmission over 2000-km nzdf Using otdm and rz-dpsk Format. *IEEE Photonics Technology*, *15*(11), 1618–1620. doi:10.1109/LPT.2003.818634

Gnauck, A. H., & Winzer, P. J. (2005). Optical Phase-shift Keyed Transmission. *Journal of Lightwave Technology*, *23*(1), 115–130. doi:10.1109/JLT.2004.840357

Hiew, C. C., Abbou, F. M., & Chuah, H. T. (2006). *Performance Analysis and Design of an Optical TDM-WDM Transmission System and Network* (Tech. Rep. No. 1). Malaysia: Multimedia University and Alcatel Network Systems.

Hiew, C. C., Abbou, F. M., Chuah, H. T., Majumder, S. P., & Hairul, A. A. R. (2004). Ber Estimation of Optical WDM RZ-DPSK Systems Through the Differential Phase Q. *IEEE Photonics Technology Letters, 16*(12), 2619–2621. doi:10.1109/LPT.2004.836759

Hiew, C. C., Abbou, F. M., Chuah, H. T., Majumder, S. P., & Hairul, A. A. R. (2005). Impact of a Post-OTDM-Demultiplexing Optical Filter on Dense OOK OTDM-WDM Transmission. *IEEE Photon. Fiber and Integrated Optics, 24*(5), 457–470. doi:10.1080/01468030590966562

Humblet Azizoglu, P. A., & Azizoglu, M. (1991). On the Bit Error Rate of Light-wave Systems with Optical Amplifiers. *Journal of Lightwave Technology, 9*(11), 1576–1582. doi:10.1109/50.97649

Norimatsu, S., & Maruoka, M. (2002). Accurate q-Factor Estimation of Optically Amplified Systems in the Presence of Waveform Distortions. *Journal of Lightwave Technology, 20*(1), 19–27. doi:10.1109/50.974814

Wei, X., Liu, X., & Xu, C. (2003). Numerical Simulation of the spm Penalty in a 10-gb/s rz-dpsk System. *IEEE Photonics Technology Letters, 15*(11), 1636–1638. doi:10.1109/LPT.2003.818664

Weiner, C. M. (1999). 40 gb/s and 4 x 40 gb/s tdm/wdm Standard Fiber Transmission. *Journal of Lightwave Technology, 17*(11), 2276–2284. doi:10.1109/50.803020

Xu, C., Liu, X., & Wei, X. (2004). Differential Phase-shift Keying for High Spectral Efficiency Optical Transmissions. *IEEE Journal of Selected Topics in Quantum Electronics, 10*(2), 281–293. doi:10.1109/JSTQE.2004.827835

Yamamoto, Y., & Inoue, K. (2003). Noise in Amplifiers. *Journal of Lightwave Technology, 21*(11), 2895–2915. doi:10.1109/JLT.2003.816887

Yu, T., Reimer, W. M., Grigoryan, V. S., & Menyuk, C. R. (2000). *A mean field approach for simulating wavelength-division multiplexed systems*. Academic Press.

KEY TERMS AND DEFINITIONS

On-Off Keying (OOK): OOK denotes the simplest form of amplitude modulation that represents digital data as the presence or absence of a carrier wave.

Optical Filter: An optical device that selectively reflects some wavelengths of light but pass other wavelengths transparently.

Pulse Width: The elapsed time between the leading edge and trailing edge of a single pulse at a point where the amplitude is 50% of the peak value.

Super-Gaussian Pulse: A pulse whose frequency components, spectral width, and edges can be can be controlled.

Chapter 15
Network Performance Analysis with Nonlinear Effects

ABSTRACT

The nonlinear Bit Error Rate (BER) performance of dense Wavelength Division Multiplexed (WDM) Manhattan Street Networks with deflection routing was obtained using a semi-analytical model. The chapter's results show that nonlinear effects impose significant performance penalties on dense WDM networks, both in terms of maximum hops attainable and average BER, and should be taken into account when modeling such networks. Simple techniques such as optimal amplifier positioning can mitigate some of the nonlinear penalties.

INTRODUCTION

Transparent all-optical cross-connected networks work entirely within the optical domain, by employing optical cross-connects (Castanon, Tonguz, & Bononi, 1997). A common network topology for multihop, wavelength division multiplexed (WDM), packet switched networks is the Manhattan Street (MS) Network (Maxemchuk, 1987; Forghieri, Bononi, & Prucnal, 1995). A model of the MS Network without optical buffers and wavelength conversion (also called Hot-Potato), employing deflection routing was presented in (Forghieri, Bononi, & Prucnal, 1995). This model was

DOI: 10.4018/978-1-4666-6575-0.ch015

used to estimate the average network bit error rate (BER) performance in the presence of linear noises (Castanon, Tonguz, & Bononi, 1997). However, the impact of nonlinear effects within the fiber interconnection links is often neglected because the WDM signal spectral density is normally low for networks (Castanon, Tonguz, & Bononi, 1997) unlike for point-to-point links (Kahn & Ho, 2004). Nowadays, as network capacity increases through the use of dense WDM, nonlinear effects will become important.

In this chapter, the impact of nonlinear effects on the BER performance of dense WDM, cross-connected networks using the Hot-Potato MS Network with deflection routing as the case study is investigated. A semi-analytical model, combining the hop distribution and node model with nonlinear Schrodinger equation (NLSE) based simulation of the fiber interconnections is used to evaluate the nonlinear BER performance.

SYSTEM MODEL

The Hot-Potato MS network with deflection routing is described using the deflection probability $p(g)$ given the packet generation probability or network load g (Forghieri, Bononi, & Prucnal, 1995). Using $p(g)$, the hop distribution $P(n)$, which is the probability density function of the number of hops, n required to travel to the destination can be obtained. The process of obtaining $P(n)$ and p for given values of g is elaborated in (Forghieri, Bononi, & Prucnal, 1995), and is not repeated here. In addition, the BER of the packets depends on the node (cross-connect) structure and the fiber link between nodes. The node structure used is shown in Figure 1(a).

All transmitters are assumed to transmit with the same average power, P_{TX}, which is the signal power of a WDM channel. Each signal consists of a pseudorandom bit sequence (PRBS) of 16384 bits where the modulation format is RZ-OOK (return-to-zero-on-off-keying) with 50% pulse duty cycle and a bit rate B_R of 42.656 GHz. We consider a high capacity, dense WDM network where the spectral density (spectral efficiency) is high at 0.4, corresponding to a channel spacing of 107 GHz. The WDM demultiplexers are modeled as second order Gaussian filters centered at the WDM channels' center frequencies. The total node loss is

$$L_{total} = L_{DEMUX} L_{coupler} L_{add/drop} L_{switch} L_{MUX} \qquad (15.1)$$

(Castanon, Tonguz, & Bononi, 1997). The receivers are direct-detection receivers followed by a fifth order Bessel postdetection electrical filter. The main switch introduces crosstalk noise, because a portion of an output link signal leaks onto the

Figure 1. Block diagram of (a) node structure and (b) fiber interconnection link (Hiew, Abbou, Chuah, Majumder, & Hairul 2006)

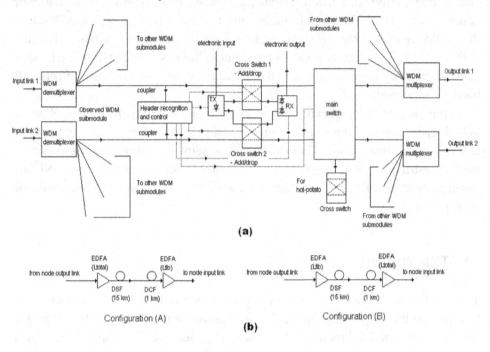

other output link, and is specified by the leakage parameter, ε. This causes in-band crosstalk, which is modeled as additive colored Gaussian noise over an effective noise bandwidth B_N, with noise power given by (Castanon, Tonguz, & Bononi, 1997).

$$P_{leak} = u\left(1 - a\right)P_{in,switch}\varepsilon \text{ if } i = 1$$

$$P_{leak} = u\left(1 - a\right)P_{in,switch}\varepsilon + |\left[uag + \left(1 - u\right)g\right]P_{in,switch}\varepsilon \text{ otherwise} \qquad (15.2)$$

where i is the current node, $P_{in,switch}$ is the power at the switch inputs, u is the link utilization and a is the absorption rate defined in (Forghieri, Bononi, & Prucnal, 1995).

Next, the fiber interconnection link is shown in Figure 1(b). All links are periodically amplified, dispersion managed (DM) links and consists of two fiber spans, one a dispersion shifted fiber (DSF) of length $L = 15$ km with dispersion $D = 4$ ps/nm/km, dispersion slope $Sl = 0.06$ ps/nm²/km, effective area $A_{eff} = 55$ µm² and attenuation $\alpha = 0.2$ dB/km. The other is a dispersion compensating fiber (DCF) of $L = 1$ km with $D = -60$ ps/nm/km, $Sl = -0.9$ ps/nm²/km, $A_{eff} = 30$ µm² and $\alpha = 0.55$ dB/km. Note that DM is ideal, and there is no residual dispersion at the output of any link. Two different amplification configurations, labeled (A) and (B), are tested. Both configurations use two erbium doped fiber amplifiers (EDFA) per link, one to compensate for fiber losses, L_{fib} and the other for node losses, L_{total}. The only difference is that the order of the amplifiers is reversed. Each amplifier adds amplified spontaneous emission (ASE) noise to the signal, which is modeled as circular complex additive white Gaussian noise (AWGN). The WDM multiplexed signal and noise, $A(T,z)$ is propagated through the fiber links using the NLSE (Agrawal, 2001)

$$\frac{\partial A}{\partial z} + \frac{i}{2}\beta_2 \frac{\partial^2 A}{\partial T^2} - \frac{1}{6}\beta_3 \frac{\partial^3 A}{\partial T^3} + \frac{\alpha}{2} A = i\gamma |A|^2 A \qquad (15.3)$$

where α is the attenuation parameter, β_2 and β_3 are the second and third order dispersion parameters, γ is the nonlinearity coefficient, T is the retarded frame time parameter and z is the distance parameter. The NLSE is solved using the split step Fourier method (SSFM) (Agrawal, 2001; Yu, Reimer, Grigoryan, & Menyuk, 2000). Thus, the main sources of signal distortion are linear noises caused by ASE, MUX/DEMUX crosstalk and switch leakage crosstalk, as well as nonlinear distortions caused by the nonlinear coefficient γ.

PERFORMANCE ESTIMATION MODEL

For OOK systems, the Gaussian approximated Q is commonly used to estimate the *BER* (Bergano, Kerfoot, & Davidson, 1993; Norimatsu & Maruoka, 2002). Here, we use

$$BER_{k,j}\left(D_{opt}\right) = \left(p_{k,j}/2\right) erfc\left(\left|D_{opt} - \mu_{k,j}\right|\big/\sqrt{2}\sigma_{k,j}\right) \qquad (15.4)$$

for bit k, rail j where $\mu_{k,j}$ and $\sigma_{k,j}$ are the mean and standard deviation of the particular rail,

$$\sum_k \sum_j p_{k,j} = 1 \qquad (15.5)$$

and D_{opt} is the optimized receiver threshold that minimizes the overall *BER*,

$$BER\left(D\right) = \sum_k \sum_j BER_{k,j}\left(D\right) \qquad (15.6)$$

(Norimatsu & Maruoka, 2002). Knowing the initial PRBS, we can classify the expected received bit sequence according to each possible received pattern of 3 bits where each pattern is assumed to possess a separate rail. This technique is more accurate in the presence of waveform distortions (Norimatsu & Maruoka, 2002) compared to the conventional method (Bergano, Kerfoot, & Davidson, 1993). The *BER* is related to the *Q* through

$$BER = \frac{1}{2} erfc\left(\frac{Q}{\sqrt{2}}\right)$$
(15.7)

(Norimatsu & Maruoka, 2002). Relating to the network, the *BER(n)*, which is the *BER* after hop *n* is obtained by evaluating the *BER* after each hop. Then, the average *BER* of the network is

$$BER_{av} = \sum_{n=1}^{\infty} BER(n) P(n)$$
(15.8)

(Castanon, Tonguz, & Bononi, 1997). In practice, this is evaluated until a suitable *n* limit where *P(n)* becomes very small and the sum terms become negligible.

RESULTS AND DISCUSSION

Results are obtained for demultiplexer optical filter bandwidth $BW_{opt} = 2B_R$, post-detection electrical filter bandwidth $BW_{ele} = 1.65B_R$, $L_{total} = 12.5$ dB and $L_{fib} = 3.55$ dB. Note that filter bandwidths were optimized first. The number of nodes N of the network was kept small with $N = 16$ (MS16 network), to reduce processing time, since our focus is on the impact of nonlinear effects. We simulate at full load with $g = 1$. Due to nonlinear effects, performance should be dependent on the power within the network, which is set by P_{TX}. Thus, the maximum number of hops attainable by the system n_{max} before it passes a performance threshold of $BER(n) = 10^{-9}$ is shown in Figure 2(a) versus P_{TX} for three configurations and $\varepsilon = -25$ dB or -35 dB.

Configurations (A) and (B) correspond to the respective amplifier configurations, while configuration (C) corresponds to the case where nonlinear effects are neglected by setting γ in equation (15.2) to zero. From Figure 2(a), we can see that without nonlinear effects, the maximum hops attainable (reach) increases steadily with transmission power over the range considered while increasing the leakage parameter ε, causes a significant reduction in reach as expected, since the in-band

Figure 2. (a) Maximum number of hops attainable by the system nmax before it passes a performance threshold of BER(n) = 10-9 and (b) the average BER, BERav; versus transmission power PTX for configurations (A), (B) or (C) and for ε = -25 dB or -35 dB (Hiew, Abbou, Chuah, Majumder, & Hairul 2006)

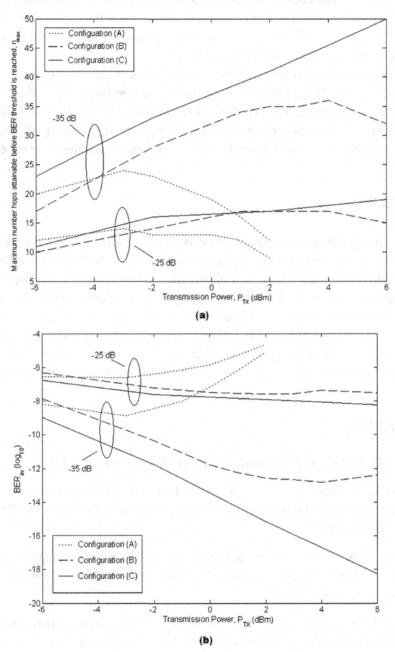

noise builds up quickly. Nonlinear effects impose a limit as the reach dips after a certain threshold power. At the optimum power, the reach of the network is significantly lower compared to the linear case. Furthermore, we can see that (B) far outperforms (A) with higher reach and higher optimum power. Remember that L_{total} > L_{fib}, and thus the amplifier that compensates for L_{total} has the higher gain. Placing it after the fiber as in (B) reduces the launched power into the fiber link, thereby reducing nonlinear effects within the fiber.

Next, we obtain $P(n)$ for our MS16 network. Example of a hop distribution is shown in (Zhu, 2002). Using $P(n)$, $BER(n)$ and a hop limit of $n = 40$, BER_{av} is computed for configurations (A), (B) and (C) and for ε = -25 dB or -35 dB, and shown in Figure 2(b) versus P_{TX}. From Figure 2(b), we confirm the significant BER performance penalties imposed on the network by both ε and nonlinear effects.

SUMMARY

The nonlinear BER performance of dense WDM Manhattan Street Networks with deflection routing was obtained using a semi-analytical model, which combines hop distributions, node models and NLSE fiber simulation. This method can be extended to other networks by simply changing the hop distribution or node models. The results show that nonlinear effects impose significant performance penalties on dense WDM networks, both in terms of maximum hops attainable and average BER, and should be taken into account when modeling such networks. Simple techniques such as optimal amplifier positioning can mitigate some of the nonlinear penalties.

REFERENCES

Agrawal, G. P. (Ed.). (2001). *Nonlinear Fiber Optics*. Academic Press.

Bergano, N. S., Kerfoot, F. W., & Davidson, C. R. (1993). Margin Measurements in Optical Amplifier Systems. *IEEE Photonics Technology Letters*, 5(3), 304–306. doi:10.1109/68.205619

Castanon, G. A., Tonguz, O. K., & Bononi, A. (1997). Ber Performance of Multiwavelength Optical Cross-connected Networks with Deflection Routing. *IEEE Proc-Commun., 144*, 114-120

Forghieri, F., Bononi, A., & Prucnal, P. R. (1995). Analysis and Comparison of Hot-potato and Single-buffer Deflection Routing in Very High Bit Rate Optical Mesh Networks. *IEEE Transactions on Communications, 43*(1), 88–98. doi:10.1109/26.385939

Hiew, C. C., Abbou, F. M., Chuah, H. T., Majumder, S. P., & Hairul, A. A. R. (2006). Nonlinear BER Performance of Dense Optical WDM Manhattan Street Network with Deflection Routing. *IEEE Photonics Technology Letters*, *18*(9), 1031–1033. doi:10.1109/LPT.2006.873554

Kahn, J. M., & Ho, K. P. (2004). Spectral Efficiency Limits and Modulation/Detection Techniques for dwdm Systems. *IEEE Journal of Selected Topics in Quantum Electronics*, *10*(2), 259–272. doi:10.1109/JSTQE.2004.826575

Maxemchuk, N. F. (1987). Routing in the Manhattan Street Network. *IEEE Transactions on Communications*, *35*(5), 503–512. doi:10.1109/TCOM.1987.1096802

Norimatsu, S., & Maruoka, M. (2002). Accurate q-Factor Estimation of Optically Amplified Systems in the Presence of Waveform Distortions. *Journal of Lightwave Technology*, *20*(1), 19–27. doi:10.1109/50.974814

Yu, T., Reimer, W. M., Grigoryan, V. S., & Menyuk, C. R. (2000). *A Mean Field Approach for Simulating Wavelength-division Multiplexed Systems*. Academic Press.

Zhu, B. (2002). *Transmission of 3.2 tb/s (80 x 42.7 gb/s) over 5200 km of Ultrawave Fiber with 100-km Dispersion-managed Spans Using rz-dpsk Format*. Academic Press.

KEY TERMS AND DEFINITIONS

Hot Potato Routing: A routing strategy used in packet switched networks to reduce the need of buffering packets. It is also known as deflection routing.

In-Band Crosstalk: Caused by imperfect isolation of optical devices, such as optical switches, multiplexers, and demultiplexers. Crosstalk signals and the desired signal, despite coming from different optical sources, have the same wavelength.

Optical Cross-Connects (OXC): An optical device used to switch optical signals in high-speed optical network.

Optimum Power: A power level at which the BER is minimal.

Packet Switched Networks: A network in which data packets are switched and routed through a telecommunication network. The packets may travel via different paths, from the source through switching points to the destination. The packets are reassembled at the destination into the original message.

334

Compilation of References

Abbou, F. M. (n.d.). *RZ and NRZ OOK OTDM-WDM Transmission System Optimizations.* Academic Press.

Abbou, F. M., Hiew, C. C., Chuah, H.T., Ong, D. S., & Abid, A. (2008). A Detailed Analysis of Cross-Phase Modulation Effects on OOK and DPSK Optical WDM Transmission Systems in the Presence of GVD, SPM and ASE Noise. *J R Laser Research Springer, 29* (1), 57-70.

Abbou, F. M., Chuah, H. T., Hiew, C. C., & Abid, A. (2008). Comparisons of RZ-OOK and RZ-DPSK in Dense OTDM-WDM Systems Using Q-Factor Models. *J. R. Laser Research. Springer New York, 29*(2), 133–141.

Abbou, F. M., Chuah, H. T., & Majumder, S. P. (2000). Limitations of Soliton Transmission in a Cascaded Optical Amplifier System. *Journal of Optical Communications, 21*(5), 165–170.

Abbou, F. M., Chuah, H. T., Majumder, S. P., & Abid, A. (2006). Semi-analytical BER Performance of a Direct Detection Soliton Transmission System. *IEICE Electronics Express, 3*(10), 203–208. doi:10.1587/elex.3.203

Abbou, F. M., Wong, H. Y., Hiew, C. C., Abid, A., & Chuah, H. T. (2007). Performance evaluation of dispersion managed optical TDM-WDM transmission system in the presence of SPM, XPM, and FWM. *Journal of Optical Communications, 28*(3), 221–224. doi:10.1515/JOC.2007.28.3.221

Agrawal, G. P. (1995). *Nonlinear fiber optics.* Sand Diego, CA: Academic.

Agrawal, G. P. (Ed.). (1997). *Fiber-optic communication systems.* New York: Wiley-Interscience.

Agrawal, G. P. (Ed.). (2001). *Nonlinear Fiber Optics.* Academic Press.

Anderson, C. J., & Lyle, J. A. (1994). Technique for Evaluating System Performance Using q in Numerical Simulations Exhibiting Intersymbol Interference. *Electronics Letters, 30*(1), 71–72. doi:10.1049/el:19940045

Anderson, D. (1983, June). Variational Approach to Nonlinear Pulse Propagation in Optical Fibers. *Physical Review A., 27*(6), 3135–3145. doi:10.1103/PhysRevA.27.3135

Compilation of References

Anderson, D., & Lisak, M. (1987). Analytic Study of Pulse Broadening in Dispersive Optical Fibers. *Physical Review A.*, *35*(1), 184–187. doi:10.1103/PhysRevA.35.184 PMID:9897942

Aubin, G. (1995). 20 gb/s Soliton Transmission over Transoceanic Distances with 105 km Amplifier Span. *Electronics Letters*, *21*(13), 1079–1080. doi:10.1049/el:19950755

Bennion, I., Williams, J. A. R., Zhang, L., Sugden, K., & Doran, N. J. (1996). Uv-written in-fibre Bragg gratings. *Optical and Quantum Electronics*, *28*(2), 93. doi:10.1007/BF00278281

Bergano, N. S. (2002). *640 gb/s transmission of sixty-four 10 gb/s wdm channels over 7200 km with 0.33 (bits/s)/hz spectral efficiency.* Academic Press.

Bergano, N. S., & Davidson, C. R. (1996). Wavelength Division Multiplexing in Long-haul Transmission Systems. *Journal of Lightwave Technology*, *14*(6), 1299–1308. doi:10.1109/50.511662

Bergano, N. S., Kerfoot, F. W., & Davidson, C. R. (1993). Margin Measurements in Optical Amplifier Systems. *IEEE Photonics Technology Letters*, *5*(3), 304–306. doi:10.1109/68.205619

Bogoni, A., & Poti, L. (2004). Effective Channel Allocation to Reduce Inband fwm Crosstalk in dwdm Transmission Systems. *IEEE Journal on Selected Areas in Communications*, *10*, 387–392.

Borne, D. V. D., Sandel, N. E., Khoe, G. D., & Waardt, H. D. (2004). Pmd and Nonlinearity-induced Penalties on Polarization-multiplexed Transmission. *IEEE Photonics Technology Letters*, *16*(9), 2174–2176. doi:10.1109/LPT.2004.833079

Born, M., & Wolf, E. (1980). *Principles of Optics*. Oxford, UK: Pergamon Press.

Born, M., & Wolf, E. (Eds.). (1980). *Principles of optics*. Oxford, UK: Pergamon Press.

Bosco, G., Carena, A., Curri, V., Gaudino, R., & Poggiolini, P. (2002). On the Use of nrz, rz and csrz Modulation at 40 gb/s with Narrow dwdm Channel Spacing. *Journal of Lightwave Technology*, *20*(9), 1694–1704. doi:10.1109/JLT.2002.806309

Bosco, G., Carena, A., Curri, V., Gaudino, R., & Poggiolini, P. (2004). Modulation Formats Suitable for Ultrahigh Spectral Efficient wdm Systems. *IEEE Journal of Selected Topics in Quantum Electronics*, *10*(2), 321–328. doi:10.1109/JSTQE.2004.827830

Bosco, G., Carena, A., Curri, V., Gaudino, R., Poggiolini, P., & Benedetto, S. (2000). A Novel Analytical Method for the ber Evaluation in Optical Systems Affected by Parametric Gain. *IEEE Photonics Technology Letters*, *12*(2), 152–154. doi:10.1109/68.823500

Bosco, G., Carena, A., Curri, V., Gaudino, R., Poggiolini, P., & Benedetto, S. (2000). Suppression of Spurious Tones Induced by the Split-step Method in Fiber Systems Simulation. *IEEE Photonics Technology Letters*, *12*(5), 489–491. doi:10.1109/68.841262

Bosco, G., Carena, A., Curri, V., Gaudino, R., Poggiolini, P., & Benedetto, S. (2001). A Novel Analytical Approach to the Evaluation of the Impact of Fiber Parametric Gain on the Bit Error Rate. *IEEE Transactions on Communications, 49*(12), 2154–2163. doi:10.1109/26.974262

Bosco, G., & Poggiolini, P. (2004). On the q Factor Inaccuracy in the Performance Analysis of Optical Direct-detection dpsk Systems. *IEEE Photonics Technology Letters, 16*(2), 665–667. doi:10.1109/LPT.2003.820475

Bouteiller, J. C., Leng, L., & Headley, C. (2004). Pump-pump Four-wave Mixing in Distributed Raman Amplified Systems. *Journal of Lightwave Technology, 22*(3), 723–732. doi:10.1109/JLT.2004.824459

Cai, J. X. (2002). Long-haul 40 gb/s dwdm Transmission with Aggregate Capacities Exceeding 1 tb/s. *Journal of Lightwave Technology, 20*(12), 2247–2257. doi:10.1109/JLT.2002.806770

Capmany, J., & Mallea, G. (1999). Autocorrelation Pulse Distortion in Optical Fiber cdma Systems Employing Ladder Networks. *Journal of Lightwave Technology, 17*(4), 570–578. doi:10.1109/50.754786

Carena, A., Curri, V., Gaudino, R., Poggiolini, P., & Benedetto, B. (1997). A time-domain Optical Transmission System Simulation Package Accounting for Nonlinear and Polarization-related Effects in Fiber. *IEEE Journal on Selected Areas in Communications, 15*(4), 751–765. doi:10.1109/49.585785

Cartaxo, A. V. T. (1999). Cross-phase Modulation in Intensity Modulation-direct Detection wdm Systems with Multiple Optical Amplifiers and Dispersion Compensators. *Journal of Lightwave Technology, 17*(2), 178–190. doi:10.1109/50.744218

Castanon, G. A., Tonguz, O. K., & Bononi, A. (1997). Ber performance of multiwavelength optical cross-connected networks with deflection routing. *IEE Proc-Communications, 144*, 114-120.

Chen, M., Wu, M. C., Tanbun-Ek, T., Logan, R. A., & Chin, M. A. (1991). Subpicosecond Monolithic Colliding-pulse Mode-locked Multiple Quantum-well Lasers. *Applied Physics Letters, 58*(12), 1253–1258. doi:10.1063/1.104327

Chiang, T. K., Kagi, N., Marhic, M. E., & Kazovsky, L. G. (1996). Cross-Phase Modulation in Fiber Links with Multiple Optical Amplifiers and Dispersion Compensators. *Journal of Lightwave Technology, 14*(3), 249–260. doi:10.1109/50.485582

Cho, P. S., Harston, G., Kerr, C. J., Greenblatt, A. S., Kaplan, A., & Achiam, Y. et al. (2004). Investigation of 2-b/s/hz 40-gb/s dwdm Transmission over 4 x 100 km smf-28 Fiber Using rz-dqpsk and Polarization Multiplexing. *IEEE Photonics Technology Letters, 16*(2), 656–658. doi:10.1109/LPT.2003.821272

Chua, C. H., Abbou, F. M., Chuah, H. T., & Majumder, S. P. (2004, February). Performance Analysis on Phase-encoded ocdma Communication System in Dispersive Fiber Medium. *IEEE Photonics Technology Letters, 16*(2), 668–670. doi:10.1109/LPT.2003.821240

Chung, F. R. K., Salehi, J. A., & Wei, V. K. (1989). Optical Orthogonal Codes: Design, Analysis, and Applications. *IEEE Transactions on Information Theory, 35*(3), 595–604. doi:10.1109/18.30982

Ciaramella, E., & Forestieri, E. (2005). Analytical Approximation of Nonlinear Distortions. *IEEE Photonics Technology Letters, 17*(1), 91–93. doi:10.1109/LPT.2004.838152

Compilation of References

Desurvire, E. (1994). *Erbium-doped fiber amplifiers: Principles and applications*. New York: Wiley-Interscience.

Doran, N. J., & Wood, D. (1988). Nonlinear-optical Loop Mirror. *Optics Letters*, *13*(1), 56–58. doi:10.1364/OL.13.000056 PMID:19741979

Dragone, C. (1989). Efficient N*N star couplers using Fourier optics. *Journal of Lightwave Technology*, *7*(3), 479–489. doi:10.1109/50.16884

Duce, A. D., Killey, R. I., & Bayvel, P. (2004). Comparison of Nonlinear Pulse Interactions in 160-gb/s Quasi-linear and Dispersion Managed Soliton Systems. *Journal of Lightwave Technology*, *22*, 1483–1498.

Elrefaie, A. F., & Wagner, R. E. (1991). Chromatic Dispersion Limitations for FSK and DPSK Systems with Direct Detection Receivers. *IEEE Photonics Technology Letters*, *3*(1), 71–73. doi:10.1109/68.68052

Elrefaie, A. F., Wagner, R. E., Atlas, D. A., & Daut, D. G. (1988). Chromatic Dispersion Limitations in Coherent Lightwave Transmission Systems. *Journal of Lightwave Technology*, *6*(5), 704–709. doi:10.1109/50.4056

Evangelides, S. G., Mollenauer, L. F., Gordon, J. P., & Bergano, N. S. (1992). Polarization Multiplexing with Solitons. *Journal of Lightwave Technology*, *10*(1), 28–35. doi:10.1109/50.108732

Fatallah, H., & Rusch, L. A. (1999). Robust Optical FFH-CDMA Communications: Coding in Place of Frequency and Temperature Controls. *Journal of Lightwave Technology*, *17*(8), 1284–1293. doi:10.1109/50.779148

Fatallah, H., Rusch, L. A., & LaRochelle, S. (1999). Passive Optical Fast Frequency-hop CDMA Communication System. *Journal of Lightwave Technology*, *17*(3), 397–405. doi:10.1109/50.749379

Feldman, R. D. (1994). Cost Effective, Broadband Passive Optical Network System. *OFC Technical Digest*, 18-20.

Forestieri, E. (2000). Evaluating the Error Probability in Lightwave Systems with Chromatic Dispersion, Arbitrary Pulse Shape and Pre- and Post-detection filtering. *Journal of Lightwave Technology*, *18*(11), 1493–1503. doi:10.1109/50.896209

Forestieri, E. (2003). Correction to evaluating the Error Probability in Lightwave Systems with Chromatic Dispersion, Arbitrary Pulse Shape and Pre- and Post-detection Filtering. *Journal of Lightwave Technology*, *21*(6), 1957. doi:10.1109/JLT.2003.812719

Forghieri, F., Bononi, A., & Prucnal, P. R. (1995). Analysis and Comparison of Hot-potato and Single-buffer Deflection Routing in Very High Bit Rate Optical Mesh Networks. *IEEE Transactions on Communications*, *43*(1), 88–98. doi:10.1109/26.385939

Francia, C. (1999). Constant Step-size Analysis in Numerical Simulation for Correct Four-wave-mixing Power Evaluation in Optical Fiber Transmission Systems. *IEEE Photonics Technology Letters*, *11*(1), 69–71. doi:10.1109/68.736394

Gnauck, A. H., Raybon, G., Bernasconi, P. G., Leuthold, J., Doerr, C. R., & Stulz, L. W. (2003). 1-tb/s (6 x 170.6 gb/s) Transmission over 2000-km nzdf Using otdm and rz-dpsk Format. *IEEE Photonics Technol*, *15*(11), 1618–1620. doi:10.1109/LPT.2003.818634

Gnauck, A. H., & Winzer, P. J. (2005). Optical Phase-shift Keyed Transmission. *Journal of Lightwave Technology*, *23*(1), 115–130. doi:10.1109/JLT.2004.840357

Goodman, J. W. (2000). *Statistical Optics*. New York: Wiley.

Gordon, J. P., & Haus, A. H. (1986). Random Walk of Coherently Amplified Solitons in Optical Fiber Transmission. *Optics Letters*, *11*(10), 665–667. doi:10.1364/OL.11.000665 PMID:19738722

Gordon, J. P., & Mollenauer, L. F. (1990). Phase Noise in Photonics Communications Systems Using Linear Amplifier. *Optics Letters*, *15*(23), 1351–1355. doi:10.1364/OL.15.001351 PMID:19771087

Gross, M., & Olshansky, M. (1990). Multichannel Cherent fsk Experiments Using Subcarrier Multiplexing Techniques. *Journal of Lightwave Technology*, *8*(3), 406–415. doi:10.1109/50.50737

Grunnet-Jepsen, A., Johnson, A. E., Maniloff, E. S., Mossberg, T. W., Munroe, M. J., & Sweetser, J. N. (1999, June). Fiber Bragg Grating Based Spectral Encoder/Decoder for Lightwave CDMA. *Electronics Letters*, *35*(13), 1096–1097. doi:10.1049/el:19990722

Hairul, A. B. A. R. (2007). *Design and Performance Analysis of Subcarrier Multiplexing Passive Optical Networks*. (Unpublished doctoral dissertation). Multimedia University, Malaysia.

Hairul, A. A., Abbou, F. M., Chuah, H. T., Moncef, B. T., Malik, T. A., & Sivakumar, L. (2006). System performance optimization in SCM-WDM passive optical networks in the presence of XPM and GVD. *IEEE Communications Letters*, *10*(9), 670–672. doi:10.1109/LCOMM.2006.1714540

Hamaide, J. P., & Gabriagues, J. M. (1990). Limitations in Long Haul IM/DD Optical Fiber Systems Caused by Chromatic Dispersion and Nonlinear Kerr Effect. *Electronics Letters*, *26*(18), 1451–1453. doi:10.1049/el:19900931

Han, Y., & Li, G. (2005). Sensitivity Limits and Degradations in od8psk. *IEEE Photonics Technology Letters*, *17*(3), 720–722. doi:10.1109/LPT.2004.842337

Haus, A. (1993). Optical Fiber Solitons, Their Properties and Uses. *Proceedings of the IEEE*, *81*(7), 970–983. doi:10.1109/5.231336

Hibino, H. (2002). Recent Advances in High-density and Large-scale awg Multi/Demultiplexers with Higher Index-contrast Silica-based plcs. *IEEE Journal of Selected Topics in Quantum Electronics*, 8.

Hiew, C. C., Abbou, F. M., & Chuah, H. T. (2006). *Performance Analysis and Design of an Optical TDM-WDM Transmission System and Network* (Tech. Rep. No. 1). Malaysia: Multimedia University and Alcatel Network Systems.

Hiew, C.C., Abbou, F.M., Chuah, H.T., and Majumder, & Hairul, A. A. R. (2004). OTDM-WDM Propagation Impairments and Techniques to Improve Performance. In *Proceedings of the IASTED International 13/16 /16 Conference on Communication Systems and Networks (csn)*. Marbella, Spain: IASTED.

Hiew, C. C., Abbou, F. M., Chuah, H. T., & Hairul, A. A. R. (2005). A Technique to Improve Optical Time Division Multiplexing-Wavelength Division Multiplexing Performance. *IEICE Electronics Express*, *2*(24), 1–6. doi:10.1587/elex.2.589

Compilation of References

Hiew, C. C., Abbou, F. M., Chuah, H. T., & Majumder, S. P. (2005). Analysis of Cross-phase Modulation Effects on a Direct Detection Optical Soliton Transmission System in the Presence of GVD, SPM, and ASE noise. *Journal of Optical Communications.*, *26*(2), 17–23.

Hiew, C. C., Abbou, F. M., Chuah, H. T., Majumder, S. P., & Hairul, A. A. R. (2004). Ber Estimation of Optical wdm rz-dpsk Systems Through the Differential Phase Q. *IEEE Photonics Technology Letters*, *16*(12), 2619–2621. doi:10.1109/LPT.2004.836759

Hiew, C. C., Abbou, F. M., Chuah, H. T., Majumder, S. P., & Hairul, A. A. R. (2005). Impact of a Post-OTDM-Demultiplexing Optical Filter on Dense OOK OTDM-WDM Transmission. *Fiber and Integrated Optics*, *24*(5), 457–470. doi:10.1080/01468030590966562

Hiew, C. C., Abbou, F. M., Chuah, H. T., Majumder, S. P., & Hairul, A. A. R. (2006). Nonlinear BER Performance of Dense Optical WDM Manhattan Street Network with Deflection Routing. *IEEE Photonics Technology Letters*, *18*(9), 1031–1033. doi:10.1109/LPT.2006.873554

Humblet Azizoglu, P. A., & Azizoglu, M. (1991). On the Bit Error Rate of Lightwave Systems with Optical Amplifiers. *Journal of Lightwave Technology*, *9*(11), 1576–1582. doi:10.1109/50.97649

Iannone, E., Locati, F. S., Matera, F., Romagnoli, M., & Settembre, M. (1993). High-Speed DPSK Coherent Systems in the Presence of Chromatic Dispersion and Kerr Effect. *Journal of Lightwave Technology*, *11*(9), 1478–1485. doi:10.1109/50.241938

Igarashi, Y., & Yashima, H. (2001). Performance of Dispersion Compensation for Ultrashort Light Pulse cdma. In *Proceedings of IEEE Region 10 Conference on Electrical and Electronic Technology*, (vol. 2, pp. 769-775). IEEE. doi:10.1109/TENCON.2001.949697

Ishio, H., Minowa, J., & Nosu, K. (1984). Review and status of wavelength-division-multiplexing technology and its application. *Journal of Lightwave Technology*, *2*(4), 448–463. doi:10.1109/JLT.1984.1073653

Jeruchim, M. C., Balaban, P., & Shanmugam, K. S. (1992). *Simulation of Communication Systems*. New York: Plenum Press. doi:10.1007/978-1-4615-3298-9

Jiang, Z., & Fan, C. (2003). A Comprehensive Study on xpm- and srs-induced Noise in Cascaded im-dd Optical Fiber Transmission Systems. *Journal of Lightwave Technology*, *21*(4), 953–960. doi:10.1109/JLT.2003.810076

Jinno, M., & Matsumoto, T. (1992). Optical Tank Circuits Used for All-optical Timing Recovery. *IEEE Journal of Selected Topics in Quantum Electronics*, *28*(4), 895–900. doi:10.1109/3.135207

Kahn, J. M., & Ho, K. P. (2004). Spectral Efficiency Limits and Modulation/Detection Techniques for dwdm Systems. *IEEE Journal of Selected Topics in Quantum Electronics*, *10*(2), 259–272. doi:10.1109/JSTQE.2004.826575

Kamatani, O., Kawanishi, S., & Saruwatari, M. (1994). Prescaled 6.3 ghz Clock Recovery from 50 gbit/s tdm Optical Signal with 50 ghz pll Using Four-wave Mixing in a Traveling-wave Laser Diode Optical Amplifier. *Electronics Letters*, *30*(10), 807–809. doi:10.1049/el:19940546

Kawanishi, S., & Kamatani, O. (1994). All-optical Time Division Multiplexing Using Four-wave Mixing. *Electronics Letters*, *30*(20), 1697–1698. doi:10.1049/el:19941153

Keiser, G. (Ed.). (2000). *Optical fiber communications*. New York: McGraw-Hill.

Killey, R. I., Thiele, H. J., Mikhailov, V., & Bavyel, P. (2000). Prediction of Transmission Penalties due to Cross-Phase Modulation in WDM Systems Using a Simplified Technique. *IEEE Photonics Technology Letters*, *12*(7), 804–806. doi:10.1109/68.853506

Kim, H., & Yu, C. X. (2002). Optical Duobinary Transmission System Featuring Improved Receiver Sensitivity and Reduced Optical Bandwidth. *IEEE Photonics Technology Letters*, *14*(8), 1205–1207. doi:10.1109/LPT.2002.1022019

Konrad, B., Petermann, K., Berger, J., Ludwig, R., Weinert, C. M., Weber, H. G., & Schmauss, B. (2002). Impact of Fiber Chromatic Dispersion in High-speed tdm Transmission Systems. *Journal of Lightwave Technology*, *20*(12), 2129–2135. doi:10.1109/JLT.2002.807777

Kovalev, V. I., & Harrison, R. G. (2004). Spectral Broadening of Continuous-wave Monochromatic Pump Radiation Caused by Stimulated Brillouin Scattering in Optical Fiber. *Optics Letters*, *29*(4), 379–381. doi:10.1364/OL.29.000379 PMID:14971759

Kumar, S. (1998). Influence of Raman Effects in Wavelength-division Multiplexed Soliton Systems. *Optics Letters*, *23*(18), 1450–1452. doi:10.1364/OL.23.001450 PMID:18091813

Kumar, S., Mauro, J. C., Raghavan, S., & Chowdhury, D. Q. (2002). Intrachannel Nonlinear Penalties in Dispersion-managed Transmission Systems. *IEEE Journal of Selected Topics in Quantum Electronics*, *8*(3), 626–631. doi:10.1109/JSTQE.2002.1016366

Kwong, W. C., & Prucnal, P. R. (1990). Synchronous cdma Demonstration for Fiber Optic Networks with Optical Processing. *Electronics Letters*, *26*(24), 1990–1992. doi:10.1049/el:19901287

Lee, J. H. (2003). All-optical tdm Data Demultiplexing at 80 gb/s with Significant Timing Jitter Tolerance Using a Fiber Bragg Grating Based Rectangular Pulse Switching Technology. *Journal of Lightwave Technology*, *21*(11), 2518–2523. doi:10.1109/JLT.2003.819123

Leeson, M. L. (2004). Pulse Position Modulation for Spectrum-sliced Transmission. *IEEE Photonics Technology Letters*, *16*(4), 1191–1193. doi:10.1109/LPT.2004.824668

Leibrich, J., & Rosenkranz, W. (2003). Efficient Numerical Simulation of Multichannel wdm Transmission Systems Limited by xpm. *IEEE Photonics Technology Letters*, *15*(3), 395–397. doi:10.1109/LPT.2003.807901

Leibrich, J., Wree, C., & Rosenkranz, W. (2002). Cf-rz-dpsk for Suppresion of xpm on Dispersion-managed Long Haul Optical wdm Transmission on Standard Single-mode Fiber. *IEEE Photonics Technology Letters*, *14*(2), 155–157. doi:10.1109/68.980482

Lichtman, E. (1995). Limitations Imposed by Polarization-dependent Gain and Loss on All-Optical Ultralong Communication Systems. *Journal of Lightwave Technology*, *13*(5), 906–913. doi:10.1109/50.387808

Compilation of References

Linke, R. A., & Gnauck, A. H. (1998). High-capacity Coherent Lightwave Systems. *Journal of Lightwave Technology*, *6*(11), 1750–1769. doi:10.1109/50.9992

Liu, X., & Lee, B. (2003). A Fast Method for Nonlinear Schrodinger Equation. *IEEE Photonics Technology Letters*, *15*(11), 1549–1551. doi:10.1109/LPT.2003.818679

Liu, X., & Wei, X. (2003). Increased osnr Gains of Forward-error Correction in Nonlinear Optical Transmissions. *IEEE Photonics Technology Letters*, *15*(7), 999–1001. doi:10.1109/LPT.2003.813443

Liu, X., Xie, C., & van Wijngaarden, A. J. (2004). Multichannel pmd Mitigation and Outage Reduction through fec with Sub-burst-error-correction Period pmd Scrambling. *IEEE Photonics Technology Letters*, *16*(9), 2183–2185. doi:10.1109/LPT.2004.833088

Liu, X., Zhang, H., & Guo, Y. (2003). A Novel Method for Raman Amplifier Propagation Equations. *IEEE Photonics Technology Letters*, *15*(3), 392–394. doi:10.1109/LPT.2002.807929

Marcus, D. (1991). Bit-error rate of Lightwave Systems at the Zero-dispersion Wavelength. *Journal of Lightwave Technology*, *9*(10), 1330–1334. doi:10.1109/50.90931

Marcuse, D. (1991). Calculation of Bit-error Probability for a Lightwave System with Optical Amplifiers and Post-detection Gaussian Noise. *Journal of Lightwave Technology*, *9*(4), 505–513. doi:10.1109/50.76665

Marcuse, D. (1992). An Alternative Derivation of the Gordon-haus Effect. *Journal of Lightwave Technology*, *10*(2), 273–278. doi:10.1109/50.120583

Marcuse, D., Chraplyvy, A. R., & Tkach, E. W. (1994). Dependence of Cross-phase Modulation on Channel Number in Fiber wdm Systems. *Journal of Lightwave Technology*, *12*(5), 885–889. doi:10.1109/50.293982

Marhic, M. E. (1993). Coherent Optical cdma Networks. *Journal of Lightwave Technology*, *11*(5), 854–864. doi:10.1109/50.233249

Marhic, M. E., & Chang, Y. L. (1989, October). Pulse Coding and Coherent Decoding in Fiber Optic Ladder Networks. *Electronics Letters*, *25*(22), 1535–1536. doi:10.1049/el:19891032

Marhic, M. E., Kagi, N., Chiang, T. K., & Kazovsky, L. G. (1996). Optimizing the Location of Dispersion Compensators in Periodically Amplified Fiber Links in the Presence of Third-Order Nonlinear Effects. *IEEE Photonics Technology Letters*, *8*(1), 145–147. doi:10.1109/68.475807

Matsumoto, M. (1998). Analysis of Interaction Between Stretched Pulses Propagating in Dispersion-managed Fibers. *IEEE Photonics Technology Letters*, *10*(3), 373–375. doi:10.1109/68.661414

Ma, W., Zuo, C., Pu, H., & Lin, J. (2002, May). Performance Analysis on Phase-encoded ocdma Communication System. *Journal of Lightwave Technology*, *20*(5), 798–803. doi:10.1109/JLT.2002.1007932

Maxemchuk, N. F. (1987). Routing in the Manhattan Street Network. *IEEE Transactions on Communications*, *35*(5), 503–512. doi:10.1109/TCOM.1987.1096802

Mecozzi, A. (2004). Probability Density Functions of the Nonlinear Phase Noise. *Optics Letters*, 29. PMID:15072354

Mecozzi, A., Clausen, C. B., & Shtaif, M. (2000). System Impact of Intra-channel Nonlinear Effects in Highly Dispersed Optical Pulse Transmission. *IEEE Photonics Technology Letters*, *12*(12), 1633–1635. doi:10.1109/68.896331

Mecozzi, A., & Shtaif, M. (2001). On the Capacity of Intensity Modulated Systems Using Optical Amplifiers. *IEEE Photonics Technology Letters*, *13*(9), 1029–1031. doi:10.1109/68.942683

Mecozzi, A., & Shtaif, M. (2004). Signal-to-noise-ratio Degradation Caused by Polarization-dependent Loss and the Effect of Dynamic Gain Equalization. *Journal of Lightwave Technology*, *22*(8), 1856–1871. doi:10.1109/JLT.2004.832424

Menyuk, C. R. (1987). Nonlinear Pulse Propagation in Birefringent Optical Fibers. *IEEE Journal of Selected Topics in Quantum Electronics*, *23*(2), 174–176. doi:10.1109/JQE.1987.1073308

Milivojevic, B., Abas, A. F., Hidayat, A., Bhandare, S., Sandel, D., & Noe, R. et al. (2005). 1.6-b/s/hz 160-gb/s 230-km rz-dqpsk Polarization Multiplex Transmission with Tunable Dispersion Compensation. *IEEE Photonics Technology Letters*, *17*(2), 495–497. doi:10.1109/LPT.2004.839372

Mori, K., Takara, H., Kawanishi, S., Saruwatari, M., & Morioka, T. (1997). Flatly Broadened Supercontinuum Spectrum Generated in a Dispersion Decreasing Dibre with Convex Dispersion Profile. *Electronics Letters*, *33*(21), 1806–1808. doi:10.1049/el:19971184

Morioka, T. (1995). Multiwavelength Picosecond Pulse Source with Low Jitter and High Optical Frequency Stability Based on 200-nm Supercontinuum Filtering. *Electronics Letters*, *31*(13), 1164–1166. doi:10.1049/el:19950759

Morioka, T., Saruwatari, M., & Takada, A. (1987). Ultrafast Optical Multi/Demultiplexer Utilizing Optical kerr Effect in Polarization-maintaining Single-mode Fibres. *Electronics Letters*, *23*(9), 453–454. doi:10.1049/el:19870326

Morioka, T., Takara, H., Kawanishi, S., Kitoh, T., & Saruwatari, M. (1996). Error-free 500 gbit/s All-optical Demultiplexing Using Low-noise, Low-jitter Supercontinuum Short Pulses. *Electronics Letters*, *32*(9), 833–834. doi:10.1049/el:19960559

Morita, I., Suzuki, M., Edagawa, N., Tanaka, K., Yamamoto, S., & Akiba, S. (1997). Performance Improvement by Initial Phase Modulation in 20 gbit/s Soliton-based rz Transmission with Periodic Dispersion Compensation. *Electronics Letters*, *33*(12), 1021–1022. doi:10.1049/el:19970714

Mu, R. M., Yu, T., Grigoryan, V. S., & Menyuk, C. R. (2002). Dynamics of the Chirped Return-to-zero Modulation Format. *Journal of Lightwave Technology*, *20*, 608–617. doi:10.1109/50.996580

Murakami, M., Matsuda, T., Maeda, H., & Imai, T. (2000). Long-haul wdm Transmission Using Higher Order Fiber Dispersion Management. *Journal of Lightwave Technology*, *18*(9), 1197–1204. doi:10.1109/50.871695

Compilation of References

Nakazawa, M. (2000). Solitons for Breaking Barriers to Terabit/second wdm and otdm Transmission in the Next Millenium. *IEEE Journal of Selected Topics in Quantum Electronics*, *6*(6), 1332–1343. doi:10.1109/2944.902187

Nakazawa, M. (2000). Ultrahigh-speed Long-distance tdm and wdm Soliton Transmission Technologies. *IEEE Journal of Selected Topics in Quantum Electronics*, 6.

Narimanov, E. E., & Mitra, P. (2002). The Channel Capacity of a Fiber Optics Communication System: Perturbation Theory. *Journal of Lightwave Technology*, *20*(3), 530–537. doi:10.1109/50.989004

Noe, R., Sandel, D., & Mirvoda, V. (2004). Pmd in High-bit-rate Transmission and Means for its Mitigation. *IEEE Journal of Selected Topics in Quantum Electronics*, *10*(2), 341–355. doi:10.1109/JSTQE.2004.827842

Norimatsu, S., & Maruoka, M. (2002). Accurate q-factor Estimation of Optically Amplified Systems in the Presence of Waveform Distortions. *Journal of Lightwave Technology*, *20*(1), 19–27. doi:10.1109/50.974814

Olsson, N. A. (1989). Lightwave Systems with Optical Amplifiers t. *Journal of Lightwave Technology*, *7*(7), 1071–1082. doi:10.1109/50.29634

Ono, T., & Yano, Y. (1998). Key Technologies for Terabit/second wdm Systems with High Spectral Efficiency of over 1 bit/s/hz. *IEEE Journal of Selected Topics in Quantum Electronics*, 34.

Pachnicke, S., Man, E. D., Spalter, S., & Voges, E. (2005). Impact of the In-line Dispersion Compensation Map on Four-wave Mixing (fwm) – Impaired Optical Networks. *IEEE Photonics Technology Letters*, *17*(1), 235–237. doi:10.1109/LPT.2004.838629

Park, J., Kim, P., Park, J., Lee, H., & Park, N. (2004). Closed Integral Form Expansion of raman Equation for Efficient Gain Optimization Process. *IEEE Photonics Technology Letters*, *16*(7), 1649–1651. doi:10.1109/LPT.2004.827968

Patrick, D. M., & Ellis, A. D. (1993). Demultiplexing Using Crossphase Modulation-induced Spectral Shifts and kerr Polarization Rotation in Optical Fibre. *Electronics Letters*, *29*(2), 227–229. doi:10.1049/el:19930156

Pauer, M., Winzer, P. J., & Leeb, W. R. (2001). Bit Error Probability Reduction in Direct Detection Optical Receivers Using rz Coding. *Journal of Lightwave Technology*, *9*(9), 1255–1262. doi:10.1109/50.948272

Peddanarappagari, K. V., & Brandt-Pearce, M. (1998). Volterra Series Approach for Optimizing Fiber-optic Communications System Designs. *Journal of Lightwave Technology*, *16*(11), 2046–2055. doi:10.1109/50.730369

Peebles, P. Z. (2001). *Probability, Random Variables and Random Signal Processes*. New York: McGraw-Hill.

Peleg, A. (2004). Log-normal Distribution of Pulse Amplitudes Due to raman Cross Talk in Wavelength Division Multiplexing Soliton Transmission. *Optics Letters*, *29*(17), 1980–1982. doi:10.1364/OL.29.001980 PMID:15455753

Petermann, K. (1990). Fm-am Noise Conversion in Dispersive Single Mode Fibre Transmission Lines. *Electronics Letters*, *26*(25), 2097–2098. doi:10.1049/el:19901350

Peterson, R. L., Ziemer, R. E., & Borth, D. E. (1995). *Introduction to Spread Spectrum Communications*. Upper Saddle River, NJ: Prentice Hall.

Proakis, J. G. (Ed.). (1989). *Digital Communications*.

Prucnal, P. R., Santoro, M. A., & Fan, T. R. (1986). Spread Spectrum Fiber Optic Local Area Network Using Optical Processing. *Journal of Lightwave Technology*, *4*(5), 547–554. doi:10.1109/JLT.1986.1074754

Prucnal, P. R., Santoro, M. A., & Seghal, S. K. (1986). Ultrafast All-optical Synchronous Multiple Access Fiber Networks. *IEEE Journal on Selected Areas in Communications*, *4*(9), 1484–1493. doi:10.1109/JSAC.1986.1146484

Ramaswami, R., & Humblet, P. A. (1990). Amplifier Induced Crosstalk in Multi-channel Optical Networks. *Journal of Lightwave Technology*, *8*(12), 1882–1896. doi:10.1109/50.62886

Razavi, M., & Salehi, J. A. (2002). Statistical Analysis of Fiber-optic cdma Communication Systems-Part I: Device Modeling. *Journal of Lightwave Technology*, *20*(8), 1304–1316. doi:10.1109/JLT.2002.800298

Razavi, M., & Salehi, J. A. (2002). Statistical Analysis of Fiber-optic cdma Communication Systems-Part II: Incorporating Multiple Optical Amplifiers. *Journal of Lightwave Technology*, *20*(8), 1317–1328. doi:10.1109/JLT.2002.800299

Sahara, A., Kubota, A., & Nakazawa, M. (1996). Q-factor Contour Mapping for Evaluation of Optical Transmission Systems: Soliton against nrz against rz Pulse at Zero Group Velocity Dispersion. *Electronics Letters*, *32*(10), 915–916. doi:10.1049/el:19960590

Salehi, J. A. (1989). Code Division Multiple-access Techniques in Optical Fiber Networks-Part I: Fundamental Principles. *IEEE Transactions on Communications*, *37*(8), 824–833. doi:10.1109/26.31181

Salehi, J. A. (1989). Emerging Optical Code-division Multiple Access Communication Systems. *IEEE Network*, *1*(2), 31–39. doi:10.1109/65.21908

Salehi, J. A., & Brackett, C. A. (1989). Code Division Multiple-access Techniques in Optical Fiber Networks-Part II: Systems Performance Analysis. *IEEE Transactions on Communications*, *37*(8), 834–842. doi:10.1109/26.31182

Salehi, J. A., Weiner, A. M., & Heritage, J. P. (1990, March). Coherent Ultrashort Light Pulse Code Division Multiple Access Communication Systems. *Journal of Lightwave Technology*, *8*(3), 478–491. doi:10.1109/50.50743

Sampson, D. D., & Jackson, D. A. (1990). Coherent Optical Fiber Communication System Using all-optical Correlation Processing. *Optics Letters*, *15*(10), 585–587. doi:10.1364/OL.15.000585 PMID:19768016

Compilation of References

Sampson, D. D., & Jackson, D. A. (1990). Spread-spectrum Optical Fiber Network Based on Pulsed Coherent Correlation. *Electronics Letters*, *26*(19), 1550–1552. doi:10.1049/el:19900995

Sardesai, H. P., Chang, C. C., & Weiner, A. M. (1998). A femtosecond Code-division Multiple-Access Communication System Test Bed. *Journal of Lightwave Technology*, *167*, 211–224.

Sartorius, B., Bornholdt, C., Brox, O., Ehrke, H. J., Hoffmann, D., Ludwig, R., & Möhrle, M. (1998). optical Clock Recovery Module Based on Self-pulsating dfb Laser. *Electronics Letters*, *34*(17), 1664–1665. doi:10.1049/el:19981152

Saruwatari, M. (2000). All-optical Signal Processing for Terabit/second Optical Transmission. *IEEE Journal of Selected Topics in Quantum Electronics*, *6*(6), 1363–1374. doi:10.1109/2944.902190

Shah, J. (2003). Optical CDMA. *Optics and Photonics News*, 42-47.

Shalaby, H. M. H. (1998). Direct Detection Optical Overlapping PPM-CDMA Communication Systems with Double Optical Hard-limiters. *Journal of Lightwave Technology*, *17*(7), 1158–1165. doi:10.1109/50.774248

Shimoura, K., & Seikai, S. (1999). Two Extremely Stable Conditions of Optical Soliton Transmission in Periodic Dispersion Compensation Lines. *IEEE Photonics Technology Letters*, *11*(2), 2. doi:10.1109/68.740703

Shtaif, M., & Gnauck, A. H. (1999). The Relation Between Optical Duobinary Modulation and Spectral Efficiency in wdm Systems. *IEEE Photonics Technology Letters*, *11*(6), 712–714. doi:10.1109/68.766794

Sinkin, O. V., Holzlohner, V., Zweck, J., & Menyuk, C. R. (2003). Optimization of the Split-step Fourier Method in Modeling Optical-fiber Communications Systems. *Journal of Lightwave Technology*, *21*(1), 61–68. doi:10.1109/JLT.2003.808628

Spellmeyer, N. W., Gottschalk, J. C., Caplan, D. O., & Stevens, M. L. (2004). High-sensitivity 40-gb/s rz-dpsk with Forward Error Correction. *IEEE Photonics Technology Letters*, *16*(6), 1579–1581. doi:10.1109/LPT.2004.827417

Spiekman, L. H., Amersfoort, M. R., De Vreede, A. H., van Ham, F. P. G. M., Kuntze, A., & Pedersen, J. W. et al. (1996). Design and realization of polarization independent phased array wavelength demultiplexers using different array orders for TE and TM. *Journal of Lightwave Technology*, *14*(6), 991–995. doi:10.1109/50.511599

Srivastava, A. K., Radic, S., Wolf, C., Centanni, J. C., Sulhoff, J. W., Kantor, K., & Sun, Y. (2000). Ultradense wdm Transmission in l-band. *IEEE Photonics Technology Letters*, *12*(11), 1570–1572. doi:10.1109/68.887758

Stok, A., & Sargent, E. H. (2000). Lighting the Local Area: Optical Code-division Multiple Access and Quality of Service Provisioning. *IEEE Network*, *14*(6), 42–46. doi:10.1109/65.885669

Striegler, A. G., & Schmauss, B. (2004). Compensation of Intrachannel Effects in Symmetric Dispesion-managed Transmission Systems. *Journal of Lightwave Technology*, *22*(8), 1877–1882. doi:10.1109/JLT.2004.832419

Subramaniam, S., Abbou, F. M., Chuah, H. T., & Dambul, K. D. (2005). Performance Evaluation of scm-wdm Microcellular Communication System in the Presence of xpm. *IEICE Electronics Express*, *2*(6), 192–197. doi:10.1587/elex.2.192

Suzuki, M. (1992). Transform-limited Optical Pulse Generation up to 20 ghz Repetition Rate by Sinusoidally Driven Ingaasp Electroabsorption Modulator. In *Proceedings of Lasers and Electro-optics* (cleo'92). CLEO.

Suzuki, M., & Edagawa, N. (2003). Dispersion-managed High-capacity Ultra-long-haul Transmission. *Journal of Lightwave Technology*, *21*(4), 916–929. doi:10.1109/JLT.2003.810098

Takada, A., & Miyazawa, H. (1990). 30 ghz Picosecond Pulse Generation from Actively Mode-locked Erbium-doped Fiber Laser. *Electronics Letters*, *26*(3), 216–217. doi:10.1049/el:19900145

Takada, A., Sugie, T., & Saruwatari, M. (1987). High-speed Picosecond Optical Pulse Compression from Gain-switched 1.3μm Distributed Feedback-laser Diode (dfb-ld) Through Highly Dispersive Single-mode fiber. *Journal of Lightwave Technology*, *5*(10), 1525–1533. doi:10.1109/JLT.1987.1075418

Tamura, S., Nakano, S., & Akazaki, K. (1985). Optical Code-multiplex Transmission by Gold Sequences. *Journal of Lightwave Technology*, *3*(1), 121–127. doi:10.1109/JLT.1985.1074148

Ting, K. C., Kagi, N., Marhic, E. M., & Kazovsky, L. G. (1996). Cross-phase Modulation in Fiber Links with Multiple Optical Amplifiers and Dispersion Compensators. *Journal of Lightwave Technology*, *96*, 3.

Tkach, R. W., Chraplyvy, A. R., Forghieri, F., Gnauck, A. H., & Derosier, R. M. (1995). Four-photon Mixing and High-speed wdm Systems. *Journal of Lightwave Technology*, *13*(5), 841–849. doi:10.1109/50.387800

Tsuda, H., Takenouchi, H., Ishii, T., Okamoto, K., Goh, T., & Sato, K. et al. (1999). Spectral Encoding and Decoding of 10Gbit/s Femtosecond Pulses Using High Resolution Arrayed-waveguide Grating. *Electronics Letters*, *35*(14), 1186–1188. doi:10.1049/el:19990783

Tu, K. Y., Forestieri, E., Kaneda, N., Secondini, M., Leven, A., Koc, U.-V., & Hocke, R. (2004). Modeling Accuracy of a Fiber-optics Test Bed Using mgf Method. *IEEE Photonics Technology Letters*, *16*(12), 2646–2648. doi:10.1109/LPT.2004.836771

Uetsuka, H. (2004). Awg Technologies for Dense wdm Applications. *IEEE Journal of Selected Topics in Quantum Electronics*, *10*(2), 393–402. doi:10.1109/JSTQE.2004.827841

Vannucci, A., Serena, P., & Bononi, A. (2002). The rp Method: A New tool for the Iterative Solution of the Nonlinear Schrodinger Equation. *Journal of Lightwave Technology*, *20*(7), 1102–1112. doi:10.1109/JLT.2002.800376

Vannucci, G., & Yang, S. (1989). Experimental Spreading and Despreading of the Optical Spectrum. *IEEE Transactions on Communications*, *37*(7), 770–780. doi:10.1109/26.31171

Compilation of References

Varvarigos, E. M. (1998). The 'Packing' and the 'Scheduling Packet' Switch Architecture for Almost All-optical Lossless Networks. *Journal of Lightwave Technology, 16*(10), 1757–1767. doi:10.1109/50.721062

Vassilieva, O., Hoshida, T., Choudhary, S., Castanon, G., Kuwahara, H., Terahara, T., & Onaka, H. (2001). Numerical Comparison of NRZ, CS-RZ and IM-DPSK Formats in 43 Gbits/s WDM Transmission. *Lasers and Electro-Optics Society, 2,* 673–674.

Vlachos, K., Pleros, N., Bintjas, C., Theophilopoulos, G., & Avramopoulos, H. (2003). Ultrafast Time-domain Technology and its Application in All-optical Signal Processing. *Journal of Lightwave Technology, 21*(9), 2895–2915. doi:10.1109/JLT.2003.816826

Wang, D., & Menyuk, C. R. (1999). Polarization Evolution due to the kerr Nonlinearity and Chromatic Dispersion. *Journal of Lightwave Technology, 17*(12), 2520–2529. doi:10.1109/50.809672

Wang, J., & Kahn, J. M. (2004). Accurate Bit-error-ratio Computation in Nonlinear crz-ook and crz-dpsk Systems. *IEEE Photonics Technology Letters, 16*(9), 2165–2167. doi:10.1109/LPT.2004.833033

Wang, J., & Kahn, K. (2004). Impact of Chromatic and Polarization-mode Dispersions on dpsk Systems Using Interferometric Demodulation and Direct Detection. *Journal of Lightwave Technology, 22*(2), 362–371. doi:10.1109/JLT.2003.822101

Wang, J., & Petermann, K. (1992). Small Signal Analysis for Dispersive Optical Fiber Communication Systems. *Journal of Lightwave Technology, 10*(1), 96–100. doi:10.1109/50.108743

Wang, Z. (1995). Effects of Cross Phase Modulation in Wavelength Multiplexed scm Video Transmission Systems. *Electronics Letters, 31*(18), 1591–1592. doi:10.1049/el:19951074

Weiner, A. M., Heritage, J. P., & Salehi, J. A. (1988). Encoding and Decoding of Femtosecond Pulse. *Optics Letters, 10*(4), 300–302. doi:10.1364/OL.13.000300 PMID:19745879

Weinert, C. M., Ludwig, R., Pieper, W., Weber, H. G., Breuer, D., Petermann, K., & Kuppers, F. (1999). 40 gb/s and 4 x 40 gb/s tdm/wdm Standard Fiber Transmission. *Journal of Lightwave Technology, 17*(11), 2276–2284. doi:10.1109/50.803020

Wei, X., Liu, X., & Xu, C. (2003). Numerical Simulation of the spm Penalty in a 10-gb/s rz-dpsk System. *IEEE Photonics Technology Letters, 15*(11), 1636–1638. doi:10.1109/LPT.2003.818664

Wei, Z., Shalaby, H. M. H., & Ghafouri-Shiraz, H. (2001). Modified Quadratic Congruence Codes for Fiber Bragg-grating-based Spectral-amplitude-coding Optical CDMA Systems. *Journal of Lightwave Technology, 19*(9), 1274–1281. doi:10.1109/50.948274

Wickham, L. K., Essiambre, R. J., Gnauck, A. H., Winzer, P. J., & Chraplyvy, A. R. (2004). Bit Pattern Length Dependence of Intrachannel Nonlinearities in Pseudolinear Transmission. *IEEE Photonics Technology Letters, 16*(6), 1591–1593. doi:10.1109/LPT.2004.826782

Winzer, P. J., & Kim, H. (2003). Degradations in Balanced dpsk Receivers. *Journal of Lightwave Technology, 15,* 1282–1284.

Winzer, P. J., Pfennigbauer, M., Strasser, M. M., & Leeb, W. R. (2001). Optimum Filter Bandwidths for Optically Preamplified rz and nrz Receivers. *Journal of Lightwave Technology*, *19*(9), 1263–1273. doi:10.1109/50.948273

Wu, M., & Way, W. I. (2004). Fiber Nonlinearity Limitations in Ultra-dense wdm Systems. *Journal of Lightwave Technology*, *22*(6), 1483–1498. doi:10.1109/JLT.2004.829222

Xu, C. (2003). Comparison of Return-to-zero Differential Phase Shift Keying and On-off Keying in Long Haul Dispersion Managed Transmission. *IEEE Journal of Selected Topics in Quantum Electronics*, *15*, 617–619.

Xu, C., Liu, X., & Wei, X. (2004). Differential Phase-shift Keying for High Spectral Efficiency Optical Transmissions. *IEEE Journal of Selected Topics in Quantum Electronics*, *10*(2), 281–293. doi:10.1109/JSTQE.2004.827835

Xu, C., Liu, X., & Wei, X. (2004). Differential Phase-shift Keying for High Spectral Efficiency Optical Transmissions. *IEEE Photonics Technology Letters*, *10*, 281–293.

Xu, C., Xiang Liu, , Mollenauer, L. F., & Xing Wei, . (2003). Comparison of Return-to-zero Differential Phase Shift Keying and on-off Keying in Long Haul Dispersion Managed Transmission. *IEEE Photonics Technology Letters*, *15*(4), 617–619. doi:10.1109/LPT.2003.809317

Yamamoto, Y., & Inoue, K. (2003). Noise in Amplifiers. *Journal of Lightwave Technology*, *21*(11), 2895–2915. doi:10.1109/JLT.2003.816887

Yang, F. S., Marhic, M. E., & Kazovsky, L. G. (2000). Nonlinear Crosstalk and Two Countermeasures in scm-wdm Optical Communication Systems. *Journal of Lightwave Technology*, *18*(4), 512–520. doi:10.1109/50.838125

Yang, G. C., & Kwong, W. C. (1997). Performance Comparison of Multiwavelength cdma and wdma+cdma for Fiber-optic Networks. *IEEE Transactions on Communications*, *45*(11), 1426–1434. doi:10.1109/26.649764

Yang, G. C., & Kwong, W. C. (2002). *Prime Codes with Applications to CDMA Optical and Wireless Networks*. Norwood, MA: Artech House.

Yao, X. S., Feinberg, J., Logan, R., & Maleki, L. (1993). Limitations on Peak Pulse Power, Pulse Width, and Coding Mask Misalignment in a Fiber-optic Code Division Multiple-access System. *Journal of Lightwave Technology*, *11*(5), 836–846. doi:10.1109/50.233247

Yu, T., Reimer, W. M., Grigoryan, V. S., & Menyuk, C. R. (2000). *A mean field approach for simulating wavelength-division multiplexed systems*. Academic Press.

Zhang, J. (2000). Bit Error Rate Analysis of otdm System Based on Moment Generation Function. *Journal of Lightwave Technology*, *18*(11), 1513–1518. doi:10.1109/50.896211

Compilation of References

Zhang, X. (2004). Noise Statistics in Optically Preamplified Differential Phase-shift Keying Receivers with Mach-zehnder Interferometer Demodulation. *Optics Letters*, 29. PMID:14971745

Zhou, Y. R., & Watkins, L. R. (1995). Rigorous approach to performance modeling of nonlinear, optically amplified im/dd systems. *IEE Proc-Optoelctron., 142*, 271-278.

Zhou, X., & Brik, M. (2004). New Design Method for a wdm System Employing Broadband Raman Amplification. *IEEE Photonics Technology Letters, 14*(3), 912–914. doi:10.1109/LPT.2004.823726

Zhu, B. (2002). *Transmission of 3.2 tb/s (80 x 42.7 gb/s) over 5200 km of ultrawave fiber with 100-km dispersion-managed spans using RZ-DPSK format*. Academic Press.

Zuo, C., Ma, W., Pu, H., & Lin, J. (2001). The Impact of Group Velocity on Frequency-hopping Optical Code Division Multiple Access System. *Journal of Lightwave Technology, 19*(10), 1416–1419. doi:10.1109/50.956128

About the Authors

Fouad Mohammed Abbou received his "Ingenieur" Degree in Electrical Engineering from Delft University of Technology, The Netherlands in 1995. He obtained his PhD degree from the Faculty of Engineering, Multimedia University (MMU), Malaysia in 2001. From April 1997 to April 2001, he was working with the Faculty of Engineering at MMU, Malaysia. In 2001, he joined Alcatel-Lucent as Multimedia Advisor and MMU as a Professor to support teaching and research activities in the area of photonics and telecommunication networks. In November 2008, he joined Al-Madinah International University (MEDIU) as Vice President for Research and Development and Dean of Postgraduate Studies. His research interests include optical transmission systems, optical networks, security in all-optical networks, and grid integration of renewable energy systems. He has authored/co-authored more than 90 papers in international journals and conferences. Dr. Fouad is a member of the Institution of Engineers, The Netherlands, Member of IEEE and IET, and he is currently a Full Professor in the School of Science and Engineering at Al-Akhawayn University, Morocco.

Hiew Chee Choong obtained his bachelor degree and his Master's of Engineering Science degree in Electronic Engineering majoring in Telecommunications from Multimedia University (MMU) in 2003 and 2006, respectively. From 2003 to 2005, he was a research officer at the Center for photonics research, innovation, and application, MMU. He joined Kasatria MSC Sdn Bhd in 2005 as a Lead Developer and became Chief Technology Officer (CTO) in 2010.

Index

A

Absorption 3-4, 26-27, 238, 263, 267, 328
Additive White Gaussian Noise 65, 83, 180, 196, 224, 232, 274, 287, 300, 312, 329
Amplified Spontaneous Emission (ASE) Noise 1, 26, 65, 83, 329
Amplitude Jitter 42, 45, 52, 58, 181, 190-191, 193, 209, 221, 229, 231, 248, 271
Amplitude-Shift Keying (ASK) 244
Arrayed Waveguide Grating (AWG) 164, 176
Attenuation 1-5, 7, 14, 26-27, 29-30, 35, 38, 40, 43, 61-62, 65-66, 78-79, 84, 149, 179, 211, 214, 229, 274, 287, 300, 312-313, 328-329

B

Back-to-Back System 275, 277, 279, 284, 293-294, 301-302, 305, 314, 316-317, 320
Bit-Error Rate (BER) 121, 139, 149

C

Carrier to Noise Ratio (CNR) 120
Channel Frequency Spacing 272, 284
Chirp 6, 31, 51, 63, 65, 73, 129, 156, 204
Chromatic Dispersion (CD) 26
Cross-Correlation 124, 149, 160

D

Deflection Routing 172, 240, 262-263, 265, 268-269, 271, 295, 326-327, 332-333
Demultiplexer (Demux) 64, 77, 244
Differential Phase Q (DP-Q) 259, 296, 298
Differential Phase Shift Keying (DPSK) 75, 96, 204
Dispersion Compensation Fiber (DCF) 17, 24, 63, 77, 84, 244
Dispersion Management (DM) 17, 178, 244, 274, 300, 312
Dispersion-Shifted Fiber (DSF) 121, 149
Distributed Feedback Laser Diodes (DFB-LD) 155, 176

E

Electro-Absorption Modulators (EAM) 176

Cross Phase Modulation (XPM) 35, 37, 58, 97, 158, 164
Crosstalk 1-2, 22-25, 37, 40, 43, 45, 47, 55, 61, 73, 97-109, 115-116, 119-120, 162, 164, 166, 180-181, 183, 185-186, 190, 192, 207, 209-210, 223, 238, 256, 258, 261, 267, 274, 277, 290, 300, 303-304, 309, 312, 316, 327-329, 333
Crosstalk Noise 97-98, 101-102, 109, 116, 120, 183, 327